VINTAGE
SYNTHESIZERS

KEYBOARD PRESENTS

VINTAGE SYNTHESIZERS

Groundbreaking Instruments and Pioneering Designers of Electronic Music Synthesizers

BY MARK VAIL

GPI BOOKS

An Imprint of

 Miller Freeman Books

San Francisco

Published by Miller Freeman Books,
600 Harrison Street, San Francisco, California 94107
Publishers of GPI Books and *Keyboard* magazine
A member of the United Newspapers Group

Distributed to the book trade in the U.S. and Canada by
Publishers Group West, P.O. Box 8843, Emeryville, CA 94662

Distributed to the music trade in the U.S. and Canada by
Hal Leonard Publishing, P.O. Box 13819, Milwaukee, WI 53213

Art Director: Richard Leeds
Page Layout and Production: Brad Greene
Copy Editor: Walter Carter
Technical Artist: Rick Eberly
Proofreader: Tom Hassett

Cover Photo: Randall Wallace
Cover Design: Richard Leeds

Additional photo credits: photos on pp. 19 (top), 20, 24, 26, 30
(top), 36 (top), 86 (top), 110, and 112 are by Dominic Milano.

Library of Congress Cataloging-in-Publication Data

Vail, Mark.
        Vintage synthesizers : groundbreaking instruments
    and pioneering designers of electronic music synthe-
    sizers / by Mark Vail.
            p.   cm.
        Includes index.
        ISBN 0-87930-275-5 (pbk.)
        1. Synthesizer (Musical Instrument)--History.   I. Title
    ML 1092.V25   1993
        786.7'419--dc20   93-24714
                                                          CIP
                                                          MN
Printed in the United States of America
94 95 96 97 98   5 4 3 2

TABLE OF CONTENTS

FOREWORD

Once upon a time, a copy of the first issue of Marvel Comics' *Fantastic Four* could be had for a mere twenty bucks — a fortune by any fourteen-year-old's standards in 1969. There were countless times I could have bought one, two . . . hell, a dozen copies during my travels to the Acme Book Store at 414 N. Clark in Chicago. Somehow, I couldn't bring myself to pop for even a single copy of Stan Lee and Jack Kirby's masterpiece. Twenty bucks could get me any three issues of a lesser book for my struggling collection of *X-men, Avengers, Strange Tales, Tales of Suspense, Spiderman, ad nauseam.*

Who knew that a mint-condition copy of Vol. 1, No. 1 of the *Fantastic Four* would sell for a couple *thousand* dollars twenty-some years later? You've probably heard similar stories about baseball cards, Barbie Dolls, toy soldiers, old cars, fine wine, and just about anything else with that indescribable quality known as VINTAGE.

Among musicians, guitarists are perhaps best acquainted with vintage voodoo. They'll spend countless hours pawing through garage sales in search of holy grails, carbon dating pawnshop prizes, and drooling over massive tomes dedicated to all things arcane relating to serial numbers, headstock decals, tuning peg placement, pickguard shapes, cutaway horn shapes, and anything else that might distinguish a '61 whozits from a '62 whozits.

On the other hand, synthesists, by nature, don't know from vintage. The entire concept runs contrary to the techno-lust that drives us to look for the next new thing, abandoning all else as obsolete. Still, when we started the Vintage Synths column in *Keyboard*, it was in anticipation of the day when synth players would long to rediscover the sound of analog oscillators beating wildly against each other in an orgy of warm fatness that would expose any modern-day digital synth's sound as so much anemic wheezing pap.

Over the last couple of years, Mark Vail has tried to apply the same exacting standards that our sister publication *Guitar Player*'s many vintage guitar gurus — Tom Wheeler, George Gruhn, Teisco Del Rey, to name a few — have applied to carbon dating guitars. It hasn't been an easy road. In many cases, manufacturers didn't keep any records of serial numbers or software updates or even production run counts. Yet MV — Bookie to his fellow *Keyboard* Chain Gangers — has done a wonderful job expanding those columns into this book. Enjoy.

Dominic Milano
Editor, *Keyboard*

INTRODUCTION
The Vintage Advantage

Perspective can make a big difference. Take television. Today, we think nothing of color on the tube, stereo broadcast TV is fairly common, and we don't have to watch any commercials thanks to VCRs and wireless remotes. (Our attention spans are minimal, but that's another story.) Now step into the time machine and let's go back 30 years. If you had a television set, it was almost certainly black-and-white. Stereo sound? Well, some new-fangled stereo albums came out in the early '60s, and I hear tell there was an FM station up in Peoria messing around with the outrageous idea of broadcasting in stereo. And when you wanted to change TV stations, you had to get up and walk over to the TV; the channel flipper was the big knob with numerals around it.

Although innovations in television took time, they were phenomenal. Innovations in the electronic music industry have been pretty amazing, too. Thirty years ago, the most common form of electronic music production entailed splicing hundreds of strips of ¼" recording tape together to create a few minutes of music. The tapes contained sounds from all kinds of natural and electronic sources. Musicians and technicians used electronic laboratory test equipment to make sounds, with performance interfaces amounting to little more than big knobs for controlling pitch. That was about all that was available before people like Don Buchla and Bob Moog made the first voltage-controlled synthesizers in the early '60s.

Since then, we've gone from modular systems to prepatched (normalized) monophonic synths, polyphonic analog synths, digital synths, and multitimbral MIDI synths. The rate at which new and "improved" instruments have been introduced is astounding, especially since the advent of MIDI (Musical Instrument Digital Interface) in 1983. There was, however, a time back in the early days of voltage-controlled analog synthesizers when evolution seemed rather slow. Back in the heyday of the Minimoog and the ARP Odyssey, when you wanted a new synth sound, you had to twirl a few knobs, adjust some sliders, and throw a switch or two. Meanwhile, you were thankful that you didn't have to fuss with a bundle of patch cords. Perhaps most frustrating of all — at least to the pianists and organists who reluctantly gave those early synths a shot — was that you could only play a single note at a time.

Today's synthesists are spoiled by 24- and 32-voice instruments with 1,001 onboard sounds available at the touch of a button. On the other hand, to do any editing from the front panel of a modern synth, you typically have to deal with a single data slider, an LCD that displays one to six parameters at a time, and dozens of parameter menus to flip through. Although there's a wide selection of computer software available for graphic editing of synth patches, you need the computer to do the programming. For these reasons, many look on the current flock of synthesizers as nothing more than preset organs.

Given the importance in popular music of fresh, novel sounds, many keyboardists have been encouraged to constantly upgrade to the latest, greatest, state-of-the-art keyboard before they begin to grasp the real potential of instruments they are replacing. Thankfully, musicians are discovering that synthesizers once considered obsolete actually have qualities and musical characteristics that aren't duplicated on newer instruments. Although many of today's 16-bit digital synthesizers can be loaded with individual sounds sampled from these elderly instruments, the actual characteristics and qualities of the original are lost. For instance, the performance interface of a modular Buchla synth — knobs, patch cords, analog sequencers, and touch plates, all of which provide more control over the resulting sound than any modern synth provides — isn't preserved in the sampling process. As more musicians discover the value of idiosyncrasies in the older instruments, these instruments are gaining in popularity.

"Vintage" is a relatively new term in the synthesizer realm. After all, the first voltage-controlled synthesizers were introduced only about 30 years ago. But in the fast-paced world of electronic music, synths less than a decade old can be labeled "vintage." This includes recent successes like the Yamaha DX7 and Roland D-50, and might even include the Korg M1 except that it's still being manufactured and continues to set new sales records.

By no means is *Vintage Synthesizers* comprehensive. There are many more instruments that could be covered in detail. For example, Serge Tcherepnin developed the marvelous Serge Modular music system in the late '70s, and oversaw its production until 1986. Serge Modulars are highly respected in the synthesizer industry. I spoke on the phone with Serge and his associate, Rex Probe, who has begun manufacturing new Serge Modular systems — making them the only American modular synthesizers still in production — but their comments couldn't be included in this volume. For information on new Serge systems, contact Rex Probe at Sound Transform Systems, 1615 Broadway, Ste. #712, Oakland, CA 94612, phone (510) 465-6896, or fax (510) 465-4656.

Rather than presenting a comprehensive historical account of the electronic music synthesizer, *Vintage Synthesizers* outlines groundbreaking instruments and their makers from 1962 on, with special focus on select instruments and discussions with their creators. Many of these articles originally appeared in *Keyboard* magazine, and they have been updated and expanded for this book. Also included is information on support services and organizations for current owners, vintage synth dealers for potential owners, and estimated values of over 200 aged instruments.

This book is dedicated to the dreamers, designers, developers, programmers, performers, technicians, users, fixers, modifiers, and future owners of vintage synthesizers. Now you have no excuse to hide that old (your synth name here) under your bed, in your closet, or in rental storage. Get it fixed and start using it again! Or find someone else who wants it.

Thanks to everyone mentioned in this book for sharing their knowledge. Thanks to the staffs of *Keyboard*, GPI, and Miller Freeman Books for the opportunity to be here doing what I do — interviewing people, reviewing new products, answering people's questions, writing magazine articles and this book, and playing music. Thanks Mom and Dad for the music lessons, the Vox Jaguar, and the Rhodes. And thanks to my wife, Christy, for love, support, devotion, forgiveness — and for letting me buy Dominic Milano's Polymoog.

Mark Vail

A PHOTO GALLERY OF VINTAGE SYNTHS

PROLOGUE

A modular system from Aries, a Salem, Massachusetts-based synth manufacturer that offered kits, assembled modules, and complete modular systems. This system was produced in 1975.

Steiner-Parker introduced the Synthacon in 1975 with a list price of $1,195. It featured a four-octave keyboard, sample-and-hold module, a multi-mode filter with variable resonance, and three 17 1/2-octave VCOs. Today a Synthacon is worth $300, or $500 from a reputable synth dealer.

The RMI Keyboard Computer KC-II came out in 1977 and was probably the first performance-oriented commercially available digital polyphonic synthesizer. It was based on technology made commercially available in 1971 on the Allen church organ. Original retail price for the KC-II was $4,750.

A small Serge Modular system (c. early 1981), comprising a pair of VCOs, the Wave Multiplier module, an audio mixer, a ring modulator, the Variable Q VCF, the Dual Universal Slope Generator, the Universal Audio Processor, and the Touch Activated Keyboard Sequencer. Serge Modular synthesizers, like those from Buchla, differed from all others in that the patch cords terminated in banana plugs, which could be stacked on top of one another. This system cost $3,250 when it was new, and it isn't worth much less now.

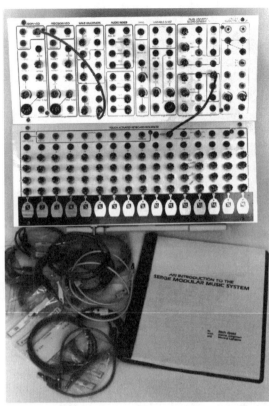

No, this isn't an alien from *Star Trek: Deep Space Nine*. It's Mike Matthews, who was responsible for many innovative products from Electro-Harmonix. Matthews is shown here at the summer '80 NAMM show, demonstrating the Electro-Harmonix Mini-Synthesizer — along with a truly bizarre pair of sunglasses. (photo by Dominic Milano)

The six-voice polyphonic Siel DK 600 came out in early '84 sporting the then-new digital interface, MIDI. The DK 600 cost $1,295. A keyboardless version, the Expander, was also available, carrying a list price of $795.

Released in 1981 at a list price of $1,095, Korg's six-voice Polysix offered four banks of eight user patches, six VCOs, a resonant filter, and an arpeggiator.

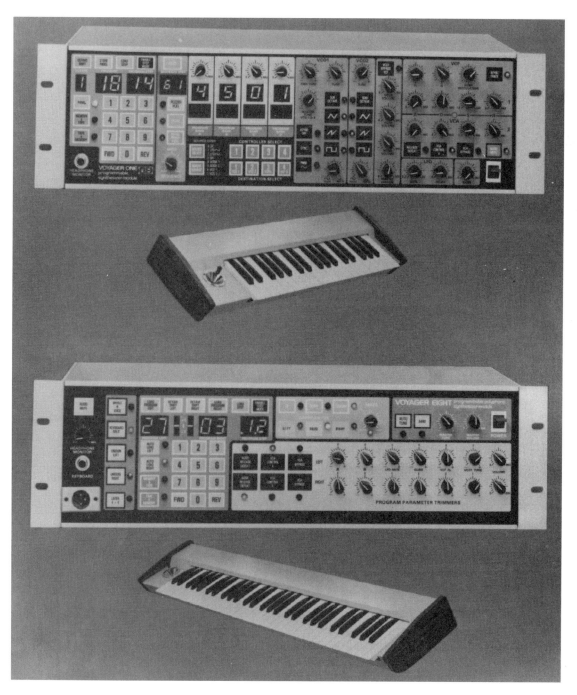

Prototypes of the last synthesizers produced by Octave-Plateau, before they went on to become Voyetra, developer of MIDI sequencer software for IBM-PCs. At the top is the Voyager One programmable monophonic synth module, along with its keyboard controller. Below these are the Voyager Eight programmable polyphonic synth module and the VPK-5 polyphonic keyboard controller. Both synth modules were actually released in '83 as the Voyetra One and Voyetra Eight, featuring the same front-panel layouts but with different color schemes. Previous to being Octave-Plateau, the company was called Octave Electronics, manufacturer of the Cat and Kitten synthesizers.

Installed in a single-piece cabinet, Aries' System III came assembled only (not in kit form) for $2,877.30 in the early '80s.

Bob Moog consulted on the design of the Spirit synthesizer from Crumar. The Spirit came out in 1983 with a list price of $895.

Polyfusion's 2058 polyphonic keyboard (c. 1980) could control up to eight analog synthesizer voices with independent velocity response for each voice.

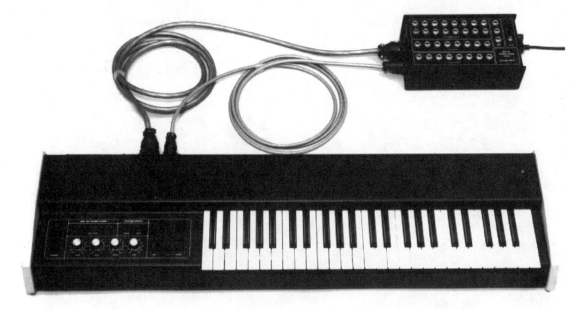

Before an enraptured audience, a ghostly Keith Emerson reaches over his Hammond C-3 to the keyboard of his monsterous Moog modular system during the *Brain Salad Surgery* tour in the early '70s. Barely visible to the upper right is another apparition, the lips of the Brain Salad face.

Since 1966, Don Buchla's first modular synth has resided at Mills College in Oakland, California. (photo by Bill Reitzel)

The ARP 2500, introduced in 1970, shown here in a 1972 product brochure.

British synthesizer designer David Cockerell finalized the EMS Synthi AKS in 1971. It consisted of the same sound-generating circuitry as the VCS3, plus a 2¹/₂-octave touch-plate keyboard and a 256-event monophonic digital sequencer. (photo by Randall Wallace)

Oberheim introduced the Four Voice in 1975 at a list price of $4,295. Based on a polyphonic keyboard designed by Dave Rossum of E-mu, the Four Voice sported a four-octave keyboard. This model includes the programmer, the module at the bottom left, which cost an additional $1,395. (photo by Randall Wallace)

Korg introduced the ES-50 polyphonic ensemble in the late '70s. One thing's for certain: It had a beautiful wood cabinet. (photo by Randall Wallace)

During the '70s, the ARP Odyssey battled the Minimoog as the most popular live-performance synthesizer. (photo by Randall Wallace)

Weighing in at 220 pounds, the Yamaha CS-80 was a true heavy-weight. Colorful, too. How many current synths can you name that have yellow buttons on the front panel? (photo by Randall Wallace)

Yamaha's programmable CS 70M provided 30 memory locations for patches, 39 parameters per patch, a keyboard with after-touch, two-way keyboard splits and voice layering, a rudimentary sequencer, and a magnetic-media data card slot for patch storage (two patches per card). Gone was the ribbon controller featured on its predecessor, the CS-80, replaced by Moog-style pitch and mod wheels. According to experts in the vintage synth field, the CS 70M is only worth from $200 to $400 today.

Roland introduced the Jupiter-8 at the summer '80 NAMM show in Chicago. Also known as the JP-8, the Jupiter-8 offered a 64-patch memory, 16 oscillators in an eight-voice configuration, and an arpeggiator that could be synced to one of Roland's Compu-Rhythm drum machines — all for a mere $5,295. (photo by Randall Wallace)

Roland's System-100M modular synth, patched and ready to play.

Roland's JX-3P programmable polyphonic synth, shown here with the PG-200 programmer.

Another "lost" instrument from the tarpits of technology, the second-generation Con Brio ADS 200-R system (c. 1982).

Sequential's Prophet-10 essentially contained the equivalent of two Prophet-5s. It could produce two different timbres simultaneously, and these could be assigned in various ways to the two keyboards. Estimated street value of a Prophet-10 with MIDI ranges from $500 to $1,200, soaring up to as much as $2,500 if you buy a mint-condition-10 from a dealer. (photo by Randall Wallace)

A short-lived animal called the Chamberlin, the Mellotron's direct ancestor, was virtually the first sampling keyboard, but its samples were stored on magnetic tape — one length of tape per key, per timbre — rather than in computer memory, which was in rather short supply when the Chamberlin first appeared in the late '50s. Shown here is a Chamberlin M-1. (photo by David Kean)

First appearing in early '64, the Mellotron Mark II featured two side-by-side, 35-note (*G* to *F*) keyboards and 70 playback heads. While the right-hand keyboard was typically loaded with lead or melody sounds, the left was split in two, with rhythm and accompaniment tracks in the lower half — recorded to play in the key of the note that you play — and fill patterns in the upper half. (photo by David Kean)

The Model 400 is the most popular Mellotron. However, many old recordings feature the Mellotron Mark II, not the 400. (photo by David Kean)

Created by Dave Biro to improve upon the Mellotron concept, the under-$2,000 Birotron was funded by Rick Wakeman. "It uses eight-track tapes arranged in loops so there's no eight-second sustain limit like on the Mellotron," Wakeman explained in a *Keyboard* interview dated March '76. "You can program different kinds of attack and sustain." (photo by David Kean)

Technos 16π (late '80s): "At last, a digital synthesizer that permits the fusion of synthesis and analysis! The 16π's touch-sensitive control panel gives access to all Dynamic Additive Synthesis parameters with unprecedented operational simplicity. With its General Audio Processor, a specialized A/D converter, the 16π can analyze and reconstruct acoustic sound with 64 harmonics, making the analysis and synthesis processes perfectly interchangeable." We've never seen a Technos 16π and believe that Technos concentrated instead on developing the Acxel Resynthesizer.

Among other venues, Technos showed the Acxel Resynthesizer at the spring '91 Musik Messe trade show in Frankfurt, Germany. By tracing shapes with your finger across its Grapher interface, you could enter waveforms and envelopes. The Acxel Resynthesizer would respond with timbral changes in real time. We haven't seen the Acxel or heard from the Canadian-based Technos since.

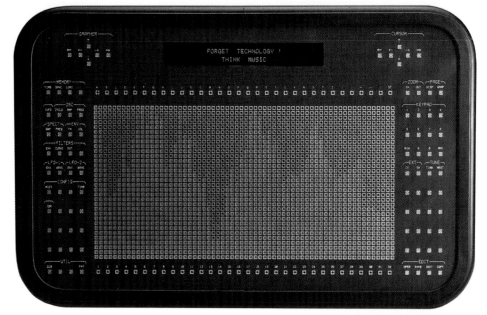

One of the newest synths that could be considered "vintage" is the popular Roland D-50, which came out in 1987 and stole lots of attention away from the Yamaha DX7II. The D-50, shown here with the optional PG-1000 programmer, was the first synth to feature built-in effects, which camouflaged the flaws of some of its waveforms.

HEARTS OF THE MODERN SYNTH INDUSTRY

SECTION 1

AMERICAN SYNTHESIZER BUILDERS

Triumphs & Crises for an Industry in Transition

BY DOMINIC MILANO
INTERVIEWS BY KYLE KEVORKIAN & MARK VAIL

merica, land of dreams and opportunity. America, land where freedom reigns, Mom's apple pie is tops, and ideas as silly as pet rocks can leave you laughing all the way to the bank. It's the land of innovation, where people like Franklin, Edison, Ford, and thousands more have transformed visions into realities that forever changed the shape of the world we live in.

America also happens to be the land of the synthesizer — its birthplace divided between East and West Coasts. Its fathers, Don Buchla and Bob Moog, were dreamers whose workbenches full of circuit boards turned the world music community on its collective ear and spawned a two-billion-dollar-a-year electronic music industry.

That industry is now over 30 years old. And many of Moog's and Buchla's offspring have come and gone, victims of the things dreamers tend to be victims of: Bad business sense. Bad timing. Bad luck. In one way or another, the money stopped and so did their companies. ARP, Moog, Linn, Oberheim, Sequential, Polyfusion, EML, and countless others, whose names may be remembered only in the tar pits of technology, are extinct.

This story on the American synth industry started out as a labor of love by Jeff Burger. It was to be a retrospective on the evolution of the American side of synthesizer manufacturing, picking up where Tom Rhea's Electronic Perspectives column left off — with the advent of the voltage-controlled synthesizer developed by Don Buchla in late 1963 and made commercially successful in 1965 by Bob Moog. But as we got closer to putting this article together, it became obvious that there was a bigger story to be told. What were the fatal mistakes that caused the downfall of industry giants? Is foreign competition at the heart of it? What are the lessons to be learned? How do companies like Ensoniq and Alesis manage to thrive in the face of increasing foreign and domestic competition? Is the picture of the future really as bleak as some might paint it, or does hard competition breed hardier competitors?

Our apologies, then, to Jeff Burger, whose historical research has been relegated to background material here. And our thanks to the dozens of representatives and former employees who took the time out from their busy schedules to talk to us. We're only sorry that space didn't allow us to use all of their comments.

Birthrights. Up to the mid-'70s, there were only two synthesizer giants, Moog and ARP. Don Buchla's early collaboration with Morton Subotnick had led to some fascinating instruments, but like so many others who would follow, Buchla had a stronger sense of instrument design than mass marketing principles. His modular synths never reached beyond the academic community into mass market profitability. In 1969, Buchla struck up a deal with CBS (which owned Fender) to manufacture his instruments. According to Don, they sold well for modular gear, but CBS was unwilling to fund any of the long-term research into instrument design that

Don Buchla with a number of his revolutionary creations, 1982. (photo by Jon Sievert)

he wanted to do, so they parted company on good terms. Not until Buchla directed his attention to designing MIDI controllers did he find measurable success. Never an advocate of 12-tone equal temperament and the traditional keyboard interface, Buchla dove into the alternate MIDI controller market with two products: Thunder, a multiple touch-pad performance interface introduced in 1990, and Lightning, an optical MIDI performance interface with hand-held wands or finger rings that are tracked in a two-dimensional space by the controller box. Lightning defied the laws of nature by following Thunder by a year.

Although the results are surprisingly similar, Bob Moog's story is slightly different. His analog modular instrument was developed a year after Buchla's original black box, which by the way is still in use at Mills College in Oakland, California. Unlike Buchla's machines, the Moog synthesizer became a bona fide success, but not without some serious trials and tribulations for Moog himself. By 1973, Moog Music, the company that built the most successful synth of the day (the classic Minimoog — 13,000 of which sold over a ten-year period), was sold to what was then the largest distributor of musical instruments in the world, Norlin Industries. Norlin owned Gibson guitars, Lowrey organs, Sennheiser mikes, and more. By 1977, Moog had left the company he founded. (The complete story in Bob's own words can be found starting on page 29.) Today, he continues to develop new MIDI controllers, consults with manufacturers on a freelance basis, and runs Big Briar, through which you can purchase new self-contained and MIDI-ready theremins — a long-time passion of Moog's. Isn't it ironic that these two pioneers of analog synthesizers, Buchla and Moog, now concentrate mainly on MIDI controllers rather than synths?

The decline and fall of Moog Music follows a pattern that you'll see repeating throughout this article. In the words of Berklee College of Music professor, electronic music historian, and ex-Moog employee Tom Rhea, "Norlin's marketing people did not come from the music business. They were from French's mustard, Gabriel shock absorbers, Beatrice foods, that sort of thing. They were all bright men, but they didn't have a handle on the music industry. Musicians accept new ideas slowly. Moog was on the leading edge, and Norlin didn't understand that they had an education problem, not a distribution problem. Few musicians understood the implications or the applications of the instruments we were selling.

"Norlin also did not spend enough money on product development. They did not have deep enough pockets, nor could they ever have competed with Japan Inc. Their outlook was too short-term. For Norlin, blue sky was a year ahead. The Japanese are capable of looking downstream 10, 15, or 20 years."

For Moog, and later ARP, innovation gave way to corporate politics and bad planning driven by eco-

An exhausted Dave Luce after a long day of demoing his prototype Polymoog (on floor) at NAMM, Chicago 1975.

nomic necessities. Supporting 200-plus employees and sizable manufacturing facilities takes capital. And instruments like the Polymoog (1975), of which about 3,000 were sold, experienced 150–200% failure rates. But mass production techniques were adopted, and spin-off products became the rule and not the exception. Unfortunately, some of them, notably the Polymoog Keyboard (1976), were unsuccessful. Unlike mega-corporations like Yamaha, Norlin's Moog couldn't sustain such failures for long. Says Tom Rhea, "You notice that Yamaha screwed up for a long time with one bad model after another before they hit on the DX7 [1983]. They could afford to keep trying. In a company like Moog, ARP, Sequential, or Oberheim, you're living from one NAMM show to the next. If you don't have a hit at one show, you'd better at the next, or you're dead."

ARP was the first industry giant to actually go down. But the story sounds all too similar: Alan R. Pearlman, for whom the company was named, was opposed to the Avatar project (1976; one of the first guitar synths). In a memo to

the board he declared, "There are formidable technical problems . . . and we have an unknown amount of R&D to produce an acceptable model." Despite his objections, he was overruled, and the $7,000,000 company sank $4,000,000 into an untested product. ARP only sold $1,000,000 worth of Avatars over two years. The hole was dug too deep for them to recover. Products like their electronic piano (1979) were shipped too early, and suffered from major flaws. In 1981, CBS acquired ARP's inventory and the rights to manufacture the Chroma and the electronic piano for a paltry $350,000. Six years later, Yamaha would acquire Sequential for only slightly more, and for many of the same reasons.

ARP's Avatar, the product that sank them.

Attrition. About the time ARP was going down, Roger Linn's Linn Electronics was born. Roger's first product, like so many other first hardware products from upstart companies of the '60s, '70s, and pre-MIDI '80s, was spawned out of necessity. "I wanted a drum machine that did more than play preset samba patterns and didn't sound like crickets," Roger recalls. The LM-1 (1980) was the first programmable drum machine to feature sampled sounds. (John Simonton marketed a programmable drum machine with electronic sounds through Paia, and Bob Moog built a mammoth 6' x 2' drum machine in the late '60s that never saw production.) Fewer than 600 LM-1s were sold — at $5,500 *each*!

Linn did considerably better with the Linn-Drum, which cost half as much as the LM-1. About 5,000 units were sold. But the fall of the company was precipitated by Roger's next product, the bug-ridden Linn 9000 (1984). "It was a good idea for a product," he claims. "But we weren't capitalized well enough. When I was engineering products myself, things went well. But as soon as I tried to get bigger, we got into trouble. But I don't think you can pinpoint any one thing. Certainly Japan-ese competition was part of it. At the time my company and Tom Oberheim's company and Dave Smith's company went down, we were really having a hard time competing against the yen/dollar situation."

Roger goes on, "I really get turned on by designing innovative products. I hate being market-driven, and I'm not sure you can do that well in a larger company situation where you need certain amounts of cash flow."

By early '86, Linn Electronics closed its doors, and by some accounts Roger lost everything. Akai subsequently took him under their wing as a consultant, and Roger developed the Akai MPC60 sampling and MIDI sequencing drum machine. What does working for a Japanese manufacturer look like from his perspective? "People warned me that the Japanese move very slowly because everything is decided by committee, but that's not the case with Akai. They're in a strong growth phase. They're trying to get up and running in the field very quickly, and they pretty much leave me alone. They trust me.

"Akai has this thing about things Not Invented Here. It's kind of a joke. They say that the company

Summit at NAMM '85. (L to R) Russ Jones, Tom Oberheim, Dave Smith, and Barb Fairhurst.

has a high N.I.H. factor. Companies like Roland and Yamaha don't have that. They have large R&D departments. They invent it themselves. They want that control. And in the long run that makes more sense, but Akai is trying to come up very fast, so they're working with Americans and Europeans who develop interesting products."

Linn also feels that Akai's product engineers are brilliant in the thing his American company was weak in — namely, building a reliable production model from a prototype. "You hear stories about the Japanese," Linn continues. "They're very rigid. Productivity and cost-effectiveness are everything. Americans are more creative, but they get into trouble over reliability and customer service. The Japanese are very egoless. They listen very accurately to what customers want. I know that when I listened to customers I filtered everything, and heard only what I wanted to hear. In doing that, I dug my own grave."

Following on the heels of Linn's fall, Tom Oberheim's Oberheim Electronics bowed to the almighty creditors and was resurrected as Oberheim/ECC in May 1985. Oberheim has been responsible for a large number of product innovations through the years. From the modular Four Voice synthesizers (1975), to the Four Voice with programmer (1976), to the programmable OB-1 monophonic (1978), to the Oberheim system (the OB-8, DMX drum machine, and DSX sequencer, 1983), Oberheim's products stood out for their sound and attention to detail. Classics like the Xpander (1984) and Matrix-12 (1985) were prolonged by Oberheim/ECC, followed by offsprings like the Matrix-6 (1986) and Matrix-1000 (1987). The company delved into the MIDI processor realm with the Perf/x series of products, comprising the Cyclone arpeggiator, Systemizer split/layer utility, and Navigator note/controller/program change mapper — all released in early '89 — followed by the early '91 release of the Strummer keyboard-to-guitar chord voicing converter and the Drummer interactive drum-pattern sequencer. Also in 1991, Oberheim began developing a rack-mount analog MIDI synth with gobs of knobs. Early on, it was called the OberM006 (to look like "OberMoog," because it had both Moog- and Oberheim-style filters). By this time, Gibson (no longer owned by Norlin) had bought Oberheim. As of early '93, production continues on the Matrix-1000, Strummer, and Drummer, as does development of the OberM006 (now renamed the OB-MX). Question is, what caused the fall of the Tom Oberheim-led company?

The story is remarkably familiar: "Cash flow is the major problem that affects all growing companies," says Tom Oberheim. "We were underfinanced. I don't think foreign competition hurt us that much." Marcus Ryle and Michel Doidic, two instrument designers who worked at Oberheim — and later helped develop the Dynacord ADS and ADS-K stereo samplers, as well as the Alesis ADAT multitrack digital tape recorder, among other groundbreaking musical products — add another perspective: "The company started out in a garage. It was a large company being run like a small company. There was no business plan. When Oberheim went under, we were actually doing a peak business. We were back-ordered. But when your sales continue to grow, you have to ride the rollercoaster of sales. You find yourself in the position of having to build up a large inventory. If you have a couple of slack months, the banks who financed the parts for that inventory start getting nervous and think about closing your doors. We don't think Oberheim should have gone out of business, under the circumstances. Their situation wasn't at all like what Linn experienced. Linn had only one product, whereas Oberheim had many, and quite a few of those are still being manufactured. They're still viable."

Interestingly, Oberheim established a relationship in the early '80s with their Japanese distributors (a company now known as Suzuki), and had some instruments built in Japan. "It was a cooperative effort," Oberheim explains. "Not only did the Japanese company make some of the equipment, they helped design it. We weren't making a move to relocate manufacturing offshore, we were looking for the best route to bring products to market. We also did some manufacturing in Mexico [primarily board stuffing], but it was only certain pieces. The final assembly and testing was always done in Los Angeles. I don't care what nationality a manufacturing company is, the biggest problem they face is that one month you need a hundred people, the next you need two hundred, and the next you don't need any. You can't keep hiring and firing, laying them off and bringing them back. So it made more sense for us to go outside the company for certain things."

Though Tom doesn't feel that Japanese competition hurt his company, he has some strong feelings about why the Japanese have done so well: "Their long-term marketing is a major factor," he explains. "Their commitment and consistency are also part of it. But the Japanese are in it for the long haul. And they have the resources to back up the commitment." Going back to Don Buchla's experience with CBS in 1969, it's interesting that Don remembers that CBS was unwilling to support a long-term research project on input structures, while at the same time Yamaha was sending their engineers to school in the U.S. to see if there was anything to the new electronic music technologies — 14 years before the DX7 catapulted Yamaha to the top of the synth market.

Tom Oberheim left his former company to form Marion Systems in 1987. His first product, a circuit board that turns an Akai S900 sampler from a 12- into a 16-bit machine, appeared on the market in 1988. More recently, Oberheim developed a SCSI interface for the Akai MPC60 sampling drum system (Roger Linn's machine). How does Tom feel about starting over again? "I think it's difficult for any company of any nationality to become a syn-

thesizer manufacturer in today's market. You have to have a proprietary advantage and lots of capital to do it. It's not very likely that my new company will become a keyboard synth company in the manner of Roland or Ensoniq. I think that's very difficult to do for any company today. The financing it would take to be competitive would be monstrous."

Bob Moog seconds Oberheim's opinion. "In the late '60s and early '70s, you could put five pounds of shit in a box, and if it made a sound, you could sell it." By contrast, today's instruments involve incredible amounts of software development and custom LSI chips. It's hard to imagine a one-man garage operation competing with Roland's 250-man R&D department.

The Oberheim modular Four Voice and its companion programmer were the polyphonic Minimoogs that most people were clamoring for in the mid-1970s. But there was one overall complaint: The programmer did not affect 100% of the four expander modules' functions (each module made up one voice in the instrument's architecture). It seemed no one would answer the problem, until the January 1978 NAMM show, where in a small booth in the Disneyland Hotel, Dave Smith, Barb Fairhurst, and John Bowen unveiled the Prophet-5. Sporting Minimoog/ARP Odyssey voice architecture and on-board microprocessor control of all the unit's functions including auto-tuning, the Prophet-5 rocketed Smith's garage operation to stunning heights.

Over the next five or six years, Sequential would become the largest American manufacturer of synths. But many of Sequential's products were spinoffs of the Prophet — the Prophet-10 (1980), the Prophet-600 (the first American-made synth with MIDI, 1983), and the Prophet-T8 (1983). In an attempt to diversify, Sequential was one of the first to bring out programmable effects. They were one of the first to try to market MIDI software and accessories for the Commodore 64 (1984), and they bravely introduced a series of multi-timbral instruments with a built-in sequencer (the Six-Trak/Max/Multi-Trak, 1984/85) and tried to sell them in department stores. Sequential's pioneering efforts often hit the market at just the wrong time, proving that it's always the pioneers who end

Sequential's ill-fated stab at the home computer market, on display at summer NAMM 1984.

up being encircled by the Indians. Casio's CZ-101 (late '84) certainly proved that multi-timbral instruments can be sold in department stores.

"We had a bad year in '85," explains Dave Smith. "We had also tried to move into the home computer market when the computer business was in a major slump. We were never fully able to recover from those blunders. We were always undercapitalized. We had never taken outside investments so we never had the luxury of getting any breathing room. That meant that if we tried something and it didn't work, we'd depleted all our profits. What we should have done was get outside venture capital. If we had done that, we could have stayed in the market and waited for it to catch up to us. As it was, if the product didn't support itself, we had to drop it."

Another factor that put a major dent in Sequential's plans was the flood of economical instruments that hit at about the same time as Sequential's low-cost Max and Prophet-600. As Smith puts it, "We found ourselves discounting our low-cost products to keep up with other people who were heavily discounting their products. That's when we switched back to doing high-end products, starting with the Prophet-2000 [1985] and following up with the Prophet-VS [1986] and the Studio 440 [1987]."

Many wonder how much the Korg DSS-1 sampler hurt Sequential's sales of the Prophet-2000, especially when Korg cut the price to a little over a thousand dollars and threw in a free copy of Digidesign's Sound Designer software. "I'm sure the DSS-1 hurt eventually," Dave admits, "but what really did it was the cluttering of the 12-bit sampler market in general. There just wasn't enough room. But we were still limping along then. We never had the chance to do adequate marketing, and even though we had what most people think was the best-sounding 12-bit sampler around, we couldn't afford to beat the bushes to tell people about it. And that makes it all the more difficult to compete."

Despite the sound quality of the Prophet-2000 and VS, Sequential never fully got out of the hole they had dug with the Six-Trak, their software and add-on keyboard for the C-64, and the Pro-FX. By late 1987, their doors were closed. A few months later, their assets (including employment for Smith) were bought by Yamaha for just over half a million dollars. Sequential's last gasp was the release of a 16-bit rack-mount sampler, the Prophet-3000. No more than 300 were made, many of which were blown out at the discount price of $1,999 by Wine Country Productions. Smith and others from Sequential worked for Yamaha for less than a year before Korg bought their contracts. At the January 1990 NAMM show, a pair of vector synthesis instruments — fruits of Dave Smith and his team's labors — were introduced: the Yamaha SY22 and Korg's Wavestation. Although the SY22 and Wavestation carried list prices about a thousand bucks apart ($1,095 and $2,150, respectively), they shared a bloodline as direct descendants of the Prophet-VS — the first commercially available vector synthesizer.

Dave Smith doesn't subscribe to anti-Japanese sentiments. Does he see any difference in the way the Japanese capitalize their firms? "I'm not a money expert, so I can't go into a lot of detail," Dave explains. "But a lot of their banking relationships are different. Japan is built more on long-term goals. Where an American manufacturer might fail, they stay in the market and try until they get it right. But that's not all. What's easy to forget is that while a Japanese company might build an instrument that doesn't make it in the States, it might be a moderate to huge success in Japan, because Japan has a very lucrative domestic market. If you look at any of the Japanese firms, a large percentage of their sales — 30 to 50% — are in Japan. Roland is a pretty good example of that. Their synthesizers sounded terrible until they brought out the JP-8, which sounded great, had the right features, and professionals accepted it. And look at the DX7. That didn't just appear. Yamaha worked on getting the technology right for years. First it was $20,000 for a non-programmable instrument. Then it was $9,000. Then it was under two grand for a programmable DX.

"You know, I don't subscribe to the idea that the Japanese just copy and don't innovate," Smith goes on. "I think that was true in the past, but it's not true now. If there's one thing they're good at, it's learning. A lot of those companies will send people overseas for a few years and then bring them back, just so they get more of an international experience."

The Triumphant. Lest we paint a completely bleak picture of American synth building, let us not forget that there are more U.S. companies thriving in the maelstrom of competition than ever before. Of these, E-mu Systems certainly deserves a medal for longevity. Founded by Scott Wedge and Dave Rossum in the early '70s, E-mu was responsible for building the digital scanning keyboard (1973), which, when connected to a number of synthesizer modules, allowed the first polyphonic synths from both Oberheim and Sequential to be developed. E-mu also developed the SSM synth module chips that made Dave Smith's Prophet-5 a reality. However, E-mu's own synth business was focused largely on modular systems until Rossum and Wedge saw the Fairlight CMI at an AES convention in 1979.

"We were delivering a paper on our Audity [a mono analog/digital hybrid with a price tag of $70,000]," Wedge recalls. "We saw the Fairlight and recognized that the one feature that people would really find useful was its sampling capability. But there was no way it should have cost $30,000, so we set out to build a dedicated sampling keyboard — the original Emulator [1981]."

The Emulator I listed for $7,900. Only 500 or so were built. Much to the surprise of all who were used to thinking of E-mu as a non-mass market company, E-mu built the Drumulator next. It was the first programmable drum machine with samples built-in for under a thousand dollars. Its closest competition was the LinnDrum at three times the price. Needless to say, it was a very successful product. As have been the Emulator II, the Emax, the SP-12, the Emulator Three, the Emax II, the Proformance, and so on. But most successful of all in the professional market is the Proteus line, with offsprings like the Procussion (1991) and Vintage Keys (1993).

But E-mu's history took a new turn in early '93, when the Santa Cruz, California-based outfit was purchased by Singapore-based Creative Technologies, who also owns Creative Labs, the California-based manufacturer of the popular PC soundcard, the Sound Blaster. Over the past few years, E-mu's synthesis technology found its way into the computer market via such soundcards. Early indications are that E-mu will continue to make its synthesis technology available to soundcard and other music manufacturers (Samick has licensed E-mu technology for their consumer line of digital pianos), while concentrating its own efforts on innovations in state-of-the-art synthesis techniques and products.

In retrospect, Scott Wedge's early 1988 comments provide an interesting perspective. "The American synthesizer industry is larger than it has ever been. I think it's unfortunate to see no active investment in this industry by the American financial community. It would be nice to see these companies get properly funded so they can survive. There's a long list of companies that went under just prior to Sequential, so it's easy to forecast gloom and doom, but E-mu grew 65% last year, and that's the slowest growth we've had in five years. Ensoniq is another success story, and I think Kurzweil is in a strong position at this point, too. [Korean piano manufacturer Young Chang purchased Kurzweil in 1989. The reborn, foreign-owned Kurzweil deserves credit for one of the most respected and talked-about synths of the day, the K2000.] And then there are Alesis and Waveframe. [The latter became a division of a new and expanding force in the digital recording industry, Digital FX — a splinter of another long-lived but recently expired American music company, Hybrid Arts.

E-mu's Scott Wedge (L) with Roger Linn at summer NAMM 1984.

Barefoot Software took over distribution and further development of Hybrid Arts software.] For every failed small company, there is one larger and stronger to take its place."

Wedge cites the yen/dollar price competition as being a pivotal factor in the success of American synth building. "Imagine if all the Japanese competition in sampling had come in at half the price it is," he explained. "It would have been very hard to compete against it. As it is, it's a fair match. Remember that during the day of the DX7, the yen was half its current [1988] value, so it was very easy for Yamaha to come in and dominate the market. It was very difficult to produce something in the United States with a similar level of technology for a similar price.

"Japan has been very good at letting somebody else open up a market, recognizing the marketing opportunity, applying very skilled manufacturing, investing very heavily, and being very successful," Wedge went on. "However, in an era with a balanced cost-competition, which is what we have now, that strategy becomes less prone to success. I think that had currency values been maintained at an appropriate level for the past decade, we'd still have a steel industry, an automobile industry, and an electronics industry."

Looking back at the mistakes made by Moog, ARP, and the rest, one gets the impression that growth got the best of them. But Wedge pointed out, "I think company size is a red herring. The issue is the relationship between a company and its customers. Moog and ARP failed to turn the corner when Sequential gave musicians a product that answered their needs better than those made by the competition. At the time the Prophet came out, ARP was putting their efforts behind the Avatar, and Moog thought the Polymoog was going to save the day. They were wrong. So it's not that the companies got too big, it's that

they didn't heed the right market trends. They misunderstood where things were going."

One of the major factors in bringing down prices and making heretofore unaffordable technologies available to the masses is the advent of the custom LSI chip. E-mu's collaboration with Solid State Microtechnologies on their analog synth chips marked the beginning of a practice that would put a number of today's most successful American Japanese builders on the map. A couple of cases in point: The Emax's E chip was essentially an Emulator II on a chip; the DX7 was built around LSI technology, as was the Roland D-50.

Ensoniq is one American manufacturer that understands the value of building custom chips. Founded in the early '80s by some engineers from Commodore, Ensoniq's first product (a software drum machine) was aimed at the home computer market. Bob Yannes, one of Ensoniq's cofounders, was responsible for designing the Commodore 64's three-voice synth chip. In 1982 he designed a portion of a PC that was similar to the sound synthesizer that ended up in the Amiga. It was this chip that was used in the Mirage (1984) — the world's first really affordable sampler — and the ESQ-1 (1986), Ensoniq's wavetable synth.

Ensoniq's Mirage, first produced in 1984, was the first mass-marketed sampler.

Unlike most of the American manufacturers who had come before them, Ensoniq did not go for the high-end market. Explains Yannes, "We have always courted the mass market in music. We know you could build high-end equipment that's really superb and that you'd be able to sell for a little while to a certain number of people, but sooner or later someone's going to come along and stomp on you because the technology will allow them to produce something that's almost as good as what you've got for less. I think our going for the larger market is more of a Japanese philosophy. There is no significant long-term growth potential in the high-end market."

Still, Yannes is quick to point out that Ensoniq has expanded their product orientation to include the high end as well as the low. "The EPS and SQ-80 are intended to address the professional market, but we know our bread and butter is in the low end." Witness the present-day Ensoniq, who serves the low-end synth market with the SQ series and the KS-32 (1992) — the most affordable synth with a piano-action, 76-note keyboard and built-in sequencer — and the high end with the TS-10 synth and the ASR-10 sampler (both 1993).

Production, American Style. Japanese manufacturing techniques are an awesome sight. Yamaha's synthesizer assembly line is entirely automated, with robots doing all the work. Even product testing is performed by computers, then verified by a human. By contrast, a typical Roland assembly line looks more like a typical American assembly line. Humans do most of the work, yet they are amazingly productive. What are Ensoniq's production techniques like? Yannes tells us, "We use automated insertion techniques to stuff our circuit boards. We have automatic testers. But all the subassembly is done manually — putting the boards in the units and screwing them together.

"Our approach," he goes on, "is to design the minimal amount of hardware to get the job done and do everything else in software. Hardware costs you money. Every time you put a component in, it's costing you. Software is a development cost that you incur up-front. After that, it's essentially free. In production, we have basically a just-in-time system. Actually, it's called materials-as-needed. Material is ordered and hits the floor only when we need it. Just-in-time is a U.S. invention that was

Product specialist John Shykun waving hello while Ray Kurzweil smiles in satisfaction that his 250 is finally in production.

brought to the Japanese. Their approach goes back to [W. Edwards] Deming, who went there after World War II and helped re-establish their industry. Deming is in his 80s now. He has a book out, *Out of the Crisis* [MIT Center for Advanced Engineering Study]. Just about everyone in the audio industry has brought him in to lecture because his mass-production insights are so useful."

John Shykun, who has worked with as wide a range of American synth companies as you can imagine — from ARP to Sequential to Kurzweil to Mellotron — has another perspective on mass-production cost-cutting techniques: "You have to be fairly well capitalized to take advantage of those procedures," he points out. "You also have to have a market base that justifies those expenditures. No American company I have worked for ever had a world view of the market, whereas the Japanese think globally. I think the first American company that's doing it successfully is Ensoniq. They're doing some of the things the Japanese have done so well.

"I think there's a really interesting parallel between Ensoniq and Kurzweil," Shykun continues. "The two companies started at about the same time. Ensoniq had trouble raising even a million dollars of venture capital. Kurzweil had a very charismatic president — Ray Kurzweil — who was able to raise $20,000,000. But look at that little undercapitalized company now. They're a big profitable force in the industry. And Kurzweil is just starting to come around."

In fact, Kurzweil finally produced the product that their marketing surveys had been telling them people wanted — a $2,500 version of the Kurzweil piano sound — the Kurzweil 1000 (1988). It featured the Kurzweil 250's famous piano sound in a box that lists for a quarter of the price of the 250, and led to the eventual production of Kurzweil's current hotter-than-hot product, the K2000 (1992).

"Kurzweil's approach to building instruments is much different than Ensoniq's," Bob Moog said in early '88, when he worked for the company. "Kurzweil starts out with a no-compromises instrument using completely new technology, and then tries to develop that technology to where it can be produced more cheaply. We've been in

business five years now, and our engineering department has 30 people in it. I don't think there is any other American manufacturer going that's putting as much into keyboard instruments."

Another American success story can be found in Alesis, whose incredibly inexpensive effects arrived with a thunderous bang in 1985. Easily their biggest splash, though, came in 1992 when — two years after showing the product at NAMM — Alesis finally shipped the ADAT multitrack digital tape recorder. Like Ensoniq, Alesis seems to be beating the Japanese at their own game — delivering products with the right features at the right price for mass market appeal.

Their strategy is much the same as Ensoniq's. Marketing director Alan Wald explains, "We try to minimize the amount of hardware. We scale it down to exactly what is needed to bring about the desired music outcome. Our HR-16 drum machine and MMT-8 sequencer (1987/88) have a lot of features, but if you look at their hardware, we kept it to a minimum. We also utilize buttons and cases that allow us to implement mass production techniques and keep the costs down. We've taken some heat for our buttons, but we try to find the fine line

The Alesis MMT-8 sequencer: A second-generation American hardware manufacturer expands into a new area.

between what's acceptable and what's not.

"When it came to our digital reverb," Wald adds, "Keith Barr [president of Alesis] made some very hard decisions as to what features to include and what to leave out in order to come out at the right price point but still have the features that would make for a usable product. And that's how we go at the market. We're able to deliver low cost but still have features that professionals will find useful. And that gets us both the pro market and the entry-level market."

As with Ensoniq, almost every Alesis product has its own LSI chip. Their drum machines — including the current SR-16 — have custom designed chips. The Microverb and Midiverb II used the same chip, as did the Midiverb and Midifex (1986).

Much of Alesis' manufacturing is done in Taiwan, with the remainder being handled in the States. "That's been very cost effective, because of the favorable economic climate in Taiwan," Wald states. "We build certain of the circuit boards and

parts over there, and ship them to the States for assembly. The Microverb II is the one product that we fully assemble over there." We're told that the ADAT digital multitrack tape machine is assembled entirely in the Los Angeles area.

What We Missed. In case you hadn't noticed, we intentionally limited the scope of this chapter to U.S. hardware manufacturers. Certainly a number of software companies are crossing over the great solder and circuit-board boundary. Opcode, with its line of sync boxes and Macintosh interfaces/MIDI patchbays, and Digidesign, with their Macintosh DSP cards and digital recording systems, come to mind. Voyetra crossed the line in the other direction. They went from building synths to making IBM software.

Scott Wedge sums things up pretty well: "When you toss America's software companies into the ring along with the hardware companies, I don't think the synthesizer industry has ever been healthier."

THE RISE & FALL OF MOOG MUSIC

Shuffle off to Buffalo

BY CONNOR FREFF COCHRAN & BOB MOOG

Last year you and I and a lot of folks like us spent something over three billion dollars, worldwide, on large and small electronic sound-generating thingies with keyboards. No kidding. This is not an unrespectable figure, being midway between the gross national products of Afghanistan and Bolivia. It's also not the way it always was.

Synths aren't toddlers any more. After 20 years, they are more like seniors in college: too young to be totally together, too old to slide by on that excuse, and too damn close to a forced choice between grad school and a real job.

We thought you'd like to hear from our beloved *father*, the guy who started it all. So, some baby pictures, if you will, from the scrapbook of a man who's had to wash out his share of diapers along the way.

Bob?

* * * *

Birth of the Bloops. When I set up shop in Trumansburg, New York, in the summer of 1963, I was finishing my Ph.D. at Cornell and suffering vague notions of getting into the kit business. I had no

A cellarful of Moogs: Bob with a selection of synths that shared his name, c. 1975.

Some early Moog products on display at a NAMM show.

The Moog System 15 was the company's smallest production modular system. One of these might cost $500 to $1,000 today.

concept of synthesizers or electronic music at all. It was just me and a couple of people in a storefront, designing a portable, battery-operated musical instrument amplifier kit — which never did go into production, because it was way overpriced. This is a lesson you learn when you go into consumer electronics: The most important parameter of any product is price, because everything is measured against price, just the same way that in music, everything is measured against time.

All through the amplifier project, I was making theremins on a custom basis. I'd been doing that

since I was 19 — it was a hobby, the output of which I could sell. My New York rep, Walter Sear — these days Walter makes Grade Z movies, but before he made Grade Z movies he made porno movies, and before he made porno movies he sold tubas and my theremins — invited me to come help him show theremins to schoolteachers at the New York State School Music Association convention, at the Concord Hotel. That was where I met Herb Deutsch.

What I knew about electronic music at the end of '63 was some vague knowledge that yes, at Columbia University there were some people who had something called the Columbia-Princeton Electronic Music Center, and yes, they gave concerts once in a while, and yes, I should probably find out more. Herb was a music instructor at Hofstra who was doing his own experimental tape compositions. He invited me down to a concert of his at the studio of a sculptor colleague named Jason Seley, who worked in welded automobile bumpers. They were beautiful sculptures. More than that, they made great percussion instruments. It was a very exciting concert. I got all turned on by the visual idea of playing a sculpture, the interaction between electronic and acoustic sounds, and the whole idea of tone color music. There was no harmony or melody; it was strictly tone color space.

Herb and I kept in touch. More or less in my spare time I built two voltage-controlled oscillators and two voltage-controlled amplifiers, and some kind of controller that could turn the sounds on and off and change the pitch and the rates of modulation. It might have been a couple of doorbells. When Herb came up with his family — he parked them at a cabin in the state park while we worked for three weeks — he just flipped when he heard what my breadboards could do. By the end of that session and the one that followed, together we had come up with the basics of a modular analog synthesizer.

Mind you, neither of us had any idea where this was leading.

We went across the border to the University of Toronto electronic music studio, which was, at that time, headed by Myron Schaeffer. *He* flipped. He was the first person from the electronic music

Although the Minimoog was billed as "a Moog for the road," the Moog Sonic Six — intended for educational use — was a bit more portable because it was built into a carrying case. Today a Sonic Six is only worth $150 to $250.

establishment to give us encouragement. Word got around, and in September I got a call from Jacqueline Harvey of the Audio Engineering Society (which was much smaller then than it is today). She called me up and said, "We hear that you people are doing something . . . interesting . . . up there." To which I replied, "Well, maybe." She explained that she had an exhibit area to give away at the forthcoming AES show, because CBS had taken a booth but decided not to use it. Now, I knew nothing about the AES. I knew nothing about conventions in New York. I knew nothing about the audio industry. I knew nothing about buying and selling and taking orders. It was still just a hobby. So I went down and set up these few handmade modules on a little card table, and on one side of me was Ampex, with their huge tape recorders, and on the other side was 3M, and across the way was Sculley. . . . I was really a David among the Goliaths, and feeling very much out of place. But Jimmy Seawright, who was a technician at Columbia-Princeton Electronic Music Center, came by and took a look and said [choreographer/composer] "Alwin Nikolais should see these." Later that day, Nikolais came by and a most unexpected event happened: He placed an order.

We actually took two or three orders at the

show, which kept us busy for about six months. And that's how it began.

Big Business. It was part-time until the summer of 1965. We were working overtime on a custom job for John Cage — by that time I had eight or ten people working for me, but it was going badly and we were behind schedule — and at 9 pm the phone rang. It was my thesis adviser. "Moog, whatever is *not* on my desk at 9 tomorrow morning is not going in your thesis." That's how I finally got my degree. I finished that night.

Once that was out of the way, we were full-time. But a business? From the point of view of competence, we were never a business. Never. We got some of the elements in place, but none of the controls or forecasting or planning that go with a well-run business. We just never had it.

We were always in the red. We had no capital. None. Zero! And yet, we managed to keep stumbling along.

A Little Bach-Ground Information. Wendy Carlos was a student of Ussachevsky's at the Columbia-Princeton Center. We first met when we all went out somewhere to have Chinese. By the time this became a business, Wendy was working as an engineer for Gotham Recording, one of the hip studios, and on the side she was putting together her own music system. She began ordering modules and of-

Composer Wendy Carlos at work in 1979 on her monster Moog system, the one featured on *Switched-On Bach*. (photo by Len DeLessio)

fering all sorts of criticisms. She really understood instinctively what I was doing right and wrong. The fixed filter banks came from Wendy. Lots of other things, too; I've lost track. It was always on the back of an envelope, or over the telephone. Wendy had already done a couple of Bach pieces, and she and Rachel Elkind — who was Goddard Lieberson's secretary at CBS — decided an electronic music record based on the works of Bach would be interesting.

I found myself giving a paper at the 1968 AES convention in NYC, on different ways of organizing electronic music studios. By that time we knew

The single-oscillator Micromoog, introduced in '75, was intended for those who couldn't afford the Minimoog. A Micromoog will currently bring only $50 to $150.

Basically an expanded version of the Micromoog, the Multimoog featured two oscillators, a pitch-bend ribbon, and a 3 1/2-octave keyboard with a force sensor for controlling functions like pitch, LFO speed, and volume. It came out in 1978 at a list price of $1,595.

about sequencers, we knew about computer control, multi-track tape recording, etc. At the end of the talk I said to this fairly big audience, "As an example of multi-track electronic music studio composition technique, I would like to play an excerpt of a record that's about to be released of some music by Bach." It was the last movement of Wendy's *Brandenburg No. 3*. I walked off the stage and went to the back of the auditorium while people were listening, and I could feel it in the air. They were jumping out of their skins. These technical people were involved in so much flim-flam, so much shoddy, opportunistic stuff, and here was something that was just impeccably done and had obvious musical content and was totally innovative. The tape got a standing ovation.

CBS had no idea what they had in *Switched-On Bach*. When it came out, they lumped it in at a studio press party for Terry Riley's *In C* and an abysmal record called *Rock and Other Four Letter Words*. Carlos was so pissed off, she refused to come. So CBS, frantic to have some representation, asked me to demonstrate the synthesizer. I remember there was a nice big bowl of joints on top of the mixing console, and Terry Riley was there in his white Jesus suit, up on a pedestal, playing live on a Farfisa organ against a backup of tape delays. *Rock and Other Four Letter Words* went on to sell a few thousand records. *In C* sold a

few tens of thousands. *Switched-On Bach* sold over a million, and just keeps going on and on.

Walter Sear had been beating a path up and down Madison Avenue, selling modular systems to commercial music producers who did work for ad agencies. He had something like 40 customers by 1968. But when *Switched-On Bach* came out, the shit hit the fan. All the record producers had to have their Moog record for 1969. We got orders from CBS, NBC, Elektra, a lot of other guys. And these guys didn't want just "one of this, and two of that. . . ." They said, "Give me your biggest system," and they expected to make money like Carlos did. I could play you some of these records. A few of them still stand up. But mostly they were cynical, inept, opportunistic things: throw together a group, lay down some strings and horns and vocals, leave some space for a novelty melody line from the synth. That was the scene in '69. Moog records.

Big Business (Bites). At our peak, we were cranking out two or three modular systems a week, and had 42 employees. We were back-ordered all through 1969 and the first half of 1970.

Right around then, three forces merged. The first was that the market became saturated. The guys who'd jumped on doing their Moog records hadn't had hits, so they'd dumped their synthesizers. The second was that now we had competition — ARP —

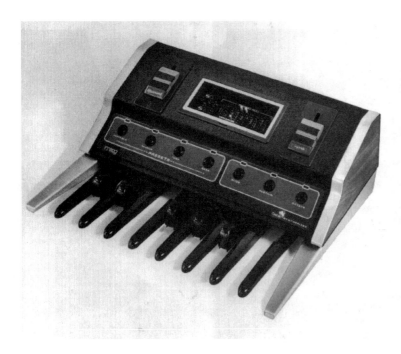

The Moog Taurus pedals unit is still popular thanks to its ability to pump out killer bass timbres.

One of the first polyphonic synthesizers was the Polymoog (c. 1975). A mass of internal circuits, it required 300 engineering changes. $200 to $600 might get you a Polymoog nowadays. (photo by Dominic Milano)

and their product had the appeal of stable oscillators and no patch cords. The third thing was a general recession that forced music producers to cut back. Suddenly we went from having a quarter-million backlog to no backlog at all. We *did* have the Minimoog. We'd been getting requests from studio musicians asking us to pack all that stuff into a nice package they could carry to gigs with them, and we'd done that, but we had no way of selling it. Music stores didn't carry synthesizers.

Zero sales, huge bills, lots of inventory, and no capital. I'd been looking for capital for quite a while, but that's another thing I was absolutely no good at. I could never inspire money people to invest in the company. So this guy Bill Waytena — who specialized in buying distressed companies, then pumping them up and selling them — took over the company. It cost him nothing except his guarantee that our personally secured debts and our suppliers would be paid off: more than $250,000.

Waytena's Ways & Means. Why was he interested? He saw a marketing opportunity. He'd actually hired a couple of engineers to design a synth called the Sonic V for a company of his own called Musonics. He told me that it would be the next rage in adult toys, that all he had to do was advertise these things in *Esquire* and he'd sell 5,000 of them. [*Waytena's own recollection is that he was aiming mainly for the educational market.*] This wasn't entirely unreasonable: Back then people were going apeshit over things that made funny electronic sounds. Anyway, as soon as he put it out he saw he wasn't going to sell 5,000. He wasn't even going to sell 500, because he didn't have a *name* and he didn't have any product experience. So he bought R. A. Moog Inc., moved it to Buffalo, merged it with Musonics into a company called Moog/Musonics, eventually dropped the Musonics part — and that left Moog Music.

The building that we moved into had been a gelatin factory for the previous 100 years. Know how they make gelatin? In one huge building, there was nothing but these concrete pits in the floor, pits six feet wide by ten feet long and six feet deep. They'd fill these pits with incredibly tough water buffalo hides (the leftovers, anyway, since between India and Buffalo the hides stopped in

Brazil, where gears and other machine parts were stamped out of them, they were so tough) and these hides would soak in lye for a year. Then they'd steam-cook the stuff in an above-ground vat, with rollers mashing it to pulp, filter the gelatin out, and dry it on trays inside a 60-foot long semi-circular ventilating tunnel, using huge fans. When this place was making gelatin, you could smell it ten miles away, and every kook and crazy in the area had a job there because you had to be nuts to work in a place like that. If you consider what Kurzweil Music looked like before Young Chang bought it, or even at what ARP Instruments looked like in the early '70s, by comparison Moog Music was a shithole. A smelly, damp, uncomfortable, unattractive, unfinished shithole that we worked in from March 1971 into 1974.

But You've Gotta Know the Territory. Dave Van Koevering was born into a family of fundamentalist southern ministers, and he was an absolute genius at entertaining people, at capturing their attention and enthusiasm. I met him when he was making a living by going around elementary schools and putting on assemblies in which he'd demonstrate novelty instruments like glass harmonicas and — this is why we met — a modular synthesizer.

Dave formed a partnership with a piano and organ businessman in St. Petersburg, Florida, and decided to sell Minimoogs. At that time there was no such thing as a synthesizer, or *any* instrument with knobs being sold in music stores. But Dave had a vision.

He would take a Minimoog into a music store somewhere in central Florida and show it to the proprietor and salesmen, and almost invariably they'd throw him out. He'd then go to the local Holiday or Ramada Inn and check out the bands. During the break he'd ask the keyboard player aside, show him the Minimoog — the guy would flip — and Dave would say, "I'm going to

The Polymoog Keyboard was a stripped-down version of the original Polymoog. Current value: $150 to $450.

arrange for you to have this thing." The next morning he'd walk into the store he'd been kicked out of, musician in tow, and say "Here's your first customer, so now you'll have to place an order for two." That is how Minimoogs got to be carried in musical instrument stores. And it began in the absolute most unlikely place: central Florida.

Van Koevering had a golden tongue and enormous hands that he used whenever he talked. He looked like a combination of Colonel Sanders and the Music Man. So we hired him as marketing manager. He stayed on board for a year and signed up a lot of European Moog distributors. But Waytena apparently felt that Van Koevering would not be perceived as an asset in selling the company off to a buyer, so Van Koevering didn't last long.

Introduced in the late '70s along with low-cost monophonic synths from Korg, Yamaha, and Roland, Moog's Prodigy did surprisingly well against the competition. In fact, it more or less dominated the field until Sequential released the Pro-One in March '81.

Moog's strap-on wonder, the Liberation (released in early '81), was too heavy (14 lbs.) for some players to haul around for extended periods. The mannequin in this NAMM display must have eaten his Wheaties to last the day. According to Sean Denton of the Starving Musician, a Moog Liberation is worth about $150 these days.

Big Business Bites (Back). Anecdote! The quintessential anecdote! Van Koevering determined that we ought to have a preset synthesizer, something equal to the ARP Pro-Soloist. I started in December 1971, with one draftsman who couldn't draw a straight line, not with all the tools in the world, and one designer who was equally inept. By

June — somehow — we had a prototype called the Satellite. At the June 1973 NAMM [National Association of Music Merchants trade show], it was demonstrated on top of a Wurlitzer organ, and every single organ manufacturer came and gawked and drooled over it. A hot product. But it wasn't in production. Waytena decided to sell the rights to make the Satellite, and at the end of the summer he landed a big fish. Want to hear astounding, appalling, unbelievable business numbers? The Thomas Organ company agreed to build Satellites into their organs for a royalty of $15 each — and to build and sell 5,000 free-standing Satellites at a royalty of $75. Each. This product was supposed to retail for $500, which meant that the music store paid $300, which meant that manufacturer's cost had to be less than $180 to be worthwhile, and out of that Waytena was soaking Thomas for $75. An unbelievably steep royalty. The usual rate is 5% of wholesale; this was at least 40%.

Next year, on Moog Music's income and expense statement, there was an item marked *Extraordinary Income* — $375,000. That was the royalty. Added to the rest of the income, and put against costs, it appeared on the bottom line as an extraordinary percentage of operating profit — at least 25%. To a businessman, a company that produces 24–25% profit is unbelievably lucrative. So Waytena took this balance sheet, this one piece of paper, and used it to sell Moog Music to Norlin. "Twenty-five percent profit before taxes!" he re-

Moog replaced the Prodigy in late '81 with the Rogue. It cost $495 and was designed to be as inexpensive as Moog could make it.

portedly told them. "What else do you have that will produce like this?" Even more amazing, apparently no one at Norlin understood the extraordinary income for the one-time thing it was. [*Waytena suggests that Moog Music's reputation for engineering expertise may also have been an important asset.*]

I don't know exactly what Norlin paid for Moog: more than two million, less than ten.

The Squeaky Wheel (& You Know the Rest). Waytena's deal with Norlin was that he would remain to manage the company for seven years at a mere $5,000 a month retainer. But he bragged that he'd be able to wash his hands of the company well before that. As soon as the ink was dry, he made himself so difficult to deal with that they decided to pay him off; it took less than a year. By Christmas of 1973, according to stories that were going around at the time, they said, "We'll send you your money. Get lost." [*According to Waytena, he was paid $50,000 a year for ten years.*]

One example: Part of the deal was an incentive he got paid based on the number of Minimoogs we sold. Well, at that point Moog Music really only had one customer, and that was Norlin. So a couple of months after the agreement was signed, Waytena approached an executive at Norlin and said, "I

have some paperwork that needs a signature." One of the sheets was a purchase order for Minimoogs — 300 a month. A few months later, an audit team from Norlin came by, and that 60-foot tunnel I told you about, where they dried the gelatin? — that tunnel was completely full of Minimoogs. Fourteen hundred of them. The audit team freaked out. But Waytena had the purchase order. . . .

Sloping Downward to the Sea, & Oblivion. By the time Waytena left, Dave Luce was running engineering and Tom Gullo was running manufacturing. I had my own little research operation with Norlin.

Tom Gullo was a capable guy wrestling with big problems. When Norlin took over, their marketing people decided to consolidate all Norlin manufacturing at the Moog facility, because Buffalo labor costs were cheap. On the basis of combined sales estimates, they sank $2.5 million into upgrades and equipment. But the estimates were

The Liberation with its interface/power supply. In his review in the Apr. '81 *Keyboard*, Dominic Milano said, "The Liberation's fat sound . . . is perhaps even a little fatter than the sound of its famous ancestor the Minimoog."

Moog's Opus 3 combined a mono synth voice with polyphonic strings, organ, and brass sounds. Introduced in 1980, it will only bring $150 to $200 on the street market today.

cally trained person who gravitated toward complicated, sophisticated, tricky, convoluted things. Tom Gullo was a self-trained manufacturing man who gravitated toward simple, straightforward, easy-to-understand things. After I left in 1977, Norlin brought in a guy named Dave Bueschel, an EE with some management training, and he tried for a while but couldn't integrate the two sides. When he left, the Norlin people, in their infinite wisdom, decided the right way to select the president of Moog Music was to hire an industrial psychiatrist and give intelligence tests to four people: Luce, Gullo, sales manager Neil Smith, and marketing manager Herb Deutsch. Dave, the MIT Ph.D. who liked complicated solutions to seemingly simple problems, won the contest and became president of Moog Music. The rest is well known.

What Prompted Me to Leave. What prompted me to stay that long, more like it. I had a four-year employment contract I had to stick out in order to cash my stock in. I would have left before, if I could.

Big Business Bites Back (& Bites Deep). After Moog Music, I built a house, did some custom work, and did some consulting before joining Kurzweil. Jim Scott, Tom Rhea, and I designed a very hip analog synthesizer for Crumar, called the Spirit. How many of those do you see around today? And I did some work on a thing called the Gizmotron.

That's a story.

Aaron Newman founded Musitronics and started the Mu-Tron Pedal line, which were very

wrong, and Tom Gullo was faced with financing this very large investment, so he went out and got subcontract assembly work. As the music business kept on stumbling — Dave Luce's Polymoog got into production, but then needed 300 engineering changes — Tom went more and more out of the company to keep the plant busy. By the late 1970s, Moog Music was more subcontractor than manufacturer.

So here was this entity with two people who had completely different personalities running the two sides. Dave Luce was a highly intelligent, techni-

Don't recognize the Moog SL-8? That's because it was never released as such. It became the Memorymoog.

popular in the early and mid-'70s. Around 1976, Lol Creme and Kevin Godley of 10CC approached him and showed him their guitar controller invention, the Gizmotron. Aaron was a guitar player. He figured that there were more guitarists than keyboard players, and that everyone was going to have to have one of these things. So he found a buyer for Mu-Tron in ARP, under royalty terms, and proceeded to do the Gizmotron development. Well, a lot of things happened: ARP lost the power to live up to its commitment and didn't pay its royalties. The Gizmotron was very tricky to build. It relied on rubber parts that sometimes worked and sometimes didn't. The molding of these parts was very expensive. Before Aaron knew it he owed $90,000 to

the mold maker, as much or more to other people — and still the thing couldn't be made. Aaron tried to raise money, because the creditors were getting more and more strident. After six months, he managed to get the SBA [Small Business Administration] to lend him $150,000, secured against everything he owned: house, car, everything. He signed the papers on a Monday morning — and that night he had a heart attack and was in the hospital for six weeks. While he was in the hospital, the $150,000 was disbursed to the creditors, but it wasn't enough, and the company was forced into bankruptcy.

Last I heard, Aaron was an insurance agent. (Quite a successful one, too.) That's what *can* happen to you in the music business.

The Memorymoog hit the market in late '82, not long before MIDI revolutionized the electronic music field. Whereas the original Memorymoog is currently worth $200 to $700, a Memorymoog Plus (with MIDI and a built-in sequencer) can go from $650 to a substantial $1,300 from a dealer or store.

THE RISE & FALL OF ARP INSTRUMENTS

Too Many Chefs in the Kitchen

BY CRAIG R. WATERS WITH JIM AIKIN

Back in 1975, when the first issue of Keyboard *hit the stands, there were only a handful of companies making synthesizers. The first polyphonic instruments had just appeared, and programmability was still several years in the future. The leaders of this fledgling industry were Moog Music and ARP Instruments, both of which were named after their founders — Bob Moog and Alan R. Pearlman. Over the years, ARP produced a number of keyboards that were eagerly embraced by musicians, including the Odyssey, the Pro-Soloist, and the Omni, and one — the 2600 — that remains a classic. Today, however, ARP no longer exists.*

What happened? To some extent, changes in technology caught up with ARP. A major part of the company's design philosophy was explicitly to recycle existing circuit boards into new instruments, which left plenty of room for newcomers in the industry, unencumbered by outmoded components and concepts, to take advantage of developments such as microprocessors. In addition, outside observers often noted that ARP seemed hypnotized by the idea that they had to design things differently from Moog. They ignored some good, usable ideas — notably the pitch-bend wheel — for no better reason than that Moog was using them. Allowing somebody else to define your products' identity in a negative sense is bound to be risky, especially in an expanding industry where there are fewer and fewer good ideas left unused.

Nevertheless, ARP built good products, and they sold well. The major problems that developed in the company were due less to design flaws than to corporate mismanagement. These problems were detailed in an article in the November 1982 issue of Inc., *a magazine for business management. The facts and figures below were marshalled by Craig R. Waters, a senior staff writer at* Inc., *and appear here unchanged except for the abridgement of a few passages and the correction of some minor technical inaccuracies having to do with synthesizers. We also spoke to Philip Dodds, formerly the vice president of engineering at ARP, who was able to rescue his entire engineering team and the nearly completed Chroma synthesizer from the ashes of ARP and give them a new home at CBS Musical Instruments, where they joined the Rhodes piano division and rechristened ARP's last project the Rhodes Chroma. Dodds' comments add another perspective to the article that* Inc. *called "Raiders of the Lost ARP."*

— Jim Aikin

David Friend (L) and ARP founder Alan R. Pearlman survey the ARP Sequencer. Stacked in the background are (top to bottom) a Pro-Soloist, 2600 keyboard, and String Ensemble (Solina).

Alan R. Pearlman never really understood the world of rock music; for him, it was groupies, drugs, and inarticulate musicians. Pearlman, 67, an engineer who had been weaned on classical piano and had spent five years designing amplifiers for the Apollo and Gemini space programs, found pop musicians inexplicable at best and flabbergasting at worst. Yet the company he founded in the late '60s quickly became one of the premier manufacturers of the synthesizers used by such people. From its inception, ARP was on the cutting edge of technology, and by the mid-'70s it enjoyed preeminence in the marketplace. It had 40% of the $25 million [synthesizer] market, surpassing Moog Music, whose predecessor, R. A. Moog, Inc., had created the first well-known synthesizers. But by 1981, Pearlman's Lexington, Massachusetts, company was dead, the victim of miscalculation and the worst form of mismanagement: no management at all.

Today, Pearlman works as a senior electronics engineer for a small electronics company in Natick, Massachusetts. "There are only two engineers in the whole place and I'm one of them," he says. "I'm enjoying it very much." Only a decade ago, Pearlman was struggling to recover face, fortune, and his faith in free enterprise with Selva Systems, Inc., a microcomputer software company. ("Yeah," he admits, "that went down the tubes, too.") As chief executive officer of Selva, he occupied a small office one flight up from a store that sold electronics kits in Wellesley, Massachusetts — only ten miles from the site of ARP's luxurious 50,000-square-foot plant. He lost $1 million in paper assets and, for a while, his peace of mind, because of what happened at ARP.

A brilliant engineer, Pearlman co-founded Nexus Resarch Laboratory Inc., a maker of solid-state analog modules (precision circuits used in amplifiers and test equipment, for example), and nurtured it to a solid $4 million sales status before selling out to Teledyne Inc. in 1967. Aroused a year later by *Switched-On Bach*, the first major recording done on synthesizer, he returned to an earlier interest, electronic music. In 1948, as a student at Worcester Polytechnic Institute, he had written a paper on the subject, saying, "The electronic instrument's value is chiefly as a novelty. With greater attention on the part of the engineer to the needs of the musician, the day may not be too remote when the electronic instrument may take its place . . . as a versatile, powerful, and expressive instrument."

Twenty years later, Pearlman made the leap from speculation to reality. "I went into the basement," he says, "and did some playing around." His tinkering yielded promising sounds and, shortly, a new company. With $100,000 of his own money and $100,000 from a small group of in-

ARP's first instrument, the model 2500 modular synthesizer, was unveiled in 1970 under the name Tonus, Inc. Along with Philip Dodds, the 2500 made a cameo appearance in *Close Encounters of the Third Kind* (1977, 1980), where it helped man communicate with alien visitors from outer space through music and mathematics. In today's math, a 2500 might bring as little as $500 (it would have to be in horrible shape), but more accurate figures probably range from $1,000 upwards to $8,000. That's on the street. Buy one from a reputable dealer and the price could soar to a cool ten grand.

vestors, he set up ARP Instruments in 1969, and in 1970 the company unveiled its first instrument, the ARP 2500.

Creating notes electronically rather than mechanically had been achieved within a few years of the invention of the vacuum tube in 1904, and the first viable ancestor of today's synthesizers, the Ondes Martenot, made its debut in 1929. But the idea of voltage control wasn't applied to musical instruments until 1964, when the first commercially available instruments, built by Moog on the East Coast and Don Buchla on the West Coast, appeared. By 1969, in part because the instrument used on *Switched-On Bach* was a Moog, Moog owned the market.

[*Perhaps because Moog and Buchla were using patch cords, Pearlman elected to do signal-routing in the 2500 with a matrix switching panel, a crisscrossing grid of horizontal and vertical lines into which pins were inserted to make electrical connections. With this system, some users reported excessive cross-talk between theoretically independent signal paths — which might under some circumstances be musically useful but would more likely cause problems.*] The 2500, however, enjoyed one distinct advantage. The oscillators used by Moog tended to drift in pitch, which necessitated frequent retuning and made live performance difficult. "We were better at analog electronics," explains Pearlman. "We knew how to keep the oscillators in tune." [*Bob Moog unhesitatingly confirms the superiority of the early ARP instruments in this respect.*]

ARP had a promising first product, but it was entering a volatile and risky market in which it had no expertise. "At Nexus, I had dealt for the most part with other engineers," Pearlman says wistfully. "We spoke the same language and were basically the same sort of people. The musical instrument business was alien — I never understood the people."

The company revolved around, and was essentially shaped by, three individuals: Pearlman, chairman of the board; Lewis G. Pollock, legal counsel and chairman of the executive committee; and David Friend, who was president from 1977 to 1980. Each brought distinctive backgrounds, personalities, and goals to the project. Pearlman was the soft-spoken engineer, a man wedded to technology but seduced by business. At Nexus, he had made the daily decisions, a chore he hoped to escape at ARP. "I thought, in starting a new company, that I could get others to do it," he says. "I wanted to do long-range R&D, long-range marketing."

Pollock, who had represented Nexus in its merger with Teledyne and had a management consulting contract with ARP, was known as "the entrepreneur's lawyer" but might better have been dubbed "the entrepreneur/lawyer." Although never an officer of ARP, he spent an inordinate amount of time overseeing the company's fortunes. "I'll bet if you looked at his time log, you'd find that he put in 40 hours a week at ARP," says Joseph Mancuso, the author of 14 books on business and a consultant to more than 340 companies, and an ARP director for three years. "If any one person ran ARP, and that's debatable," says another insider, "then Pollock was that person."

Catering to performing musicians who wanted a smaller synth, ARP introduced the Odyssey in 1972. Note the pitch-bend knob at the lower left of the control panel. This was later replaced with the PPC (proportional pitch control) pitch-bending system, which consisted of three pressure-sensitive pads that bent the pitch sharp or flat, or induced vibrato. An Odyssey is worth $100 to $250 street value, up to $450 for a beaut from a store.

Friend was the whiz kid, a talented and ambitious young man with a background in engineering and music, but none in business. Discovered by Pollock and recruited from graduate school at Princeton, at 21 Friend was the youngest member of ARP's inner circle.

These three men sat on ARP's board, along with two outside directors brought in by Pollock, and made up the executive committee that ran the company. Created by the board at Pollock's suggestion, the committee — an unusual form of management for a small business — was entrusted with its operation. The egos and goals of the three frequently clashed, and their management skills were open to question. None had ever run a "glamour" company before. Pearlman, in his ivory tower of long-range planning, was initially blind to the severe shortcomings of his management team.

And there were other problems. From the outset, ARP was under-capitalized. In 1973, the company went public, raising $750,000 [by selling stock]. "We needed the money," says Pearlman. "There was a critical mass we had to achieve in order to pull ahead." In 1973 and 1974, ARP borrowed a total of $600,000 in the form of convertible debentures [a form of loan in which the lender has the option of taking stock in the company instead of repayment]. In addition, it had an ongoing line of credit with First National Bank of Boston, primarily to cover [the cost of building up] inventory and to finance receivables [amounts owed to the company]. "It was always a borderline company in terms of cash flow," notes Friend. "It lived from hand to mouth the entire time I was there."

A quickly saturated market, pressure on prices, Japanese competition, changing musical tastes, and the vagaries of the instrument business all added to ARP's woes. "Whether or not a product catches on," Friend argues, "is largely a matter of how well you can get in the front door to see Stevie Wonder. You rise or fall with each new product." [*Artist endorsements are certainly a major factor in musical instrument marketing, but in the long run engineering is at least as important. It's doubtful whether endorsements would have helped generate wide-spread acceptance of such ARP blunders as the ill-fated Avatar guitar synthesizer or the PPC pitch-bending system, both of which were developed and implemented largely by Friend.*]

Over the years, ARP created enough winners to hold the odds at bay. The 2500 proved popular with university music departments, and the 2600, Pro-Soloist, Odyssey, and Axxe became the favorite lead synthesizers of a generation of keyboard players. The company's all-time best-seller was the Omni, introduced in 1975. [*Like the Poly-moog, which appeared at about the same time, the*

Omni had a fully polyphonic keyboard whose oscillators used the same top-octave divide-down scheme that had been used for years in electronic organs; this was mated to some synthesizer technology to create these first polyphonic synthesizers. Simultaneously, Tom Oberheim was developing the Oberheim Four Voice using a different kind of polyphonicity, with four separate integrated voice modules assigned to the notes played on the keyboard. The scanning system used for assigning keys to modules was developed by Dave Rossum and Scott Wedge of E-mu Systems, and it is this type of polyphonicity that has ultimately proven more useful except in inexpensive instruments.] About 4,000 Omnis (1980 price, $2,450) were sold.

Annual sales climbed from about $865,000 in 1971 to a peak of $7 million in 1977, with net earnings running a lean $232,000. When it had loss years, ARP managed to snap back. Bob Moog recalls that ARP had problems with quality control and excessive cost of sales (as high as 20%). "The killer, for me, with ARP was that, two or three years after they began, they had a negative net worth of $400,000," Moog recalls. "I thought I was a rotten businessman — I was under-capitalized, and I didn't manage things properly. But the worst we ever had was a negative net worth of $11,000."

Pearlman's company not only managed to maintain its precarious balancing act but generally made the performance look like an inspired success. "ARP was a movie-star company," notes Mancuso, "and Pearlman had the time of his life —

he was donating ARPs to the Metropolitan Museum, his name was in the paper, Diana Ross was dropping by. These three guys loved the glamour of running the company, but they weren't doing it in a businesslike way."

When he joined ARP's board in 1976, Mancuso promptly made several elementary management suggestions. The company had done cost-plus pricing, but when it introduced the Omni, Mancuso suggested seeing what the market would bear. With a price tag $1,000 higher, the instrument sold better. Mancuso also recommended that higher-margin domestic orders be filled more quickly than overseas sales, a move that bolstered the company's cash flow. "Mancuso had a lot of good ideas," concedes Pearlman.

In 1977, income and profit soared — the company had record sales of $7 million, an amazing recovery from the $33,000, 8¢-a-share loss it had suffered in 1974. As a result, ARP management grew more expansive. New Chevrolet Blazers were passed out to members of management, and at least one board meeting was followed by an elaborate dinner party. "Each bottle of wine cost about $60," recalls Mancuso.

But the problems that had plagued ARP remained, as the Pearlman-Pollock-Friend combination became more unwieldy. Each man pursued his own vision for the company, aligning himself with others to further his own ideas and interests. Memos show Pearlman increasingly alienated from his own company, Friend jockeying for the

The Quadra (1978) consisted of an Omni, an Axxe, and the equivalent of a couple of other synthesizers strapped together in one box under the control of a microprocessor. (Current street value, $150 to $400; dealer/store, $650.)

presidency, and Pollock insisting that ARP perform as a sane company.

In a July 21, 1976, memo to the directors, Pearlman groused that he was being kept in the dark about a guitar synthesizer that was being developed. "I may be oversensitive," he wrote, suspecting "that Dave Friend and [engineer] Tim Gillette were laying down a smokescreen of concealment for fear that I would prematurely criticize their efforts."

At about the same time, in a memo to Pearlman, Friend said, "I believe Lew [Pollock] is exhibiting the classic Freudian behavior of a parent who sees his child emerging as an independent adult. . . . Lew feels that he is in control of ARP now and views my acquiring the title of president as diluting that control."

And in a July 13, 1977, memo to the executive committee, Pollock insisted: "The company is a rather mature company, and for it to be considered a growth kind of opportunity for investors, acquisitions, etc., the company must, *must*, have about a 10% pretax earning. Waiting for next year is no longer excusable."

"It was difficult to tell who was running the company," comments Mancuso. "They were doing what I would call management by turns — 'Pollock is away a week, I'll run it'; 'Friend is away a week, I'll run it.' And Pearlman would run it by default when the two of them were away."

Mancuso saw no solution to the strong ambitions and intransigent positions; none of the men was willing to yield power, either to one of the others or to a chief executive officer who might have been brought in. At one point, as he watched his own authority evaporate, Pearlman considered waging a proxy battle to regain control, but — advised against it by his own attorney — he resigned himself to the status quo. "I didn't know how to fight," he concedes.

Instead, ARP embarked on the most ambitious and dangerous product-development project it had ever undertaken, one that intensified and underscored the rivalry within the executive committee. After having spent eight years acquiring expertise in building keyboard instruments, ARP undertook to create a guitar synthesizer, the Avatar. The reasoning was that there were four times as many gui-

This prototype (one of the two in existence) of the ARP Centaur is on display at the New England Synth Museum. The Centaur was shelved in '77 in favor of developing the Avatar. (photo courtesy of David Wilson, New England Synth Museum)

tarists active in rock bands as keyboard players. Whether those guitarists were willing to pay nearly $3,000 for a synthesizer was a question that was never answered by market research.

The 1977 business plan written by Friend called for a research and development commitment so major that a polyphonic keyboard synthesizer under development had to be shelved. [*The shelved project was the ARP Centaur, a polyphonic synthesizer that was originally intended to have both guitar and keyboard incarnations. According to Philip Dodds, "The Centaur was the biggest boondoggle you've ever seen. There were 115 printed circuit boards in that unit. It was to be the polyphonic guitar synthesizer that would do it all. I agreed to get involved in the project provided that it would parallel the keyboard version, since that was our forte. But Dave Friend killed the keyboard version and put all his money on the Centaur. During all the dissension, Al Pearlman did a failure analysis on the unit and determined that the average time between breakdowns was about two hours. It was a brute-force approach to polyphonic synthesis, with everything implemented using available technology, and as a result it would probably have retailed for between $15,000 and $20,000 — if you could keep it running."*]

As far as Pearlman was concerned, throwing the company into the Avatar project was "dropping the bird in the hand and going for the bird in the bush." In a memo to the board, he declared, "This project is the riskiest one we have ever undertaken. . . . There are formidable technical problems of sound analysis, as well as synthesis, and we have an unknown amount of R&D" to produce an acceptable working model. [*The problems of sound analysis concerned the performance of the pitch-to-voltage converts that sensed the vibrations of the guitar strings and turned them into DC voltages the synthesizer could work with. The R&D on the synthesizer part of the instrument was less complex, because the Avatar used the same oscillator and filter boards found in the ARP Odyssey.*] By the time of this memo, though, Pearlman had virtually lost his voice at ARP. At one point, he actually feared the board might dismiss him. "It became a political party — the guitar party," he explains. "It was blasphemy to question anything about it."

Friend, who had been largely responsible for several of the company's major successes, including the Omni, and whose standing at ARP prospered as a result, was the driving force behind the Avatar. "Pearlman was opposed to the Avatar," Friend concedes, "but several of our best sellers had been developed over his objections." Aligning himself with Pollock, Friend obtained approval to proceed. The executive committee voted to fund the project, a move the board supported. "Everybody thought it was going to be the hottest thing since the wheel," notes Friend.

The ill-fated ARP electronic piano.

"They decided to go for $4 million in the first year," says Pearlman. "Our R&D budget was almost $500,000, and most of it went into the guitar synthesizer. Not only that, we also started to buy inventory for $4 million a year."

The notion that a $7 million company could sell $4 million worth of an as-yet-untested product struck Pearlman as rather naive. "On the basis of objective reasoning, rather than 'bandwagon emotions,'" he wrote the board, "it seems that we are planning to spend over 25% of our 1977 R&D money . . . to make a product which . . . is more likely to be a disaster than not."

Friend's contagious enthusiasm carried the day, but Pearlman's premonition proved more accurate. Avatar flopped. Although it extended the resources of the synthesizer to guitar players, it didn't do it well enough. Players had difficulty producing a clean sound [because of the imperfections of the pitch-to-voltage converters] and disliked the high price tag. Once the lackluster sales were documented, the Avatar was marketed as a loser. "What you want to do is create a demand," Mancuso explains. "But they were begging people to buy it. If you bought two of them, you got a deal. A guy bought six, they shipped him seven — that kind of marketing."

ARP sold only $1 million worth of Avatars in the two-year life span of the instrument. "In 1979, we had an operating loss of about $700,000 and an inventory write-off of about $300,000," Pearlman recalls. "Essentially, we blew our brains out on that instrument."

In the meantime, Mancuso had been desperately trying to peddle the company. "I was trying like hell to sell it," he says with a laugh. "I thought one day I'd slip a letter under their hands and have them sign it — 'Ha, ha, we fooled you, it's sold!' They'd have been a lot better off." Mancuso got as far as an informal offer of $10 per share from Gulf+Western Manufacturing Co., when the stock was trading at about $4 per share. But the board remained intransigent. For his efforts, Mancuso was fired.

The same disunity and political infighting that had marked the birth of the Avatar prevented the sale of the company. Pearlman, more and more confident that insolvency awaited, was eager to explore the possibility, but he wasn't able to. The board passed a motion prohibiting any officer from talking to a prospective buyer until the offer had been cleared by ARP's law firm — that is, by Pollock. Pearlman found himself reduced to holding an "unofficial" meeting with an interested party at Boston's Logan Airport.

Feelers from CBS Musical Instruments were accorded cool and, according to one insider, occasionally arrogant responses.

But even then, with its cash reserves depleted and time fast running out before the company went under, ARP was not without options. "We could have cut our losses," Pearlman sighs. "We could have said, 'We'll rent out half the building, we'll go very lean, we'll operate in a survival mode.' The biggest mistake was thinking we could turn it around by playing catch-up."

In 1979, ARP introduced a 16-preset electronic piano. "It was supposed to rescue us," says Pearlman. But a switch on the piano failed: "It was one of those things that went up too fast because we didn't have the time or money to do it right," he admits. "When you left the unit in, say, the back of a hot car, the Mylar insulation in the switch would melt." [Dodds comments, "The product was released well before it should have been. It was flawed in two major ways. It was terribly noisy, and the membrane switch had an inherent design flaw. I felt terribly bad about that, because it was my design. At several points I requested that manufacturing be shut down until the problems could be corrected, but the management decided that we couldn't do that or the company would be out of cash and out of business within a month. So over my protests they continued to manufacture."] The pianos began coming back in for repairs nearly as quickly as ARP shipped them out. "The company's sales plummeted, repair costs went up — all sorts of things started going wrong at that point," Pearlman recalls. That year, the board asked Friend,

who had master-minded the Avatar and become president *non grata* in the process, to resign.

Pearlman returned as president, and another "bailout" product was developed — the Chroma, a microprocessor-operated touch-sensitive polyphonic synthesizer that would eventually prove quite profitable for another company. [*Unlike the Quadra, which was designed, under the direction of David Friend, as a "synthesizer sandwich" consisting of an Omni, an Axxe, and a couple of other synthesizers strapped together in one box under the control of a microprocessor, the Chroma was a new product from the ground up. "The Chroma marked a major departure in R&D direction for ARP,"* Dodds explains. *"And the fact that it didn't make it in time could be considered partly my fault. There were two occasions on which I froze the project, brought it back into R&D, and said, 'It's not ready.' But one of those is what's paying off in spades now. We decided to configure the instrument so you could have individual channels under computer control. I had to stop the project and do a ground-up design to do that. The decision was a risky one, and it may have added to the company's troubles."*]

By this time, it was too late for ARP. Suppliers were providing parts on a COD-only basis, First National Bank was making angry noises, and, instead of coming to grips with its destiny, management was trying to keep the show going with sleight of hand. Desparately trying to turn 1980

Among other features, the ARP Solus offered two phase-syncable VCOs, a four-pole lowpass filter, a ring modulator, and system-interface jacks for external control to or from another synthesizer. It came out in 1980 at a price of $790.

Never commercially produced by ARP, the Chroma was picked up and manufactured briefly by CBS Musical Instruments — alongside latter day Rhodes electric pianos — in 1981. A total of around 3,000 were ultimately produced. Several at least are still in use for live performance by advocates like virtual realist Jaron Lanier and *Electronic Musician's* Steve Oppenheimer.

ARP musician Jean Claude (played by ARP vice president of engineering Philip Dodds, top) plays a five-note sequence on a huge ARP synthesizer while Dr. LaCombe (Francois Truffaut, left) and Roy Neary (Richard Dreyfuss) watch the "mothership" come in for a landing in the Columbia film, *Close Encounters of the Third Kind.*

into a break-even year, Pearlman lent ARP $168,000 so it could ship a $1 million backlog in November and December. "In January, we discovered we had created a $300,000 loss," he recounts with obvious regret.

Eventually, ARP found itself pushed beyond desperation; frantic to stay alive, it began playing games with money. Philip Dodds, who later helped First National unravel ARP's tangled finances [and arrange sale of the Chroma to CBS],

explains that "we were shipping units to dealers with the promise that, if they didn't sell them, we'd take them back and credit them . . . for the purpose of inflating receivables. The purpose was to generate enough cash flow to get to the point where the practice wouldn't be necessary." But when First National — which ARP owed $1.8 million, including nearly $1 million in receivables financing — found out, it decided to pull the plug.

The bank took ARP to court. After listening to First National and the company's other creditors, the judge appointed a trustee to oversee ARP's liquidation. On May 13, 1981, the trustee took over and on September 11 presided over the sale of all the company's tangible assets. [*The sale was arranged in large part by Philip Dodds, whose memories of this period are vivid: "The first thing the trustee did was to fire all of the management except me. He then required me to operate the balance of the company, which was tricky, because the week before I had been trying to figure out how to*

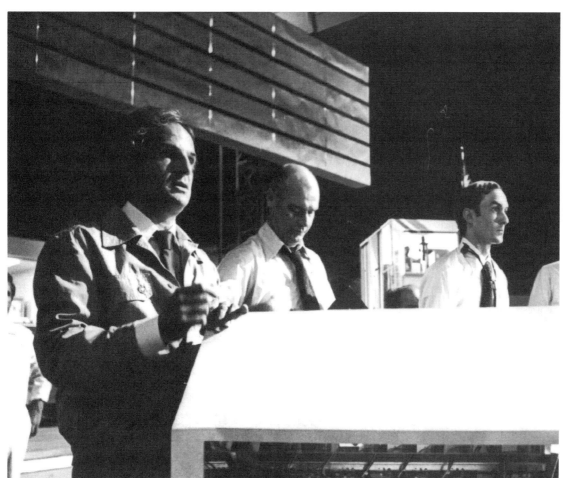

meet the payroll. Then I didn't hear from him for weeks, and he was the only one with the power to sign checks, which made operating the company somewhat difficult.

["I did manage to get a couple of things through. I convinced him to keep the service department on, so that we could get repaired units out, and ship parts — you know, keep ourselves ethical. But each week he asked me to cut more and more. The first department that had to be cut in its entirety was, not surprisingly, research and development. He had me scale the company back until there was literally no one left, except for the two service techs and one person in accounting. So for a period of three months, I came to work in an empty 50,000 square-foot building, and spent all day on the phone looking for a buyer. I recontacted CBS and struck a deal with them to sell only the engineering department and the Chroma, convincing them by sheer brute force, just by not letting them alone. I called them four or five times a day for three weeks running.

["I originally tried to get them to buy the whole company, but they rejected that out of hand. A bankrupt company is a liability, not an asset. So I said, 'Well, how about the Chroma? It's a hot product.' And there was enough belief in that that they said okay, it might be worth it. So they made an offer, with the provision that I had to contact all the people in R&D who had been laid off for three months and get them to sign contracts guaranteeing that they would come to work for CBS if the deal went through. Well, I went out and did that. But when the deal was finally arranged, the trustee felt that CBS would be willing to pay more. He told me to tell CBS to go fly a kite. So I went to the bank and told the bank, 'Hey, look, your trustee is about to blow the deal.' At that point, they intervened and struck the deal with CBS. By the middle of September I had rehired the entire department, relocated ten miles north of the old factory, and we were hot and heavy back on the Chroma again."]

CBS Musical Instruments acquired ARP's inventory for $300,000, and, for an additional $50,000, picked up the manufacturing rights to the Chroma and the [four-voice] electronic piano. In its first year with the product, CBS sold more than $3 million worth of Chromas. But stockholders and creditors lost more than $4 million when ARP went under; Pearlman and members of his family lost a total of nearly $500,000 in cash.

David Friend, who now runs Pilot Software, a $50 million Boston-based communications software and database company, maintains a studied indifference to the ARP affair. "We were in a risky business, and we made one bad move," he explains, referring to the Avatar. "On top of that, we had some lousy management that blew away what little we had — that was the end of the ball game."

Pollock prefers to place ARP's failure in a broader context by citing "companies with larger resources, market conditions, and worldwide competition" as elements that contributed to its demise. When pressed, he concedes that the Avatar was the critical factor.

Mancuso has a simpler explanation: "Among the three of them, I couldn't get one full-time chief executive officer. Alone, they're each worth about 0.4 on a scale of 1 to 10; together, they add up to about a 2. There was no reason ARP should ever have gone out of business," he concludes. "It's a sin. It's a tragedy to see a beautiful little company, and 200 jobs, go under because of bad management. All three of them should physically have to go to jail and serve six months for screwing up a beautiful thing like that."

[*Philip Dodds sees things a bit differently. "One person who was very much maligned during the troubles at ARP was Al Pearlman," Dodds comments. "And he was, throughout, the one who categorically defended the correct path, or what ultimately proved to be the correct path, the one who fought the dumb decisions. And right down the line he was ridden over like a Mack truck. I don't think he's ever gotten credit for being the defender of what was ethical and what was correct. The guy definitely ought to be given a little more credit."*]

THE EURO-SYNTH INDUSTRY

Classic Sounds
Exotic Hybrids
Lost Opportunities

BY PAUL WIFFEN & MARK VAIL

Pick a synthesizer, any synthesizer. Chances are it was manufactured in either Japan or the United States. Not a big surprise, right? But while it may look as if those countries have the market sewed up, there is a thriving electronic music industry in Europe. Unfortunately, over the last quarter-century, a number of innovative products have been introduced, flourished, and died there without being noticed elsewhere.

Thankfully, worthy instruments have surpassed the European boundaries and continue to trickle into the U.S. and other countries. Familiar synthesizers range from yesteryear's PPG Wave 2.3 and the OSCar to the current crop, which includes the Waldorf Microwave and Generalmusic S2.

But other companies that tried to make inroads into the American market met with disaster. More often than not, failure was due to circumstances beyond their control, not because their product was inferior. For example, Italian manufacturer Siel introduced the Opera 6, a six-voice, velocity-

sensitive, polyphonic synthesizer that might have sold quite well on the world market — if only it hadn't come out at the same time and same price as Yamaha's DX7, which boasted 16 voices. That kind of failure made other European companies think twice about taking their new pride-and-joy synthesizer out of their own backyard and subjecting it to the harsh realities of the international pro music industry.

This microcosm deserves more worldwide acknowledgment from a historial viewpoint, because you can bet that innovations will continue to appear from Europe in the future. And plenty of European synthesists would feel lost without some of their native gear in their performance rig. What could it be about European synths that make them so different? Is it just pure chauvinism, or are European companies onto something that other manufacturers are missing?

Until the mid-'80s, American manufacturers stayed clear of digital oscillators, claiming digital sounded cold and thin. On the other hand, most

Japanese companies accepted digital sound generation in order to gain greater tuning reliability and more control of harmonic content. The European approach has been to use the latest digital technology in conjunction with analog signal processing. The PPG Wave 2.3, one of the most esteemed European synths in America and forerunner to the Waldorf Microwave synth module and newer Wave keyboard synth, was based on a digital-oscillator-based instrument that Wolfgang Palm built in the mid-'70s. And until the early '90s, there wasn't a European synth that omitted analog filters. (Wersi's Pegasus is the first we're aware of with digital filters. Waldorf reportedly spent the latter half of 1992 trying to get digital filters to sound like the analog ones in PPG synths, but they have given up and the new Wave will feature the same analog filter as its predecessors.) Perhaps the hybrid nature of European synths

gives them a distinctive character. Or maybe there's more to it than that.

There have been variations in synthesizer design from one European nation to another as well. The personalities of these nations may be reflected by the synthesizers they produce. Let's have a look at some key synths categorized by their respective countries of origin.

England

British technological innovation, whether in aviation, computers, or any other field, always seems to follow the same sad pattern: British geniuses take their ideas for manufacture elsewhere and another nation reaps the profits. (On the other hand, certain Japanese manufacturers do the lion's share of their research and software development in the U.K.) Nowhere is this more evident than in British synthesizer manufacturing.

One of the first companies to make its mark in the field of electronic music was EMS (Electronic Music Studios), founded by Peter Zinovieff. The majority of designs during EMS's most successful and influential period were done by Dave Cockerell. Dave was involved in the first prototypes of the Electronic Studios I and II in late '69 and early '70. He also designed EMS's most famous product, the VCS3, which probably did more to change the face of the British electronic music scene than any other synthesizer. Basically, the VCS3 was a modular system reduced to a reasonably portable size without losing the flexibility of patch cords and multiple oscillators, filters, and envelopes. It worked in conjunction with the DK2 voltage-control keyboard. Every university and college in the U.K. seemed to have a VCS3. It was marketed in the U.S. (with limited success) as the Putney, so named for the London district where EMS was at one time based.

The VCS3 was also a major part of the experimental work of bands like Pink Floyd and Roxy Music. On *Dark Side of the Moon*, every member of the Floyd is credited with VCS3 "performance." Brian Eno put Roxy's vocals, drums, and everything else through his VCS3 filters, and he wasn't above playing synth solos using the potentiometer knobs. (Listen to the first three Roxy albums.)

In 1974, EMS introduced the Synthi 100, designed for those who didn't need a portable system. As Cockerell put it, "You had to take walls down to get it into studios." The Synthi 100 was originally based on three VCS3s, and grew from there to encompass 12 oscillators and associated filters, envelopes, etc. It also had a three-track monophonic digital sequencer and two 64 x 64 patch matrices. The Synthi 100 sold for around £10,000 (U.S. $25,000 at the time), which limited the number of units sold, but it was the only thing Britain ever produced that could compete with the modular systems from American manufacturers. One Synthi 100 went to the BBC Radiophonic Workshop, which does electronic music and sound effects for a myriad of TV programs, including *Doctor Who*.

Then EMS did an about-face and introduced the Synthi AKS, a briefcase-enclosed VCS3 with a

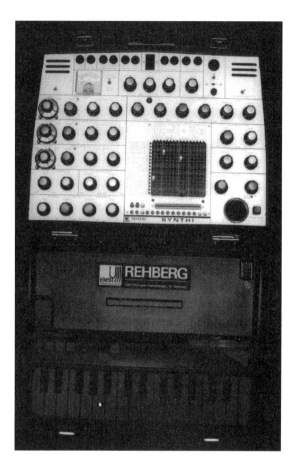

The airlines won't let you carry your modular synth on the plane? You might try the EMS Synthi AKS, the synthesizer in a briefcase. (photo by Matthew Vosburgh)

touch-sensitive, plastic membrane keyboard mounted in the lid. The AKS was so successful that EMS also released a smaller version, the Synthi E, for the educational market. The Synthi E didn't have a keyboard; a low-cost ribbon controller was used to determine its pitch.

At that time, EMS wanted to widen their focus to include other musicians. Before leaving EMS to work for Electro-Harmonix in New York, Cockerell designed the Synthi Hi-Fli, a multi-effect guitar processor. Apart from a one-year break in 1976, when he supervised the installation and setup of the electronic studio at IRCAM in Paris, Cockerell worked for Electro-Harmonix until their demise in 1985. He then returned to the U.K. and began working as a designer for Akai. Dave's been involved in the development of samplers like the S900 and S1000, and newer S2800 and S3200, as well as Akai's DD1000 digital recording system.

Tim Orr, another seminal British designer who was involved in producing the Synthi E, devised the plans for EMS's vocoder. Between 1975 and 1977, three distinct vocoder models were developed, and many of those are still giving sterling service. Orr went on to design many electronic instruments for Powertran, a British mail-order company that sold synthesizer kits (*à la* America's Paia). Among his designs were several synthesizers, a vocoder (his speciality) and, shortly before the company went out of business in 1986, a MIDI-controlled monophonic sampler. Tim now lectures on electronic instrument design at the London College of Furniture — which has offered courses in acoustic instrument design for many years, and expanded in the '80s to include electric and electronic instrument design.

Peter Eastty designed the next EMS product, the Computer Synthi. It was based on a Synthi 100 that was controlled by a PDP-8 microcomputer. Eastty devised digital-to-analog converters and wrote software to control the synthesizer components. As you can imagine, the Computer Synthi was very pricey, but specific details of the instrument remain shrouded in mystery.

In 1979, Datanomics purchased EMS and moved its production site to Wareham, Dorset, on the south coast of England. The first product under the new management was the Polysynthi, designed by Graham Hinton. Datanomics struggled

on with the line until 1982. Their last product was the ill-fated Datasynth, which had a 16 x 16 matrix of switches to memorize the configuration of the machine, but unfortunately not any of the knob positions. The Datasynth never saw the light of day. Graham Hinton now runs Hinton Electronics, a company that produces various MIDI peripherals and custom software applications.

When Datanomics gave up in 1982, the reins of EMS (as well as the rights to the name) were taken over by Robin Wood, who had joined EMS when it was six months old. He described his original position with the company as "floor cleaner/demonstrator." Apparently, Peter Zinovieff had never been too keen on demonstrating the VCS3, so Wood found himself doing it. He became what nowadays would be called product specialist and sales coordinator, although he was never officially a salesman. During the Datanomics period, Robin was the only means by which anything was sold simply because he was the only one who knew the outlets for EMS.

Today, EMS still exists in this form. Tim Orr's vocoder designs were refined and two rack-mount versions — the 2000 and 3000 — are available. (Although the original EMS vocoders looked like rack-

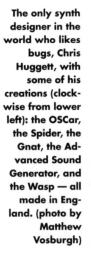

The only synth designer in the world who likes bugs, Chris Huggett, with some of his creations (clockwise from lower left): the OSCar, the Spider, the Gnat, the Advanced Sound Generator, and the Wasp — all made in England. (photo by Matthew Vosburgh)

mounts, either they didn't fit or half of their electronics were exposed.) Both are 16-channel vocoders, and the 3000 has an individual attenuator for each channel. The majority of these units are sold in Germany. It's interesting that EMS, one of the first manufacturers of vocoders in the modern era, is the last company still making and selling vocoders profitably. In addition, EMS will manufacture VCS3s and Synthi AKSs by special order, and reconditions and sells older models. Newest in the EMS product line is an alternate MIDI controller called the Sound Beam. Using sonar — high-pitched clicks that you can scarcely hear — the Sound Beam transmits MIDI commands based on the distance to any object that breaks the plane of its sound beam. Robin Wood tells us Sound Beams are currently being used as therapeutic aids for physically disabled students.

The other main strain of English synthesizer history follows the career of designer Chris Huggett. In 1977, after working for Ferrograph, for 3M in their digital multi-track division, and as a freelance studio maintenance engineer, he met up with synthesist Adrian Wagner, who had ideas for an inexpensive synthesizer. While it might compromise on cosmetic appeal and the playing interface, Adrian's synthesizer would not suffer in flexibility and sound quality. Wagner and Huggett started working together on specs and features: Adrian suggesting and explaining synthesizer functions, and Chris developing cheap ways to implement them. Eventually, it became clear to Huggett that, other than the analog filter, the whole synthesizer could be digital. However, a microprocessor would be too expensive, so they had to use TTL (transistor-transistor logic).

After Huggett put together a prototype of the synth, he and Wagner took it down to Rod Argent's Keyboards. (At that time, Argent's was the only all-keyboard store in London.) After the directors of Argent's learned how much it would cost to produce the new synth, they put up £10,000 ($25,000) for Chris and Adrian to set up manufacturing under the company name Electronic Dream Plant. In return for this loan, Argent's reserved the distribution rights of the new synth. The first models were delivered in the fall of 1978.

The synthesizer was called the Wasp because of its black and yellow coloring. It had two oscillators with a variety of wave-shapes, lowpass and highpass filtering, and separate three-stage envelopes for amplitude and the filter. The Wasp listed for an incredibly low £199 ($695 in the U.S.), less than half the price of any comparable synthesizer. Of course, there were compromises like the flat, two-octave touch-sensitive keyboard and a plastic case. Many people couldn't afford a proper amplifier to play the Wasp through, so they only listened to its tiny built-in speaker. In fact, the Wasp sounded very professional when properly amplified, but many people preferred the sound of the cheap radio speaker resonating within the plastic case.

Perhaps the most innovative feature of the Wasp was the seven-pin DIN digital interface, which allowed bi-directional communication along one cable. A number of Wasps could be connected together and played from any one Wasp keyboard. [In 1981, co-author Paul Wiffen successfully connected more than 50 Wasps for testing before they were shipped to the London Education Authority.] All EDP products featured this interface.

The Wasp became a great success; they were selling at the rate of 30 to 40 per week soon after the initial release. However, there were reliability problems and the cellar at Argent's became a Wasp graveyard, because it was easier to replace a broken-down unit than to try to repair it. But these problems didn't stop many influential players from using them. Dave Stewart of the Eurythmics loved to put a mike on the Wasp's speaker to capture its distinctive sound in the studio. Dave Greenfield of the Stranglers used four Wasps on stage for many years. Jean-Michel Jarre took one on his Chinese tour and let people from the audience play it during his performance. Others may have been too shy to be seen with such a tacky-looking device, but they weren't ashamed to use them in the studio. These performers included Pink Floyd and Genesis. Rick Wakeman and Patrick Moraz reputedly gave Wasps to friends as Christmas presents. The Wasp was also the first synth for many influential synthesists, including Thomas Dolby, Dave Stewart, and Nick Rhodes.

To complement the Wasp, Huggett and Wagner

wanted to release a sequencer. In 1980, Chris began working with Steve Evans from the Oxford University engineering department to produce the Spider, a 256-note digital sequencer that recorded in real-time or step-entry and would interface with the Wasp through its digital interface or with an analog synthesizer through control voltage and gate outputs. The Spider was even cheaper than the Wasp, and it compared quite favorably to clumsy analog sequencers with voltage settings and an eight- or 16-note limit. Of course, the Spider had a few problems of its own: Real-time sequences played back slightly faster than they were recorded, there was no quantization, and it was the devil itself to sync to a click. But the Spider was years ahead of its time, having more in common with MIDI sequencers of today than with its contemporaries, because of the digital encoding of musical pitches.

During 1979, things began to go wrong for EDP. Production was proving more expensive than anticipated, but prices weren't increased to make up the difference. Wasps and Spiders were produced at a loss, and Wagner was investing heavily in studio gear. Huggett resigned as a director at the beginning of 1980, although he worked freelance on the next product, the Caterpillar. This was a real keyboard that could control up to four Wasps simultaneously for polyphony (one of the first master keyboards). Unfortunately, it was practically impossible to get four Wasps to sound exactly the same. (Wasps were like guitars: There were good ones and bad ones, because of the variability of the components.) Another disadvantage was the price. Four Wasps and a Caterpillar cost around £1,000 ($2,500), which could buy you somebody else's polyphonic synth all in one box. But the Caterpillar was a precursor to MIDI keyboard controllers, since it had a switch to send program change commands to a future product (which EDP never produced).

EDP's final product was the Wasp Deluxe. It added separate oscillator volume controls, multiple triggering, and a real three-octave keyboard. Somehow, though, the magic of the original Wasp sound had been lost.

Such was not the case with the Gnat, a single-oscillator version of the Wasp that Huggett began work on just as EDP went under due to large debts owed to component suppliers and distributors. Soon, however, Adrian had started a new company, Electronic Dream Plant (Oxford) Ltd., which took over production of all EDP's models. Chris was then able to finish the Gnat. This monster-sounding little box made up for its lone oscillator by featuring preset pulse-width modulation as one of its available waveforms and a warm, fat-sounding filter. It was the only synth able to impersonate Moog's Taurus pedals.

This second company survived long enough to market the Gnat, but then a business and marital split left Adrian Wagner's wife and her mother in charge of EDP(O). Wagner relaunched as Wasp Synthesizers, Ltd., and produced deluxe versions of the Wasp and Gnat in wooden cases with a classier-looking black-and-gold color scheme. However, neither company lasted very long. By the end of 1981, production of Wasps, Spiders, Gnats, and Caterpillars had stopped. Precise sales figures aren't available, but it is estimated that 3,000 Wasps were sold in its four-year history, along with 1,000 Spider sequencers. The failure of both the Caterpillar and the Wasp Deluxe is reflected in the fact that less than 100 of either was made. The Gnat, which sold for half the price of the Wasp, sold over 1,500 in its six months of production, and its sales probably would have eclipsed the Wasp in its first year if EDP(O) had survived.

Fortunately, the end of EDP was not the end of Chris Huggett's work in synthesizer design. He spent a year refining the basic concept of the Wasp, Spider, and Gnat to include presets, memory, additive synthesis, and full sequence editing. In 1983, Huggett reemerged with the OSCar, produced by the Oxford Synthesizer Company, which was financed and run by Huggett's parents. The OSCar used digital synthesis, but Chris went out of his way to make the synth sound analog. Its sales took off very quickly despite the fact that it was monophonic and cost almost as much as a Roland Juno-60. But then MIDI arrived and sales slumped. Undaunted, Huggett designed a MIDI retrofit and simultaneously increased available

British synthesizer designer Chris Huggett created the Oxford Synthesizer Company OSCar in the early '80s. Although the original version didn't feature MIDI, Huggett later implemented the digital interface as a retrofit. Currently, a dealer-tendered OSCar can go for as much as $1,000 — equal to the synth's original list price. (photo by Jon Sievert)

patch memory to 36. Sales picked up, and the OSCar found its way into the setups of some very influential performers, including Ultravox, Keith Emerson, Geoff Downes, Guy Fletcher of Dire Straits, and Stevie Wonder. A second product, the Advanced Sound Generator, which combined sampling with digital and analog synthesis, was abandoned because of its non-competitive price. Chris Huggett now works as a freelance designer. One of his clients is Akai, for whom he finished the S3200 operating system in early '93.

No history of Britain's contribution to electronic music would be complete without mention of Simmons or the Mellotron. Dave Simmons' drum system was another product carried only by Argent's in the early years of the manufacturer's life. Nobody else thought the unique-sounding electronic drums were worth bothering with. Bill Bruford helped popularize the former Simmons flagship SDS5 electronic drum system. The subsequent SDX 16-bit sampling drum kit offered features, quality, and flexibility that compared with many keyboard-controlled samplers. In 1987, Simmons demonstrated a tendency toward a more generalized market approach by dabbling as an early competitor in the programmable mixer market with their SPM8:2. This eight-channel MIDI-controlled mixer had a price tag of a mere $999, considerably cheaper than competing units like the Akai MPX 820 ($1,995) and the automated-

fader Yamaha DPM7 ($3,995). Simmons went belly up in 1989, but Dave Simmons continues to produce the Trixer II drum trigger/sound module system and Drum Huggers trigger system. Rights to manufacture the SDX were acquired by someone else, but no one to our knowledge has continued software development for the device.

The Mellotron was ironically based on an instrument from California, the Chamberlin Rhythmate. In 1962, a representative for Harry Chamberlin brought a couple of Chamberlins to England, where he met and contracted three brothers — Leslie, Frank, and Norman Bradley, founders of a company that manufactured semi-professional tape recorders and magnetic heads — to improve on Chamberlin's design and carry through with the instrument's manufacture. The radical design actually used a tape recorder head and magnetic tape for each key to play back recorded sounds. As such, it must be considered a first-generation sample player. Developed in the late '60s, it helped shape the sound of a whole generation of progressive rockers, including the Moody Blues, King Crimson, the Strawbs, Yes, and Genesis. The flutes at the beginning of Led Zeppelin's "Stairway to Heaven" were played by John Paul Jones on a Mellotron. Without the instrument, would "In the Court of the Crimson King" have made such a dramatic impact? Not since the invention of the electric guitar had one instru-

VINTAGE SYNTHESIZERS   **57**   THE EURO-SYNTH INDUSTRY

ment been so responsible for developing a new strain of popular music.

Of course, such innovation was not without its problems. The tapes ran for about eight seconds, so a curious playing technique had to be developed for sustained chords. The performer had to lift each finger independently to allow that note's tape to be rewound and start playing again. This process had to be repeated for each finger within six or seven seconds, or else the chord would come to an abrupt halt.

Then there was the reliability (or lack thereof) of the tape mechanism. Anyone who toured with the Mellotron usually took two or three on the road, because they broke down with a regularity that would make today's most temperamental synthesizer seem a paragon of reliability. The mechanism would jam or tapes would break in the middle of a gig, so another Mellotron needed to be available instantly.

In an attempt to deal with the reliability problems, Mellotron developed several models after the original. On the Mark II, according to Tony Banks of Genesis, some chords sounded much better than others, probably because of inaccuracies in the tuning of the original recordings. Banks actually composed the introduction to "Watcher of the Skies" exclusively using those chords that sounded good on his Mellotron. Then he traded up to the Model 400. It was much more reliable and had superior sound quality, but those chords just didn't sound the same on it.

Like other English electronic instruments, the Mellotron fell on hard times, caused both by its unreliability and the arrival of string synthesizers. (The Mellotron was used first and foremost for its string sound, although its tape library included many more sounds.) Eventually, the company could no longer continue and everything was put up for sale. Streetly Electronics acquired the rights to the design, but since the name "Mellotron" had already been sold to an American manufacturer, they called their instrument the Novatron. This version was more reliable, but string synths were in their heyday by that time. Sales dwindled until manufacturing stopped entirely in 1984.

Although the history of the British synthesizer industry has included stories of a number of bankrupt manufacturers and uncultivated native designers, the future looks promising. Part of this optimism is due to the success of Welsh manufacturer Cheetah, which began life in 1982 making peripherals for personal computers. In 1988, Cheetah released the MS6, a single-space rack-mount synth module developed by Ian Jannoway, that sonically and (for the most part) functionally duplicates what the Oberheim Matrix-1000 can do. Both are six-voice analog-oscillator MIDI synth modules — the MS6 is also multitimbral — that simulate the sound of vintage analog synths like the Minimoog, Oberheim OB-X, and Sequential Prophet-5. Cheetah also made a diverse line of master MIDI keyboard controllers, the SX16 16-bit rack-mount sampler, several drum machines, and a wavetable synth module.

At the January '93 NAMM show in Anaheim, California, Cheetah released a new version of their MS6 hybrid (digital oscillators/analog filters) single-space rack-mount synth. The MS6II ($799) has stereo outputs, built-in effects, auxiliary inputs for processing other instruments, 416 patches (320 ROM, 96 RAM), and 64 performance memories. Cheetah also escalated the master keyboard race with the introduction of two comprehensive keyboard controllers, the Master Series 7000 ($1,380) and 8000 ($1,499). Both are full 88-note keyboards, the 8000 having a weighted action. The pressure-sensitive keyboards (channel and polyphonic aftertouch) generate both velocity and release velocity data. Besides three wheels (pitch-bend, mod, and MIDI volume), there's a programmable joystick, six programmable sliders, eight programmable switch controllers, four programmable expression pedal inputs, eight programmable switch controllers, and six soft function/edit buttons. These controllers have two merging MIDI ins with data filtering, two MIDI thrus, and four MIDI outs, provide controller remapping functions, eight overlappable zones, four programmable note layers per zone, and extensive arpeggiator and MIDI echo capabilities, and are touted as being General MIDI/Roland GS compatible. Memory count: 255 performances, 16 controller setups, 16 input map setups, 16 performance memory chains, and 32 programmable sys-ex strings.

In the digital audio recording realm, Cheetah introduced Soundscape ($2,249), a Windows 3.1-compatible low-cost 16-bit system for expanding the average MIDI musician's home studio or a low-budget recording studio with four, eight, 12, or 16 audio tracks. Each unit provides four tracks, with two-track recording and four-track playback. Up to 16 Soundscape units can be combined for a maximum of 64 tracks.

After showing these new products, Cheetah — who continues to manufacture joysticks, track-balls, and mice for computers and game machines — pulled out of the music industry for financial reasons. Thankfully, a spinoff company, Soundscape Digital Technology, Ltd., will continue to manufacture all the new products introduced at the January 1993 NAMM show.

After developing the original Cheetah MS6, Ian Jannoway went on to form Novation, who makes the MM10 MIDI keyboard controller. It only has two octaves of velocity-sensitive keys, pitch-bend and mod wheels, four buttons, and a two-digit LED display, but it's the smallest and — at $219.99 — cheapest MIDI keyboard with full-size keys that we've ever seen. For maximum portability, the MM10 will run off six AA batteries and weighs only 4 lbs. Owners of the Yamaha's tiny QY10 synth workstation shouldn't overlook the MM10, whose case includes a divot perfectly designed to cradle the QY10 at an angle, leaving easy access to the QY10's control panel. (An adapter for Yamaha's new, slightly larger QY20 is also available.) Novation also provides a 15" micro-snake (with audio, MIDI, and power cables) for interfacing the QY10 and MM10 together. The MM10 is available in the U.S. from Music Industries.

Most of the British designers we've covered so far are associated in some way with the city of Oxford. But there is another strain of British synthesizer design from Cambridge, the other main university town in England. Dr. Mike Lynch and his company Lynex Systems are behind these various products. His first, in 1988, was the Lynex, designed for and marketed by Commander Electronics. It was an eight-voice 16-bit sampler that used an Atari ST as the control interface. Cooperation with German software houses Steinberg and C-Lab meant that you could trigger the samples directly from Pro-24 and Notator sequencer programs on the same Atari in the same way as with Digidesign's SampleCell or MacProteus on a Macintosh. In fact, this system predated the Digidesign products and was the first time the facility to do both sampling and sequencing was available on a personal computer.

The Lynex sold several hundred pieces in Europe and is still supported today by the Lynex User's Group — or LUG — who are still developing their own software with typical British ad hoc ingenuity. Commander Electronics returned to being the distribution company they started out as. Lynch, undaunted, turned the Lynex into the stand-alone rack-mount sampling module that Cheetah formerly manufactured called the SX16. Federal Communications Commission regulations prevented sales of this device in the U.S. His firm, Lynex Systems, has done development work on hard disk recording for several Japanese manufacturers and designed the ADAS series of direct-to-disk recorders for Plasmic, a British manufacturer of jack fields (patch bays) — using the brand name Mosses & Mitchell — that are featured in SSL, Neve, and many other top-end mixing consoles. The ADAS exists as a line of supplementary components for Atari ST, Macintosh (from Plus up to Quadra), and IBM-PC compatible computers, as well as a stand-alone rack-mount module currently in use by pop radio giant KIIS ("KISS-FM") in Los Angeles and Stevie Wonder (the ADAS SA, i.e. Stand-Alone, being the only direct-to-disk that can be used by a non-sighted operator).

FCC problems again stopped the computer-based systems from being sold in the States, but brought Lynch to the attention of Atari. While Atari's new Falcon030 computer was still in very early development, Lynch was invited to develop a bundled piece of software for it. This neatly resolved the FCC problems his designs had had in the past, as the hardware is now Atari's responsibility. This led to the formation of a new Lynch company, D2D Systems, whose first product, Falcon D2D, will be shipped as a bundled, package with every Falcon sold. This is a beginner's guide to hard disk recording and DSP effects, and will act as a consumer-level introduction to the technology. For the more professional user, D2D has produced two other packages: a stereo editor, D2D Edit, and a four-track hard disk recorder with effects, 40FX. (All Plasmic and D2D products are distributed in the U.S. by Digital I/O.)

Germany

Of all the European synthesizer products that have made the long trip across the pond to the U.S., the German-made PPG is probably the best known and most widely used. The PPG originated in a fairly humble manner. At first, it was unknown beyond the local area of Hamburg, where designer Wolfgang Palm turned what started as a hobby into a successful business. He began in the early

This is how German engineering stacked up: PPG's Expansion Voice Unit, the Wave 2.3, and the PRK Processor keyboard. (photo by Matthew Vosburgh)

'70s servicing and modifying analog synths and modular systems. By 1975, he was producing his own products. Perhaps his most important customer was the German synth band Tangerine Dream. Palm did a lot of custom work for them, and he implemented their ideas on his commercial products.

In 1976, Palm introduced the 1003 system, one of the first programmable synthesizers. However, it was the System 340 (1978), which featured the Wave name and technology, that was to make PPG world-famous. Palm had turned to digital techniques in an attempt to gain greater control over the harmonic content of the oscillator waveforms, making him one of the pioneers of digital synthesis. The System 340 was an eight-voice machine with separate keyboard controller, synthesizer brain, and video display. It used wavetable synthesis, reading a list of numbers representing a waveshape, and turning the digital information into an analog audio output. The oscillators could change from one waveform to another using envelope control or by reversing the direction of the wavetable in real time. The effect is similar to pulse width modulation on analog synths, but is not restricted to percentage variations of one waveshape. Using PPG-style wavetable synthesis, you can make much more radical timbre changes than with analog techniques.

In today's market, few instruments offer PPG-like synthesis techniques. First, there are the PPG's direct descendants, the currently produced Waldorf Microwave and Wave — instruments based on Wolfgang Palm's PPG designs. In addition, Ensoniq's VFX, VFX-SD, SD-1, SQ-1, SQ-2, and SQ-R allow waveform modulation, a sequential playback of a specific range of single-cycle waves in their order in memory. Only these instruments share this synthesis capability with PPGs. (Korg's Wavestation will perform wave sequencing, which is a slightly different technique.)

In any case, the all-digital nature of the machine was not popular in 1978. As Wolfgang Palm has said, "Everybody wanted analog warmth." Some musicians were also intimidated by computer video terminals. These complaints led Palm to design the classic PPG combination found in the Wave 2.2 and its descendants: the flexibility of digital oscillators and the warmth and familiarity of analog filters and VCAs. These instruments also featured the event generator, a 16-channel sequencer first implemented on the Wave 380.

The Wave 2.2 had other aspects that added to its acceptance by musicians. Gone was the computer display, so the entire instrument could be housed in one keyboard unit like a conventional synthesizer. The digital oscillators offered rock-solid tuning, as opposed to other polysynths that needed periodic tuning (an automated process that could take anywhere from five to 30 seconds).

Due in part to the marketing efforts of Andrew Thomas, the 2.2 was very successful, finding its way beyond the German market to worldwide distribution. The design evolved (not without a few upgrade problems) into the Wave 2.3, which added multi-timbral sequencing with separate audio outputs. The 2.3, which represented the limit of wavetable synthesis in such an implementation, was PPG's most successful product and was produced until 1987.

To take the wavetable concept further required a visual display and a better human interface. Therefore, PPG developed the Waveterm as an expansion to the capabilities of the Wave synths. With the Waveterm connected, waveforms could be seen and edited, sampling and additive synthesis became alternative sound generation techniques, and more complex sequencing functions were added.

The original Waveterm A was 8-bit and used 8" disks for data storage. The more convenient 5¼" disks were used in the second, smaller version of Waveterm A, which could decode 16-bit factory samples. The Waveterm B offered 12-bit user sampling and longer sample times (up to three seconds). In its heyday in the mid-'80s, the Wave/Waveterm combination was state-of-the-art, with what many people considered better quality sampling than the Series II Fairlight.

The Wave synths came to an end because the hardware limited samples to very short time periods. (The Wave memory was not expandable, and all functions were controlled by a single, overworked 6809 computer chip.) Instruments like the

Emulator II and Prophet-2000 began to make inroads into PPG's market. PPG tried to compete with these instruments by producing the PRK Processor keyboard, which allowed playback of samples without needing the Waveterm and also featured a 100-track sequencer with four separate MIDI outputs that provided 64 discrete MIDI channels. But the PRK was very difficult to program because it communicated all information through a two-character LED.

In a strange change of direction, PPG introduced the Hard Disk Unit, a direct-to-disk recorder that could be synced to MIDI and provided extensive stereo processing. It raised a lot of interest because of its ability to speed up and slow down playback without altering the pitch of the material. Unfortunately, the process distorted the sound quality. Sales of the $17,000 unit were few. PPG's next move was the introduction of the Realizer, a mega-system that replicated other synthesis methods digitally. When the Realizer was shown at several trade shows, it was emulating the Minimoog and an FM synthesizer. In a last-ditch effort to sustain his company, Palm began producing Wave 2.3s (which were suddenly in demand after being discontinued in late '86). The effort failed, and PPG ceased trading at the end of '87. Fortunately, TSI (Steinberg's distributor in Ger-

Direct-to-disk recording, variable playback speed, and stereo processing for a mere $17,000, compliments of PPG's Commander and Hard Disk Unit. Sales were slow, but Wolfgang Palm deserves credit for being six years ahead of everyone else.

many) hired Wolfgang Palm in 1988, and his contributions in that company's Waldorf division have led to the Microwave rack-mount synth module, which has been available for several years. For the past year, Waldorf has shown an impressive new keyboard synth — the Waldorf Wave (who would have guessed) — at music trade shows. Slated for release in the third quarter of 1993, the new Wave's front-panel/programming interface is to die for! Buttons, knobs, and sliders galore, and a beautiful 480 x 64-pixel LCD. You can tilt the control panel to different angles, just like on the Minimoog. The Wave is eight-part multitimbral and offers 16-note polyphony, which you can bump up to 32 or 48 notes with additional voice cards. The basic version comes with a 61-note keyboard, although a 76-note model will also be available. This kind of instrument doesn't come cheap. Projected retail for the basic Wave is around 10,000 DM (Deutsche marks). According to Russ Jones Marketing, who imports Waldorf products to the U.S., the Wave will go for an estimated $7,000 to $8,000.

Another successful German music manufacturer is Dynacord, who has been making P.A. gear and effects processors for years. From 1989 to 1991, Dynacord also delved into the musical instrument business. In collaboration with the American design team Fast Forward — namely Marcus Ryle and Michel Doidic, who later helped develop the Alesis ADAT digital multi-track tape machine — Dynacord introduced the ADD-One drum brain. In conjunction with the ADD-Drive, this worked as a sampling unit. Later fruits of the Dynacord/Fast Forward collaboration were the ADD-Two (a 16-bit version of the ADD-One) and the 16-bit ADS and ADS-K stereo samplers. While Dynacord has since ceased production of its musical instrument line, the sound generator that was used in their ADS samplers was the basis for Digidesign's SampleCell soundcard.

Waldorf isn't the only German manufacturer that still produces synthesizers and related gear. Doepfer has offered master MIDI keyboard controllers for several years, and their MAQ 16/3 MIDI sequencer is something to behold. Reminiscent of the Moog 960 analog sequencer module, the MAQ

has three rows of 16 knobs. Each row can transmit a note-on for each knob — the note itself determined by the setting of the knob — over a single MIDI channel. You can activate all the knobs in the row, or only some of them, and independently assign the row to play forward, backward, back-and-forth, or randomly. Or each vertical stack of three knobs can be assigned to control the note, duration, and velocity of a single-voice 16-step (or less) sequence. It isn't surprising that the MAQ 16/3 was developed in cooperation with the fabled German band Kraftwerk. Outside of Germany, Doepfer products are distributed by Cedos.

On a larger scale, there's Wersi, manufacturer of keyboard synths, synth modules, master keyboards, digital pianos and organs, auto-accompaniment instruments, and the Pegasus multi-purpose workstation. This winged horse offers 16-part multitimbral operation, a *really* impressive 54 notes of polyphony, General MIDI compatibility, 18-bit DACs, 10Mb of sampled ROM, 120 drum sounds, 150 ROM presets, 80 RAM patches, a 3.5" floppy drive, and — here's the *wow* factor — a touch-screen display for programming. Two Pegasus models are available: a keyboard version with built-in speakers, and a three-space rack-mount module.

Quasimidi also caters to the MIDI musician with a line of MIDI accessories and processors and auto-accompaniment instruments and products. Their QM-One is a five-octave, 64-voice polyphonic keyboard with split-keyboard functions that include programmable left-hand-controlled accompaniments with bass, drum, and rhythm tracks. General MIDI compatible, the QM-One includes a 3.5" floppy drive and will play back sequences stored on disk in MIDI file format. If you prefer a rack-mount version, there's the QM-One-EX.

Joining the growing list of stage-worthy MIDI sequencers is Quasimidi's Style-Drive, a rack-mount unit that records and plays MIDI files on 3.5" disks, and can store sys-ex data for other MIDI devices. In addition, Style-Drive provides 32 auto-accompaniment styles for playback by a General MIDI-compatible synth; you can also create your own accompaniments. If you don't need the recording capability or disk drive, and you only want an auto-accompaniment sequencer that will accept Quasimidi's QM-E-Cards, a series that has drum, bass, and rhythm tracks for driving a General MIDI synth, you can opt for the company's Third-Hand.

Quasimidi also offers the QM-2016 programmable MIDI patchbay processor, a rack-mount unit with 20 MIDI ins, 16 MIDI outs, 128 patches with program changes stored separately for each MIDI out, and merging on five of the MIDI ins. Two MIDI ins and outs are conveniently positioned on the unit's front panel. The QM-Merge is a table-top device providing three merged MIDI ins and a single MIDI out, a one-to-three MIDI thru, multi-channel data filtering, and a footswitch input for hands-free transmission of an all-notes-off message.

Musitronics survives by developing upgrades for existing instruments. In particular, they have concentrated on the Roland D-50, introducing a multitimbral mod, a chip that improves the D-50's response time to incoming MIDI commands, and a system for burning custom PCM cards with your own samples for playback in the D-50, as well as Roland's D-70, U-20, and R-8. These products are imported into the U.S. by Valhala Music, Inc.

In the software realm, Steinberg continues to be a force in MIDI sequencing and digital recording products for Atari, IBM, and Macintosh computers. Another familiar software developer, C-Lab, dissolved in late '92 due to internal differences, but reappeared soon thereafter as Emagic, with the same lineup of MIDI sequencing, utility, and editor/librarian products for the Atari and Mac as before.

Another German company, Überschall, survives as a sound developer, with over a dozen sampling CDs and DATs of samples for the Akai S1000/1100. Valhala distributes Überschall's products in the U.S.

As any of these companies will attest, the German synthesizer industry is alive and kicking.

Italy

First things first: In 1964, Paul Ketoff constructed the Synket in Rome. This was around the time that Bob Moog and Don Buchla independently began shopping their modular synthesizer wares. Instead of sporting a conventional organ-style keyboard, the Synket featured three two-octave keyboards that could move from side to side as well as up and down. This additional control aspect transcends what can be done with a normal keyboard. Although such a keyboard isn't commercially available, synth pioneer Bob Moog and composer John Eaton have co-designed a complex controller called the Multiple-Touch-Sensitive Keyboard, whose 49 keys each recognize finger position front to back and side to side, the amount of finger touching the key surface, the depth each key is depressed, and the amount of pressure exerted on each key once it has been fully depressed (polyphonic aftertouch). John Eaton also collaborated with Paul Ketoff on the creation of the Synket. That was in Rome. Now, class, take your seats.

The Italian musical instrument industry is based, like a more famous Italian organization, very much on family lines. The founder and namesake of Crumar was Mario Crucianelli, and Piero Crucianelli was the president of Elka until it was sold to GEM.

The majority of Italian music instrument manufacturing is centered in the town of Castelfidardo on the Adriatic coast. The industry grew up here from humble origins: Accordion maker Paolo Soprani first set up shop in Castelfidardo in the last century. The area became famous for accordions.

It was a natural move into organs, first of the bellows variety and later electronic. Electronic organs became the area's principal product, and they were very popular in the home consumer market until the late '70s. When this market began to weaken, the Italian manufacturers entered the market that had eroded the organ market: portable and combo keyboards.

The first wave of these falls roughly into two categories: electronic pianos with names like Compac, Roady, Roadracer, and Roadrunner, and string machines like Performer and Orchestrator. The pianos were mainly electronic, so while the sounds weren't terribly authentic or pleasing (unlike the Rhodes and Wurlitzer, which survive as distinct sounds to this day), there wasn't a problem with tuning or breakage of tines or reeds. These pianos were fairly rugged and were very successful as live-performance keyboards for the road. On the other hand, the string machines were of much better sound quality and saw a lot of professional use in Europe.

Crumar's real breakthrough came in 1977 when they combined the electronic piano and string machine together in one keyboard package, the Multiman. It offered piano, harpsichord, and string sounds, plus a rudimentary brass synthesizer. The piano sounds hadn't been significantly improved, but the real power of the instrument lay in its ability to provide all its sounds simultaneously. You could supplement the thin piano sound with synthesized brass and strings. (This was co-author Paul Wiffen's first keyboard purchase.)

At about the same time, Elka had a great deal of success with its piano/string machine, the Rhapsody. It found its way into the hands of many big-name acts. The most commonly used picture of Tangerine Dream in Britain featured the Elka Rhapsody at center stage as the only identifiable keyboard amongst towering modular systems. This was no doubt responsible for many Rhapsody sales to keyboard players who were into that style. Jean-Michel Jarre used a Rhapsody to create his string-wash backdrops. Elka also produced a high-quality electronic piano with the most authentic piano sound available at the time.

Siel also had a line of electronic pianos. In the early '80s, one of these was marketed in the U.S. by Sequential Circuits under the name of Piano Forté.

Unfortunately, the arrival of Yamaha's FM-based PF10 and PF15 keyboards spelled the end of the market for the Italian electronic piano manufacturers. Crumar, Elka, and Siel all turned their attention to organs and synthesizers. Perhaps the best of these was Elka's Synthex, an eight-voice polysynth with an on-board four-track digital sequencer. The Synthex began as an outside project by Mario Maggi, but was developed, manufactured, and distributed by Elka in an attempt to break into the professional keyboard market. It boasted more features than its contemporaries, the Prophet-10 and the OB-Xa. The Synthex had a multi-mode filter, cross-modulation capabilities, three levels of good quality chorusing, and a sequencer that was a breeze to use — a rarity in the pre-MIDI days. The fact that it bore the Elka name seemed to put a lot of people off. Elka persevered, however, making the sequencer multi-timbral and adding MIDI as a retrofit. Just when it seemed that the Synthex would disappear without a trace, a few people started buying them. Public visibility of the instrument greatly increased when Keith Emerson, Geoff Downes, and Jean-Michel Jarre started using them onstage. More recently, after production of the Synthex had been halted, Stevie Wonder used co-author Paul Wiffen's Synthex extensively in the production of Wonder's *Characters* album [Motown, 6248], so Elka consented to produce one last Synthex for Wonder.

In the early '80s, Elka and Crumar had some success with portable organs that, like Korg's BX-3 and CX-3 and Roland's VP-70, emulated the Hammond B-3 through a Leslie speaker. Crumar's Organizer actually went so far as to offer dual manuals and drawbars. Their Toccata covered church

The Synthex is one of Jean-Michel Jarre's all-time favorite synths. It featured more goodies than the Prophet-10 or the OB-Xa. It wasn't very successful partly because it was made by Elka, and people figured an Italian organ manufacturer couldn't design a proper synthesizer.

In an attempt to avoid the organ-manufacturer-designer-synth syndrome, the Italian company Crumar released a line of professional products under the Bit name.

organ sounds. Elka's X50 was more of a multiple-preset instrument, but actually came much closer to the B-3/Leslie sound. As a result, Elka relaunched the X50 with MIDI in 1988 because of European public demand. It was in production until 1991.

Crumar and Siel were working on polyphonic synths from the end of the '70s, but models like the Crumar Stratus and Trilogy and the Siel Cruise didn't make much of an impact in the world market. However, in 1983 both companies completely revamped their image by introducing a new breed of polysynths that looked like professional instruments, not machines produced by organ manufacturers. Crumar even changed the name under which their products were marketed to Bit. To match the new look, there was a new sound quality and attention to professional features like velocity sensitivity and intermodulation. The Siel Opera 6 was the first to hit the market, but Yamaha's DX7 stole the spotlight (tough competition for any synth). Crumar was luckier with the Bit One, an eight-voice, multi-timbral polysynth that was considerably cheaper than the DX7; it sold quite well in Europe.

The trend toward MIDI-controlled rack-mount synthesizers led both Crumar and Siel to produce versions of their own. The synths were analog, and their warm sound mixed nicely with that produced by Yamaha's DX series. They sold quite well as inexpensive expanders.

The next step was to put two synths into one keyboard/module (à la Roland's JX-10 or Yamaha's DX5). Siel obliged with their DK80 (1984), while Crumar countered with the Bit 99 (1985). Both companies also brought out master keyboards, the Bit having a built-in sequencer for very little money. Around this time, the Crumar Bit keyboards were marketed in the U.S. under the name Unique. The American distributor changed the appearance of the keyboards again — this time for the worse — to disguise their origins.

Before all this activity at the lower end of the synth market, Crumar had also broken new ground at the top end. They had formed a design/distribution collaborative with New York-based Music Technology. Crumar and the MT designers worked in conjunction with some respected names in electronic music to produce the GDS (General Development System) and the

One of Siel's last synthesizers, the DK-80. In 1988, Roland bought Siel and subsequently made use of its Italian-based factories. (photo by Matthew Vosburgh)

Synergy. These leviathans, which used additive synthesis technology and phase modulation, were bulky and cumbersome, but they were state-of-the-art in 1981. Although few could afford the sort of money involved, the GDS created lots of interest. Perhaps this was due to Wendy Carlos' work with the instrument on projects including the movie *Tron* and many of her more recent albums, starting with *Digital Moonscapes* and including *Peter and the Wolf* and *Beauty in the Beast*. Sadly, Crumar ceased trading in 1987, just as they were about to launch a high-quality sampler at the lower end of the market.

In 1988, Roland purchased a controlling interest in Siel in order to use the Italian facilities to manufacture its own products for European distribution. Once the remainder of Siel's product line had been sold, the name disappeared from the market.

In mid-1987, Elka re-entered the picture with a range of synths that catered to lovers of digital and analog technology. The EK44 — available in keyboard and rack-mount versions — actually used Yamaha chips and offered multi-timbral FM sounds before Yamaha released the TX81Z. The EK22 was multi-timbral, and everything but the filter was digital. In addition, Elka was an active master MIDI keyboard manufacturer for semi-pro and professional use. Their top-of-the-line model, the MK88, boasted 88 weighted keys with programmable velocity response, multiple split/lay-

ering, and master MIDI clock control. Elka also kept its roots in mind by releasing a MIDIed accordion, often used in performance by Michael Mac-Neil of Simple Minds.

Actually, Elka is owned by Italy's leading torchbearer in electronic music manufacturing these days, Generalmusic. Other members within this conglomerate include Bachmann, LEM, and GEM. In late '92, Generalmusic released the S2 and S3 sample-playback synths with built-in MIDI sequencing, effects processing, and 3.5" floppy disk drive. Both the S2's 61-note keyboard and the S3's 76-note keyboard offer polyphonic aftertouch response, a rare but eminently more expressive means of control than the monophonic (channel) pressure response provided by a vast majority of keyboards. With polyphonic aftertouch, you can articulate individual notes via pressure on each key.

While the Bachmann division of Generalmusic continues to generate a competitive line of consumer-oriented digital pianos and automatic accompaniment instruments and modules, the LEM branch recently made a splash with the introduction of an automated mixing system. Dubbed the Sound Engineer, this monster "center of signal exchange" is an analog mixer that can be controlled by digital techniques. All its functions are automated, via MIDI and SMPTE codes, and can be memorized and controlled externally. Sound Engineer comes with virtual mixing software (currently for Atari, with Mac and IBM versions to come) that displays faders and potentiometers that can be controlled with mouse movements. The mixer itself takes up five rack spaces. Its front panel is devoid of sliders and other controls, featuring instead a disk drive slot, a headphone jack, MIDI data reception indicator, and a panic button. The rear panel features 64 inputs and eight outputs (main and sub stereo outs and four aux sends). Each input channel features balanced inputs, gain, three-band EQ with parametric mid-range and defeat switch, four aux sends (switchable to pre- or post-fader), pan, cue (pre- or post-fader), VU meter, volume control with adjustable maximum and minimum levels, and noise gate. Channels can be linked into groups without limitation. Sound Engineer can also be outfit with the optional DSP Quad board, which offers four simultaneous effects (two different reverbs and two multi-effects). Assignment of effects to the aux sends is programmable via matrix routing. What's the cost? Under $10,000 for a 32-channel system with DSP.

Another rising Italian force in the software market is Intersound & Soft, who supports many Akai and Roland samplers with graphic editing software for the Atari ST.

France

Probably the most enduring name in the French synthesizer market is that of RSF Kobol. Its designer, Rubin Fernandez, produced several synthesizers in the early '80s. The first of these was the Kobol, a programmable monophonic keyboard unit with two banks of eight memories. A rackmount expander without memory was also available; the master programmer held the patch data for the expander. Quite a few of these have found their way into the arsenals of well known European synthesists like Jean-Michel Jarre, former Depeche Mode producer Daniel Miller, and Hans Zimmer — who used, among other instrumentation, Kobol synthesizers in the production of the soundtrack for *The Last Emperor*.

RSF also did quite well with the Black Box, a product based along the same lines as the EML Poly-Box. The Black Box allowed you to turn a monophonic synth, such as a Kobol or Sequential's Pro-One (which sold very cheaply in France at the time), into a pseudo-polyphonic synth with separate oscillators for each voice. All audio signals were passed back through the filter and envelopes of the monophonic synth.

The big project for RSF was the PolyKobol, which appeared at several trade shows in '83 and

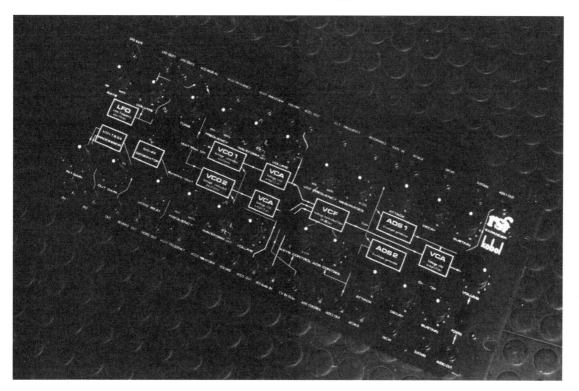

Though not a traditional Chinese instrument, the French-made RSF Kobol Expander was used in the soundtrack production of *The Last Emperor*, a film scored by Hans Zimmer. Wes Taggart of Analogics tells us street value for a Kobol runs from $300 to $500, with dealer prices ranging from $800 to $1,200. (photo by Matthew Vosburgh)

The original RSF Kobol programmable and monophonic synth.

'84. It was a velocity-sensitive polyphonic synth with programmable memories very similar in conception to Sequential's Prophet-T8, but with the unique feature of being able to select waveforms continuously between square, pulse, triangle, and ramp. Envelopes or LFOs were used to move between these waveforms in a manner similar to PPG's Wave synthesizers. Unfortunately, the PolyKobol was too expensive to develop and cost around $8,000 to $9,000. RSF was liquidated after delivering only a handful of PolyKobols.

However, the RSF name reemerged in 1985 with a couple of digital drum machines, the DDR10 and DDR30. The latter featured 12-bit user sampling. Although he no longer produces musical instruments, Rubin Fernandez manufactures PA systems with his brother Serge in Toulouse.

Another French company, MDB, produced a polyphonic sequencer, designed by Eric Lamy, to work with the Kobol synths. Only about 20 of these were sold, together with multiple Kobols as big synth/sequencing packages. This was in the pre-MIDI days, before such facilities became ridiculously cheap and commonplace. MDB later collaborated with Giant Music of Switzerland (a synthesizer manufacturer that doubled as a distributor) to produce the MDB Window Recorder. This 16-bit linear sampling device was like a cross between a studio production device and a music instrument. Although it was only monophonic, it provided a great deal of editing flexibility, including the ability to mark off zones in the "window" for reversed or different-order playback. Like many other well known products by European manufacturers (PPG, Dynacord, Oxford Synthesizer Company), it was distributed in the U.S. by Europa Technologies, which was based in California until its demise in 1987.

MDB also planned to make a sampling drum machine called Giant Drums, which was to use the same digital sampling circuitry as the Window Recorder. However, the product never made it to market. Lamy was more successful in consulting for a keyboard instrument for Furstein called the Night & Day. This normal-looking upright piano, distributed by Comus SpA, transmits MIDI data from its keyboard. Not only that, but when you plug in headphones and depress the middle footpedal, you'll only hear the piano through the headphones! The acoustic piano sound will be muted, so that you can play without disturbing others.

Micro Performance appeared around 1986 with a reasonably priced MIDI sequencer that compared quite favorably with more expensive models of its day like the Roland MSQ-700 and Yamaha QX1. It sold very well for a while in France, until super sequencers like Roland's MC-500 and sequencing packages for the Atari ST computer came along and devoured the market. Micro Performance went on to introduce trigger-to-MIDI interfaces similar to those available from Simmons, and is still in business as of early 1993.

One of France's Unsung Hero stories centers around two foresighted Frenchmen whose quest was to improve the original Yamaha DX7. Designer Dan Armandy and musician/marketer/ear-nose-and-throat specialist/plastic surgeon Alain Seghir collaborated to create SuperMax. Europe's answer to the Grey Matter Response E! board, SuperMax adds superb arpeggiation functions, two-, three-, and four-way voice stacking with independent transposition and tuning for each layer, internal voice and MIDI echo and delay, velocity-controlled cross-switching, microtonal tuning, automated patch generation, and MIDI controller capabilities to the DX7, along with expanding patch memory to eight or 16 banks. SuperMax was imported into the U.S. for a short period by Glynn Thomas of Group Centre Innovations. Co-author Mark Vail, who reviewed SuperMax for the May '88 issue of *Keyboard*, has owned a SuperMaxified DX7 since 1989. It's still the master unit in his MIDI performance rig. In March of '91, after attending the Frankfurt Musik Messe in Germany, he traveled to southern France to meet Armandy and Seghir and to buy the last SuperMax they had in stock for a friend. At the time, Armandy was experimenting with computer-controlled audio mixing components, which led to the development of an automated audio level-control device called the VideoMix, a product much like the Niche Audio Control Module or CM Automation's MX-816. Not to degrade the development of such a handy device, but we can't help but wish that Dan Armandy and Alain Seghir could again collaborate to improve a current synthesizer the way they enhanced the DX7.

Digigram has been a persis-tent member of the music industry. Back in early '88, they introduced a hand-held pitch-to-MIDI converter called the Midimic. It looked like a cross between a microphone and a high-tech plastic spatula, but it's one of the more accurate pitch-to-MIDI converters that we've played with. Unfortunately, the FCC disapproved of the Midimic design and stopped their importation into the U.S. More recently, Digigram developed an IBM-based hard disk recording system mainly for broadcast applications, and it is still available today. According to French music dealer Francis Mandin, Digigram is doing very well.

Holland

Electronic music in the Netherlands (or the whole of Benelux — Belgium, Netherlands, and Luxembourg — for that matter) is supported on the shoulders of one company, Synton. Over the years, the head of Synton, Felix Visser, was involved in most aspects of the business: manufacturing, distributing, organizing the Dutch show Syncom, and so on. From '85 through '88, Visser headed Ensoniq's European operation based in Brussels, Belgium. Felix is the man behind the bizarre Ensoniq stands that appeared at the

Known for their vocoders, Dutch manufacturer Synton also produced modular synths. Today, a Synton modular can cost up to several grand from a dealer of vintage synths.

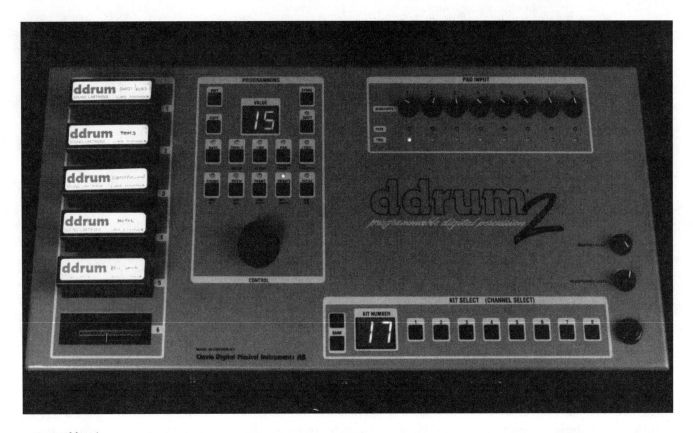

Up tto ddate in the Swedish ddigital ddrum rrealm is the ddrum2 ffrom Clavia. (photo by Matthew Vosburgh)

British Music Fair and Frankfurt Musik Messe shows of that era. In 1989, Ensoniq moved all manufacturing back to the U.S.

Synton produced a series of synthesizers starting with large modular systems in the late '70s. They developed this market until 1983, when they introduced the Syrinx, an extremely versatile monophonic machine. Unfortunately, it hit the market just as the rest of the world was going programmable, polyphonic, touch-sensitive, and MIDI, and everyone was embracing Yamaha's DX7 and other polysynths of the period. Despite having none of these features, the Syrinx sold quite respectably in Europe (several hundred were produced). It was nicely implemented, with pressure-sensitive pads for modulation and pitch-bend, and multiple format filters. These allowed you to exaggerate certain frequency bands into resonance, making the Syrinx great for vocal-type sounds and solo string voices. (Remember, this was pre-sampling.) The only problem was that it was difficult to get the same sound twice because there were so many parameters and often the slightest movement of a knob completely changed the sound. But the Syrinx has found an honorable

retirement in several studios, where it makes a source of great sounds for sampling — thereby making it polyphonic, programmable, touch-sensitive, and MIDIed.

After Ensoniq's withdrawal in 1989, Felix Visser approached E-mu to distribute their products in Europe. He invested all his money in this venture. Unfortunately, when E-mu found other distribution, he went bankrupt. Visser currently makes a living overdubbing alternate languages in foreign films.

These days, the only active Dutch music manufacturer is Zadok, whose SAM1 reads samples stored on disk in Korg DSM-1 and T1, Akai S950 and S1000, and Digidesign Sound Designer formats and allows you to play the sound data on a Korg M1, M1R, M3R, T1, T2, T3, or Wavestation synth.

Sweden

Fortunate owners of the relatively antique Sequential Pro-One discovered Per Linnè's expander mod for that synth. It increased the Pro-One's sequencer to a capacity of 255 notes and provided some programmability.

The only current product from Sweden that

we're aware of is the ddrum AT. (That's no typo; ddrum is the name of the Swedish manufacturer.) This electronic drum module offers unprecedented dynamics and trigger-tracking abilities, but comes at a hefty price of nearly $5,000.

The Future

You've probably noticed this isn't an all-inclusive overview of the European electronic music industry. We apologize to those manufacturers and developers who were left out of the story.

England's strength these days seems to be primarily in software and design development, whether you consider Chris Huggett and Dave Cockerell behind the best-selling Akai samplers or Mike Lynch developing D2D products for the Falcon. Soundscape Digital Technology and Novation continue to produce keyboards and have a few surprises up their sleeves for late '93.

Germany and Italy are the only European countries where the economy can support major manufacturing companies. Italy's Generalmusic products should continue to make an impact in the U.S. in 1993 and beyond.

Other European influences will continue to be seen especially in the software realm. Steinberg and Emagic, in particular, will continue to dominate the sequencing market. Indeed, the European approach generally seems best suited to software, as manufacturing capacity and financing in Europe is being more ravaged by the early '90s worldwide recession than in the U.S.

Only time will tell, but the Waldorf Wave looks like Europe's best hope for a Phoenix-like revival of the European synthesizer tradition and its alternative sounds with the new Wave's unique hybrid combination of digital wave creation and analog filtering.

IT CAME FROM THE MUSIC INDUSTRY

BY TED GREENWALD & JEFF BURGER

PART 1: DREDGING THE TAR PITS OF TECHNOLOGY

You can see them in the vaulted, airy halls of just about any natural history museum: hulking skeletons, their huge ribcages folding around snake-like spines that end in long, unwieldy tails. These bones, painstakingly dug from the earth and reassembled like jigsaw puzzles, are all that remain of the dinosaurs. The evolution of keyboard instruments has also left behind its skeletons. Instruments have left their imprints in the sediment of ancient record albums, Christmas wish lists, artist interviews, and musical-instrument-for-sale classifieds, but for the most part they remain buried beneath the shifting sands of musical fashion and technological innovation.

The history of keyboard design — from undifferentiated protoplasm to lungfish, if you will — is

pretty well documented in the literature, and a detailed account of the tail end of that development can be found in Tom Rhea's Electronic Perspectives column, which ran in *Keyboard* from 1977 through 1981 [reprinted in *The Art of Electronic Music*, 1982, compiled by Tom Darter, GPI Publications (out of print)]. Rhea's columns dealt with the early post-acoustic period, when the first electronic prototypes like the Cahill Telharmonium dragged themselves by the fins from the murky depths of vacuum tube technology toward the brave new world of the integrated circuit. The remains of other long-forgotten instruments — mostly early synthesizers such as Electronic Music Systems' synth-in-a-suitcase Portabella, Paul Ketoff's Synket, the Sonic Six, and gargantuan modular rigs like the Coordinated Electronic Music Studio built by Joel Chadabe and Robert Moog — can be tracked down in a number of texts, among them *The Development and Practice of Electronic Music*, edited by Jon Appleton and Ronald Perera (Prentice-Hall, 1975) and *The Evolution of Electronic Music* by David Ernst

(Schirmer, 1977). [*Lots of this stuff is also detailed in these very pages. — MV*]

But time seems curiously compressed in the latter half of the 20th century. During the last few decades, keyboard instruments seem to have passed through their Jurassic, Triassic, and Cretaceous periods. The monstrous instruments that once lumbered across the landscape have given way to the multiplicity of today's small, sleek, aggressive keyboard designs, each of which is well adapted to its own niche. Some of the lungfish, as it were, have developed fur, and some now lay eggs.

For a while, some of them had fur *and* laid eggs. Not to mention a few that howled at the moon. In place of discolored bones, the remains of these creatures are preserved on paper: the advertisements and press releases generated during the life cycle of a post-acoustic musical instrument vying for a niche in the commercial environment. Dig through some dusty back issue of *Keyboard* and you'll come across a few of them.

You won't need a pick and shovel for this dig. Dr. Keyboard has done the dirty work for you, sifting wheelbarrows full of promotional material for a fragment of a jawbone, probing the dark recesses of the collective memory for a glimpse of NAMM shows primordial. Follow us, if you dare, through the Hall of Keyboard Evolution. What you'll see will astound you.

Lest this seem too much like a stroll through a circus freak show, it should be noted that many of these instruments were the first embodiment of ideas that have since become the Latest Thing (c. 1986). Some grew from undeniably great ideas that — greatness never having been a guarantee of commercial survival — promptly sank without a trace. (An obscure whammy-bar mod for the Hohner Clavinet, marketed by one Edward Gfell, fits this description.) Like the pterodactyl's wings, many of the ideas behind these dinosaurs were simply ahead of their time. And, in a few cases, they appear never to have been anything more than ideas, propped up by a healthy dose of PR and a few splashy artists' conceptions.

Riding the Oblivion Express

During the late '70s and early '80s, when digital synthesizers first appeared, new instruments seemed to fall from the sky. Most of them landed with a dull thud. But a few hit the ground running, notably Yamaha's DX7 and two large-scale systems, the Fairlight CMI and New England Digital's Synclavier. Others, like Passport's Sound Chaser, were retired after a fairly successful run to make way for newer technologies.

The hype that accompanied instrument introductions during this period was particularly pungent, probably because digital technology at the time cost so much money that aggressive advertis-

Coupland Synthesizer (1978): "Every performer knows keyboard synthesizers are not really designed for live performance. So we built sophisticated synthesizer technology into a real musical instrument. A performance instrument that can be played. Without faking. Without limitations. That's what the artist notices first. Then he realizes that he is playing in his own style, not the synthesizer's style."

Overhead view of the Coupland.

"Rick Coupland: genius, musician/composer, computer programmer, inventor, and well-dressed-man-about town." His instrument came from the heart.

picting sexy keyboards clad in a wispy negligee of LEDs and hyperbolic prose, Micor Inc.'s 1978 promo boldly pictured this vaguely nerdy fellow whose glasses were held together by a safety pin. ("Rick Coupland: genius, musician/composer, computer programmer, inventor, and" — no kidding — "well-dressed-man-about-town.") The sexy digital keyboard was pictured inside, however, lying in alluring soft focus like a sultry maiden across the booklet's center spread. And boy, did it look good!

But what the heck did it do? Glad you asked. Micor did give some specifications — "tentative" specifications, that is — describing 12 independent waveform generators, each with 16-voice polyphony, 256 Fourier harmonics, dual five-stage envelope generators for amplitude and frequency, AM and FM inputs, and variable phase angle. The Coupland's velocity-sensitive keyboard was reportedly splittable for each waveform generator, and a variety of pedals regulated modulation. Finally, an on-board sequencer offered 20 sequences and quite extensive editing capabilities.

Unfortunately, as far as we know, nobody ever actually played one. Those who entered Coupland's flying-saucer-shaped booth for a demo at the 1978 NAMM show were treated to a recorded "simulation of a real-time performance" on the instrument, and those who remember visiting Rick Coupland's hotel room for a peek at the thing itself also recall that the inventor spent most of his time trying to figure out why it wasn't working. Mysterious, to say the least, especially in light of the fact that representatives of Ramada International Inc., which financed the Coupland (apparently Rick was in with the Inn crowd), swear they don't remember anything about it. But if it had sounded anywhere near as good as that svelte photo looked, maybe we'd all be playing Couplands today.

It Slices, It Dices . . .

Although the limited size of the market and the enormity of the task must have been apparent to anyone with his or her eyes open, more than a few fledgling companies trampled each other in the rush to develop the elusive Machine That Does It All. The vision of a single keyboard instrument ca-

ing campaigns and glossy brochures were a given. The Coupland is a case in point.

Micor Coupland. In the line of American inventors that began with Ben Franklin, Rick Coupland aspired to squeeze in somewhere between Robert Moog and Ray Kurzweil. While other synthesizer manufacturers printed full-color brochures de-

Con Brio ADS 100 (1980): "At last, a synthesizer that throws open the whole sound universe while throwing aside electronic limitations. The Con Brio ADS 100, developed only after extensive human ear tests were performed, is designed to exceed the capabilities of the ear itself. With the ADS 100 the artist can finally realize any sound in his imagination. Why settle for anything less?"

pable of real-time synthesis, expressive performance, multi-track recording and mixdown, and automated score entry, editing, and printing has led to some of the more intriguing entries in the race to keyboard oblivion. The technologies, both mechanical and conceptual, existed, but they hadn't yet had time to develop far enough for realistic commercial applications such as musical instrument manufacture. Baking a cake is a tall order if you have to start by growing the wheat.

Con Brio ADS 100, 200, & 200-R. After designing sequencer software for Sequential, Syntech, and Sonus, Tim Ryan went on to found Midiman, a successful MIDI, audio, and synchronization interface and accessory manufacturer. Clearly Ryan has had a productive career. He got his start in an unlikely place though, with a lanky digital flop called the Con Brio, which was built by Ryan and two Cal Tech chums, Don Lieberman, and Hal Danziger. Con Brio's first model, the Advanced Digital Synthesizer 100 (according to the promo, "the first synthesizer that deserves to be called a musical instrument") was introduced amid a

flurry of publicity in 1980. It never got past the prototype stage.

The ADS system comprised a dual-manual splittable keyboard, a video display for the envelopes, a "control cube" the size of a filing cabinet for disk drives and computer hardware, and a rainbow-buttoned front panel for 64-oscillator additive synthesis and real-time sequencing that would have looked at home on the Starship Enterprise of the *Star Trek* of your choice. The analogy is apt, in fact — the ADS 100's most notable public appearance was in the sound effects for *Star Trek: The Motion Picture*. No price was given when the ADS 100 was introduced, but it sure looked expensive.

Well — to reduce a three-year tale to a few words — it was. "We wasted three years," Ryan recalls. "We never made a dime off the thing."

A midget all-in-one-box version, the ADS 200, followed soon after. Its display now sported musical notation, the sequencer played back four tracks, the rear panel offered CV and gate interfaces, and the microprocessor count had jumped from three to five. Happily, the multicolored but-

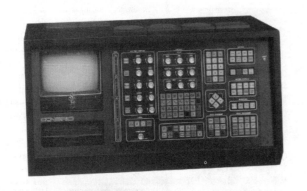

The Con Brio
ADS 200-R, an
alternate config-
uration of the
second Con Brio
instrument, car-
ried a base price
of $20,500.

tons remained and the filing cabinet was nowhere in sight. With the ADS 200, Con Brio's synthesis facility finally rated a description: "Additive synthesis, phase modulation, frequency modulation, nested phase and frequency modulation, and combinations of all modes."

"It was totally configurable in software," Ryan says, "and we had 16-stage envelope generators for both frequency and amplitude, so it was kind of like the grandfather of the Yamaha DX7. On ours, you could build your own algorithms, using any or all of the 64 oscillators in any position in the algorithm. If you wanted additive, you could add 16 of them together. The phase modulation was similar to what Casio did with their CZ series. You could designate any tuning you wanted and save it. You could split the keyboard, stack sounds, model different parts of the keyboard for different parts of the sound, and save that as an entity — the kind of things that are common now." Compared with the first version, Con Brio's second model was a hit: Of the three instruments manufactured, one was actually sold — for $30,000.

By 1982, the Con Brio had dropped one of its two manuals and, with it, a few thousand from the price tag. The ADS 200-R featured a 16-track polyphonic sequencer with 80,000-note storage capability and editing functions available from the scoring screen. The 32-voice version, expandable to 64, sold (or rather didn't sell) for $20,500, with an additional $25,000 worth of options. Only one was ever built.

Why did Con Brio take a turn up an evolutionary blind alley, while other companies have had great success with similar concepts? "It was a labor of love," Ryan says reflectively. "We didn't have much sales savvy, and that was eventually our downfall. Another thing was the intimidation factor: It had something like 190 buttons on it. We figured that no musician would ever want to enter commands, so we went to the trouble of putting on all those buttons. But obviously that approach was just as cryptic as a computer language would have been. It was an amazing feat technologically, but with complete disregard for the people we had to sell the thing to."

KineticSound Prism. Around the same time, another behemoth was vying for the digital big time. For $45,000, the KineticSound Prism claimed to offer "All of the expected features of a digital synthesizer plus a wealth of unique new ones," but since very few musicians at the time had even gotten their hands on a digital instrument, it was hard to know just what that meant. The 24-voice machine sure looked flashy, with its two-manual keyboard, extensive routable left-hand control section, numeric keypad, loads of LEDs, and its own version of the old filing cabinet routine. The ad copy sounded good, too: FM (using any waveforms), additive synthesis (128 harmonics), and waveform plotting (although individual wavetable values had to be entered from the QWERTY keyboard without graphic feedback). Also mentioned were dynamic timbre modulation, real-time amplitude panning in quad, and on-screen viewing of waveforms.

The Prism was the brainchild of James Stephenson Jr., armchair organ builder and president of a high-tech firm in Lockport, Illinois, called Kinetic Systems, and cohorts Sandy Laman-

tia, Brian Swindells, Ed Dyer, Mike Skubic, and Rick Arial. Beginning in 1979, this team designed some very forward-looking capabilities into their instrument. Each of four envelopes per voice (volume, timbre, pitch, and location) boasted eight segments. The timbre envelope smacks of NED's timbre window system of resynthesis, and according to Stephenson, it was "the heart of the invention. You could store 168 waveforms and use them as points on the timbre envelope. The sound would blend from one to the next."

Furthermore, envelope segments were independently loopable, a development not seen in the affordable world until Sequential's Prophet-VS appeared in 1986, and hardly seen since. Dynamic voice allocation to the eight-way keyboard splits and layers presaged the E-mu Emulator. Not to mention an eight-track polyphonic sequencer featuring independent track tempi, independent track looping, track merging, real-time entry, and step editing, all stored in an innovative "bubble memory."

Although bubble memory proved a technological dead end, even today the Prism looks pretty impressive on paper. Apparently it didn't come across as well in demos at NAMM shows in '81 and '82. "The price was too high," Stephenson explains, "and at that time sampling became fashionable, and MIDI and velocity-sensing keyboards became important. For a small company like us, it became overwhelming. Also, Kinetic Systems' market is

government laboratories throughout the world. We knew how to deal with that kind of customer, but not with the music industry." Only two Prisms were built. One was sold, only to be repossessed when the company realized that they wouldn't be in the synthesizer business for long. Stephenson never tried to sell the project to another company. "That would have been like selling a child," he says. As of early '93, both Prisms are still in working condition and reside in a musical room at Kinetic Systems, where Stephenson still works.

Adaptive Systems Synthia. The Synthia was yet another bid for the obviously limited high-end market for computerized all-in-one-box ultra-keyboards. Although the Synthia's projected price was more reasonable than that of the Prism — a mere $20,000 — few musicians seem to have had a close encounter with a working model. The most, um, interesting aspect of the Synthia was its touch-responsive plasma screen, a computer display-cum-data-entry device that followed the user's finger as he or she sketched around bar graphs — the ultimate in intuitive user interfaces. No more eating Doritos while you edit patches, friends. Among the touch-responsive displays were editing screens for harmonic content (up to seven partials), envelope parameters, keyboard setups, controller assignments, and, once again, an implementation of the timbre window concept (called "time slices").

The Synthia's controller section was also partic-

Spiegel, who worked on later versions of the instrument. "In many ways they were absolutely wonderful, and in other ways absolutely infuriating."

The McLeyvier's functions reportedly included notational score display, editing, and printout ("push a button and printed sheet music appears in publishable form"). A disk memory was capable of storing six hours of music material, and played it back via analog hardware with up to 128-voice polyphony. The computer was to accept commands "in any language," including Braille. Priced between $15,000 and $30,000 depending on the options, the McLeyvier appeared at successive trade shows as the Interactive Music Processor and the Amadeus, before sinking without a trace. "With the indomitable spirit of David facing Goliath," in the words of the press release, Hazelcom proved itself not quite up to the job.

"One of the big problems," Spiegel states, "was that the company put out a computer-controlled analog system in the very year when digital synthesis was becoming the big thing." When McLey decided that music was more important to him than instrument manufacture, Spiegel was put in charge of redesigning the software to fit the proposed new digital hardware. Soon after, however, Hazelcom's attention became diverted to other ventures, and the project was scrapped. According to Spiegel, "Only about eight of them were ever in serious use.

"It was a very special instrument," she goes on. "It was unbelieveably reconfigurable, on the assumption that there is no best way to set up an instrument; it varies from person to person, and from piece to piece. Instead of coming up in any fixed way, the first thing it did when the program booted was to run an initialization program so that the user could customize it completely. As an integrated music environment, I don't think there's anything as good out there. You memorized a couple hundred commands, and you could use them at any point, so your world wasn't chopped up into a lot of separate editors. You had random access to everything all the time. Also, it was a musical language, an operating system for music composition. The vocabulary consisted of things like 'invert,' 'ostinato,' and 'transpose.' It had cer-

ularly impressive. Four panel positions were available for sliders, joysticks, and touch plates, which could modulate a number of parameters including the pitches of individual harmonics. There were also three expression pedals, three switch pedals, and of course a velocity- and aftertouch-sensitive keyboard. The accompanying computer, or "control unit," was housed in a separate box, and could accommodate incoming data from four keyboards.

Whatever happened to baby Synthia? Dr. Keyboard must leave that mystery unsolved.

Hazelcom McLeyvier. Like an object caught in the Starship Enterprise's malfunctioning transporter, the McLeyvier shimmered between existence and limbo for a few years beginning in 1981. Designed by composer/technologist David McLey and aggressively (not to mention prematurely) marketed by Hazelcom Industries of Canada, this high-end digital system was to be another all-in-one-box performance/production wonder machine. "Only a few people really know the McLeyvier intimately," says composer Laurie

tain limitations," she concludes, "but it could do things that nothing else today can."

Digital Egg Snatchers

While these saurian systems were competing for the high-end niche, several manufacturers stayed lower to the ground, stealing digital eggs from the larger instruments and incorporating them into more limited, more specialized, and hopefully more marketable designs. These, perhaps, were the immediate ancestors of past success stories of instruments like the Yamaha DXs, Casio CZs, Roland JXs, and Korg DW synthesizers.

Strider DCS I & II. The first Digitally Controlled Synthesizer from Strider Systems of Norman, Oklahoma, wasn't much to look at from an aesthetic point of view, but there sure hasn't ever been anything else that looked like it. Its four-octave keyboard, recessed in a bulky wooden cabinet, was flanked on either side by numeric keypads, one of which sat beside an on-board cassette deck — as though an organ and a calculator had fallen in love and their child had been delivered at a Radio Shack. What filled the DCS I's $4,500 cabinet appears, by 1976 standards, to have been more promising: 12 analog oscillators, three noise generators, three resonant lowpass filters, four LFOs, eight "software-generated programmable contours" (sounds like envelope generators to us), and enough digital memory to store ten patches and four 256-note sequences. (That's where the cassette deck came in.)

Strider's next version, the DCS II (1979), looked a lot more like a synthesizer, but with a few interesting twists. No knobs or sliders: All pa-

rameters were marked on the front panel in a rectangular matrix, bordered by a row and a column of switches. The user selected a parameter by touching a button in the appropriate row, followed by one from the appropriate column. A value for the cross-referenced parameter could then be entered or controlled from a joystick — very logical, and ergonomically sound. The DCS II's price ranged from $2,495 for a single voice to $4,995 for six voices. The front panel's austere silk-screened graphics made the instrument look just a little cheap, though, an impression apparently substantiated by Strider's warranty: 90 days labor, 180 days parts if shipped without a Calzone case; 180 days labor, one year parts if you bought the case, too.

Gray Labs Basyn Minstrel. The Basyn Minstrel leaped out of the woodwork in San Jose, California, in 1981, daring to compare itself feature-for-feature with such five-figure behemoths as the Synclavier and the Fairlight. In that context, it may well have been a bargain; the Minstrel threatened to put only a $3,995 dent in the wallets of prospective buyers.

The four-voice instrument featured an uncluttered front panel of a dozen or so buttons and an LED display, which required users to remember what parameters corresponded to which numbers. The Minstrel's angle, though, was a programmable wavetable that allowed the user to define a voltage level for each of 64 steps: totally user-definable waveforms.

A "transform filter" function was reported to interpolate among four waveforms, in sequence over a definable amount of time, mimicking ADSR ef-

Strider DCS (1976): "Will the DCS I ever become obsolete? Not for at least five years. The tape cassette will allow for the interchange of new patches and new versions of operating systems for the microcomputer."

Gray Labs Basyn Minstrel (1981): "The digital technology that we apply to our synthesizers is ideal for the synthesis and manipulation of sound because it can create any possible audio waveform. We developed and designed a musical instrument using technology developed for the computer industry instead of trying to turn a computer into a musical instrument."

fects and producing timbre envelopes of novel character — an NED-style timbre window approach that our shovels have struck a few times in this dig, and one that, to our knowledge, was only available in the Synclavier (which went out of production when NED folded on July 1, 1992). "Obtaining the effects that the transform filter produces," according to Gray Labs' product literature, "has been one of the major obstacles to building a viable digital synthesizer." Presumably we're still tripping over it, as neither transform filters nor Basyn Minstrels are exactly falling from the trees these days.

Buchla Touché. Legendary synthesizer designer Don Buchla used the emerging computer technology in 1980 to build a 24-oscillator, eight-voice, split/layerable keyboard called the Touché. The $8,500 Touché's primary *raison d'etre*, though, was to fulfill its inventor's vision of a keyboard-controlled real-time performance instrument.

"It was optimized for performance," Buchla says, "rather than for creating something for subsequent playback, what's called sequencing these days. It incorporated things like recording a pattern, a riff, a rhythmic element, or a tune in real time, and recovering it during the performance. As you were performing you could hit a panel control that would say 'remember until I tell you to stop,' and then you could repeat that section *ad nauseam*. You could condition a particular key to signal the end, and then when you struck that note, that was the end."

A Touché built for Suzanne Ciani passed through Laurie Spiegel's apartment en route to its owner, and Laurie subsequently played the instrument in concert. "It let you define notes as pro-

grams," Spiegel remembers. "You could trigger a note, an envelope would start, then it would move the pitch from that note to this note, the envelope would drop to zero amplitude, trigger 14 notes in an ascending scale, and so forth. You hit a key and it began a process, rather than just playing a note."

"The keyboard split would follow the hand motion," Buchla adds. "It also had the capability of continuously fading from one instrument selection [patch] to another. You'd hit a few buttons to decide the fade time, then select the new instrument and continue playing, and the instruments would gradually be transformed."

Buchla very frankly considers the Touché "a bomb." Only four or five of them exist, he says, mostly at universities. "They all wound up with friends of mine who happened to be skilled keyboard players and liked the instruments." As with so many other innovative instrument designs, technological changes made the Touché impractical. "It was pushing the technology at the time," Buchla observes, "and it wasn't the kind of thing you could sell in a retail store. The technological changes at the time were extremely rapid, and so it became economical to design a new system almost immediately after it was introduced. That became the 400 series."

Morenz-Perkes 1200. The origins and capabilities of the Morenz-Perkes synthesizer are among the Great Questions of keyboard paleontology (although we can take a guess about its fate). A brochure appeared in the early '80s picturing the reputedly eight-voice digital keyboard, its ultra-hip player, and an adoring, doe-eyed, buxom female fan, all virtually smothered in an overgrowth

The Morenz-Perkes 1200, outside the flower patch.

of daisies. The copy inside speaks of "any number of harmonics in any mixture," "any shape envelope," and "scales other than equally tempered." Peek past the vegetation, if you will, and take a gander at that control panel. What? That can't be. It's blank! No buttons, switches, sliders, pots, not even silk-screened labels or diagrams!

To be honest, it's not completely blank; there's a single four-digit LED display set against that classy woodgrain backdrop, presumably to display parameter numbers and values. So how do we get at those harmonics, those involved envelope shapes, those non-tempered scales? It's really very simple: You, um, do it "using the instrument keyboard in create mode." Is the filter resonance $D\flat$ or $F\sharp$? Low C seems to turn it down, but I want to crank it up. . . .

Action on the Home Front

Everyone can see the tremendous impact that personal computers have had on electronic keyboard design and marketing. Back in 1980, though, when the only consumer computer was

the Apple II and the only digital synthesizers were clunky systems employing special-purpose computers, linking synthesizers and microcomputers was a visionary proposition. Two companies jumped into the fray, and into direct competition: Passport, with the Sound Chaser, and Syntauri, with the alphaSyntauri, both priced well under $1,500 (not including the Apple). While Passport went on to become a leader in the MIDI software market, the alphaSyntauri's star didn't shine so brightly.

Syntauri alphaSyntauri. The professional market for a computerized musical instrument may have looked small at the time, but nobody knew what to expect from the consumer and educational markets. The Syntauri team (Charlie Kellner, Scott Gibbs, Laurie Spiegel, Ellen Lapham, Robin Jigour, Steve Leonard, and Bob Hoover) gambled on the latter, the company ad evoking family togetherness with photos of generic Mom, kindly Dad, and two full-o'-smiles kids, all gathered around a blazing computer. Despite the domestic imagery, the alphaSyntauri eventually de-

Morenz-Perkes 1200 (c. 1980): "We've broken the sound barrier. Unprecedented flexibility in control of timbre, envelope, pitch, pedal function, and keyboard modes. Make chords, echoes, arpeggios, drones, glides, sequences, glissandi, all in great variety. Unlimited instrument sounds are created by using the instrument keyboard in create mode."

Syntauri
alphaSyntauri
(1980): "A new
age in music.
Infinitely simple
to use. Simply
infinite in capa-
bility. Limitless
as the future."

veloped into a computerized music production environment to be reckoned with.

Syntauri began with a 61-note, six-voice velocity-sensitive keyboard, real-time note displays on the CRT, and real-time recording with a storage capacity of 7,000 notes. Early on, in a paper presented at an Audio Engineering Society conference in late 1980, Laurie Spiegel detailed an FM software implementation that was subsequently scrapped because one of the team members considered the capability "too far out and weird" to sell as part of the system. Over the next few years, software updates provided ground-breaking implementations of notational display and score editing, 16-track polytimbral sequencing, drum-machine and tape sync, educational programs, special effects, user-defined scales, and user-drawn waveforms. The latter program allowed the user to design timbres visually, after which the computer analyzed, reproduced, and made them available for editing via additive techniques. This package cost only $29.95 in 1982; comparable goodies couldn't be had at the consumer level until 1986.

It is possible that Syntauri's biggest hurdle was the mutually exclusive nature of the computer and musical instrument markets at that time. "If you went to a computer store, they didn't know anything about music," recalls hardware designer Bob

Hoover, "and music stores didn't know anything about computers." Syntauri's other difficulties, though, had less to do with the market or the product than with management. "In their last month, they sold more stuff than they had in the previous year," Hoover asserts. "MIDI was just hitting, and basically they just missed the boat. MIDI output was available to Syntauri, and they decided not to take it. The world was finally ready for them, and they decided to stop." By Hoover's count, several thousand units were sold.

Although Syntauri dissolved in 1984, Mimetics supported the system before it stopped doing business in 1988, offering MIDI software and upgraded synthesis cards. "A lot of people are still making a living off of the Syntauri, even though the technology seems incredibly outdated," Hoover commented in 1986. "It's not a dead instrument."

Casheab Syn10. We know it's kind of hard to swallow, but dramatic new evidence indicates that proto-humanoids were hooking up keyboards and computers as far back as the Stone Age. Well, maybe not as far back as the Stone Age — we only said that to get your attention — but at least before the Apple II. And in those days, mind you, you had to stray pretty far from your cave to get involved in computer music. Most small computers used the CP/M operating system and a communications bus called S-100, but there wasn't a convenient way to interface them with synthesizers. In 1978, a pioneering two-man operation in San Diego called Casheab (after Cesar Castro and Alan Heaberland) designed a synthesis card to run on such machines. The Casheab board came with rudimentary software, but by and large you had to program it yourself (which is precisely what one early Casheab owner, synthesist *extraordinaire*, and frequent Utopia keyboardist Roger Powell, did). It was, however, one of the only synthesis cards available, and one of the most powerful.

So what does that have to do with keyboards? Not much; at least it didn't until freelance keyboard designer David Rayna teamed up with Casheab to produce the Syn10, a complete synthesizer package that included two Casheab cards, extensive synthesis software, and a keyboard interface.

The new software configured the boards for additive, FM, and "direct digital" synthesis ("where a recursively generated phase is mapped into a waveform") of as many as 32 voices, and also for sequencing with keyboard entry. Each oscillator had ADSR-type volume and frequency envelopes, and the keyboard could be programmed with user-defined 12-tone scales. The computer's keyboard was also available for user-defined controls. "One thing that I found useful," Rayna recalls, "was to change keyboard splits and timbres rhythmically through the score. With every quarter-note, the keyboard would change its sound." The Casheab system's FM capability prompted a letter from Yamaha, who owns a license for a patent on digital FM technology. (This patent license is due to expire in 1995.) "We just started calling the FM a "vibrato feature" or something like that," Rayna explains.

The small company, however, wasn't much of a threat to the Japanese conglomerate; Casheab went out of business shortly afterward. "I think only one keyboard system was sold as a package, and two more were sold piecemeal," says Rayna, who developed a custom 576-key microtonal keyboard for a performance group in Massachusetts in 1986. "Most people bought the cards and wrote their own software. About 70 of the cards were sold to universities and experimental musicians. It was a self-motivated garage business, so the system wasn't really marketed. That was before marketing

consciousness had come about in the computer music field."

Another problem becomes evident upon reading Casheab's owner's manual, which would give MIT graduates a run for their money. The CP/M software approach was adopted to provide maximal flexibility with minimal hardware, but when musicians with minimal computer chops encounter pages full of BASIC code, tables of hex figures, and equations that evoke memories of that calculus course you failed in college, flexibility goes out the window — along with the instrument.

—Ted Greenwald & Jeff Burger

PART 2: MUTANTS AND MISSING LINKS

Somewhere back in the deep dark recesses of prehistory lies a rational explanation for the confusion of today's complex world. The key to the origins of such technological mysteries as the eight-stage rate-level envelope generator, the wireless remote keyboard controller, and even MIDI itself lie buried in the press releases and advertisements of *Keyboard*'s antediluvian past (roughly 1978 through late 1986). In Part 1, we reconstructed the brief rise and spectacular fall of such high-end digital dinosaurs as the Synthia and Prism. Now we're digging a little higher up the slopes, where erosion has uncovered the remains of a number of other extinct species. While their forms range from the vaguely familiar to the unrecognizable, their descendants can be found today frolicking on stages and in music stores worldwide, and perhaps even in your own keyboard rig. We may not arrive at a rational explanation for much of anything, but it sure is fun poking around among the petrified bones.

From Stage-Left to Spotlight

You say you've got the itch to run up and down the stage with your band's guitar players while

Paia Oz (1976):
"As Larry Fast
of Synergy puts
it, 'When I don't
want to pack
up my big
poly-machine,
my Oz pro-
cessed through
a smaller
synthesizer
makes a good
substitute.'"

playing keyboard? Don't fool yourself; it ain't no new thing. Remote operation was all but built into the voltage-controlled systems of the '70s, and Poly Keyboard Interface was there to prove it.

PKI Freedom I. The Freedom I keyboard (1979) offered most of the features of today's portable MIDI masters, including remote pitch-bend, program change, and multi-instrument splitting and layering for any six Oberheim, Sequential, Moog, Yamaha, Korg, ARP, and/or Crumar synthesizers.

That's not all: An extra few hundred clams made your remote connection wireless ("Look Mom! No cords!" shouted the promo). Wireless system price: $2,869. And to bring your pre-control-voltage instruments into the modern age, PKI modified non-synthesizer keyboards — including acoustic pianos, Hohner Clavinets, Hammond organs, and Rhodes electric pianos — to operate as master controllers for about $500. As the French are fond of saying, the more things change, the more they stay the same.

Paia Oz. Speaking of remote controllers, the Oz, introduced by Paia in 1976, was surely one of the first. Funny thing, though — it only had 18 keys. Chopped off above the octave, the Oz had an amputated look about it. It was, nonetheless, a fully polyphonic six-and-a-half-octave mini-organ/amp/speaker that could also provide monophonic control voltages, gates, and triggers, all for $84.95. The Oz even sported an external touchplate for pitch-bending, and in combination with Paia's Gnome Mini-synthesizer, it earned an endorsement from Larry Fast.

COI KB 2200. "On the ground or in the air, you now can be anywhere." What a slogan, and what an instrument — the KB 2200 Dual-Sided Mobile Remote Electronic Keyboard by California Optoelectronic Industries of Palo Alto really wins the

COI KB 2200
(c. 1979): "On
the ground or in
the air, you now
can be any-
where with the
California Opto-
electronic Indus-
tries KB 2200
Dual-Sided
Mobile Remote
Electronic
Keyboard."

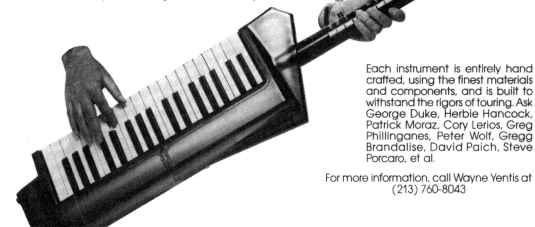

CLAVITAR

...the "full dress" remote keyboard for all single voice lead synthesizers. Lightweight, solid, comfortable to hold and play, the CLAVITAR provides access to the front line for the performing electronic keyboardist.

prize as far as designer remote controllers go. The dual-keyboard look is what does it: Strap this on, and you too can look like a Siamese twin onstage. Covering the player's chest with three-octave manuals to the right and left, this remote gave keyboardists the freedom to finger lead lines, punch out chords, and shield themselves against airborne tomatoes all at once.

Davis Clavitar. If it weren't for the rock-and-roll world's perverse tendency to shovel lead synthesists into the guitar-hero mold, the remote controller idea might never have gotten off the ground. Even before Moog's guitar-necked portable Liberation synthesizer, remote controllers were appearing with everything but frets and strings. Case in point: The Davis Company's Clavitar, surely the duck-billed platypus of keyboard phylogeny.

Although strap-on keyboard instruments have been with us for at least as long as the accordion, Dominic Milano recapped more recent developments up to that point in his April '81 Keyboard Report on the Liberation: "Not too long ago, Edgar Winter and Billy Preston were dancing around with Univox electric pianos or ARP 2600 keyboards around their necks. Jan Hammer put a customized Moog 15 keyboard around his neck. Gary Wright did the same thing with a Minimoog and a customized controller for his Oberheim Four Voice. And then we had a flood of superstar types using something called the Clavitar. . . ." Favored by the likes of George Duke, Herbie Hancock, and Patrick Moraz, this baby's Corvette contours dripped high-tech, and its strap-on design marked an evolutionary watershed: Keyboards had forever left the safety of their stage stacks for the warmth and adulation of the spotlight.

PMS Syntar. The next step, as Moog demonstrated, was to build a self-contained synthesizer version. The Liberation had to defend its turf, though, against the Syntar by Performance Music Systems. In the guitar-inspired tradition, the monophonic Syntar's truncated-rectangle body housed a three-octave keyboard and an analog voice of two VCOs, a VCA, a multimode VCF, an

bending, however, this $1,195 axe provided nine user-programmable "expression keys." Each key activated a preset filter, amplitude, or pitch effect for exact replication of filter sweeps, vibratos, tremolos, and pitch-bends, performance after performance. Presto, no more accidental chalk-on-blackboard quarter-tone bends or police-siren vibratos — Syntar had you covered.

Gleeman Pentaphonic Clear. While getting a slick-looking haircut is certainly the most popular — as well as the most direct and cost-effective — way to compete with the guitarist in the band, you can bet that more than one company has banked on the idea that keyboard players might go for a slick-looking synthesizer instead. Enter, in 1983, the Gleeman Pentaphonic Clear — "Born for the Spotlight" — a variation on Gleeman's 1981 Pentaphonic model. Indeed, the spotlight would have shone straight through this instrument's portable plexiglas shell, drawing the audience's attention not to your fingers, not to your music, but to all the shiny new capacitors in its innards. To a standard analog-style voice, Gleeman's $3,395 instrument added eight digital

LFO, two EGs, and a ring modulator, while a neck-like protuberance housed the left-hand expression controls. In place of the usual wheels, joysticks, or ribbons for modulation and pitch-

waveforms, storage for 100 patches, chorusing, and a polyphonic sequencer.

According to designer Al Gleeman, the Clear was a response to "customer demand. We had a few customers who preferred the more radical look of the clear case. The original idea, I think, came from a clear Rhodes piano that somebody built, and we started getting requests for it." Something under 50 were built during its limited production run, and here's hoping that Clear owners refrained from throwing stones. Gleeman tried to develop a digital synth to compete with the DX7, but wasn't satisfied with the results after completing one voice, so he scrapped the idea. Gleeman now does electrical engineering for a medical firm, designing a laser system for dental applications. Pentaphonic Clear parts and a MIDI retrofit (for reception only) are still available from Gleeman; write to *Keyboard* [411 Borel Ave., San Mateo, CA 94402] for details.

Realton Variophon. Yet another way to bring lead keyboardists into the foreground — one that doesn't involve aping guitarists — has been with us for quite some time in the form of that funny little plastic keyboard-cum-harmonica, the Melodica. It was only a matter of time before the Melod-ica spawned a mutant electronic keyboard. A German firm, Realton, introduced the Variophon at the Ars Electronica festival in Linz, Austria, in 1980 and marketed it in the States soon afterward. Surprisingly, the sounds were digital recordings of genuine wind instruments, dynamically altered with real-time filtering, but since the sound module's front-panel labels were in German, it's hard for us stay-at-home types to tell from the photographs precisely how it worked. Realton's promo, advertising "humanised electronics trough (*sic*) creative blowing," proved, if nothing else, that the Japanese aren't the only keyboard manufacturers to suffer a language barrier.

Star Starwind. A Stateside Melodica/synthesizer, the Starwind from Star Instruments (the Connecticut manufacturer of the Synare percussion synthesizer), appeared in 1982. Probably the most striking aspect of the Starwind was its price: $195. For your money you got a one-octave keyboard with breath-controlled amplitude and filtering, plus pressure-sensitive controls for octave transposition (over a five-octave range), sub-octave oscillator, filter resonance, waveform variation, and portamento. Sounds cool, huh? In the Weird Science department, Star also offered an optional FM

Star Instruments Starwind (1982): "If you play any wind instrument, you'll play Starwind because it's a very expressive, rich-sounding instrument. If you're a keyboard player, you'll immediately be able to play Starwind's simple keyboard. If you're a synthesizer owner, you'll value a synthesizer where you can literally put yourself into each note."

radio transmitter, allowing Starwind owners to play "through any FM radio or FM receiver without connecting to it." Not a bad way to get some airplay without sacrificing your artistic integrity.

The Reign of the Proto-Sampler

Remember the Mellotron? Something of a milestone in the history of electric keyboards, this instrument — if we are to believe the critics — engendered an entire subgenre of art-rock called the "sweeping Mellotron sound" (early Moody Blues, Genesis, and King Crimson). The Mellotron's direct ancestor, a short-lived animal called the Chamberlin, was virtually the first sampling keyboard, but its samples were stored on magnetic tape — one length of tape per key, per timbre — rather than in computer memory, which was in rather short supply when the Chamberlin first appeared in the late '50s. Although its very success disqualifies the Mellotron from inclusion in our rogue's gallery, any of several clones designed to exploit the market it created are prime choices. Among these unfortunates were the obscure Birotron and the ill-fated Orchestron.

Birotron. The Birotron is an enigmatic beast, never having stirred up so much as a press release. Created by one Dave Biro to improve upon the Mellotron concept, and funded by Rick Wakeman, the under-$2,000 instrument apparently never saw the light of day. "The choir and strings are really frightening," Wakeman gushed in a *Keyboard* interview dated March '76. "It uses eight-track tapes arranged in loops so there's no eight-second sustain limit like on the Mellotron. You can program different kinds of attack and sustain, and the keyboard is light; you can play as fast as you like, which you can't do on the Mellotron."

Three years later, however, the instrument was still in the beta-

test phase. "It's my fault that the Birotron didn't come out," Wakeman admitted in the February '79 *Keyboard* cover story. "The last thing I wanted was an instrument that was rushed out. I don't mind having the teething problems to deal with myself, but I don't think it's fair to have other musicians paying for instruments and then having to deal with teething problems." At that time there were "30 to 35 working models" in the world by Wakeman's count, and there certainly haven't been many more since. "I doubt we'll ever make our money back," he commented, "but that's not the object of the exercise. We just wanted to do an instrument that no one else was doing right."

Vako Orchestron. Ex-Moog executive David Van Koevering was also out to one-up the Mellotron in 1975 with the Vako Orchestron. Laser-optical encoding technology, somewhat like an analog CD, was the name of the Orchestron's game. Orches-

Vako Orchestron (1975): "The drama of great new beginnings surrounds the entrance of the laser optical Orchestron into the music world. But, as always in drama, and in great new beginnings, the wonder of the event does not originate entirely in the present moment. The Orchestron cannot be assessed apart from its heritage and apart from the tradition from which it springs. Which is to say, the Orchestron is the product of Technical Research Institute, an organization led by a unique musicologist and marketing master, Dave Van Koevering."

tron strings, brass, and so forth were recorded in an optical format to be read as variations in a concentrated beam of light. Models ranged from the one-manual version at $2,495 to the gargantuan four-manual, pedal-equipped top of the line. One of the first of the fully polyphonic beasties was built for Patrick Moraz, and one custom model included a six-track control-voltage sequencer. Phonograph-sized memory disks, read by an unwieldy remote scanning unit, cost $110 each. The disk readers in some of the larger systems could read three disks at once for layering effects.

The kicker, though, is that Van Koevering adapted the concept of the laser disc keyboard from a toy called the Optigon. "Mattel manufactured and distributed it through Ward, Sears Roebuck, K-Mart, catalogs, discount stores," he confirms. "Over 100,000 home units were sold. The Optigon's soundtracks had rhythms, riffs, little turnaround arrangements, and so forth. It was essentially the same technology."

Vako converted the Optigon for professional use and continued searching for a better way. "We prototyped the first digital devices that rolled a sample over in order to loop it," Van Koevering recalls. Unfortunately, such innovations weren't enough to keep the company afloat. A million dollars and 1,000 Orchestrons later, Van Koevering ran out of steam and Vako ran out of R&D money. "I have many regrets about the project," he reflects. "We were too early, we came in with too few dollars, and we were more dreamers than realists. I didn't want to see the company picked up, and found what Bob Moog and Roger Linn have found. We didn't have the resources to remain independent." Last we heard, Van Koevering was busy introducing MIDI technology to Christian churches throughout the U.S. and living in the Nashville, Tennessee, area.

Computer Music Melodian. Of course, time has shown digital memory to be the most practical technology to come along for sampling keyboards, and one of the pioneering efforts in that direction was Computer Music Inc.'s Melodian. Appearing in 1979, the very first of these instruments had no keyboard of its own, but used control-voltage and gate outputs from ARP and Moog synthesizer key-

boards for its pitch and timing information. Stevie Wonder gave the prototype Melodian a workout on his *The Secret Life of Plants* soundtrack, and the last we heard from it was the bass line on "Happy Birthday," from *Hotter Than July*.

Monophonic Monstrosities

While the monophonic market wasn't exactly flourishing after the polyphonic explosion ignited by the Sequential Prophet-5, small companies could dodge competition and cut costs at the same time by producing one-voice synthesizers. At the turn of the '80s we blinked, nearly missing such instruments as the Jen Synthetone SX1000 (boasting "the most sofisticated" [*sic*] features on the market) and France's programmable variation on the Minimoog, the RSF Kobol.

EDP Wasp. One to keep your ears open for, though, is the Electronic Dream Plant Wasp. This reportedly all-digital British import was one nifty little synthesizer, not to mention cheap at $695, and its documentation featured sex-obsessed comic-book illustrations that bordered on the offensive. Legend has it that back in '78, entire techno-pop groups would jump on stage armed only with a bunch of these little buggers.

The Wasp's two-octave capacitance touchplate keyboard fired two oscillators, a low/band/high-pass filter, two rather funky envelope generators (release and decay times were determined by the same setting), a noise generator, and an LFO. The thing was also battery powered and had its own speaker, for those intimate musical moments. The *pièce de résistance* was a couple of jacks that allowed "up to 50 Wasp units to be connected together in chorus." Let's see — that's only $34,750 for an all-digital modular synthesizer with 50-note polyphonic capability, folks. Boggles the mind.

SMS Voice 400 & Digital Keyboard 430. Small Modular Systems of San Francisco put in its bid for the monophonic market remarkably late, introducing the Voice 400 in 1983. This boxy module contained two VCOs (one with oscillator sync and one with linear FM), a resonant multimode VCF, a VCA, one AR and two ADSR EGs, and an LFO. A 1,024-note sequencer and an analog delay rounded out the SMS voice, which was fully programmable.

SMS Voice 400 & Digital Keyboard 430 (1983): "The fastest, most versatile and musical synthesizer voice available. Unique effects such as AR-swept hard sync and linear FM put the Voice 400 in a class by itself. . . . Emphasis has been placed on making [the Digital Keyboard 430] the most musically engineered controller available."

The Digital Keyboard 430 was designed as a controller for the 400 or any other voltage-controlled instrument. Innovations in the keyboard included last-note priority (as opposed to the low-note priority of most monophonic synthesizers), a patch-select keypad, and a three-axis joystick modulation controller hard-wired to oscillator pitch, filter cutoff, and LFO modulation. At $3,225 for both sound module and keyboard, the SMS system was one expensive monophonic axe, but as a lead voice or bass instrument, it was remarkably well equipped.

EML Poly-Box. While we're on the subject of mono synths, it would be a shame to pass over what is probably the strangest accessory ever designed for one-voice systems, the Poly-Box. Electronic Music Labs, an early manufacturer of high-quality modular synthesizers in Vernon, Connecticut, introduced this $475 oddity in 1977. It only had 13 keys, but each pitch, or a transposition thereof over four octaves, could be memorized by the instrument. Once a chord was held in memory — up to 26 simultaneous notes — the Box would track the output of an external monophonic synthesizer, providing automatic parallel harmony. Not great for the *Two-Part Inventions*, we'll allow, but a real godsend when you were trying to get through the solo rendition of "Smoke on the Water" using only a Roland Bassline.

The Poly-Box's voices were pretty simple, consisting of 30% pulse waves, filtering, chorusing, and detuning, but if your monophonic instrument had the right inputs, you could impose its envelope over the polyphony. Not bad for a one-octave keyboard.

Dubreq Stylophone. With the Stylophone, the number of keys wasn't even an issue. Instead, the Stylophone 350S, manufactured by Dubreq Ltd. in 1977, had a three-and-a-half-octave conductive touchplate. Notes were specified and triggered by touching the appropriate section of the plate with a metal stylus. The sounds were more or less preset, with a sustain/decay switch providing some control over envelope shapes, switchable vibrato, and a photoelectric amplifier (block out the light with your hand, and the volume decreased). Oddly enough, several other manufacturers produced instruments of the touchplate keyboard variety, including the EDP Wasp and Paia Gnome (mentioned above), Electro-Harmonix, and in the realm of serious instruments, Serge and Buchla.

Creatures from the Black Lagoon

In the depths of the Marianas Trench (an undersea Grand Canyon that is reputed to be the deepest in the world) dwell creatures of an otherworldly cast: ghastly fish with teeth like daggers and phosphorescent lamps for noses, demonic manta rays with 40-foot wingspans, organisms exhibiting such alien modes of existence that they scarcely seem alive at all. We have arrived at the outer reaches of the world as we know it. Follow us into a nether region of keyboards so bizarre, so oddly conceived, so unmarketable, that you'll hardly believe they're musical instruments.

Computer Automation Musecom. Computer Automation, a manufacturer of — you guessed it — computers, socked musicians right in their classical guts with the assertion that "Beethoven's last symphony may very well have been his Nineteenth instead of his Ninth," had he owned one of their revolutionary new instruments. In an age of increasing miniaturization, the Musecom II was "no bigger than a standard upright piano." Pouring out of that piano's headboard was a stream of sheet music corresponding to the player's finger

motions. And lodged in its left side was a video screen displaying notation of same.

The system was touted to handle 20 staves at a time, and the notation display was reputedly scrollable and editable. "The one thing the system won't do is create music," admitted the promo. "That's still up to the composer."

Vandervoort Keyboard. As far as we know, the Vandervoort keyboard never reached the market in any form, but it was exotic enough to deserve a mention. Inventor Paul Vandervoort found the various fingerings required to play the scales in different keys to be an intolerable, or at least unnecessary, imposition on keyboard players. And another thing: If the keys were narrower, and the spaces between them wider, players would have an easier time avoiding keys they didn't wish to play. Hard to argue with that; we'd all rather be watching Letterman than practicing Hanon.

The solution was inspired by the keyboard designs of a nineteenth-century Hungarian, Paul von Janko. The Janko design has four rows of keys, each sounding a whole-tone scale. The first and third rows are duplicates (C♯, E♭, F, G, and A), as are the second and fourth (C, D, E, F♯, A♭, and B♭), which keeps the hand from having to go through all sorts of contortions. The advantages of this system are significant: Transposition to at least six keys requires no change in fingering, the octave span is shorter, grace notes obtained by sliding the finger from a flat or sharp to a natural note can be played from and to any pair of adjacent notes, and entire chromatic chords can be slid up and down in a similar manner. Pretty cool, no?

Keyboard reported on Vandervoort's invention in December 1976. At the time he was said to be working on a consumer model (a self-contained module designed to be mounted on top of, and play, any existing keyboard), but we're afraid the project never made it out of the Trench.

Motorola Scalatron. What would you expect of a keyboard made by a conglomerate television/communications/defense-systems manufacturer? Why, the Motorola Scalatron, of course. The ideas of geniuses often appear laughable in their own time, so we'll allow that maybe the Scalatron was a brilliant invention. Maybe. But you've got to admit that, on the face of it, George Secor's "generalized keyboard" (another variation on the Janko design) looks a tad loony. Take the designer's own remarks on the subject: "Even if it were completely impractical musically, it would make a wonderful prop for a futuristic movie." Or maybe for *The Cabinet of Dr. Caligari*.

Actually, Secor's generalized-keyboard Scalatron was an extension of the original instrument built by Motorola engineers Don Ryon and the late Dick Harasek, with help from now-retired DePaul University Professor Herman Pedtke, to play non-tempered tunings. Their Scalatron had a standard black-and-white keyboard, but Secor's multicolored arrangement of 240 push-button keys was adopted to make the instrument's variable-tuning hardware practical with virtually any microtonal scale. The designer himself (a specialist in microtonal theory and musical temperament) toured with it, performing the works of Harry Partch and Ben Johnston. Of course, any technology has its limits. "There is not much point," Secor writes, "in using this alternative keyboard for systems below 31 tones in the octave." If you're into playing standards, don't bother looking for this baby on the used market. Two Secor-style Scalatrons were built — compared to about 12 with the standard keyboard — in the few years after the instrument's introduction in 1974.

While Secor mentioned in a 1976 newsletter that "the synthesizer functions of the Scalatron seem to have been almost as important as the keyboard in putting the instrument over," those functions look a little rudimentary even by contemporary standards, especially for a $6,500 machine. The square-wave oscillators, one for each note, were kept in tune by a reference frequency gener-

ated by Motorola's television technology. From there the waveforms were subjected to filtering and attack/release envelope control. Seven user-definable tuning programs were provided at an additional cost of about $1,000. "I use mine all the time," says Professor Easley Blackwood of the University of Chicago, "but only for research." Blackwood still keeps a standard-keyboard Scalatron in his office. "It's on the fritz now, but I'll be getting it fixed soon. It has rock-steady tuning capabilities; you can always count on it to be right. But I would never consider it for live performance."

The Crocodile Rock

Brushing the sand from these dry old bones, it's easy to forget that dinosaurs continue to walk the earth even in the MIDI Age. Remember the crocodile? Like the Minimoog, a very successful dinosaur indeed, and one that's likely to be with us for ages to come.

More to the point is the story of the coelacanth, a rather ugly prehistoric fish. It was assumed to be extinct until an unsuspecting fisherman hooked one back in the '50s. Which only goes to show that you never know what may be swimming around in obscurity, waiting patiently for the lure of a stable financier to bring it to the surface. We leave you, then, not with a dinosaur, not even with a turkey, but rather with a coelacanth: the Beilfuss.

Beilfuss Performance Synthesizer. The Beilfuss was introduced at the summer NAMM show in 1984 after ten years of initial development. In many ways this $6,000 instrument represented the antithesis of contemporary synthesizer design. While everyone else was streamlining, the Performance Synthesizer's front panel boasted 32 knobs, many in a one-pot/one-function relationship,

Beilfuss Performance Synthesizer (1984): "The varied, easily recognized controls and switches of the Beilfuss allow you to give full attention to the sound you're getting, and not to 'what-does-the-manual-say-is-the-control-code-so-that-I-can-get-access-to-the-control-I-need?'"

some the size of a Peppermint Patty. "That instrument was the bare-bones prototype of a new method of tone generation," says inventor Keith Williams of Evanston, Illinois. "Since then the software has increased by a factor of eight."

The Beilfuss' ten-note polyphonic keyboard (eight octaves, weighting optional) is divided between two independent sound generator units. Operating after the fashion of a graphic equalizer, a 16-slider signal control section allows the user to shape each unit's 15-segment amplitude digital filter envelopes according to the right-to-left configuration of the sliders.

The Beilfuss really begins to look unusual, though, when you find that the sliders also shape the digital waveform directly. "It's like subtractive synthesis, but the harmonics aren't there to begin with," Williams comments cryptically. "You're not adding or subtracting anything, you just digitally create what you want to create." The transitions between the 16 points along the waveform are selectable as sloped (smooth) or stepped (abrupt), a choice that the owner's manual insists makes the difference between "analog" and "digital" sounds.

The instrument's first appearance at NAMM was intended to stimulate financial backing, which has proven elusive. Nonetheless, Williams continues to develop his instrument in isolation — toiling as a messenger during the day to finance his project. As of early '93, the first production model is near completion — "99% ready for production," he says. Although Williams can't quote a price yet, he estimates the Beilfuss will cost about twice as much as originally projected. We're certainly curious to see what Williams finally comes up with, and offer his parting remark as a summation not only of this chapter in keyboard history, but of the entire eternal mechanism of evolution itself:

"It's a long development process."

—Ted Greenwald

MODULAR SYNTHESIZERS

SECTION 2

BUCHLA'S FIRST MODULAR SYSTEM

Still Going Strong
After 30 Years

BY MARK VAIL

Sometimes we take our MIDI-laden music systems for granted. Turn on a few switches, push a button or two, and instant nirvana. It's all so easy.

It hasn't always been so. Let's jump in the time machine and travel back three decades to the 1960s. Electronic music was produced differently then. The most familiar method of creating new sounds was *musique concrète*, in which acoustic sounds and bleeps and bloops output by electronic test equipment were recorded on ¼" magnetic tape, which was meticulously cut into short strips and spliced back together to make music. Creating a few minutes of taped music could take weeks or months. Thankfully, several groups of forward-looking electronic pioneers began to work on instruments that could simplify the music-making process; otherwise, we might all still be holed up in tape studios with razor blades, splicing blocks, Scotch tape, and thousands of strips of magnetic tape strewn about the floor, wound around 7" plastic spools, and pinned to the walls.

Some of the earliest efforts to replace *musique concrète* techniques took place at the San Fran-

cisco Tape Music Center, founded by Morton Subotnick and Ramon Sender in the early '60s. "Ramon and I were trying to move away from cutting and splicing to get something that was more like an analog computer," Subotnick explains. "From around 1959 or 1960, we had the idea of a kind of open-ended palette or black box for composing. Instead of having to go to a big studio, composers could have this inexpensive instrument in their own home and be able to compose. We had approached a number of different people, but Don Buchla appeared to be the most interesting of everybody. So we commissioned him to make a system for the Tape Center. I think we got a grant of $500 from the Rockefeller Foundation to build it, which is sort of ridiculous, but that's what we got. Buchla's first synthesizer was the beginning of an answer to the vision we'd had. It allowed me to really do what I believed I wanted to do — and much more — although it took a different shape than I thought it was going to."

What was Buchla's perspective? "I was doing *musique concrète* using tape recorders at the time," he recalls. "I went over to some of the concerts at

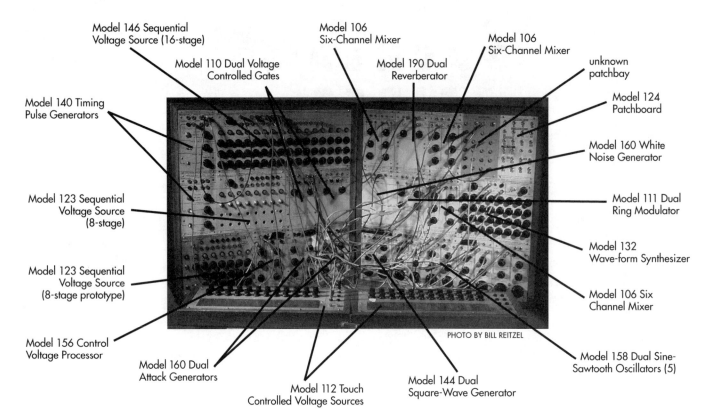

Model 146 Sequential Voltage Source (16-stage)

Model 110 Dual Voltage Controlled Gates

Model 106 Six-Channel Mixer

Model 190 Dual Reverberator

Model 106 Six-Channel Mixer

unknown patchbay

Model 124 Patchboard

Model 140 Timing Pulse Generators

Model 160 White Noise Generator

Model 123 Sequential Voltage Source (8-stage)

Model 111 Dual Ring Modulator

Model 132 Wave-form Synthesizer

Model 123 Sequential Voltage Source (8-stage prototype)

Model 106 Six Channel Mixer

Model 156 Control Voltage Processor

Model 160 Dual Attack Generators

Model 112 Touch Controlled Voltage Sources

Model 144 Dual Square-Wave Generator

Model 158 Dual Sine-Sawtooth Oscillators (5)

PHOTO BY BILL REITZEL

321 Divisidero, the old San Francisco Tape Music Center, and noticed that they had more tape recorders than I did, seeing as I had only one monophonic Wollensak and they had this wonderful three-track Ampex. They were making music with war-surplus electronics and Hewlett-Packard oscillators, things like that. I asked, 'Why don't we make intentional musical instruments?' Nobody had thought of that, at least in that area of studios that were classically fitted out with surplus electronics. I suggested that we design a voltage-controlled musical instrument, and they supported it."

The result is the instrument you see pictured above, Buchla's first modular synthesizer. If you were able to focus closely on the individual modules, you could see "San Francisco Tape Music Center Inc" stenciled on most of them. "We just called it 'the Buchla,'" says Subotnick. "Don named it the 'San Francisco Tape Music Center' because he thought we were going to go into business with him, but we didn't want to do that. So he later changed his company's name to 'Buchla and Associates.'"

Buchla started designing the synthesizer in early '63, drawing on his knowledge of physics and electronics and his experience in building acoustic and electro-acoustic instruments of

welded steel and other materials. "I took a very scientific attitude about sound," he says. "The reason we called it a 'synthesizer' was because we started with the elements of sound. I know that synthesis means something else now: It's come to mean imitation. But at that time, the correct interpretation was the building of sounds from basic elements, like pitch, timbre, amplitude, and a few other things. We used envelope generators from the very beginning, and of course oscillators, filters, and voltage-controlled amplifiers. I called them 'gates,' but they're correctly known as voltage-controlled amplifiers."

Perhaps you're wondering where the keyboard is. Actually, there are two of them right there in the picture. But they aren't in the black-and-white form you might have expected. "The input devices were an important aspect to that system," Buchla explains. "They were all capacitance-sensitive touch-plates, or resistance-sensitive in some cases, organized in various sorts of arrays."

Subotnick explains the touch-plates further: "They were pressure-sensitive. One had 12 keys and you could tune it straight across the board. You could get a chromatic scale if you chose to. It had three control voltages per position. The other one had ten keys and one output per key. We often used this one to control the amplitudes of *concrète* tapes during playback. You could literally play ten loops with your fingers."

Those familiar with analog synthesizers may remember the term "volts-per-octave," which defined the increase in voltage needed to boost an oscillator's pitch up an octave. Early on, most synth manufacturers couldn't agree on a volts-per-octave standard. Moog synths had one scale, ARPs another, and so on. What volts-per-octave scale did the Buchla follow? "Our original oscillators were actually linear rather than exponential," Buchla explains. "In fact, the original ones weren't even linear, they were something in between. So I can't give it a volts-per-octave figure."

One aspect shared by early analog synths was the instability of certain components, most obviously demonstrated by pitch drift in the oscillators. Some synths were more stable than others. The question was, what did the manufacturer consider a tolerable amount of pitch drift? "We felt that it was more important for the Buchla synth to have lots of things that were slightly less stable than to have it be so expensive you could only afford a few modules," says Subotnick. "As I recall, the determination of how long the oscillators would stay in tune was how long a violin stayed in tune in a concert. I figured if you had to retune a violin halfway through, why not an oscillator?"

Buchla is also credited with developing the first analog sequencer. "The sequencer came pretty early," he reveals, "and it had its basis actually in tape music, I would say, as a tape replacement. I thought of the sequencer as a way of rapidly sequencing a series of predetermined pitches and avoiding a number of tape splices. The traditional way at that time of assembling a tone row was to take an inch and a quarter of *A*, followed by three-quarters of an inch of *B*, and so on, and then splice all your pitches together. It was a tedious way of making a tape."

Three sequencers were fit into the first Buchla synth, two with eight stages, the third with 16. Morton Subotnick explains how they worked and the importance of having more than one: "There were three voltage-controlled outputs for each stage. I used to cascade two sequencers so that they would run simultaneously, giving you six voltages per stage. One voltage would control pitch, another spatial location, the third amplitude. Then one, which was really clever, would control the pulse generator that was controlling the sequencer, so that you could determine the absolute rhythm. You could literally program a very complex rhythm over a long period of time, for example, by running five stages against 13."

According to Subotnick, Buchla's approach to synthesizer design wasn't as orthodox as that launched by his East Coast rival, Bob Moog, who

A Buchla 400 (c. 1983), rare because it has a keyboard instead of the Buchla-preferred touch pads.

began developing voltage-controlled modules almost the same time as Buchla. "I think people feel more comfortable with the Moog," Subotnick suggests, "which is more like a traditional instrument. Moog's envelope generators controlled voltage-controlled amplifiers. The envelope generator in the Buchla wasn't intended to govern the loudness of the sound. It was a generic envelope that could be used for any number of things. For instance, I could use an envelope generator to control the pitch of an oscillator. I could route a single voltage from the sequencer for a stable tone, then use an envelope generator with a very fast attack and decay to create a transient at the beginning of the sound. It was much like dealing with an FM synthesizer today. All the envelopes that you have with an FM sound were equivalent to analog envelopes and they are applied in exactly the same way, except that you could apply them to anything, because they were wires. You could apply it to the filter, you could make an accelerando and ritard by applying it to the pulse generator that drove the sequencer."

In the summer of 1966, the San Francisco Tape Music Center was moved to Mills College in Oakland, California, where it was renamed the Center for Contemporary Music, or CCM for short. Meanwhile, Subotnick had moved to New York, taking along another synthesizer, very similar to the first, that Buchla built for him. Subotnick used this system to record two of his early albums, *Silver Apples of the Moon* and *The Wild Bull*. (Both of these are currently out of print, but Subotnick is in negotiations to get them and historical recordings made at the San Francisco Tape Music Center rereleased on CD.)

Buchla's first synthesizer has been in residence at Mills for more than a quarter of a century. For much of that period, it sat unused in a closet while students made use of newer technologies. Early in 1992, though, a CCM student pulled it out of the mothballs to see if it still ticked. "When I first fired it up, it made the most incredible sound," Christopher Koenigsberg tells us. "Just plugging in one oscillator and not even touching it produced this enormous range of variations, as if someone was triggering it with the sequencer. I guess it was heating up and cooling off, but it was wailing and making awesome music! It was like waking up dinosaurs."

Not much else worked on the instrument at that point, but things improved after a visit from Bill Maginnis, CCM's first technical director. Maginnis got the Buchla up and running again, and soon thereafter, Koenigsberg decided to use it — along with some '90s-vintage gear — to record music for his upcoming concert. "I modified some patches that somebody had already set up and basically improvised for a while, recording it onto DAT. I did a little bit of editing on a Macintosh with Digidesign's Sound Tools to filter out some 60-cycle hum and cut out a couple of dead spots. It came out pretty well, I think."

Koenigsberg sums up working with the old Buchla as opposed to today's digital synths: "This is more like taking a lump of clay and kneading it with your fingers on the knobs and touch-plates. You can interact with the sound in complex ways. The problem with most equipment nowadays is there's a lot of bandwidth coming out, they can make a lot of different sounds, and the signal-to-noise ratio is really great. But there are a lot of parameters to change using these awful little LCDs. You don't get the sense that you're getting any bandwidth from the performer — the bandwidth of a human making expressive motions."

EMS VCS3 & SYNTHI A/AKS

British Modular Systems

BY MARK VAIL

Although Brian Eno fingers his Minimoog in this photo, the EMS AKS in the background was also dear to his heart. At that time, Eno told *Keyboard* readers about an interesting quirk that the AKS had developed: "If I feed a loud input signal into the ring modular it will trigger the envelope. . . . It's very useful, because then you can use the envelope to trigger any other function in the synthesizer. . . . When I get it serviced I have to put little notes all over the thing saying 'Don't service this part. Don't change this.'" (photo by Ebet Roberts)

While most of the synthesis attention in the late '60s here in the United States was focused on the creations of Bob Moog and Don Buchla (and soon thereafter, those from ARP), there was only one ballgame to follow in Europe. Out of an advanced — for 1969 — computer-music studio in London came a tabletop modular synthesizer known here in the States as the Putney.

Developed and marketed by EMS, the VCS3 — its true name, which stood for the voltage-controlled studio, attempt #3 — was tiny compared with its behemoth American counterparts. Instead of dozens of jacks spread across several square feet or more of front-panel space, the VCS3 offered a tiny, square patch-board matrix. Whereas American synth modules were connected together using handfuls of patch cables, small pins were inserted into

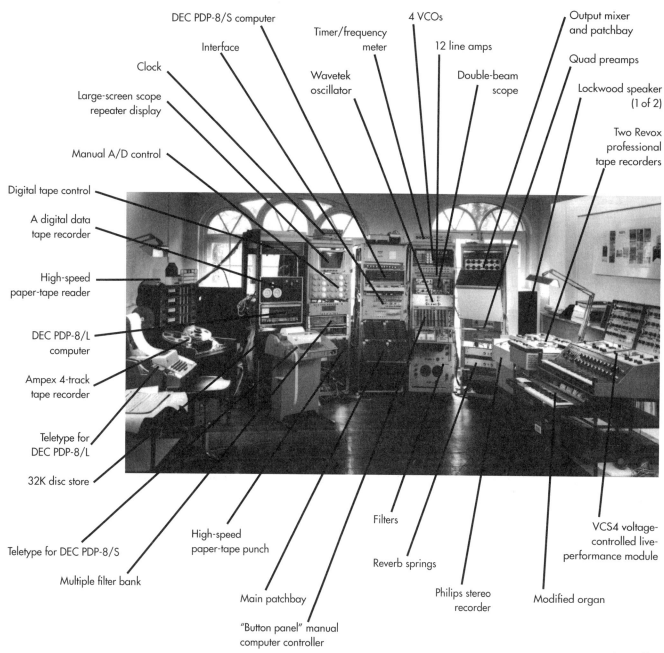

DEC PDP-8/S computer

Interface

Clock

Large-screen scope
repeater display

Manual A/D control

Digital tape control

A digital data
tape recorder

High-speed
paper-tape reader

DEC PDP-8/L
computer

Ampex 4-track
tape recorder

Teletype for
DEC PDP-8/L

32K disc store

Teletype for DEC PDP-8/S

Multiple filter bank

High-speed
paper-tape punch

Main patchbay

"Button panel" manual
computer controller

Timer/frequency
meter

Wavetek
oscillator

4 VCOs

12 line amps

Double-beam
scope

Output mixer
and patchbay

Quad preamps

Lockwood speaker
(1 of 2)

Two Revox
professional
tape recorders

Filters

Reverb springs

Philips stereo
recorder

Modified organ

VCS4 voltage-
controlled live-
performance module

**Peter Zinovieff's
"Musys" studio
at Putney (Digital/Analog Computer Studio),
1971. (photo
by Ravenna
Studios Ltd.)**

the VCS3's patch board to route control and audio signals through the device. "There was actually a very good reason for using that patch board," explains David Cockerell, designer of the VCS3. "We got a good deal on them surplus. We got a few hundred of them pretty cheaply."

Since 1965, Cockerell had worked for Peter Zinovieff, who'd purchased a DEC (Digital Equipment Corporation) PDP-8, the first minicomputer, and put together one of the early computer music studios. According to Robin Wood, who joined

EMS in 1970 and currently runs the company, "At least half of EMS was a very expensive computer studio where DEC computers were used to control prototype analog systems, not only for generating simple analog synthesizer sounds, but also for some very sophisticated filter bank systems that could analyze sounds. David Cockerell designed this 64-channel analyzing filter bank. It was a bit like a vocoder, only it was all under computer control. The company was heavily into this kind of advanced computer research."

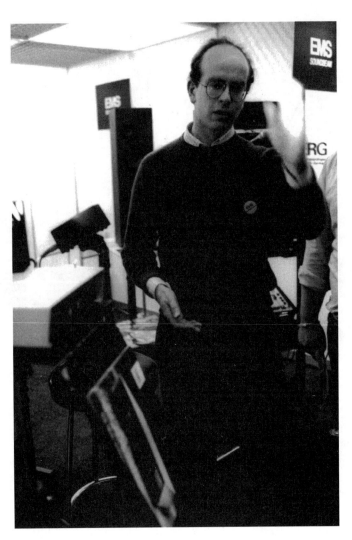

plate keyboard with a 256-event monophonic digital sequencer. This fit inside the Synthi A's lid. A combination of the Synthi A and the KS was called the AKS.

While Cockerell did all the designing, Wood was busy with other duties. "Half of my jobs were to do with keeping the studio in order: tidying, lining up tape machines, sweeping up, making tape copies. The other half was actually concerned with demonstrating the equipment to quite a lot of notable pop stars, who would come by and decide whether they wanted to buy something." Ready for a list of who-was-who in the European rock scene? Go ahead, Robin: "Pink Floyd, the Who (the organ on 'Won't Get Fooled Again' was processed with the VCS3's envelope shaper), Roxy Music [Brian Eno's band], King Crimson, Tangerine Dream, Klaus Schulze, Moody Blues, Curved Air, Jean-Michel Jarre, Gong, and Yes. Todd Rundgren (one of your own) used the VCS3; there's a good picture of it on the inside cover of *Something/Anything*. Many other groups bought EMS gear but never seemed to make use of it: Rolling Stones, Led Zeppelin, Fleetwood Mac, Jethro Tull, and Deep Purple."

Like the American analog synths of the time, EMS's oscillators tended to drift. "They were a bit dodgy onstage," Cockerell reports. "You had to keep tuning them up." Wood concurs, "They're rather temperamental with regard to tuning and pitch stability. People who used them onstage deserve a lot of credit for their bravery. If you wanted to use one with a keyboard in performance, you had to let it settle down for about half an hour before you could set the tuning. Even then, if someone were to open the door and let in cool air just before your lead solo, you could easily be in trouble. Lots of people used them live. Pink Floyd used them for quite a long time. But a lot of their stuff wasn't pitched; it was just effects. There were many applications where the machines were just used as effects generators. Jean-Michel Jarre is

"There was a group of three of us," Cockerell explains, "Peter Zinovieff, myself, and Tristram Cary. They were both into avant-garde music, what you would call serious music in the classical tradition. It was toneless, and they thought the keyboard was of secondary importance. The VCS3 wasn't really a keyboard instrument to start with. We sort of added the keyboard on as an afterthought." The keyboard in question was the DK2, a three-octave, duophonic mechanical affair installed with control electronics in a wooden cabinet that matched the VCS3.

Portability was an afterthought as well. "The VCS3 was pretty awkward to carry around," Cockerell asserts. "It would have to be in a box as big as a tea chest. It didn't fold over or anything." By 1971, Cockerell had squeezed his VCS3 electronics into an oversized briefcase, and the Synthi A was born. He also designed the KS, a 2½-octave touch-

VITAL STATISTICS

Produced: 1969 to present (out of production for a short time in 1980).

Total Number Made: VCS3, estimated 550; Synthi A/AKS, 850.

Manufacturer: EMS (Electronic Music Studios), Trendeal Vean Barn, Ladock, Truro, Cornwall TR2 4NW, United Kingdom. 44-726-883-265. Owned by Peter Zinovieff from 1969 to 1979. Datanomics took over until 1983, when current owner Edward Williams stepped in.

Current U.S. Contact: Don Hassler, 2409 Hewatt Rd., Snellville, GA 30278. (404) 972-9176.

U.S. EMS Servicing: Everett Hafner, EMSA (Electronic Music Studios, America), 11 North Main St./Box 767, Williamsburg, MA 01096. (413) 268-3588.

Description: First commercially manufactured portable analog synthesizers (electronically identical), conceived by designer David Cockerell and avant-garde composers Tristram Cary and Peter Zinovieff. VCS3 comes in an L-shaped hardwood cabinet for tabletop use; measures 43 x 44 x 42cm (roughly 16 3/4" x 17 1/4" x 16 1/2"); weighs 9kg (almost 20 lbs.). Synthi A is in a black ABS briefcase for portability; measures 48 x 38 x 12cm (roughly 18 3/4" x 14 3/4" x 4 3/4"); weighs 7.5kg (about 16 1/2 lbs.).

Features: Two audio oscillators (0.5Hz to 20kHz, one with sawtooth and variable-shape sine waveforms, the other with variable pulse-width square and rising- or falling-ramp triangle waveforms), an LFO (0.025Hz to 500Hz, variable pulse-width square and rising- or falling-ramp triangle waveforms), noise generator, lowpass filter (18dB/octave, variable resonance, 5Hz to 15kHz, sine-wave oscillation), ring modulator, envelope shaper, dual-spring reverb, joystick controller, signal level/control voltage meter, dual input channels (1/4" mono, mike, line, and CV levels), two outputs (1/4" mono, via VCAs for audio or pre-VCA for CV), headphone and scope outputs. Built-in stereo amplification/speaker system. Optional 3-octave duophonic DK2 mechanical keyboard with internal oscillator and velocity-sensitive dynamics, and 2 1/2-octave KS capacitive touch-plate keyboard and 256-event monophonic digital sequencer (fits inside Synthi A's lid, resulting in the AKS).

Insider Information: The VCS3 is better known in the U.S. as the "Putney," perhaps due to EMS's original address in Putney, a suburb of London. . . . David Cockerell now works for Akai; he designed the hardware used in the S1000, S1100, and S3000 samplers and the DR4d multitrack hard disk recorder. . . . Tristram Cary is a Professor of Electronic Music at Adelaide University in Australia. . . . Current EMS owner Edward Williams, a contemporary classical and electronic music composer, is perhaps best known for scoring music for television broadcast. Among his projects is the long-running nature series "Life on Earth," narrated by David Attenborough.

Original Retail Prices: VCS3, £330 (about $825). Synthi A, £198 (about $495). AKS, £420 (about $1,050). [U.S. dollar to British-pound exchange rate in 1971 was 2.5 to 1.]

Current Retail Prices: New: VCS3, £1,450 (about $2,393). Synthi A, £1,375 (about $2,269). AKS, £1,675 (about $2,764). Reconditioned: VCS3, £850 (about $1,403; Synthi A, £800 (about $1,320); AKS, £988 (about $1,630). [Calculated on a U.S. dollar to British-pound exchange rate of 1.65 to 1.]

Current Street Prices: £250 to £650 in England. In the U.S.: Synthi A, $300 to $1,000. Synthi AKS, $400 to $800. VCS3, $500 to $800.

Current Dealer Prices: Synthi A, $800 to $1,500. Synthi AKS, $1,000 to $1,500. VCS3, $1,000 to $1,500.

probably the best-known performer who still uses them. He's got six of them in a big rack."

Rock stars haven't been EMS's only supporters. "Educational people consider that the VCS3 has never been bettered as a tool for teaching people about sound processing, acoustics, and analog audio synthesis," Wood points out. "We've also got the jingle and effects professionals, broadcasters, people like that. There are younger enthusiasts who may have seen Jean-Michel with his enormous array of VCS3s, and they want to make sounds like he does. We get young musicians who have listened to early Tangerine Dream stuff, when they used a lot of VCS3s. We haven't only attracted people from the pop end. There have been young people influenced by avant-garde music, acid rock, or Jean-Michel Jarre."

Of all the synths covered in the Vintage Synths column in *Keyboard*, only the EMS lineup of VCS3, Synthi A, and AKS is still being manufactured — albeit on a custom-order basis. In fact, they were out of production only briefly during 1980. And if you don't want to pay for a custom-built one, you can save a bit of money by ordering a factory-refurbished unit. But don't look for MIDI connectors. "We were asked by the shop that markets those rack-mount Midimoogs and Prophet-5 modules [Studio Electronics] to MIDI the VCS3 and put it in a rack," Wood recalls. "The trouble with that is it would take up an enormous amount of panel space. It would be a monster. None of it would be preset, you have to make all the connections for the audio and control lines, and you have to modulate all its controls in real time. It seems like too much of a sweat to start tinkering with the old design. Why not just tell people to go out and buy a MIDI-to-CV converter and keep the design the same, so as not to confuse the issue? It doesn't feel right to me, having one of them in a rack. Besides, the AKS is quite handy as it is."

Not that there weren't some design changes along the way. "The most significant changes came in early '72," Wood explains. "We call them the MkI and MkII. We're still on the MkII to this day. It has a redesigned power supply, which can deliver a lot more power in order to drive the KS's monophonic digital sequencer. The original design also used a different output amplifier. On the MkII, you can trigger the envelope using an external audio signal. When the amplifier reaches a certain threshold, it triggers the envelope generator, which wasn't possible on the MkIs. The patchboard matrix layout was also slightly changed. On the MkI, there were separate rows for the two oscillator waveforms: sine and sawtooth. You could route the sine wave to, say, ring-modulate some sounds while sending the sawtooth off through the envelope generator to do something else. On the MkII, these are mixed together on one row."

According to Cockerell, there were electronic circuit changes as well. "In the first VCS3s, there weren't any integrated circuits. It was all done with transistors. That's my excuse for it not working very well."

Talk about excuses — check out Cockerell's modest explanation for bringing the VCS3 to life: "It was just a means of raising money for Zinovieff's studio."

KEITH EMERSON'S MOOG

The World's Most Dangerous Synth

BY MARK VAIL

Alone, it stands 4¼' tall and 4' wide. With its tour case, it weighs 550 pounds. The stainless-steel doors that provide rear access to its innards weigh over 80 pounds. In concerts, it stands majestically overlooking everything else, including a poor, misused Hammond L-100 organ. Earlier, less complex and imposing versions of it appeared in a jazz concert in New York and on the hit tune "Lucky Man." In spite of its girth, it's been lugged to and from England, the States, and Japan. One individual who was quite intimate with it between the summers of '91 and '92 calls it "the most dangerous synth in the world."

Welcome the monster modular Moog synthesizer that has been Keith Emerson's companion, on and off, for 21 years. In the beginning, there were three more like it. For a long time, though, it's been unique.

"In the summer of '70," synth pioneer Bob Moog recalls, "we were commissioned to build a quartet of live-performance modular synthesizers for a concert series to be held in the Museum of Modern Art in New York City. It was called 'Jazz in the Garden.' We built these four things out of standard modules, and we designed special preset boxes so that, instead of changing all the knobs and rerouting patch cords, you could just press a button and get a new preset.

"After the concert, we wondered what the hell to do with these things. We let our representatives know that we wanted to sell them. One of them, a Londoner named Dag Fellner, told me that maybe he could sell one to a young musician by the name of Keith Emerson, because their new group was doing an album. That winter, I visited Dag. By that time, Keith already had this damn thing in his possession. Dag asked me if I wanted to meet this guy, and of course I said, 'Yes.' I found out later the group was right in the middle of making *Emerson, Lake & Palmer*, their first album. 'Lucky Man' was the first song they used it on. I don't think they had intended to use the system in 'Lucky Man' until Keith actually got it and they heard what he could do with it."

If you've never seen ELP live, you're probably unaware of Emerson's antics. Moog was pretty as-

Keith Emerson's massive modular Moog system, in an earlier form (photo at right) and the way its modules are configured today (diagram on facing page). For the most part, the arrangement of modules hasn't changed that much. A fixed filter bank, a 904A lowpass filter, and a television that displays fake waveforms now reside at the upper right of the system, in the space once occupied by a frequency counter. Although seven programmers are shown, only six are functional. None of the modules across the bottom row work; they're merely there for show. How old are some of the components? Date-stamped yellow tags indicate when each Moog module passed its final tests. Will Alexander tells us the 901A and B oscillators are dated 1967. (photo by Val Podlasinski, diagram by Rick Eberly)

tounded the first time he saw the band in concert, but not nearly as much as an acquaintance of his. "In 1971, I got a call from Keith saying he was going to be on tour. It might have been their first American tour. I was still in upstate New York, and the closest they were going to get was New York City. They were playing at a place called Gaelic Park. I tried and tried to find out where Gaelic Park was. Nobody at the New York City Parks Department had heard of it. Finally, somebody found out

that Gaelic Park was a little soccer field way up in the Bronx or Manhattan. In fact, it was at the end of the subway line, because there was an elevated track all the way around it, where the train looped around before going back. Keith had invited me to come wherever backstage was. He and I piled into his mandatory limousine and we went through the mud, rocks, and broken glass — which is what you expect to find underneath the tracks of a New York City subway train — onto the soccer field. He got

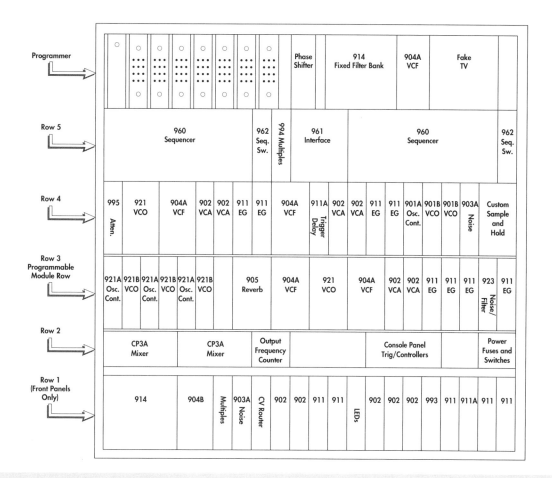

YOU CAN'T BLAME THEM FOR TRYING

Would you say "no" to Keith Emerson? Moog Music had to early on, as shown below. Louis Newman of Media Sonics/Discrete Audio faxed the following letter, which he procured along with major portions of Moog's inventory and documentation when it shut down. The late Tony Stratton Smith was the manager of Keith Emerson's trio, The Nice.

January 16, 1970
Mr. Tony Stratton Smith
7 Townsend House
22 Dean Street
London W.1. England

Dear Mr. Smith:

Thank you for your letter of January 7th concerning the Moog Synthesizer and the possible use by "The Nice."

We have never offered instruments to groups for promotional use, first because of the cost of the unit and secondly, because of the small size of our company. It would also be quite unfair to the groups (such as the Beatles, Stones, etc.) in England who have purchased the equipment.

An additional problem would be that some time and training is necessary before the Moog can be used. Although it is a keyboard instrument, various patch cord arrangements are needed before the instrument would produce any sound whatsoever.

I am enclosing some literature and should you option to add a Moog Synthesizer to the equipment of the Nice, we could make immediate delivery from inventory of most models.

Thank you for your interest in the Moog Synthesizer. Should you or the group be in New York in the near future, please come up to the studio which I have which contains a collection of various electronic instruments.

Very truly yours,

Walter E. Sear

Walter Sear now runs Sear Sound, a recording studio in New York City.

Judging from this photo and the performance and pose-for-effect photos that follow, Emerson's modular Moog and Hammond C-3 were a neglected pair.

out with the rest of the group and they walked onto the field up to this wooden platform stage out by one goal. At the other end of the field, there was a line of ten or 12 portajohns.

"There were about 10,000 young white males packed in there. I don't remember any seats; people were just trampling on the soccer field. That's where I saw Keith do his number with the organ and knives, with pieces of keys flying off.

"Lo and behold, who do I meet there but a customer friend of mine, Gershon Kingsley. Gershon was a successful middle-aged professional studio musician who had lived in Israel and Germany. He and a guy named Jean Jacques Perrey had already made a couple of synthesizer records with tape-splicing techniques. One was called *The In Sound from Way Out*, and it was sort of commercial, novelty stuff. Anyhow, I meet up with Gershon by the row of portajohns, and he's completely disoriented and freaked out. In back of us, you can smell all the shit and piss and the doors to the johns are banging open and closed. And in front, here's this guy throwing an organ around, making keys go flying off, and making the instru-

ments scream. All of a sudden, Gershon shrieks, 'This is the end of the world!'"

Evolution. Emerson's Moog has undergone lots of changes during the last 21 years, growing considerably from the original configuration of a single row of modules. According to his technician, Will Alexander, Emerson added a second cabinet when the band recorded *Trilogy*, and a third cabinet with two Moog 960 analog sequencers for the *Brain Salad Surgery* tour. During those early ELP days, Emerson often brought the modular system back to the factory for additions and alterations. Somewhere along the line, Alexander says Bob Moog, Dave Luce, Tom Rhea, and Rich Walborn designed custom circuits and primitive hardware programmers to assist Emerson in live performance with the Moog system.

Tours tend to be really tough on gear. However, the synth was pretty sturdy. According to Moog, "There was one point in the early '70s when ELP was onstage at a stadium in Jersey City, New Jersey. There was a freak thunderstorm with high winds that blew away a big tent-like canopy that was protecting the equipment, knocking over a lot of gear, including the synthesizer. It actually filled up with water. After the storm, they emptied out the water, let the instrument dry out, and it worked. I was always rather proud of that."

Then came a sad time when Emerson no longer used the Moog system, and it ended up in a situation that it couldn't handle. "I found out from people at Moog that it sat outside in its case in Buffalo throughout the winter," Alexander reports. "I got it for the first time in September of 1990, before Emerson went on tour in Japan with the Best." Joining Emerson for this tour were guitarists Joe Walsh and Jeff Baxter, bassist John Entwistle, drummer Simon Philips, and singer Rick Livingstone. The once-mighty modular Moog wasn't quite what it had been.

"We went to Japan and we set it up right out of the case," Alexander says, "having no idea what condition it was in. We got it to make noise, and we did the Japan tour with it."

To help out with the now under-the-weather Moog, Alexander contacted Gene Stopp, a dedicated vintage keyboard and synth enthusiast who designed and constructed his first modular synth from scratch while he was still in high school. Stopp elaborates on the Moog's condition: "When we first got it out of its case, we looked at the patch diagram and bought $500 worth of Audio-Technica patch cords. When we plugged it in and turned it on, the thing wheezed, crackled, and squeaked. It was not musical. There were bad modules and blown-up transistors. Every single trim pot was out of adjustment. All the pots and switches were dirty. It was in sad shape, but that was its condition for this tour."

Restoration. After the Japanese tour, Alexander

Emerson lashes at his $50,000 triple-manual Yamaha GX-1, ignoring the Moog and Hammond C-3 in a freezing, empty Olympic Stadium in Montreal in 1980. The GX-1 was a forerunner of the CS-80. (photo by Michael Putland/Retna)

returned with the Moog to his home in the Los Angeles area, where Stopp was anxiously waiting for an opportunity to dig in and restore the once mighty system. "Will left a cryptic message on my answering machine," says Stopp. "It was the sequence from the end of 'Karn Evil 9, 3rd Impression' [on *Brain Salad Surgery*]. That was all. Of course, I knew exactly what it was: 'Hey, Will's got the Moog. All right!'"

For the next eight months, Alexander and Stopp worked on the modular system whenever they could. "All the power buss connectors were rusted," Alexander reveals. "They were pure rust. We pulled out the entire power harness and replaced it with brand new wiring and soldered connectors instead of using twisted wires in screw clamps. We also put additional filters on the power rails throughout the system. That's a design philosophy that has evolved since this thing was built. This removed the ripple from the power supplies. These analog circuits are notorious for drifting, and they drift because there was current ripple from the power supplies.

Attention-starved, it beckoned. "Play me," cried the Moog, "play me!"

"I also replaced all the 741-type op amps with 411-type op amps, which are low-drift, low-offset, so that when they heat up they stay stable. They're also FET-input instead of bipolar, so they don't draw current. When I changed all of those parts, the oscillators just went at attention.

"Then we went through and cleaned every module, made all the jack points work, and calibrated all the trim pots. In addition, we pulled out everything that was superfluous. There was a Polymoog interface built into the center panel, and we took it out."

"There were some blinking LED circuit boards," Stopp adds. "They were dead weight, so we took those out too."

They didn't, however, remove the most impressive visual display in the top row of modules. "It's a TV screen, but it's just a visual effect," Alexander explains. "It displays a simulated waveform that goes faster as you speed up the sequencer. Also, the whole lower panel is facade. There aren't any electronics associated with the module panels."

One of the main problems involved the loss of power as more and more modules were patched together. "The Moog uses S-triggers, which is short for shorting triggers," Alexander continues. "There's voltage on the line and when it's pulled down to ground, the envelope generator triggers. If you started plugging in patch cords to various trigger modules, you'd come to a point that it would stop working."

Then there was the big metal box. "It contained photo transistors that were silicon-glued to LEDs to control the time constants of all the envelope generators," Stopp tells us. "The box was to hide the photo transistors from external light, but there was all kinds of cross-talk, because one LED would trip the neighboring envelope generator. Also, at some point, all of the Moog 911 envelope generators had been modified, but since then some of them had been replaced with non-modified modules. We modified those to match the modified 911, then took out the metal box and soldered photo couplers to the envelope generator pots. That worked a lot better."

Alexander agrees: "These new opto couplers are basically photoresistors with an LED in a

sealed package. They were superior to the LEDs that were silicon-glued to photoresistors."

All told, Alexander estimates the two spent 150 hours working on the Moog. That doesn't include play time. "When we'd fix something, we'd play with it for three or four hours," he admits. "I know I drove my neighbors completely bananas."

The result of this work? "The thing is extremely accurate now," Stopp testifies. "The oscillators, the calibrations on the front panel, and the linear envelopes are all very precise."

Ribbon Controllers, Reverb, & Why It's So Big. While Emerson rarely fails to throw his Hammond L-100 about the stage, he once told Bob Moog that he never took knives to his modular Moog. He does, however, scamper about quite freely — both onstage and into the crowd — while triggering the Moog and some pyrotechnic fireworks from a ribbon controller. Sometimes, the ribbon controller has fought back.

"Keith's roadie just before me was named Rocky," says Alexander. "Rocky would load the pyro-launcher, which was basically copper tubing inside the original ribbon controller — which was

a lot bigger than the new ribbon controller, but is now non-functional. The pyro-launcher was loaded with glow plugs that heated up when Keith pushed the switches; the glow plugs would fire the gunpowder and shoot out the flash-paper stuffing. Keith would get more and more ambitious, wanting to make it bigger every time. One time, he was demonstrating it in rehearsal for the fire marshal and it blew Keith's thumbnail off. Because I have ultimate respect for his hands, I removed the switches that were right on the launcher. Now, they're six inches away, so I don't think there's any possibility of him getting hurt, or at least not that severely.

"He's told me some great stories, like the time he picked the controller up wrong and fired the pyrotechnics right at the front row. He said everybody was cheering."

Whereas Emerson's ribbon controller used to have 100 feet of cable connecting it to the Moog, he's now limited to 25 feet. Sometimes he forgets how far he can go. "During the Japan tour," Alexander tells us, "the band was playing in Osaka at a baseball stadium. They were set up in the out-

Keith can't keep his hands off that Yamaha. (photo by Neal Preston, 1977)

field and the audience was about 150 feet away, up where home plate was. So Keith started playing with the ribbon controller and he went running at the audience, when all of a sudden he reached the end and it knocked him down. It made the Moog go berserk. He got up, turned and bowed to the audience, and went running back to the stage."

According to Gene Stopp, one reason Emerson's Moog sounds particularly good is due to its reverb. "It's got the Moog 905 spring reverb, a very important part of the sound. It has a timbre to it — that *Trilogy* lead sound. Digital reverbs don't sound like that. Now that we're in the '90s, you might look at that and say, 'Nix the springs; get them outta here.' Don't ever do that."

Considering the modular Moog's size, you'd probably think it's stuffed full of electronic components. Not so. "Actually," Alexander says, "it looks really massive, but by today's standards, the

amount of electronics is extremely minuscule. There's a lot of air space in there."

But the size is important, as Stopp explains: "You need that panel space. You need big knobs far apart and big patch cords, because what do we have arms for anyway? This thing puts it all right in front of you. Everything is laid out for you. For improvising on a synthesizer, it stands today as the best way to do it. How do you improvise on a Korg M1? During a jam, you want to solo. Okay, what do you do? You change patches. That's all you can do. Or you have a Roland JD-800. Great, you can open up a filter and stuff like that. But this is the ultimate for improv, because you can do so much with the sound."

What It's Worth. How much would you pay for Keith Emerson's modular Moog? Or one that's similar? It depends on who you are and what your perspective is. We got several opinions.

Will Alexander first: "It's priceless, as far as I'm concerned. It's irreplaceable."

Hurray! Keith Emerson wields the ribbon controller/ pyro-launcher that drives the big Moog. (photo by R. A. Erdmann, 1980)

"You have to consider what it would take to duplicate something like that digitally," says Bob Moog, offering a different perspective. "You can't duplicate it exactly digitally, but there are instruments costing $1,000 that come close — as close as current digital technology can come. On the other hand, if you had somebody custom-build something with analog sound-producing capabilities and digital control technology, that might run well into five figures, because it would cost a lot of money. So, depending on how you looked at it, you can say anything from less than $1,000 to more than $10,000 is what something like that might cost today."

We also contacted Louis Newman at Media Sonics/Discrete Audio [2416 S. Chestnut Ave., Broken Arrow, OK 74012; (918) 451-0680]. According to Newman, an established collector and distributor of Moog and other analog modular synths, "In my best estimate, the Emerson modular Moog would sell for about $12,500, plus or minus $2,000 due to its condition. Cosmetics are very important, as is the general working order. However, Keith Emerson is such an important figure in synthesizer (and musical) history, there might be a buyer that would pay more, simply because it was Keith Emerson's.

"This isn't always the case. In fact, it is very rare that a name player will get more for a unit than anyone else. Sometimes, it even works in reverse. I mean, that Moog has been blown up, stabbed, left out in the New York weather, and God knows what else. You can bet if it was part of ELP that it has been used."

Why the Fuss? You probably wonder why Emerson still uses this huge analog modular system. Not only does it look so impressive, standing tall above all else onstage, but the modular Moog has some rather special sonic capabilities. Will Alexander explains: "The beauty of this instrument versus today's synths is that it goes from DC to 100kHz. This system has none of what I call 'padded-cell technology.' It can hurt you. It's the world's most dangerous synthesizer."

"It has no D/A converters," Stopp concurs. "It doesn't know that it can blow out your tweeters."

Emerson's modular Moog as it appears today.

"Luckily, I had circuit breakers on my tweeters," Alexander continues. "I was resetting them every day. Everybody says that we hear from 20Hz to 20kHz, but I think that we perceive a lot more than that. Digital has a frequency limit. The best digital instruments — the Fairlight, WaveFrame, Synclavier, Roland S-770, Akai S1100, whatever you want — start falling apart at 15 or 16kHz. The cheap samplers are far below that. This instrument has a sizzle that is absent in all other instruments."

"Compared to this, something like the Roland D-50, a Minimoog, or an ARP Odyssey sounds like there are pillows in front of the speakers," Stopp swears. "This thing is so crystal clear. It's just right up front."

Alexander voices another opinion: "Unfortunately, synthesizer engineers have engineered out all the distortion. But that's a desirable thing in electronic music and synthesizers. Once you make it distortion-free, it's dead. To make really thick digital sounds, you have to stack sounds up together. You can take one oscillator on this instrument and it can sound unbelievable."

Unbelievable as this beast may sound, it's most startling to hear what Emerson's main modular Moog patch emulates: "Basically, it's a Minimoog," Stopp reveals. "Three oscillators, VCF, and VCA, with extensive modulation capabilities."

ARP 2600

Most Popular Modular Synth

BY BOB MOOG

The ARP Instrument Company introduced its line of high-tech analog modular synthesizers, the 2500 series, in 1970. These instruments featured matrix-switch patching (no "patch-cord jungle") and stable oscillators. ARP's founder, Alan R. Pearlman, recognized the importance of teaching musicians how to use the technology, so he designed a new instrument with a fixed selection of basic synthesizer functions. This instrument, dubbed the Model 2600, was an integrated system with the signal generating and processing functions in one box and the keyboard in another. The functionality was borrowed from the original ARP modules, but instead of using matrix switches (which were expensive and bulky) for patching, Pearlman devised a system of factory-installed "normal" connections between the modules. These connections could be added to or replaced by patch cords. Thus, a beginning user could work the system relatively simply. When the user desired to develop more complex sounds, patch cords could be added as needed.

Pearlman believed that schools with small or medium-sized music departments were the main market for this new instrument. To further enhance the 2600's educational value, Pearlman put graphics on the console's front panel so that the signal paths were easy to follow, and used sliders and slide switches so that the control and switch settings were easy to see. The first production run had blue panels, painted sheet-metal cases, and polished wood handles. "That's not what I wanted," Pearlman recalls. "I wanted the instrument to be housed in a rugged case that would travel safely. But those were the days when nobody would listen to you if you were over 30, so the young designer had his way." Musicians and retailers, however, quickly shot down the "Blue Marvin" or "Blue Meanie" design in favor of the vinyl-covered luggage-style case with the dark gray panel that remained in production from 1971 to 1981.

Into the Hands of Musicians. The ARP marketing people quickly determined that the key to promoting the 2600 was to show musicians and retailers what could be done with the instrument. David Friend and Roger Powell toured the United States, putting on demos and talking to musicians and dealers. Powell (who left ARP to become a synthesist with Todd Rundgren and currently works for Silicon Graphics) recalls, "David and I traveled all over the place in a red Chevy van. We tried to sell the 2600s in hi-fi outlets as well as music stores. We got thrown out of most of them. For most musicians of that time, the instrument was hard to use. On top of that, it was monophonic. The turning point was when [the music retail store] Sam Ash decided to take on the 2600, late in 1971. They were really forward-looking. They gave us credibility among retailers, and exposed our instruments to all the musicians in New York."

Edgar Winter was the first high-profile musician to pick up on the 2600. He had the keyboard equipped with a long extension cord, which enabled him to wear the keyboard around his neck like a guitar. Pete Townshend, who also had a 2500 modular system, was another early 2600 user. Stevie Wonder had the control panel of his 2600 labeled in Braille.

Many talented musicians took on the 2600 and, with sustained determination, mastered the new technology. Powell remembers Joe Zawinul's early experience. "Joe came up to Boston to play at the Jazz Workshop. I met him and showed him the 2600. It took him a little time to pick up on some of its features. For instance, the 2600 lets you route the

The ARP 2600.

output either through the VCA or directly from the VCF. If the output came from the VCF, the sound would always be on. After Joe had his instrument for a week or so, he called and said, 'Hey, man, the sound is *fantastic*. Now tell me, how do you make it stop?' But he kept at it, and became one of the 2600's leading musical innovators. Eventually he

VITAL STATISTICS

Produced: 1970 to 1981.

Manufacturer: ARP Instruments, Newton and Lexington, MA (out of business).

Description: Patchable monophonic analog synthesizer (two-voice polyphonic keyboard after 1975).

Features: Three VCOs, 4-pole lowpass VCF, VCA, ring modulator, two envelope generators, sample/hold, noise source, mike preamp, spring reverb, voltage processor, four-octave keyboard. Post-1975 models have two-voice keyboard with built-in delayed vibrato.

Retail Price: $2,600 to $2,900 during the early '70s. $3,600 from 1975 to 1981.

Current Street Value: $300 to $1,000.

Current Dealer Price: $700 to $1,500.

Insider Info: The ARP "Blue Meanie" was the first version of the 2600, built in a garage before the ARP plant was open. With its all-aluminum case, designed by an aerospace engineer, Blue Meanies were essentially unserviceable and, according to ARP vice president of engineering Philip Dodds, "We would cringe when one came in for repair."

One of ARP's prominent artist endorsements came from Josef Zawinul. In this mid-'70s advertisement, he is playing two-voice counterpoint on a pair of 2600s.

ARP 2600 PATCHES

These two patches only begin to illustrate the wealth of sonic resources that are available in an analog modular system of this size. The second patch, used by Edgar Winter in his song "Frankenstein," illustrates two important features of the ARP 2600, as well as of other instruments with related design philosophies. First, real-time access to all of the front-panel controls is an important musical resource. And second, completely new, unconventional sound material can be produced with only a few functions, controls, and patch connections.

These patches are shown as block diagrams so that you can better understand the principles of signal routing in a modular system.

Patch 1: Breaking Glass. The sample/hold module samples a noise (random) waveform, producing voltage steps of differing heights. These steps control the frequency of the VCO. The VCO square-wave output is then used to clock the sample/hold. The result is a waveform at the output of the sample/hold that consists of steps of random height and width, and another waveform at the output of the VCO that consists of

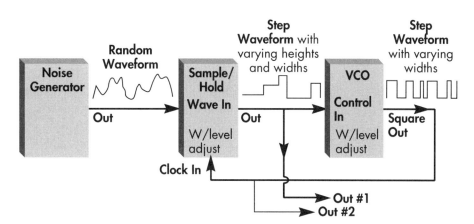

**Patch 1.
Breaking Glass.**

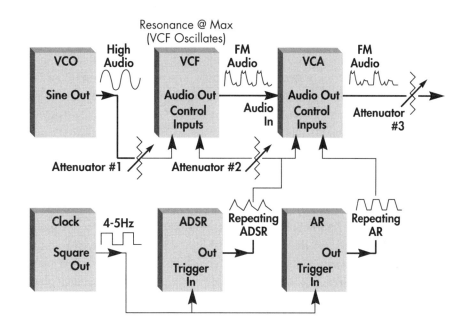

**Patch 2.
Edgar Winter's
"Frankenstein."**

steps of uniform height and random width. By varying the noise level, sample/hold level, and VCO frequency, you can produce a wide range of crashing and breaking sounds, which can then be fed through a VCF and VCA.

Patch 2: Edgar Winter's "Frankenstein." The sine wave from the VCO is used to frequency-modulate the VCF, which is set to oscillate.

The VCF output is a raunchy FM sound. The degree of raunchiness is controlled by attenuator #1.

Two envelope generators are used. The ADSR envelope generator produces a short, percussive envelope, while the AR produces a sustained envelope. Both envelope generators are triggered by a clock that produces a trigger four to five times per second. The VCF is swept by the ADSR; the sweep of the depth

is controlled by attenuator #2. The VCA is controlled by both the ADSR and the AR. The level of the audio output is controlled by attenuator #3.

To produce the complete sound: (1) Turn up attenuator #3 so that the sound becomes audible. (2) Change the filter frequency. (3) Turn down attenuator #1 to reduce the amount of FM. (4) Jerk attenuator #2 up and down in time with the beat of the music.

had two 2600s, one of which was controlled by ARP's model 1601 16-step analog sequencer." Zawinul also took advantage of the function that allows the 2600's keyboard voltage to be inverted, which results in pitches that are mirror images of those on a normally tuned keyboard. He would then simultaneously play the identical fingering on two keyboards, one of which used the reversed tuning. The effect was far from conventional.

From Monophonic to Two-Voice. A couple of years after the 2600 was introduced, Tom Oberheim came out with a kit that would convert the 2600 into a two-voice instrument. The kit worked by converting the keyboard so that it would produce both high-note and low-note voltages. Since the instrument had three oscillators, you could use one or two of the oscillators for the high note, and another oscillator or two for the low note.

In 1975, ARP incorporated Oberheim's idea into its standard production models. The keyboard circuitry was redesigned to include not only the two-voice mode, but also delayed vibrato, interval latch, single and multiple trigger, and improved pitch-bend capability. Mark Minter-Smith, ARP's musical tester for six years (and now an instructor at the Berklee College of Music) points out, "Just the addition of delayed vibrato freed up a VCO, the VCA, and an envelope generator." The new keyboard had the model number 3620, whereas the monophonic keyboard model numbers were 3601 and 3604. (The console model number was always 2600.)

The 2600 color scheme remained black, gray, and white until 1978, when the look of the entire ARP product line was changed. After 1978, the panel graphics were white and orange, and the panel itself became a darker gray.

The Service Situation. The critical circuits of the early 2600s were cast in epoxy blocks that are almost impossible to repair. Around 1975, ARP switched to potting the circuits with silicone rubber, then topping them with epoxy, which is less difficult to repair. A few years later they stopped potting altogether, resulting in circuits that can be easily fixed.

When ARP went out of business in 1981, Music Dealer Service in Chicago bought a large quantity of ARP parts at the bankruptcy auction. From then

until recently, MDS was the main source of replacement parts, and they repaired many 2600s as well as other ARP instruments. Although MDS recently stopped doing business, service and parts for the 2600 are still available; see the list of service centers and technicians who support ARPs starting on page 275.

Although no one is advertising MIDI 2600s, the instrument can be integrated into your system using a stock MIDI-to-CV converter such as the Clarity Retro or Paia MIDI/Control Voltage Interface. This is easy because it is a trivial matter to disconnect the keyboard. Another bonus is that the 2600's oscillators are more stable than other early-model synths, such as the Minimoog, so you needn't worry too much about the instrument staying in tune.

Wrapping Up. As Roger Powell says, "The 2600's main assets are the same things that made it hard to sell initially. The 2600 boiled down virtually all analog synthesis capabilities into a single box. You could experiment with it or use it pre-patched. It was a magic mix — definitely enough stuff to use musically. On top of that, it stayed in tune and was reasonably robust and roadworthy.

"As analog synths went, it was easy to use. You could easily see and recognize panel setting patterns — even in the darkness of the stage. As one well-known 2600 user said many years ago, 'It's the only synth that I can operate while I'm drunk.'"

TECH TALK WITH A TALKATIVE TECH
Realizing the 2600's Sonic Potential

By Timothy Smith
As told to Mark Vail

In contacting people as resources for my Vintage Synths column in Keyboard, *I've come across many an interesting individual. Such a description can easily be applied to Timothy Smith, who started taking apart EML synthesizers when he was in junior high school. He went on from doing repairs for a local music store to become a regional technical rep for Moog and ARP, and continues to service and modify old and new synthesizers. These days, he's got a gripe against synthesizer manufacturers who use less-than-state-of-the-art components in their instruments, a subject that he'll delve into here. Smith works with his partner and fellow engineer David Weyer as The Audio Clinic/Weyer-Smith Labs, developing audio upgrades for digital synthesizers.*

Smith singled out the 2600 as a candidate for some semi-major overhauling that would bring it up to today's standards of operation. Unfortunately, his level of detail transcends the technical scope of this book. While we present much of Tim's verbal description of what can be done, we suggest you contact him at The Audio Clinic/Weyer-Smith Labs [3461 Canyon Dr., Billings, MT 59102. (406) 652-1564] for his 2600 modification package. The price of this package will depend on exactly which modifications you want, but Smith estimates it will start around $100. If you send your 2600 to The Audio Clinic for the basic upgrade and minimal repairs, prices start around $300.

Wes Taggart of Analogics [5261 Maple Ave. East, Geneva, OH 44041. (216) 466-6911] reports that he has epoxy-encapsulated ARP modules available, with prices ranging from $100 to $295. He has the 4072 filter for $295, but doesn't offer the 4012. Although most of Tim's technical talk deals with the 2600, there are topics of interest to other readers as well. —MV

The ARP Filter & 26 Other Truths. The filter that ARP originally used was called the 4012, and it was essentially a copy of the Moog filter ladder. That was what Moog patented. At some point, Moog Music sued ARP and asked them to please stop using their filter design. So ARP came up with their own design called the 4072, and it is a four-pole voltage-controlled lowpass filter with performance very similar to the Moog filter, but it doesn't use the Moog filter ladder. The problem that occurred, unbeknownst to most people, was that there was a design error. ARP specified in their technical literature that their filters would go from 16Hz to 16kHz. Most 4072 filters will not go beyond 11 or 12kHz, and that's a problem. Nobody

exactly knew why, but it seems like everybody historically knew that the Moog filter had a much better high end. It wasn't because the ARP filter wasn't capable of that high a response, it was just that unfortunately some circuit values were incorrectly calculated. However, these are easily repaired to have a frequency response out past 20kHz.

Which ARPs did this filter appear in?

Everything: the 2600, the Omni, the Odyssey, the Axxe — every ARP instrument that had a four-pole lowpass VCF used the 4072. The old white-faced Odysseys had the Moog filter. A certain number of 2600s — particularly those that were called the "Blue Meanie" — had the 4012 filters. The ARP Axxe originally had the Moog filter.

Interestingly, ARP had designed a circuit called the linear-voltage-to-exponential-current converter. That circuit converted linear control voltages to exponential currents. Moog stole that from ARP. It was used in the Moog filter in, for example, the Sonic Six and the Prodigy. Also, Moog may have used it in their later VCO designs. Phil Dodds told me that ARP had seriously considered suing Moog for the use of that circuit, but evidently they never got around to it. That's a little known fact.

It was really, in the words of Philip Dodds, an elegant, extremely accurate, and simple little circuit, and the truth is that ARP's VCOs were actually very, very stable. The instability that comes from ARP synthesizers, in terms of tuning, is probably more related to the keyboard circuitry and control-voltage processing circuitry than it is the VCO itself. Phil explained to me that he thought this was an extremely elegant little circuit and it was probably responsible, if anything was, for the excellent frequency stability of the ARP oscillators.

[Philip Dodds confirms Smith's summary of the ARP/Moog conflict: "The so-called 'fat sound' of Moog filters was a big thing in the early '70s, and it was really based on a ladder filter of transistors. I can draw the schematic for you if you really care, which is scary because it's almost 20 years later.

["ARP came up with a filter design that was real close to it, and Bob Moog had a patent on it. That ended up in litigation, because the ARP and Moog filters looked really similar. The reason they looked

similar is because they were. ARP was flat-footed infringing. But it turns out that there was a linear-voltage-to-exponential-current converter that Moog tried to use.

["I will tell you bluntly, and it was known internally at ARP, that when things came to fisticuffs, Moog said, 'You're infringing on our patents.' And at ARP — I was a lowly guy then, but I was an observer and I could hear it happening internally — we scratched our chins and said, 'Oops, they're right.' So we went to them and said, 'Yeah, but you're infringing on our linear-voltage-to-exponential-current converter.' 'Oh.' And there was a lot of chin scratching. At the end of it, we said, 'Maybe we can cut a deal here.' But I can tell you that it was Alan R. Pearlman, in particular, who said, 'This

The Octave Cat's smaller offspring, the Kitten.

isn't right. We really are infringing, and we shouldn't do this.'

["So the Moog filter design is indeed unique, and ARP's version of it was sufficiently different that ARP's filters never sounded quite the same, but it

was close enough that it still infringed on the patent. Of course, under the agreements that followed, there were no problems thereafter, but we basically had guns pointed at each other's head before we all said, 'Oh, forget it.'

["There was another ARP patent that put the Cat synthesizer company out of business, because they infringed directly. The Cat was a knockoff ARP Odyssey clone that was built in New York. ARP had a two-voice synthesizer scheme that was used in the Odyssey, principally, which allowed you to play two notes at once. It was based on a resistor chain, a resistor basically between each note, and if you pressed two notes you could measure the current difference between the top and bottom of that resistor chain and derive the voltage difference and create an idea of what the second note was. We're talking years before polyphonic synths appeared. ARP had a patent on the second-note technology, and it was a really clear patent.

["So when Cat introduced a synth that infringed on our patent, we nailed them right to the cross; they were infringing right down the line. They literally copied the design right out of the service manual. We said, 'Excuse us.' It was so blatant. We succeeded very quickly in getting a cease-and-desist order, and they were out of business. Their Odyssey knockoff was so complete, you could go from the left of the panel to the right, and it was all there. The only thing they did was change some of the sliders to knobs. Apart from that, they were identical."

[Other sources dispute this claim. The Cat was manufactured by Octave Electronics Inc., which later became Octave-Plateau and subsequently the current-day IBM software developer Voyetra Technologies. According to Carmine Bonanno, the former president of Octave Electronics and now at the helm of Voyetra, ARP lost their suit against Octave Electronics and the Cat synthesizer remained in production from 1977 to 1981.

[Dodds continues, "The 2600 was a product that refused to be killed and die. Each year, because I ran engineering in later years, I went through the issue of 'Why don't we refurbish it.' The marketing guys would say, 'No, no, no! It's dead.' But it just kept selling, so we kept doing engineering changes and upgrades all the way through. We finally did one mas-

sive upgrade, and we couldn't make enough of them. The last version of the 2600s was the best. They're distinguishable because they have orange screened graphics on a black front panel, whereas all the previous ones were gray with white lettering."]

Fix Your Filter. If you have a 2600 that has a 4072 filter, you can modify it for an extended frequency response. If it has a 4012 filter, there's no need to bother with it because it's really the Moog filter. The 4012 has a frequency response that goes out to about 35kHz, so obviously there's no modification necessary. To find out which filter you have, remove the six front-panel screws and the top four handle screws, gently lift the panel out of the cabinet, and right behind the frequency cutoff controls for the filter is the module. If it's a 4012, it will say so on it, it will be wrapped in a copper shield, and that will be encapsulated in epoxy. If it's a 4072, there will be a circuit board with circuit traces visible.

The filter fix itself involves the addition of four resistors to the underside of the 4072. I can supply the plans for doing this, or it's included in my 2600 fix-up kit.

How Not to Fry Your Speakers. Another 2600 problem is the fact that there's a DC offset that appears on the sawtooth and square wave outputs of the VCOs. If you hook those signals into the VCF input mixer, the filter is actually DC-coupled, as is the entire signal path, out to the 2600's output. If you use fast attack and release times, there will be a characteristic thumping sound as this offset is turned off and on by the VCA. This is why ARP cautioned people who had DC-coupled power amplifiers not to hook them up directly to the 2600, because a DC voltage could drive a DC-coupled amplifier, such as a Crown, directly into saturation, which will destroy all of your speakers, besides generating this obnoxious thumping sound.

The fix is as follows: If you look at the ARP filter input mixer, you'll notice that there are five sliders, and they're all DC-coupled. What you can do is insert a coupling capacitor in between the pot and the jack on the front panel. You want to choose a capacitor that has a large enough value so that it doesn't introduce any low-frequency rolloff into the signal path; I would say something

around 22, 33, or 47mF would be fine. These capacitors should be 35- or 50-volt units, and you can purchase them for 35¢ each at Radio Shack. Leave one of the sliders DC, though, in the event that you want to use the 4072 as a voltage-controlled lag processor. If you capacitively couple all of the inputs, you'll destroy its ability to do that. You might want to leave the one that's called Ring Mod unmodified.

Replace the Reverb. The next issue to address is the 2600's reverb circuit. When ARP designed it, they were afraid to overdrive the input transducer on the reverb tank. So they turned the gain up quite high in the reverb pre-amps, but by doing that they made them very noisy. The signal-to-noise ratio of this reverb circuit is very poor, which is why every time you raise the reverb sliders on a 2600 and you have it patched into an audio system, all of a sudden you have some white noise as part of your signal, which may or may not be musically useful. It's quite loud and it's annoying.

By shifting the gain structure — increasing the drive gain and reducing the receive gain — you've dramatically improved the signal-to-noise ratio, because the noise is principally coming from the reverb pre-amps. By reducing their gain by a factor of 5, you've also reduced their noise output by a factor of 5. You've lowered the noise by about 14dB. It becomes quiet and pleasant, much nicer to work with. If you want to go absolutely first class, you want to use the Analog Devices 711 or 712. New and better op amps are coming out by the week. Contact Analog Devices, National Semiconductor, Linear Technologies, Texas Instruments, and Burr Brown, and request a catalog or data books, which are often available at no charge.

You might also want to replace the old 6" two-spring reverb tank with a 17" three-spring reverb tank, available from Magic Parts [1537 Fourth St., Suite 198, San Rafael, CA 94901. (800) 451-1922. Fax (415) 453-1111]. You don't have to do that, but the 6" tank has a not terribly pleasant sound. The response characteristics of a bigger tank with more springs are much, much smoother and nicer than a 6" tank.

Slew Rates & The Dreaded 741 Op Amp. Any synth that has early high-offset, high-drift op amps isn't performing as well as it could. This includes the EML 101, a modular Moog, and the ARP 2600. The 741 op amp is the worst internally compensated operational amplifier in use in terms of DC performance. In fact, you couldn't find anything that was worse if you tried. The 1458 is a dual version of the 741, and the 4558 is an ever-so-modestly improved version of the 1458. Any time you see any of those op amps in any vintage synth, they should be replaced with either the National Semiconductor LF-353 or the LF-351, or the LF-411 or the LF-412.

In the modular Moog system, at least one version of mixer used the 741. The slew rate of that mixer circuit was half a volt per microsecond, which is very poor. Also, the 921B oscillator, the 923 module, the 952 keyboard for the Moog 15, and the Bode frequency shifter all used the 741 and could be upgraded for enhanced performance. The slew rate of an audio circuit is its ability to transfer transient information from input to output. What happens in an electronic circuit that has a poor slew rate is that there isn't enough current available in the circuit to charge and discharge its internal capacitance as rapidly as the audio signal is occurring. In simple terms, slew rate is the ability of an audio circuit to handle transient information or to pass high frequencies undistorted. It's very critical, because the human ear is sensitive to distortions at high frequencies. If you listen to two power amps, one with a very poor slew rate and the other with a very good slew rate, the one with the good slew rate will be sonically much superior. Slew rate is one of the most critical audio characteristics of a circuit, along with noise.

You can get an audio circuit that has extremely low total harmonic distortion and still sounds extremely bad because it has a slew rate of less than one volt per microsecond. If you measure the distortion at 1kHz and it's .001%, it could be 5% at 20kHz. Conversely, in a circuit that has a slew rate of 20 or 30 volts per microsecond, the distortion at 1kHz might be .001% or .002%, and at 20kHz it's .003%. Circuits that have a poor slew rate have a rapid climb in distortion as the frequency increases, and their ability to handle large voltage swings is also very poor at high frequencies.

Power amps back in the early '70s could have THD figures down to a thousandth of a percent that sounded terrible. Why is that? The Crown DC-150, for example, has a slew rate of five or six volts per microsecond, as opposed to a Crest power amp that has a slew rate of 60 volts per microsecond. One person explained it to me this way: It's like taking a blanket or a tarp off of your speakers. It's critical, and modern audio circuits are designed with the slew rate as a consideration, whereas when op amps like the 741 were originally available, nobody was terribly concerned about slew rate, because they didn't realize that it was critical in terms of the performance of the audio circuit.

There are literally thousands of electronic devices out there that would become dramatically different devices if their op amps were replaced with modern high-slew-rate op amps. That includes equalizers, mixing boards, synthesizers, whatever. You take an old mixing board that's full of sloppy, slow, noisy op amps, replace them with modern, quiet, high-slew-rate op amps, and the board becomes a different machine. I've made a fair amount of compensation over the years doing that kind of work. Pots have no slew rate, faders have no slew rate, EQ circuits have no slew rate or noise performance. It's really the active elements in any audio device that are critical. In electronic music, that turns out to be op amps.

Discrete vs. Integrated Circuits. Here's another issue: Why do discrete circuits sound better than integrated circuits? The reason is this: Discrete circuits have a high ratio of passive-to-active devices. In electronics, passive devices are essentially linear and active devices are essentially non-linear. If you have a high ratio of passive-to-active devices, the circuit is thought to be more linear and more sonically pleasing. In integrated circuits, you have a high ratio of active-to-passive devices. Transistors are essentially non-linear devices that have to be cajoled and threatened into linearity. They don't like to be linear, so this is one of the reasons that vacuum tube electronics is thought to be sonically superior to solid-state. Vacuum tubes have an extremely large linear region, they are essentially linear devices, and they don't use much negative feedback. Modern op amps have a very linear response, as well.

One of the reasons that early Moog synthesizers sound so good is that they have almost no integrated circuits in the audio signal path. The Minimoog has no integrated circuits whatsoever in the audio signal path; its op amps are constructed from discrete devices. However, modern op amps (for example, the LF series by National Semiconductor or chips from Analog Devices) are linear enough to where the issue isn't so critical — in fact, as linear or more linear than discrete circuits.

There are modern op amps made by a Massachusetts company called Analog Devices that are really monolithic op amps. They're essentially discrete circuits in a chip form. They sell for $3 or $4 apiece and are available from Old Colony Sound Lab [P.O. Box 243/305 Union St., Peterborough, NH 03458. (603) 924-6371. Fax (603) 924-9467]. Hi-fi people use them in the outputs of their CD players as an improvement over the chips that come with them. You can buy op amps for $125 a chip that are laser-trimmed and so on, but there's no need for that.

Other 2600 Fixes. ARP offered two different keyboards for the 2600. One was called the 3604, which was monophonic; the other was called the 3620, which was the two-voice interval-latching keyboard that they offered later. There's a single op amp in either keyboard that can be replaced to dramatically improve the stability of either keyboard.

ARP used a chip that was especially selected. Selected means that they actually fired the thing up, measured its characteristics, and then put a little code on it. The chip was called the SL19986, and it was nothing more than a selected LM-301. The reason ARP selected them was for their DC performance. But because they aren't of very high input impedance and even though the DC performance is selected, they are not as good as an LF-351, 411, or other high-performance op amps.

There's an SL19986, for example, in the lag processor circuit, which brings me to another 2600 foible. A lot of people use the 2600's lag processors to portamento one oscillator and not another. It's a nice effect. But if you plug a keyboard controller through that circuit and hook it

up to a VCO, it will make the VCO instantly go out of tune. As you adjust the lag processing time, the VCO will change pitch, which is very annoying. You can replace each SL19986 with a modern op amp; that problem will instantly vanish and make your lag processor painless to use. (Any time you exchange an LM-301 with a high-performance op amp, you have to remove the 30 picofarad frequency-compensating capacitor between pin 1 and pin 8 — simply cut it off the circuit board — because most modern, high-performance op amps are internally compensated and have no need for that device.)

There's another issue in audio about which capacitors sound best. Walt Jung's studies showed that electrolytic and ceramic capacitors generate tremendous amounts of THD and cause problems with audio circuits. His conclusion was that film capacitors — polystyrene, polypropylene, and polycarbonate — had much better performance in the audio signal path. This is an issue that's relatively important in electronic music circuitry.

On the 2600, there are ceramic capacitors in the feedback loops of certain op amps. Those capacitors are designed to roll off the response of the circuit above the audio frequency spectrum — it's bandwidth limited — so that it doesn't become unstable. I've removed all those in my 2600. It turns out that the signal path is completely stable and has absolutely no tendency whatever toward oscillation. I didn't like the idea that the circuit was band-limited, because circuits that have responses that extend way out past the audio frequency range (20Hz to 20kHz) are thought to have some advantages over circuits that just have an audio frequency response. I think there's something to that.

Straightening out the signal path, the reverb, getting rid of the DC offset problems, improving the VCF, straightening up the lag processor, changing the sloppy op amps in the keyboard circuit . . . if you'll do all those things to a 2600, it's a transformed instrument. It will be a precise, tuning-stable, clean, quiet, smooth, predictable synthesizer. It's really a very different experience to use a synthesizer like that than the original 2600. We aren't adding extra boards or circuitry (although we certainly can do that, too); we're just straightening out the problems. Improvements in op amps and other electronics allow us to do that.

Wash Behind the Ears. If you replace an integrated circuit operational amplifier, or any other electronic component on a circuit board, take either denatured alcohol or a keytone solvent like acetone and some Q-tips, and scrub away the flux or rosin, because it can introduce a leakage path at very high impedances and potentially cause some quirky or unstable behavior in DC circuits. It's probably a good idea to do that in audio signal paths also.

If an instrument has been sitting around for several years, contaminants that are airborne can accumulate on the circuit boards themselves and introduce leakage paths that weren't supposed to be there. This is especially critical in keyboard sample-and-hold circuits in early synthesizers, where when you press a key there's a capacitor that actually stores the charge that you've selected on the keyboard that's a very high-impedance circuit. It's critical to keep that part of the circuit board clean. If you've ever played a synthesizer where you set a very long release time, you push a note, and you hear the sound slowly drifting in pitch downwards at the end, that could be due to contamination on the PC board around the sample-and-hold circuit, or it could be due to a leaky FET, the so-called gating FET, which is the one that switches the keyboard control voltage into the capacitor.

When you work on or handle a piece of equipment that has been in a bar for a long time, you can smell the nicotine and tars on your fingers. All that stuff will have accumulated on the circuit boards inside the unit and can potentially cause trouble. Isopropyl alcohol would be good. Don't use rubbing alcohol because it contains lanolin, which is a lubricant and you don't want that. Ace-

tone is probably the most powerful and best cleaner, but when handling it you have to be careful because it's a very strong solvent. Keep it away from plastics because it will melt them. People have dripped it on keys, and it causes nice little cosmetic blemishes on the keys. Use rubber gloves, because it's rapidly absorbed into the capillaries in your extremities, and can accumulate in your body. It's a known carcinogen, so don't breathe it either; be sure to use it in a well ventilated area. But having the circuit board clean of contaminants, fluxes, rosins, and so on is a good idea, particularly in sensitive analog circuits.

For Further Reading. Walt Jung is one of the world's leading experts on op amps. He discovered TIM distortion, interface intermodulation distortion (IIMD), and other forms of distortion as well. Jung, who has changed audio design because of his discoveries, has written a book called *The Op-Amp Cookbook*, which has been revised and updated. It is useful reading for any electronic music enthusiast, because in there are all the explanations of op amps and their characteristics. Really, electronic music synthesizers — at least the analog type — are nothing more than analog computers. They're nothing more than various configurations of assorted operation amplifier circuits. So key to the understanding of analog synthesis circuitry is a very good understanding of how op amps work.

For people who are interested in electronic music and audio electronics, there's a magazine called *Audio Amateur*, which also comes from Peterborough, NH [same address and phone number as Old Colony Sound Lab]. *Audio Amateur* often talks about how to update and modify audio electronics. There are frequent construction articles, and people like Walt Jung are frequent contributors.

EML SYNTHESIZERS

Affordable Alternatives to Moogs & Arps

BY MARK VAIL

During the early '70s, the two most successful synth manufacturers were ARP and Moog. They eclipsed a handful of smaller synth companies who had to scramble for spillover business. One of these was a Connecticut-based cartel of electrical engineers who did business as Electronic Music Laboratories. Although EML was nowhere near as prestigious as ARP or Moog, an EML synth could be had for a lot less cash, even though it could do essentially the same job.

Strange Beginnings. EML started doing business in 1968 in an unusual fashion. "All of the original founders — Dale Blake, Norman Milliard, Dennis Daugherty, and myself — were electrical engineers working for a company called Gerber Scientific," Jeff Murray explains. "It looked like things were getting tough and some of us might be laid off. So we talked about the possibility of starting our own company, pretty much as a survival effort. We had no particular route in mind, really.

"A friend of mine named Fred Locke owned a hi-fi store in Hartford. Out of the blue, he called me up and said he had built some electronic mu-

sic instruments for some local schools the year before. It was an experimental project, sponsored by the Department of Education of the State of Connecticut, that required some simple modular synthesizer equipment. Fred had bid on the job, got it, and made several of these instruments, but he lost money doing it. The next year, some other schools ordered the same equipment, but Fred wasn't interested in doing the job because he could see himself losing more money. So he called me and asked if I'd be interested in designing and building some of this equipment. He told me that he'd bought ready-made components — oscillators, amplifiers, mixers, whatever — for the first instruments. He put everything together in a great big plywood box. Fred thought if he could make a system with components designed specifically for this job that would share one common power supply, and didn't have redundant cabinetry and so forth, it could probably be done profitably.

"I talked with the other three guys and we thought we'd give it a whirl. We built the equipment down in my cellar, pretty much to Fred Locke's original specs, supplied the instruments to

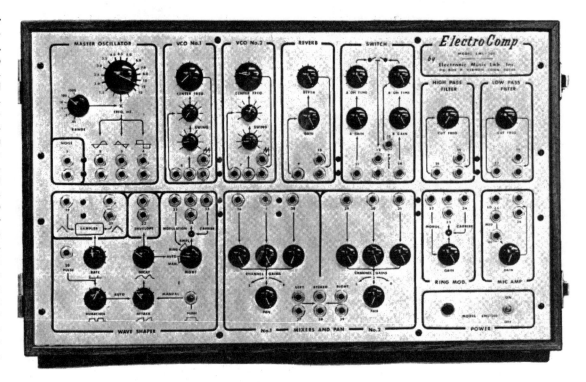

One of the first synths manufactured by EML (c.1969) was the ElectroComp 200, which included two oscillators, an LFO, high- and lowpass filters, two ring modulators, sample-and-hold, pan controls, and spring reverb. Its companion 300 manual controller (not shown) offered a 4 x 4 key matrix and associated pitch knobs, along with its own oscillator, envelope generator, and voltage-controlled amplifier.

the schools, and made a little money on the deal. That was about the time Norm was laid off from his job at Gerber — because he was working on these instruments. After we had completed the first batch of ten, we thought if we had a chance to do it again, we'd do it differently. When Norm got laid off, we took the profits that we'd earned and made a prototype of an instrument that we thought was a better solution."

What kind of problems were inherent in the educational synths, fondly known as "black monsters"? Besides the fact that concrete blocks had to be installed in each unit to meet the 200-pound weight requirement — so as to discourage students from ripping them off — no one involved in the venture knew exactly how to design a proper synthesizer yet. "We didn't know what the hell a synthesizer was," Milliard recalls. "We listened to what the teachers thought they wanted and then we made these God-awful units. The teachers were happy with them, but we were more forward-thinking because we knew what was possible with electronics. This was a transition time when people were going from using discrete to integrated components."

The EML founders soon discovered who they were competing with. "Moog was one step ahead

of us," says Murray. "We were following closely at Moog's heels, but using different techniques. Most of Bob Moog's early equipment used discrete transistors, which tended to drift. You had to continuously tune the components. We used a slightly different approach: Linear integrated circuits called op amps were becoming feasible for consumer-type equipment at about the time we got involved with this business, so we relied heavily on those to get better performance from our circuitry. We earned a reputation of making equipment that was rock-solid and dependable."

Norman Milliard had an interesting experience when he first took an EML synth to a trade show. "My first trip to face the real world was a music educators' convention in Harrisburg, Pennsylvania. We had a little booth there. On the way to the show, I stopped in New York City to see one of our customers. In broad daylight, while I was in his apartment, my car was broken into and all my clothes stolen. All I had to wear were ratty jeans, a holey sweater, and sneakers, and since this happened in the '60s, I'm sure I had very long hair and a beard. I figured I'd have time to buy new clothes before the show. When I got there, I was setting up my booth and the head of the Pennsylvania Music Educators Association came up to me and said,

'Bob Moog is a featured speaker here. There are 2,000 people sitting in that room to hear him speak.' I said, 'Oh, that's nice. I'll probably go and stand in the back and listen myself. I've never met him or heard him speak.' But then he told me that Bob's plane was snowed in at the airport in Buffalo, New York, and he said, 'We need someone who knows electronic music to speak to these people.' I said, 'You certainly do, but I'm not the guy.' He finally suckered me into it and it changed my life, because public speaking was never a problem again."

Not only was Milliard's presentation a success, he also drummed up some business for his company. "Norm came back from the music educators' show with a bunch of orders," Murray says. "So I quit my job and started ordering parts and designing and building the components. Norm was primarily a salesman. Shortly after that, Dale Blake quit his job to help me, and soon thereafter we moved out of the cellar into a rented building."

Murray's work led to the production of EML's first instruments, the ElectroComp 100, 200, and 300. Whereas the 100 was a duophonic keyboard-based synth designed to compete with the Minimoog, the 200 served as an expander for the 100 and as a lab-oriented modular synth. Alternate controller fanatics take note: Along with a few rudimentary synth components, the ElectroComp 300 manual controller offered calculator-type

VITAL STATISTICS

Manufacturer: Electronic Music Laboratories, Inc. (stopped doing business in 1984). Remaining inventory purchased by Timothy Smith of The Audio Clinic, 3461 Canyon Dr., Billings, MT 59102. (406) 652-1564.

Products: ElectroComp 100 and 101 keyboard synths, ElectroComp 200 modular synth, ElectroComp 300 manual controller, 400 series sequencer, ElectroComp 500 performance synth, Poly-Box chording accessory, model 1500 and model 2001 SynKey (non-programmable and programmable, respectively).

Production Dates: Educational "black monsters", 1968. ElectroComp 100, 1971–72. ElectroComp 200, 1972–80. ElectroComp 300, 1972–79. ElectroComp 101, 1972-82. ElectroComp 400 series sequencer, 1970–84. ElectroComp 500, 1973–84. Poly-Box, 1977–84. Model 1500 SynKey (non-programmable), 1978–84. Model 2001 SynKey (programmable), 1979–84.

Approximate Numbers Made: "Black monsters," 10. ElectroComp 100, 200. ElectroComp 101, 1,000. ElectroComp 200, 400. ElectroComp 300, 400. ElectroComp 400 series sequencer, 300. Poly-Box, 130. SynKey, 75.

Original Retail Prices: ElectroComp 101, $1,395 to $1,695. ElectroComp 200, $950. ElectroComp 300, $325. 400 series sequencer, $1,000. ElectroComp 500 performance synth, $895. Poly-Box, $475. Model 1500 SynKey, $925. Model 2001 SynKey, $1,350.

Current Street Prices: ElectroComp 101, $300 to $600. ElectroComp 200, $200 to $500. ElectroComp 300, $150 to $250. ElectroComp 400 series sequencer, $100 to $350. ElectroComp 500, $100 to $200. Poly-Box, $75 to $500. Model 1500 SynKey, $250. Model 2001 SynKey, $300.

Current Dealer Prices: ElectroComp 101, $800. ElectroComp 200, $400 to $600. ElectroComp 300, $300. ElectroComp 400, $400 to $600. ElectroComp 500, $350 to $400. Poly-Box, $150 to $800. Model 1500 SynKey, $350. Model 2001 SynKey, $500.

Insider Information: Frank Zappa bought two of the last production model 1500 SynKeys. Syntars were made for guitarists John McLaughlin and Rick Derringer.

Genealogy: EML co-founder Norman Milliard, along with John Borowicz and David Kusek, left EML in 1976 and started Star Instruments, whose most familiar products were the Synare line of percussion synthesizers. In 1980, Borowicz and Kusek founded Passport Designs. Borowicz went on to start Coda in 1986, which he left in 1988; now he works in geographic information systems.

EML's most popular synthesizer was the Electro-Comp 101, whose 3½-octave keyboard was duophonic. Whereas most of its competition only had two or three oscillators, the 101 had four. Like the ARP 2600, the 101 had hard-wired or "normaled" components, allowing the user to produce sounds with or without patching modules together with cords. Such flexibility allowed a wider range of sonic possibilities than a strictly hard-wired synth like the Minimoog.

pushbuttons and pitch knobs. According to an EML product brochure, "The 300 was originally suggested by a professional composer who wanted to escape from the traditional keyboard with its equal temperament and the patterns it suggests."

No Habla Música. Once the EML ball was rolling, the founders realized the company lacked one important element: None of them were musicians. They rectified that situation in May of 1973 by hiring John Borowicz, whose input helped the company develop more musically oriented instruments. Here's what Borowicz had to say about the early EMLs: "Each of the 300's keys could be independently tuned, so it wasn't exactly anything to do *The Well-Tempered Clavier* on, but for the banging-metal-pipe sector of the electronic music artist community, it was just fine.

"After that, they started to get a little more savvy to the market. For its time, the ElectroComp 100 was a nice little machine for the money, but it didn't have the 'ballsy' sound. The waveform generation on the oscillators was truly from an engineering point of view. For example, it could produce a sine wave and a rectified cosine wave. I asked them, 'What the hell's the difference?' 'It looks different on the scope,' they said. One oscillator did a sawtooth, and about the richest you got

on the others were square waves. So the timbral palette was, shall we say, restricted. And the multi-mode filter, although a nice idea — with lowpass, band-reject, bandpass, and highpass — was a 6dB-per-octave filter, so it wasn't much better than a car stereo.

"They got feedback on those types of things almost instantly. The layout, I thought, was one of the best. Plus having the patchbay on top allowed you to override the internal connections, *à la* the ARP 2600. It was a nice design. Since it had more musically useful oscillators, the 101 was a much better machine than the 100.

"One thing that was nice about the EMLs, and something that Moog adopted later, was that you could basically dial up a combination waveform."

EML's ElectroComp 101 turned out to be its most popular synth. If you examine its photo above, you'll see no familiar pitch-bend and mod wheels. Like every other early '70s synth manufacturer, EML avoided the Moog-popularized wheels and optionally provided an alternate — though common for the period — pitch controller. Borowicz explains: "The flat, formica-covered piece of plywood to the left of the keyboard could be replaced with a metal plate and a large knob on a potentiometer. That cost an extra $25 or $50. The pot had a center detent the size of Rhode Island, but you could wear it down after a while. Pitch-bends required a little more artistry, as we liked to say."

By today's standards, the 101's ten-year production lifetime is impressive. "It was kind of like a Volkswagen," Jeff Murray offers. "There were some internal improvements that were made over the years — better or less expensive components would become available and we'd take advantage of those, or we'd figure out a way to make something a little bit easier — but the functionality of the instrument remained about the same from day one.

"We were a small and informal enough company that we were able to satisfy a lot of our customers' special requests. There were a lot of 101s with custom doodads to satisfy somebody's particular requirements, such as a pitch controller, an extra oscillator, or more inputs."

EML's Performance Synthesizer & Sequencer. Given the popularity of the Minimoog and ARP Odyssey, EML took a shot at the same market with their ElectroComp 500 performance synth. "The 500," Murray explains, "was designed to be a little less expensive than the 101. It used less expensive components, such as sliders instead of rotary pots, and it was designed to be a little more Moog-like for people who had their hearts set on a Moog."

Following the traditions of Moog, Buchla, and other early synth developers, the EML engineers crafted an analog sequencer that bears little resemblance to today's MIDI sequencers. "The 400 series sequencer was my baby," Borowicz admits. "I loved that box. It was a killer. I'd say that was one of the first hybrids, because it was analog and digital. One of the problems with analog circuits was tuning the bloody things. So we built a voltage quantizer. As far as I know, EML was the first to use a quantizer, and then ARP jumped on the bandwagon, since they were the big boys on the block. Our quantizer was basically set up for 12-tone diatonic, but you could tune it to play microtones too, and it would still maintain its quantizing feature, which was pretty hip.

"It also had voltage-controlled envelope generators, which as far as I know was a first, too. You could patch that thing, load it up in increments of 16 stages, and the control voltages could be either

locked in — quantized — or you could set it to be variable, either way. By patching, you could get the thing to do retrograde permutations: It would go through the sequence as you programmed it with all the rhythms, and then you could start to do permutations by jumping around in a very programmatic fashion to different stages. It could go through stages 1–16, and then 1, 15, 2, 14, 3, 12, and so on. You could line up the patterns however you wanted. That was an amazing little box.

"It also had a voice module with it, the 401, which was basically a scaled-down 500: dual oscillators with switch-selectable waveforms, a multimode filter, and the voltage-controlled envelope generators. At that point, you only had A/R [attack/release] envelopes, but you could get multiple stages by gating the voltage correctly."

The Poly-Box. On the heels of introducing some fairly straightforward synth equipment, EML did an about-face and came out with one of the strangest accessories ever designed for mono- and duophonic synths: the Poly-Box, which had only a one-octave keyboard (*C* to *C*). If you sent one or more notes into the Poly-Box's audio input and played a chord on its keyboard, the Poly-Box would output a chord based on the incoming note (the root) and the notes depressed on the Poly-Box keyboard. Each key was programmable within a four-octave range, and memory could store up to 26 notes for automated pitch-following of a synthesizer. "The Poly-Box was kind of a cool instrument," says Murray. "A lot of early synthesizers were just one- or two-note devices, but with the Poly-Box you could play chords. It had phase-lock-loop circuitry so that it could follow the frequency of an incoming audio signal. Then you could hit a chord on the Poly-Box and it would synthesize all the other frequencies of the chord."

Dissension & the SynKey. By 1975, internal disagreements at EML eventually led to a parting of the ways. Co-founder Norman Milliard and musician John Borowicz, along with a few others, left the company in '76 — "because we could no longer influence the direction of the company," Milliard explains. "People left over basic business issues. You must recognize that neither Dale Blake nor Jeff Murray understood musicians or how our

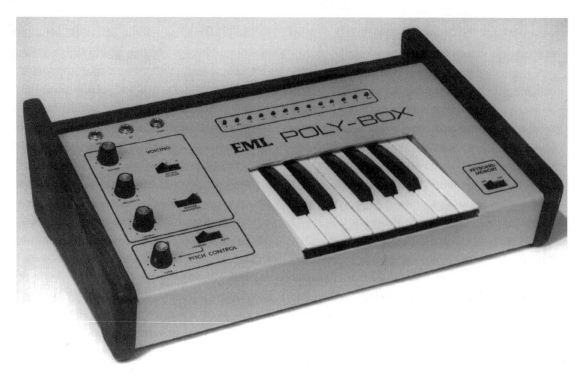

products were used. I did not fully understand the music part of our business, but I listened well to what our customers wanted, which were polyphonic instruments that were easy to use."

Borowicz describes the turmoil from his perspective: "EML was a hell of a company in the early days. It was a real brotherhood, and there was a real commitment to doing the best technology we could. But things changed. It became hard to bring new technology into EML, at least in the last days I was there. There was a general cultural and mood change from a very progressive atmosphere to one that was very xenophobic.

"The SynKey was the last project I worked on. We had been trying to develop a polyphonic synthesizer for a while, but the president of the company, Dale Blake, said it couldn't be done. He said a polyphonic synthesizer just wasn't viable. As he put it, 'It will sound like a reverb-y piano.' We said, 'Even if it isn't the greatest thing in the first iteration, at least we'll be a contender in the marketplace.' But he'd say, 'It will cost too much.' Norm tried his best to bring these wayward souls back into line with reality, and he worked at developing new oscillator and filter circuits for a polyphonic system. I thought he was doing quite well. The audio results were promising, I thought. But the cor-

porate leaders decided to take another tack, using the octave-divider chips that were then coming on the market. We told them, 'It sounds too much like an organ. It will always sound like an organ.' The divider chips only put out square waves, and doing any other kind of waveform manipulation was . . . well, it did some, it just didn't come off right. It was bogus stuff. Those kind of 'chord organs' were already out there. Calling it a synthesizer, we thought, was a bit brash.

"The divider chip was the foundation of the SynKey for tone generation. We wanted to use four, six, or eight oscillators, with individual filters. But they just said, 'No, it costs too much.'

"Another thing about the SynKey was its wonderful programming interface. It used a punched card. We absolutely bristled at this idea. We were looking at this new stuff called RAM, which was pretty pricey then. All this information could be stored in RAM and the user wouldn't have to do anything other than press a button. But the company Amp, Inc., was going to give us a deal on these card readers, which was about $5 less than the total cost of RAM. (I don't know if it was that close, but it was a small differential.) So they put this friggin' card reader in there and you had to program it by punching holes in these cards. I mean, how archaic can you get? It was just an embarrassment for anybody who worked on this project. It was like two steps backward and not even a nudge to the forward."

"The SynKey concept resulted from a patent I received for a guitar synthesizer," Milliard recalls. "Originally, the product's name was to be the Syntar. Its electronics were designed to be versatile, so that you could drive it from a keyboard or a guitar controller."

"We were going to develop this instrument for Kaman Music, the Ovation guitar people," says Jeff Murray, who stayed at EML until its demise in 1984. "But the project kind of fizzled as far as Ovation was concerned. So we were stuck with inventory that we started to build up in anticipation of having to supply Ovation with instruments. So we just took on the product ourselves.

"In ways, the SynKey was similar to the 101. There were a bunch of front-panel knobs for adjusting all kinds of functions, but any one of those knobs could be overridden by punching some holes in a card. The knob was digitized to eight positions when it was programmed with these punch cards. It wasn't infinitely programmable, but it was good enough. The idea was that this instrument was more suited to live performance, so that the performer could develop settings that gave him the sounds that he wanted, and then in a performance situation he didn't have to fiddle around with the knobs and try to quickly readjust everything. He could just pop in the appropriate card and instantly get the setup that he wanted. Eventually memory got cheaper, which would have been a better way, but that's the way it's always been in electronics."

EML's Demise. Murray cites the mid-'70s onslaught of synths from Yamaha and other Japanese manufacturers as one of the reasons EML went out of business. Another problem was more global in nature. "It was the oil crisis," he explains, "which put a cap on a lot of the school budgets. When they had to make a choice between buying electronic music instruments or oil to heat the schools, they chose to heat the schools. The kids that wanted to be rock stars, if they had to decide between driving their car or buying an instrument, they usually opted for their automobile."

As business began to slide, Murray and his remaining cohorts were able to sustain their company's life by utilizing the manufacturing skills they had developed making synthesizers. "We were always a small outfit that survived hand-to-mouth, and we saw the handwriting on the wall. Starting in the latter '70s, we continued to make all our existing music products, but in order to survive and make a living we did a lot of consulting work for other companies in this area, mostly in Connecticut. We had about 50 active clients that we helped to develop products, all sorts of things. If a company wanted a prototype or a small quan-

The good news: EML's SynKey was one of the first programmable synthesizers and its keyboard responded to pressure ("second touch"). The bad news: SynKey patches were programmed by manually punching holes in a card numbered to correspond with front-panel knob settings.

tity of some special gadget, we were capable of doing that. That's what we did until 1984."

Norm Milliard doesn't buy Murray's analyses of EML's financial difficulties. "The reason EML failed," Milliard offers, "was that it became out of touch with the customer and therefore could no longer deliver what the customer wanted.

"The first polyphonic synthesizer was built at EML," Milliard continues. "The SynKey's card reader was a mistake. EML, a company born of technology, the first to use integrated circuits in synthesizers, forgot a few lessons and stopped riding technology. They never used memory or microprocessors. I believe that a company that knew technology and knew what the customer wanted could have made the necessary changes to its products and survived. Realize that the people that left EML founded a company [Star Instruments] that sold over 30,000 electronic drums over a seven-year period."

Jeff Murray, whose designing career didn't stop when EML's doors were shut, couldn't care less. "I've spent my whole life designing new things," he says. "I guess I like the newness of stuff. It really doesn't matter much what it is. For example, now I design machines for making eyeglass lenses very quickly and efficiently. Before that, I helped design a machine for making billboards using some new techniques. Music, billboards, eyeglasses: There's really no common denominator in any of those products, except that there were new ways of going about it and that's what I enjoyed. And they had to be honorable products; I didn't want to design bombs."

E-MU MODULAR SYNTHS

Springboard for an Active Industry Leader

BY BOB MOOG

L ike many science and engineering students who grew up during the '60s, Dave Rossum and his friends from Cal Tech dabbled in analog synthesizers while they were still in college. The dabbling resulted in the Eμ 25, an actual working analog synthesizer. (The symbol "μ" is the Greek letter *mu*, hence the company's name, E-mu.) The first model was built in the summer of '71, and the second (and last) shortly after that. The Eμ 25 was a stand-alone instrument, with many of the basic synth functions on a one-piece front panel.

"We sold them for about as much as the parts cost us," Dave recalls. "While we were working on the second Model 25, Scott Wedge, a friend of mine from high school, joined us. From our involvement with the 25 we learned that modular systems were a lot more fun than fixed-front-panel instruments, so in 1972 we got our business license and started to design a modular system." It was a garage-based shoestring operation, the sort of stuff that high-tech legends are made of. Dave lived in the back of the garage and Scott lived with his parents. They printed a brief but folksy catalog,

We aren't sure who this mysterious Eμ programmer is, but we'd love to find one of those T-shirts.

and advertised their products in *Popular Electronics* and in *Electronotes*, a newsletter for engineers and serious experimenters.

An Eμ modular synth with its 4060 microprocessor keyboard. In the center rack, the two columns at the left contain oscillators, the third column contains lowpass filters, and the fourth contains VCAs. Dual envelope generator modules are along the lower right.

Although they had the needs of the hobbyists and experimenters in mind, Dave and Scott produced designs that were fully professional. The module panels were made of heavy, rugged aluminum, and the panel components were made of high-quality, heavy-duty parts. Connections between modules were established by full-sized audio patch cords, and the user could install firmwire connections that went into effect when the patch cords were not used. By 1973, E-mu's catalog listed modules that were capable of performing virtually all of the then-popular synthesizer functions. Especially noteworthy were the keyboards that Dave and Scott designed. The first was a monophonic keyboard that was digitally scanned, resulting in a more reliable mechanism than the then-common analog keyboards. A short time later, E-mu introduced their digitally scanned polyphonic keyboard, which featured a built-in digital sequencer.

The First Musician Customers. Several well-known musicians bought early Eμ modular systems. Among the first was Leon Russell. At that time, Russell was working with synthesizer programmer Roger Linn, who introduced the Linn LM-1 digital drum machine a few years later.

Another important Eμ owner was Patrick Gleeson, an electronic musician and studio operator in San Francisco. (He also wrote a synthesizer technique column for *Keyboard* from Sept. '78 to Nov. '79.) Gleeson used his large, custom system to produce several records during the mid-'70s.

VITAL STATISTICS

Produced: 1973 to 1981.

Manufacturer: E-mu Systems, Scotts Valley, CA.

Description: Patchable modular analog synthesizer. Systems assembled to order from standard modules.

Features: Audio generators and processors include voltage-controlled oscillators, amplifiers, and filters, ring modulators, and reverb units. Control generators and processors include transient generators, envelope followers, analog sequencer, digitally scanned keyboards, sample/holds, and lag processors.

Original Retail Price: $1,500 and up for a complete system.

Current Street Price: $1,000 to $5,000. (Depends on module configuration, degree and quality of modifications, and overall condition.)

Current Dealer Price: $2,000 to $8,000. (Ditto.)

Frank Zappa is perhaps the best-known Eμ modular user, and one of the few who actually used their instruments onstage. Other well-known Eμ users were Daryl Dragon (of the Captain and Tennille) and Lenny Pickett (Tower of Power). Ned Lagin, in a group with Phil Lesh of the Grateful Dead, actually interfaced his Eμ system with a minicomputer, using software written by Scott Wedge.

A total of about a hundred Eμ modular systems were produced. A large percentage went to universities throughout the world, where they have been used to teach the principles of synthesis.

The Audity — The Last Great Analog Project. Throughout 1976 and 1977, E-mu continued to manufacture and sell their modular systems, but did little in the way of new modular product development. They were still designing digital scanning keyboard circuits for other manufacturers, including Sequential Circuits and Oberheim, and they were collaborating with Solid State Music on designs for analog synthesizer chips. Around this time, E-mu received a large development contract from Peter Baumann of Tangerine Dream. Baumann wanted a computer-based synthesizer that used analog tone-generating technology. So Rossum, Wedge, and their crew came up with a very large, fully programmable analog "voice card," and built 16 of them for Baumann. E-mu then built a proprietary computer card to run the voice cards, and wrote software to make the whole system work. By 1979, this had all been shipped to Baumann.

Next, Dave and Scott decided to package their newly developed technology as an integrated, computer-controlled synthesizer. They dubbed their new instrument the Audity and prepared to unveil it at the May 1980 Audio Engineering Society convention. They knew that it would take at least a year or two to promote and sell an instrument as large and expensive (about $50,000 for a typical configuration) as the Audity. And a lot of money would have to be invested in advertising and education before the Audity line would be profitable.

Dave and Scott figured that with the income from the royalties on their digital scanning keyboards that Sequential Circuits was paying them, E-mu could survive until sales of the Audity picked up. So at the AES convention, they presented the Audity as an instrument that was fully designed and ready for production. They generated a lot of interest, and identified some potential customers.

Three weeks after the AES convention, Sequential Circuits notified E-mu that they did not believe that they owed any more royalties. The royalty payments stopped! What to do now? Without the cash flow from Sequential, it would be very risky for E-mu to try to develop the Audity into a product line. So Rossum and Wedge proceeded to design a new instrument from scratch, one that would be cheaper to put into production and easier to sell. They took note of the growing success of the Fairlight computer-based sampling instrument, and decided to come out with a simpler, less expensive version. Starting in May 1980, they designed their new instrument, wrote the software, and built a working prototype in time for the January 1981 NAMM show. They called their new instrument the Emulator. When Stevie Wonder heard it and played it, he gave it a big hug. Wonder received Emulator serial no. 1 in July of that year.

And that's the story of how yet another manufacturer of classic analog synthesizers responded to the turbulent changes in today's musical electronics.

Patrick Gleeson (L) observes as Herbie Hancock tweaks the Eμ modular system in Gleeson's Different Fur recording studios in San Francisco sometime in the mid '70s. In the background is an ARP 2600. (photo by Tom Copi)

PATRICK GLEESON: ANALOG VIRTUOSO GONE DIGITAL

Patrick Gleeson purchased one of the first Eµ modular systems. In 1973, he used it to realize *Beyond the Sun* [Mercury, out of print], an electronic orchestration of Gustav Holst's *The Planets. Beyond the Sun* was hailed by Wendy Carlos and others as a work of unique musicianship and masterful application of the electronic music medium.

Gleeson was one of the first to explore the technique of sequencing as applied to traditional orchestral music. In order to produce as many sounds as possible in real time, he assembled a four-voice modular system and a group of 16 voice cards, each of which was a complete six-oscillator synthesizer voice. (This was one of the largest and most customized systems E-mu built.)

The modular voices were controlled from a large analog sequencer, while the voice cards were controlled by the digital sequencer in his polyphonic keyboard. Later, Gleeson added two of the first Prophet-10s, which were also controlled by the digital sequencer. Having two complete banks of sound generators running off the digital sequencer allowed Gleeson to switch rapidly from one bank to the other in real time.

Rainbow Delta, Gleeson's second album done on his Eµ system, was, in his words, "essentially a series of live performances that were linked together in the style of a drum machine sequence."

Gleeson took his system on the road for a brief college tour. It was "an exciting failure" because, in Keith Emerson's words, "Performing on a modular synth is a desk job." In other words, it doesn't have the visual appeal of a traditional instrumentalist. And the more complex the system is, the more difficult it is to sustain visual appeal as a performer.

In 1978, Gleeson switched from analog to digital when he sold his Eµ modular and acquired a Synclavier. "I believe that was the right decision for me," he says. "I am now primarily a TV and film music producer. In my business, deadlines are important, and they're getting shorter all the time. With an integrated digital system like my Synclavier, I can meet those deadlines."

So what does an artist who was deeply involved with analog synthesis think of digital sampling? "You can deplore sampling, but you can't ignore it. There's no way that you can be without it in today's commercial scene. But when I collect samples, I look for idiosyncratic and distinctive sounds that can be modified. In this way, I can keep my material fresh-sounding, but still have the sonic richness that sampling offers."

FAMOUS ANALOG SYNTHS

SECTION 3

MINIMOOG

The Ultimate in Antique Analog?

BY BOB MOOG

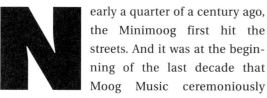

Nearly a quarter of a century ago, the Minimoog first hit the streets. And it was at the beginning of the last decade that Moog Music ceremoniously slapped brass plaques on the last 25 Minis off the assembly line and sent them out to fetch inflated prices. Yet the instrument's distinctive sound is very much with us today. In particular, its fat, three-oscillator bass sound has transcended novelty and fashion and become a timbral staple, joining a small number of instruments — the Hammond B-3 organ and the Rhodes electric piano are two that come to mind — in the keyboard hall of fame.

Over 12,000 Model D Minimoogs were made and sold during its lifetime. A whole body of lore has emerged about the Minimoog, ranging from which serial numbers sound the best to whether or not it is possible to accurately simulate its classic sound with a digital instrument. I'd like to separate the myths from the realities, and to comment on some of the instrument's enduring assets — as well as a few of its shortcomings. I was with

Moog Music when we put the first Minis into production, and I remained with the company until the end of 1977, so what I'm about to tell you is mostly first-hand testimony.

The Gestation Period. Back in 1969 and '70, Moog Music was not yet in the musical instrument business *per se*. Our modular synthesizers were sold as pieces of professional audio equipment. They were made to order, and we considered them to be too complex and high-tech to survive on the floor of a musical instrument store. Our original concept for the Minimoog was to take some of the basic features of our modular instruments and integrate them into a compact performance synthesizer that could be programmed without patch cords. We imagined that Minimoog customers would consist primarily of studio musicians who wanted a cut-down version of a Moog modular system to take on their gigs. (Modular synths either were in fixed locations or were moved to each gig like a piano or organ.) We figured that we might sell as many as a hundred Minis before it would be time to update the design.

We had no idea of what a small portable synthesizer should look like, so we asked our industrial engineers for some suggestions. They came up with drawings for some very sleek packages indeed — white sculptured plastic cabinets that suggested computer terminals, gleaming multicolored panels, and strikingly shaped controls. We then polled our musician friends to see which designs they liked. Were we in for a surprise! Nearly everybody shot down the sculptured plastic in favor of natural wood and simple lines. We simplified one of our designer's concepts to the point where we could actually make the cabinets in our own modest wood shop, then proceeded to create the Minimoog.

The only Minimoog that was ever put into production is called the Model D. There were Models A, B, and C. The Model A was built from standard Moog modules early in 1970. It had a short keyboard and sliders instead of wheels. Compared to a typical modular system, it was manageable, nonintimidating, and user-friendly. You couldn't do much with it, but you could create some basic analog sounds, and — more importantly — you could play the instrument in real time. Remember, this was a long time before synthesizers had presets. The Model A had few controls, so a musician could remember how everything was set without having

to stop and study a front panel jungle. For that reason, every musician who tried the Model A liked it.

Next came the Model B. Instead of being assembled from modules, its front panel was a single piece of sheet metal, and signal routing was done with hardware switches instead of patch cords. Its functions included the most popular ones found on the larger modular systems: three oscillators, a noise source, a mixer, the "Moog Filter," and a voltage-controlled amplifier. There were two envelope generators, one for the filter and one for the VCA, and one LFO. Next came the Model C, which had the now-familiar hinged front panel and the pitch-bend and modulation wheels, and was rugged enough for field-testing.

Finally, the Model D emerged, as ready for manufacturing as we knew how to make it. It was a group engineering effort, shared by Jim Scott, Bill Hemsath, Chad Hunt, and me. We adapted some of the circuitry (such as the filter section) from the modular instruments, but designed other circuitry (such as the oscillators and contour generators) from scratch. In fact, Moog's first temperature-compensated oscillators were designed for the Minimoog.

Dick Hyman debuted the Minimoog in a public performance at the Eastman School of Rochester, New York, in the summer of 1970. Later that year

VITAL STATISTICS

Produced: 1970 to 1981 (Serial nos. 1017–13259).

Manufacturer: Moog Music, Buffalo, NY (out of business).

Description: Monophonic analog synth.

Features: Three VCOs, four-pole lowpass VCF, two envelope generators, 44-note (*F* to *C*), single-trigger, low-note priority keyboard, pitch and mod wheels.

Original Price: $1,495.

Current Street Price: $300 to $700.

Current Retail Price: $500 to $750. Rack-mounted and MIDIfied version, the Midimini, available from Studio Electronics [18034 Ventura Blvd., Ste. 169, Encino, CA 91316. (818) 776-8104] for $2,195, or $1,495 if you supply the Minimoog.

we showed it to the general public at the Audio Engineering Society convention in New York City — the same convention at which ARP unveiled their Model 2600.

The Birth. As 1971 began, a saturated synthesizer market, a recession, and a general lack o business smarts (on our part) caught up with us. R. A. Moog, Inc. was merged with Musonics to form Moog Musonics, and then Moog Music, Inc. As part of the merger, our sales efforts were di-rected away from the professional audio market and toward musical instrument retailers. We exhibited the Minimoog at the National Association of Music Merchants convention in June, 1971. It was our first exposure to the musical instrument industry — and the industry's first exposure to synthesizers. We did not experience a warm reception. Most of the dealers didn't know what to make of a musical instrument with words like Oscillator Bank and Filter printed on the front panel.

The glamor of new technology. This layout was the centerpiece of a Norlin Music brochure on the Mini in 1974.

minimoog... a whole new freedom of expression

Retailers would pass our booth and ask questions such as "What's that?", "Whaddaya do with it?", and "You expect me to sell *that* in my store?" Al Pierce (later the head of Polyfusion) and I found a few interested retailers, but most passed us by in favor of more comprehensible hardware. To be honest, it wasn't all the dealers' fault. Although we could explain how the Minimoog worked, we couldn't demo it with convincing musicianship.

No Minimoog story would be complete without a mention of David Van Koevering, a super-salesman with a predilection for musical novelties. Starting in central Florida(!), Van Koevering introduced the Minimoog to musical instrument retailers on their own turf, wielding his unrestrained enthusiasm to close sales. Today the

MINIMOOG TIPS & TRICKS

MIDIFYING A MINI. The latest trend in the used Mini market is to hot-rod the instrument by adding MIDI, sawing off the keyboard, and putting the electronics into a rack-mount case. Where can you get it done? Studio Electronics is the most popular source, although we're sure many custom-houses will do it on a one-off basis. Why would anyone go to the trouble and expense ($2,195 for the Midimini if Studio Electronics supplies the Minimoog, $1,495 if you do) of getting a rebuilt Minimoog when its sound could simply be sampled and stored on floppy or hard disk? First, analog sounds are hard to sample accurately, even though they are electronic in origin. This is especially true of bass sounds, because samplers sometimes have difficulty reproducing extreme low and high frequencies simultaneously. Second, and perhaps more importantly, old analog synths — unlike most modern samplers — allow real-time access to sound parameters. Once you understand what the front-panel knobs do, it's easy to reach up and fine-tune the

sound until it perfectly fits your music — even if you're in the middle of playing a note!

Mini Tricks. There's more to the classic Minimoog sound than just plugging the instrument directly into a mixing board and playing. Most players prefer to run their Minis through effects — fuzz boxes, overdriven Marshall-style tube amps, delay lines of all sorts, flangers, and who-knows-what-else. Here are a couple of other tricks in not-so-common usage during the Mini's heyday:

• *The feedback loop trick.* (1) Route an audio cable from the low output to the external input. (2) Turn the external input switch in the Mixer section on and set the external volume to the point where the overload light blinks intermittently. This produces a fatter sound.

• *Double-stop pitch-bends.* A trick common to guitar playing is to play two notes simultaneously and bend one but not the other. This technique can be simulated on a Mini by becoming very skilled at detuning the second oscillator using its front-panel tuning knob. (1) Play the desired key on the keyboard. (2) Bend the pitch of

the second oscillator by the desired amount.

• *Audio-frequency modulation.* Most players use the third VCO as an LFO — setting it to the "lo" frequency mode when modulating pitch or the filter cutoff frequency. But by setting osc 3 to the audio range, many interesting "modular" and FM-like sounds can be produced. David Sancious made great use of these effects on his early solo albums.

Tuning. If you get hold of a Minimoog and you're new to analog technology, be prepared to deal with tuning your instrument regularly. You'll want to let the machine warm up for at least ten minutes before you try to tune it. And you'll want to check the tuning often — much the way guitarists spot-tune their instruments. Depending on the stability of your particular Minimoog, you'll also want to "range and scale" the oscillators every couple of months. This is a time-consuming process for which you'll need a plastic non-conducting screwdriver. (The exact details are described in the owner's manual.) Ranging and scaling analog oscillators means adjusting them to be in tune across the entire range of the keyboard.

Minimoog is so widely accepted that it's hard to imagine a time more than 20 years ago when it took a person of great persuasiveness to sell a Minimoog. However, if it were not for Van Koevering, the rest of us might have concluded that Minimoogs were unsalable.

Credit for the acceptance of the Minimoog as a *bona fide* musical instrument goes not to us engineers, nor to the salesmen, but to the supertalents who first played the Minimoog in public and showed us all what the instrument was capable of. Keith Emerson nailed its analog sound into the vocabulary of rock and roll, first on his modular behemoth and then on his Mini. Then came Jan Hammer, who developed incredible chops with the left-hand wheels. The playing styles developed by both Emerson and Hammer, along with Chick Corea, Rick Wakeman, and many others transformed people's ideas of the Minimoog from something akin to a box full of knobs to an expressive musician's axe.

Meanwhile, Back at the Factory. The Model D became Moog Music's first standard production instrument. By the latter part of 1973, production had increased from a few instruments a week to a peak of 300 Minis a month. This required a change in manufacturing techniques — especially in the areas of testing and quality control. Throughout those early years, Moog manufacturing's professionalism increased steadily. I'm not mentioning this to pat myself on the back. In fact, I personally had almost nothing to do with manufacturing back then. The reason I'm mentioning the steady improvement is to contrast it with the electronic folk tale that says that the earliest Minimoogs were better because they had more "human element." I've heard this story more times than I care to admit. Don't believe it! Of course,

Minimoogs — like most analog instruments — do vary somewhat from instrument to instrument, so you may find an old Minimoog with really great sound and a minimum of reliability problems (the first one, serial no. 1017, was released in 1970), but overall, the later instruments are much more reliable, and they sound better, too!

We never did get to improve on the functional design of the Minimoog. There were, however, many manufacturing design changes, the most important of which was a new oscillator board that provided greatly improved stability. All instruments with serial numbers greater than 10175 have this new board. In addition, many older instruments had new oscillator boards retrofitted in the field.

On to Vintage Status. After 1974, small analog synthesizers appeared on the market in great profusion, and Minimoog sales began to decline. By 1980, microprocessor-controlled polyphonic analog synths were all the rage. Moog Music decided to stop manufacturing the Mini, partly be-

Three proposed designs for the Minimoog. Developed by industrial engineers, these concepts had little appeal for the musicians Moog consulted.

Musicians preferred these more naturalistic designs. The upper drawing was the basis for the Minimoog, while the lower drawing evolved into the Moog Sonic Six.

cause the new microprocessor-controlled Moog Source was intended to fill the Mini's slot in the marketplace. The last 25 Minimoogs off the production line were deluxe instruments with solid walnut cases (just like the very first Minis), illuminated wheels, and numbered brass plaques. The last one made (serial no. 13259) was given to me at a press luncheon — one to commemorate the "historical impact of the Minimoog Synthesizer on contemporary music" — at the 1981 NAMM convention in Chicago.

By 1983, digital instruments with MIDI interfaces were stealing the show, and for a while analog sounds were out of favor. Now they're back in, especially the Minimoog bass sounds. During the mid-'80s, it was possible to pick up a Mini on the used market for under $300. Nowadays, we've seen stock Minis in excellent condition selling for upwards of $1,000. If it's been adapted for MIDI, a Mini could run you $2,000 or more. And if you live in Europe or Japan, it can run much higher. [*The*

Minimoog has even spawned an accurate — though updated with complete MIDI capabilities — reproduction in the Studio Electronics SE-1. This is a triple-space rack-mount monophonic synth based on the original Mini's electronic design. A full complement of knobs are laid out on the SE-1's front panel, along with a numerical display of the current patch number, of which there are 128. At a list price of $1,295, the SE-1 doesn't come cheap, but it's $200 cheaper than the original in its heyday and around $1,000 less than a vintage Minimoog that's been rack mounted and as MIDIfied as possible by the same Studio Electronics.]

Why the Minimoog Is So Popular. Like the Hammond B-3, the Gibson Les Paul, the Fender Precision bass, and the Rhodes electric piano, the Minimoog has become a venerable instrument. Why is this so? How can an instrument assembled entirely from standard electronic parts have the sort of unique character that is generally associated with hand-crafted instruments? The

STUDIO ELECTRONICS MIDIMINI

Midimini: $2,195.00. Conversion of owner-provided Minimoog: $1,495.00. Studio Electronics, 18034 Ventura Blvd., Suite 169, Encino, CA 91316. (818) 776-8104. Fax (818) 776-1733.

Pros: MIDI control of rack-mounted Minimoog. Enhanced capabilities and performance controls.

Cons: Expensive. Rack-mounted control panel less accessible.

Attention, Minimoog Devotees: The king of vintage synths has been spotted in different garb of late,

shrunken and rack-mounted, keyboardless, but with MIDI in and thru connectors. The Midimini comes from the guys at Studio Electronics, who have been collecting, modifying, MIDIfying, and resuscitating Minis for a couple of years now. If you've been dying to get a Minimoog into your MIDI rig, this is a smart way to go.

The Studio Electronics engineers were able to compress the Mini's control panel to a four-space size, while generally maintaining the layout of its knobs and switches. Many of the original Moog knobs have been retained, but all of the Mini's rocker switches have been replaced by more compact toggle switches. There are also almost a dozen extra switches that you won't find on the stock Mini-

moog, and several new knobs. Welcoming you into the '90s is a MIDI data reception LED.

Several of the Minimoog modifications offered by Studio Electronics have been performed by technicians for years, such as a switch to sync oscillator 2 to oscillator 1, a three-way octave switch for transposing all three oscillators at once, a pitch-bend range knob (from zero to a full octave), and a separate LFO with a frequency knob, freeing oscillator 3 for purposes other than modulation. Studio Electronics' auxiliary LFO is limited to a triangle wave, which means it isn't as flexible as oscillator 3, but it works fine for vibrato. The N/M switch lets you choose between noise or the

Studio Electronics' Midimini will take up four spaces in your rack, but it's only 6½" deep. All of the Minimoog's audio outputs (low, high, and head-phone) and the external signal input were retained, but the footswitch inputs for controlling glide and decay were sacrificed. On the Midimini's front panel is a decay switch, but glide is enabled via MIDI controller 65 instead of with a hardware switch. The MIDI receive channel is set using the lower left knob; omni mode isn't supported. (photo by Paul Haggard)

correct answer is, "Nobody knows for sure." Most synthesists agree that the Minimoog's sound sets it apart from all other brands, but no scientist or engineer can pin down the difference in sound to something that can be measured. I believe that the Minimoog sound comes from a balance of several factors: the warm, low-order distortion introduced by the VCF and the VCAs, the rapid attack times of which the contour generators are capable, the small amounts of noise in the oscillators that keep them from locking together at very small frequency differences, and the fre-

dedicated LFO for modulation; the Mini's Mod Mix knob now mixes between the third oscillator and the added LFO or noise as the modulation source. One of the new knobs, labeled "Sweep," controls the amount of oscillator 2 signal that gets routed to modulate either the filter envelope or oscillator 3's frequency; the destination is determined by the Sweep F/O (filter/oscillator) switch.

Switches allocated to MIDI functions are for velocity control of filter and amplitude envelopes, assignment of mod wheel to control filter cutoff or modulation amount, and aftertouch control of filter cutoff and modulation amount. (Velocity and aftertouch control of the Minimoog? Wow! It also responds to

MIDI volume data.) The velocity-to-filter switch is accompanied by a knob to control the filter's sensitivity — sort of an analog velocity amount control. There's also a switch for single- or multi-trigger mode, and another switch to define note priority (low, high, or last).

One aspect to consider here is whether rack-mounting one of the most playable synths ever is a sensible thing to do. To really play the Minimoog, you have to tweak its knobs quite often. Reaching into a rack to adjust knobs on the Midimini's vertical faceplate isn't as seductive as interacting with the Minimoog's control panel, which lies flat or props up to any of four different access angles, resides at a handy location just above

the keyboard, and provides generous space around various controls. To get the most out of the Midimini, prepare to mount it in a convenient place that you can easily access while triggering it from your controller.

Now for the big question: Is a ten-year-old monophonic analog synth with MIDI worth $2,200? We think the Midimini is! Remember, the Minimoog is one mighty popular vintage synth (for good reason), and we know that's about what you should expect to pay for a Minimoog with MIDI, no matter who you buy it from. You'd be hard pressed to find one in better condition than one of these, and we know of none that will do more.

— Mark Vail

A Minimoog modified by Rivera Music Services (RMS) in the late '70s or early '80s. The mods include single- and multi-triggering, a dedicated LFO to free up osc 3 for audio purposes, and oscillator sync.

quency response of the instrument as a whole. I also believe that musicians like the Minimoog because its controls have a comfortable feel: The keyboard isn't mushy, the switches are easy to hit, the knobs are large and smooth-acting, and the left-hand wheels fit the natural hand motions. But I am not *sure* that these are the important elements of the Minimoog's popularity.

In order to be scientifically certain of why the Minimoog sounds and feels good, one would have to engage in an extensive, expensive research project. For us who designed the Minimoog over two decades ago, our own intuition and discretion were our most important tools. In this respect, we performed like artists rather than engineers.

OBERHEIM SEM MODULE

Building Block of an Early Polyphonic Synth

BY BOB MOOG

Throughout the early '70s, Oberheim Electronics was a highly reputed manufacturer of electronic effects devices. Their phase shifters, ring modulators, and envelope-controlled filters, marketed by Norlin Music under the Maestro brand name, were prized by tens of thousands of guitar players and keyboardists.

In addition to designing and building effects boxes, Oberheim Electronics was an ARP dealer for about a year and a half. Many of their ARP customers asked about a sequencer for their synth, so Oberheim designed their DS-2, one of the first digital sequencers. It featured data entry from the synth's keyboard, and a memory of as many as 144 notes.

As soon as the DS-2 was on the market, Tom Oberheim noticed that many of his customers wanted to set up a sequence, then play their synth from the keyboard at the same time that the sequence was playing back. In addition, many ARP Odyssey and Minimoog owners were looking for a way to fatten up their sound. So Tom drew up plans for a fairly simple analog voice module that could serve either as a tone generator for his se-

quencer or as a backup tone generator for a monophonic analog synth.

Labelled the SEM (Synthesizer Expander Module), Oberheim's new instrument had an audio chain with two VCOs (each with sawtooth and rectangular waves), a VCF, and a VCA. The VCF was a multimode, two-pole filter. "Multimode" means that it could be set to perform as a lowpass, highpass, bandpass, or band-reject filter. "Two-pole" refers to the shape of the filter response. In any mode, this was different from the four-pole response of the Moog or ARP filters, which were popular at that time. Tom reasoned that musicians would welcome this type of VCF for two reasons: First, the variety of possible sounds was greater than if a single-mode filter had been used, because the filter could operate in one of four distinctly different modes. And second, when the SEM was used to fatten up the sound of a synth that had a four-pole filter, it would be more effective if its filter were of a different type than that of the synth itself. "There was always the assumption that the SEM user would already have a synth with a four-pole lowpass filter," recalls Tom.

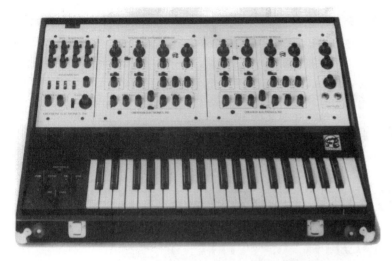

The SEM's control sources were very simple: A single LFO with triangular waveform, and two Minimoog-style ASR envelope generators, in which a single control was used for both decay time and release time. The front panel controls and switches determined the operating parameters and modes: No patching was available from the front panel. However, the module's control, trigger, and sync connections were available on small color-coded connectors on the circuit board itself. You could wire these connectors to a set of jacks, and then use patch cords to interconnect two or more modules, or connect a module to an external controller. Or, you could wire the connectors directly to some sort of master programming device.

The System Emerges. Tom Oberheim recalls, "At first, we didn't think of ourselves as being in the synthesizer business. We were in the accessory business, and some of our accessories were designed to work with synths. But Norlin forced us to rethink our position. Early in 1975, Norlin canceled several large orders when sales to their dealers dropped off. In order to stay in business, we had to come up with some new products — and quickly. So we combined our SEM modules with a

Oberheim's early synthesizer product line was based on the SEM. Besides being available as a stand-alone module, it came with a three-octave keyboard in the Two Voice polyphonic (top), or in the programmable Four Voice, which had a four-octave keyboard (below, with built-in programmer).

VITAL STATISTICS

Produced: 1974 to 1979.

Manufacturer: Oberheim Electronics, currently a division of Gibson, 1818 Elm Hill Pike, Nashville, TN 37210. (615) 871-4500, fax (615) 889-3216.

Description: Analog, two-oscillator voice module with some external programming capability.

Features: Two VCOs, two-pole multimode VCF, VCA, two ASR envelope generators, one LFO. Circuit board connectors provide access to control inputs and outputs.

Original Retail Prices: $695 for one free-standing SEM module with power supply and enclosure; $2,000 for the two-voice system; $4,000 for the four-voice system; $8,000 for the eight-voice system.

Current Street Prices: SEM, $50 to $350. Two Voice, $250 to $1,000. Four Voice with programmer, $400 to $1,500. Eight Voice with programmer, $600 to $2,000.

Current Retail Prices: SEM, $150 to $450. Two Voice, $400 to $1,000. Four Voice with programmer, $600 to $1,700. Eight Voice with programmer, $900 to $2,750. Rack-mounted and MIDIfied version with twin SEMs available from Studio Electronics [18034 Ventura Blvd., Ste. 169, Encino, CA 91316; phone (818) 776-8104] for $2,095.

In a late '70s sales brochure, the Oberheim Eight Voice programmable polyphonic synthesizer was described as "the ultimate live performance/studio keyboard system available." Its eight SEM modules could be assigned to the two manuals in rotating order, or in a 6-2, 4-4, or 2-6 split. Most SEM parameters could be controlled from the on-board Digital Programmer, which held 16 presets.

digitally scanned keyboard and a little analog sequencer, and came up with the Two Voice and Four Voice instruments. They were the first polyphonic synths to use individual voltage-controlled synthesizer circuits for each voice. In addition to the SEM, we showed the Two Voice and the Four Voice at the June 1975 National Association of Music Merchants show. That was the first NAMM show at which Oberheim exhibited products under its own name, and that's how we got into the synthesizer business."

The SEM System was designed to accommodate up to eight modules. The Two Voice was a fixed-configuration instrument, but with the Four Voice, you could expand it to up to eight modules. Then, in 1976, Oberheim introduced its programmer for the SEM System, which enabled the user to store the knob settings of the voltage-controlled parameters of each module. It was the first programmer of its type made available to the public. The SEM System remained as Oberheim's poly-

phonic product line until 1979, when the OB-X was introduced.

Early Users. Tom Oberheim remembers that one of the first really visible musicians to use an SEM module was Jan Hammer. Jan's famous "guitar sound" of the '70s and early '80s was often a Minimoog supplemented by an SEM module. But Oberheim is especially proud of the way Josef Zawinul used a Four Voice to record "Birdland" with Weather Report. Shortly after Zawinul had gotten the instrument, Tom paid him a visit. Though he spent the whole evening with Zawinul, explaining in detail how the SEMs worked, Tom left convinced that Zawinul didn't understand anything he had said, and that the new instrument would be pushed into a corner to gather dust. Then, about a week later, Zawinul invited Oberheim over to hear the rough mix of "Birdland." Tom remembers being bowled over by the great big-band sound Josef had created on his Four Voice. And "Birdland" became one of Weather Report's biggest hits.

Oberheim released the polyphonic and programmable OB-X in 1979. Available in four-, six-, and eight-voice configurations, it offered 32 program memories, polyphonic portamento, and polyphonic sample-and-hold. The eight-voice version listed for $5,995. Today, it's worth $300 to $700.

Forward to the Present. The development of the entire Oberheim synthesizer line, right up to the present time, has been a continuous evolution that began with the SEM modules. In 1977, the OB-1 was introduced. A monophonic instrument with virtually the same sound chain as the SEM, it was the first completely programmable synth of its type to hit the market. The OB-X came in 1979, offering complete programmability and either four or eight voices. The OB-Xa, introduced shortly after the OB-X, offered the ability to split the keyboard, or to double up the voices so that two voices would sound for each key that was depressed.

The first instruments using the "Oberheim parallel buss" were introduced in '83. These included the DSX digital sequencer, the DMX drum machine, and the OB-8 eight-voice synth, the circuitry of which was redesigned to include a VCF that could be switched from two-pole to four-pole. The Xpander (1984) was Oberheim's first synth product that was designed from the ground up with MIDI in mind; outgrowths of the Xpander development include the Oberheim Matrix-6 (1986),

A complete Oberheim system (c.1982), comprising (from the bottom up) the OB-Xa synth, DSX polyphonic digital sequencer (L), DMX drum machine, and OB-Xpander (not to be confused with the later Oberheim Xpander — see facing page). The units interfaced together using a pre-MIDI network.

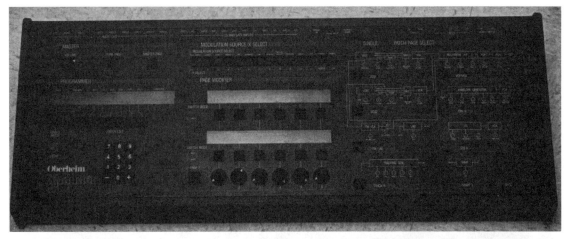

Oberheim introduced the MIDI-compatible Xpander in 1984. An absolutely killer synth, it's still worth about $1,000.

The current Oberheim Matrix-1000, introduced in 1987, provides super analog synth sounds in a single-space rack-mount MIDI module. It lists for $599 new, but can be had for around $350 used.

the Matrix-12 (1985), and the Matrix-1000 (1987).

In May 1985, Tom Oberheim's Oberheim Electronics failed and quickly resurfaced as Oberheim/ECC. Besides maintaining production of the Matrix-12 and -1000, the new company developed some MIDI processors — dubbed the Perf/x line — starting with the Cyclone arpeggiator, Systemizer split/layer utility, and Navigator note/controller/program change mapper, all released in 1989. These were followed in '91 with the Strummer keyboard-to-guitar chord voicing converter and the Drummer interactive drum-pattern sequencer. During that same year, Gibson purchased Oberheim, and development began on a

Want your Oberheim OB-8 in a rack-mount box under MIDI control? You need the Obie-Eight from Studio Electronics. (photo by Paul Haggard)

The monophonic, programmable Oberheim OB-1 came out in '78 at $1,895. Unlike early Oberheim synths, the OB-1's VCF was switchable for two- or four-pole response. Expect to pay from $100 to $200 for one on the street, or up to $350 in a store.

rack-mount analog MIDI synth called the OB-MX. Originally dubbed the OberM006 (to look like "OberMoog," because it will feature both Moog- and Oberheim-style filters), the basic OB-MX is slated to cost from $1,500 to $5,000, depending on its voice configuration, and will reportedly offer 12-voice polyphony, 12-way multitimbral operation, matrix modulation, and four multi-stage envelopes. The OB-MX's front panel is crowded with knobs, surely a welcome sign to vintage-synth enthusiasts. As of early '93, development continues on the OB-MX, as does production of the Matrix-1000, Strummer, and Drummer.

Tom Oberheim is now head of Marion Systems, Inc. His recent work includes upgrades for Akai samplers, as well as design work for computer and audio companies. Referring to "the Oberheim sound," Tom told me, "I think the early designs — the SEM, the OB-1, the OB-X, and the OB-Xa — have somewhat better sound than the OB-8 and the instruments that followed it. I think that's because the sound of the earlier designs is dirtier in subtle ways, and therefore seems to have more guts. The OB-8 is a more perfect design. The auto-tune routine tunes the oscillators more perfectly. But the sound is clean . . . too clean."

SEQUENTIAL CIRCUITS PROPHET-5

Defining the Future of Poly-Synths

BY MARK VAIL

The date: January 1978. The place: The Disneyland Hotel convention facility in Anaheim, California. The event: The winter NAMM (National Association of Music Merchants) show. Moog and ARP were reveling in their heyday — synth-industry giants in the days when Roland and Yamaha were still trying to figure out how to make a synthesizer that would sell in the U.S.

Tom Oberheim's modular Four Voice and Eight Voice synths, Moog's Polymoog, and ARP's two-voice 2600 were just about the only synthesizers able to sound more than one note at a time (other than by putting out unison chords). The Oberheim was the only polyphonic synth with the capacity to remember patches, but it couldn't store all of its parameters in memory.

Two landmarks were unveiled at this particular NAMM show. In a medium-sized private exhibit room, Yamaha's John Gatts previewed the CS-80, an eight-voice polyphonic synth with the first polyphonic aftertouch keyboard and hardwired memory capability. Meanwhile, tucked away in a tiny booth on the lower level of the con-

vention facility, a barely working prototype of the Prophet-5 was being shown by Dave Smith, former Moog clinician John Bowen, and businesswoman Barb Fairhurst — the staff of Sequential Circuits, a self-funded outfit that started in the confines of Smith's San Jose, California, garage selling a digital sequencer and a generic synth programmer.

Sequential was hardly the kind of mega-company you'd expect to send industry leaders running for cover, but while Moog and ARP were battling over the relative merits of pitch-bend wheels vs. ribbons vs. spongy little rectangles called PPCs (proportional pressure controllers), Sequential was cranking out exactly the kind of instrument, with exactly the kind of sound and features, that musicians needed.

By today's standards, those features may look a bit lacking: a whopping 40 user-programmable presets (later revs had 120 programs), five non-multitimbral voices, a non-touch-sensitive keyboard, etc. But the Prophet was the first polyphonic synth in which every parameter could be stored in computer memory.

A rev 3 Prophet. Note the tape cassette control buttons at upper right. The poly-mod section at the left end of the panel, which allowed osc 2 to be modulated by osc 1 or the filter envelope, was an important ingredient in the Prophet's sound.

Its voice architecture, contrary to popular myth, had more in common with the ARP Odyssey voice than with the Minimoog, since it featured two audio oscillators per voice with its third oscillator being a dedicated LFO. The VCO pulse width was continuously variable (the Mini only offered three fixed pulse-widths), osc 1 could be synced to osc 2 (an Odyssey feature available only on modified Minimoogs), and the two envelope generators were ADSRs (the Mini's were ADS, release time being governed by the decay knob and a switch).

If there was a single feature that defined the Prophet sound, it was the poly-mod section, which enabled you to use the filter envelope and osc 2 to modular the frequency of osc 1, the pulse-width of osc 1, and/or the filter cutoff frequency. These modulation routings, combined with osc 1's sync function, produced the trademark (and at one time hopelessly overused) oscillator sweeping

VITAL STATISTICS

Produced: 1978 to 1984ish.

Total Number Made: About 7,200.

Manufacturer: Sequential Circuits (later just Sequential), San Jose, CA. Out of business after being bought by Yamaha.

Description: The first fully programmable polyphonic analog/digital hybrid synthesizer.

Features: Five-voice polyphony (a ten-voice model in the same chassis was available for a short time). Each analog voice contained two VCOs, a lowpass VCF, and two ADSR envelope generators. Additional features included 40 user-programmable presets (later models have 120 presets), a poly-mod section, digital noise source, 61-note non-touch-sensitive keyboard, pitch and mod wheels. Later models include digital bus, cassette interface for program storage, and various MIDI implementations.

Insider Information: Revisions (revs) included: Rev 1 (serial numbers 0001–0182), rev 2 (0183–1300), rev 3 (1301–2469), rev 3.2 (2470–?), and rev 3.3 (serial numbers not known). SSM chips were featured on rev 1s and 2s, while Curtis Music chips were used in all rev 3 machines, which is why rev 1s and 2s sound different than rev 3s.

Original Price: $3,995 to $4,495.

Current Street Prices: $400 to $800.

Current Dealer Prices: $500 to $2,000 for rev 3.3 with MIDI. Rack-mounted version available from Studio Electronics [18034 Ventura Blvd., Ste. 169, Encino, CA 91316. (818) 776-8104] for $3,395, or $2,195 if you supply the Prophet-5.

In late 1989, Prophet developer Dave Smith said a rack-mount Prophet-5 was inconceivable, because it would be prohibitively expensive and people wouldn't settle for a mere five voices of polyphony. In spite of Smith's skepticism, Studio Electronics — who specializes in rack-mounting and MIDIfying old analog synths — offers the P-Five, which compensates for the limited polyphony with extended MIDI capabilities like velocity and aftertouch response for control of volume, VCF cutoff, VCF resonance, and poly-mod envelope amount.

sync sound, usually variations on what was originally factory preset 33.

Revs. There have been a number of different models of the Prophet, each a slight improvement (theoretically) from the last version or revision (rev for short). The original Prophets came to be known as rev 1s. Few of these have survived over the years, since they were hand-built, without the serious bench testing for quality that was implemented much later. Rev 1s were shoved out the door as quickly as possible so Smith and company could pay their bills. As a result, rev 1s were buggy and fragile beasts. You can generally tell a rev 1 from a rev 2 by the reddish Koa wood used for its case (most rev 2s and all 3s used a walnut case). Other distinguishing features are the placement of the power on/off switch — rev 1s feature it on the front panel, and it's on the back panel on rev 2s — and the tune and edit switches on the rev 2s. Rev 3s added cassette interface controls to the front panel.

In addition to these physical characteristics, there are sonic differences. Rev 1s and 2s have a fatter, ballsier sound than rev 3s. SSM (Solid State Music) chips were used in 1s and 2s, while Curtis chips were used in later models because they were more consistent and reliable.

MAINTENANCE & MIDI

Wine Country Productions [1572 Park Crest Ct., #505, San Jose, CA 95118. (408) 265-2008] services and upgrades all Sequential products. They also sell reconditioned Prophet-5s for $1,299, including manual, the most complete MIDI implementation, and full 120-program memory. Wine Country's Dave Sesnak, a former Sequential employee, gives us the following Prophet survival tips:

• **Don't throw away broken Prophets.** If you're a collector or a Prophet owner and you come across a beat-up Prophet, buy it even if it's unplayable. It can be scavenged for spare parts, which are worth their weight in gold.

• **Prophet-5s are all due for a battery change.** The advertised life of the battery used to retain patches in RAM was ten years. Replacing them isn't that hard, but you do need to be technically oriented, since they're soldered to a circuit board. Replacement isn't necessary if you leave your Prophet plugged in and turned on 24 hours a day; even so, we recommend replacement.

• **MIDIing.** To MIDI a Prophet using Wine Country's MIDI kit ($249), the machine has to be brought up to rev 3.2 level. Rev 3s can be upgraded to rev 3.2, but it requires major brain surgery of the transplant variety — the computer board has to be replaced and a new power supply installed. This will run you about $400–$500.

VINTAGE SYNTHESIZERS **159** SEQUENTIAL CIRCUITS PROPHET-5

When it was introduced in late 1980, the dual-manual Sequential Prophet-10 carried a steep list price of $7,795. A few single-manual versions were made, but the smaller cabinet contained so many components that overheating and oscillator tuning instability were constant problems.

Rev 1s did not have a cassette interface for memory storage, though chances are any rev 1 you find today will have had this feature added. Auto-tuning was accomplished by pressing program select switches 1 and 8 simultaneously on rev 1s. Editing a parameter required hitting two switches simultaneously, after which turning a knob would add to or subtract from the value as stored in memory. On rev 2s, this system was changed so that turning a knob would instantly jump the parameter to the knob's absolute setting, overriding whatever was in memory.

The circuit board placement was changed with the rev 2 design, so that they are easier to service than rev 1s. For example, in order to do a routine cleaning of the keyboard contacts in a rev 1, you've got to remove the circuit board with the Z-80 on it. If you accidentally plug that board in backwards, you end up with a fried microprocessor. Ouch! Rev 3s included the ability to alter the tuning of each note in an octave and store this setting as part of a patch.

Rev 3.2 or 3.3 machines are the only units that can be MIDIed, though some ex-Sequential em-

Released in late '83, Sequential's Prophet-T8 had a weighted-action 76-note keyboard, wooden keys, and MIDI. Each key had a spring-loaded wooden hammer assembly and two sets of optical sensors for sensing velocity. Calibration of the sensors can be tricky because of slight warping in all the T8's wooden parts. David Sesnak of Wine Country Productions says that some T8 keyboards are better than others, and that humidity and transportation are factors in the keyboard response.

ployees were rumored to be working on a relatively expensive rev 2 MIDI mod. MIDI implementations range from basic (omni mode only) to extensive (poly mode, 16 channel assignments, program change commands, pitch-bend wheel in three ranges, and data dumps). Six versions of MIDI software were done in all. Interestingly, none of them supported the mod wheel — there just wasn't enough room left in ROM.

Mods. A number of oddball modifications were done to Prophets by Sequential staffers looking to make some extra bucks on the side. Suzanne Ciani had voltage and gate outputs added for individual voices. You may also find Prophets with octave switches, rev 1s with rev 2 output stages (the 2s were hotter), LFOs with different waveforms (negative-going sawtooth in particular) and a wider range, memory expansions, and heat sinks to help stabilize the oscillators.

The quality and reliability of modifications may vary greatly, but shouldn't really hurt the value of the machine. In fact, depending on its usefulness, a modification should add value.

Accessories. Sequential marketed a digital polyphonic sequencer that connected directly to rev 3s via a pre-MIDI proprietary serial digital bus that was 30 times faster than MIDI. Only a few hundred of these were made, according to Dave Smith. They sold new for about $1,300.

Prophet-10s. In 1978, a handful of ten-voice Prophets were built in the same case as the rev 1 five-voice machines. Patrick Gleeson and Josef Zawinul are two players who took delivery on these

The vector-synthesis techniques developed by Dave Smith and his team in creating the Sequential Prophet-VS later appeared in the Yamaha SY22 and Korg Wavestation. Original list on the VS was $2,599, and they still can bring from $700 to $1,200 on the street today.

machines. These Prophet-10s, not to be confused with the two-manual monster that came out in 1980, suffered from severe tuning instability caused by heat buildup. There just wasn't enough room in the chassis for the heat to dissipate from two voice boards. Even adding heat sinks didn't help.

Heed This. So you want to invest in a Prophet-5, or any other vintage synth? David Sesnak of Wine Country Productions offers some suggestions and warnings: "Usually the word 'vintage' means that it's not generally open to the public. It's for collectors, people who know what they want. It isn't for someone who would say, 'What's the Prophet-5? I think I'm interested. If I could hear one, maybe I'll like it.' That guy needs to go someplace else, preferably to a Japanese manufacturer, because they're more suitable for his style.

"Be prepared to deal with a vintage instrument, which you have to look at as a collector's item. They're out of manufacture. Not many people know a whole hell of a lot about them, either operationally or technically, because the company's gone. A vintage instrument is difficult to operate and even more difficult to repair, but not impossible by any means. If you're qualified, it's a good challenge."

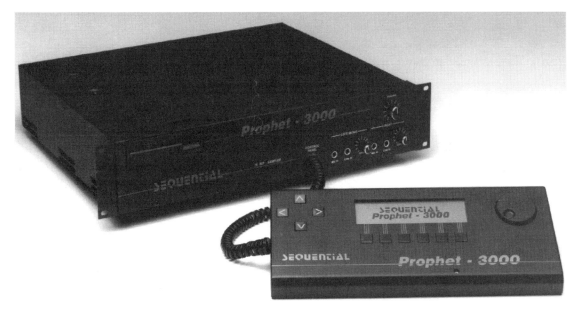

Introduced soon before Yamaha announced that it was buying Sequential in the early fall of '88, the Prophet-3000 16-bit sampler came too late to bolster the company's existence. Yamaha blew the 3000s out at unheard-of prices, and the sampler gained a good reputation before it faded into the sunset.

YAMAHA CS-80

Heavyweight Champion of the Early Polyphonics

BY MARK VAIL

In 1976, synthesizers that allowed you to play chords instead of single notes finally appeared. Even by today's standards, the competition was pretty intense. The Polymoog, ARP Omni, Oberheim Four Voice, and Sequential Prophet-5 — all American synths — led a host of notable polyphonics. Meanwhile, Yamaha — whose only previous campaigns into the synthesizer domain were the little-known SY-1 and SY-2 — tossed their microprocessor-controlled, analog CS-80 into the fray.

Actually, tossed isn't the most accurate term. Tipping the scales at a hefty 220 pounds, the CS-80 was no lightweight. Neither was its price: $6,900. Even though the CS-80 didn't crush the competition, it offered a distinctive sound and some unique controller features. It found its way into the arsenals of Stevie Wonder, Herbie Hancock, Michael McDonald, Steve Porcaro, Vangelis, Hans Zimmer, and Michael Boddicker, among others.

"There was no question that ARP, Moog, Sequential, and Oberheim were dominating the market," remembers Yamaha's John Gatts, Product Service Manager of their Combo Division at the time. "But nothing out there sounded like the CS-80. It was an incredibly fat-sounding synth, and it was easy to use. It appealed to players who weren't necessarily into synthesis. They could turn it on and play it like a piano."

Richard Luebbing, a CS-80 expert with David L. Abell, Inc., in Los Angeles, has had a real love-hate relationship with the CS-80. "It was a turkey on a bunch of levels, but there was absolutely no other synth at that time that a piano player would like as far as touch and responsiveness. When it was all set up, it was really a joy to play."

Controllers. The CS-80 ushered in a few new controller ideas. It was one of the first synths with a velocity-sensitive keyboard. Another CS-80 innovation was polyphonic aftertouch, which allows you to push down harder on a single note within a chord and increase the volume of, or add vibrato to, that note independently, without affecting the other notes within the chord. Finally, instead of the now-familiar Moog-style pitch-bend wheel, the CS-80 had a ribbon controller. Some Moog synths had ribbons as well, but the CS-80's ribbon was different. Moog's ribbon had a constant center

It ain't my brother, but it's heavy. The keyboard on the 220-pound CS-80 looks like that on any ordinary five-octave synth, but it was different. Not only was it velocity-sensitive, it offered polyphonic aftertouch, the first to be offered in a production synth. Stretched across the front panel above the lower three octaves of the keyboard is the one-of-a-kind pitch-bend ribbon. Hidden behind the etched graphics to the upper left of the control panel are the controls for creating the four programmable user presets.

point, so that touching the ribbon anywhere but the center caused the pitch to jump an interval corresponding to the position of your finger. On the CS-80, wherever you put your finger on the ribbon became the center point, and moving away from that point created pitch-bends. Also, by starting at either end of the ribbon, you could bend notes further than with a typical wheel or Moog ribbon of that era. (Back then, synths didn't offer programmable pitch-bend ranges.)

"The pitch ribbon was really cool," recalls Gary Leuenberger of G. Leuenberger Yamaha in San Francisco. "You could just reach up and do these nice little pitch-bends with that thing. It had a very

VITAL STATISTICS

Produced: 1976 to 1979.

Total Number Made: About 2,000.

Manufacturer: Yamaha. Manufactured at Nippon-Gakki, Ltd., factory in Hamamatsu, Japan.

Description: One of the first polyphonic synthesizers, one of the first synths with a velocity-sensitive keyboard, and the first production synth with polyphonic aftertouch. Two audio channels, each with eight analog oscillators capable of generating variable-width square and sawtooth waves and white noise, eight voltage-controlled filters (high- and lowpass), eight voltage-controlled amplifiers, and 16 envelope generators. Built-in tremolo/chorus and ring modulator. Selectable portamento (continuous glide)/glissando (stepped) control between notes. Twenty-two factory presets (11 per channel), four user presets (two per channel). User presets programmed using four miniaturized versions of the control panel, found hidden behind a front-panel hatch. Sixty-one-note keyboard. Pitch-bend ribbon controller. Left/right stereo and mono outputs; footpedal, footswitch, and control voltage inputs. 220 lbs.

Original Retail Price: $6,900.

Current Street Price: $500 to $1,000. Stand and accessories increase value. $300 to $500 for inoperative unit to be gutted for spare parts.

Current Dealer Price: $500 to $1,500.

natural feel. As time progressed, they probably looked at other manufacturers' pitch-bend and mod wheels and thought, 'Well, that's what most people like Chick Corea are used to, so let's go back to the wheels.' Every time I've been in product development meetings, I've said, 'Bring back that little ribbon controller.'"

We've never heard of a synth's wheels, joysticks, or levers wearing out, but the CS-80 ribbon? "The guy who really loved it, and the only person that I've ever seen wear one out physically, was Stevie Wonder," Luebbing says. "It actually wore smooth;

the fabric came off and we had to replace it." Stevie could afford the installation of a new ribbon; according to Gatts, Wonder owned four CS-80s.

Hidden Assets. Programmability in synths was a fairly recent development when the CS-80 happened on the scene. Each manufacturer implemented programmability in their own way. Yamaha's may not have been the weirdest, but it was quite different. "You opened up a little door on the CS-80's front panel," Leuenberger reveals, "and there were four miniaturized versions — little toggle switches — of the control panel. That was your programmable memory."

Tuning. Weight wasn't the only hassle inherent in the CS-80; like many analog synths, its oscillators tended to drift in pitch. "The tuning was stable for about 20 minutes, and that's on a good one," Luebbing claims. "There were problems with air circulation inside the unit. Cooling wasn't the same for all of the oscillator cards, so they would drift at different rates."

According to Luebbing, this air circulation problem made the tuning process ugly. "You couldn't keep the lid open for more than a minute — preferably 30 seconds — when making an adjustment, because the interior temperature would drop. You had to prop the lid open with a pencil, reach in, tweak a trim pot, close the lid, and let the temperature stabilize for about three minutes. I had a little egg timer and two digital thermometers that would tell me what the internal temperature was above the ventilation grills. Whenever the temperature started to fluctuate, I would notice that my tuning would not be accurate."

As you can imagine, tuning the CS-80 wasn't much fun. It was both lengthy and expensive. "My procedure took three days and I charged $300. Most of the synths I saw came in on a periodic basis. They were owned by professionals like [L.A. session ace] Ralph Grierson. Tuning is a religion with him; he would bring his in every two weeks."

Three hundred bucks? Maybe tuning was covered under the CS-80's warranty. "No," Luebbing admits, "but we'd get you in the ballpark the first couple of times for free."

Even the CS-80's case design had a detrimental effect on tuning. "There were four casters that could be inserted into holes on the CS-80's back panel and lid," Luebbing explains, "so that you could roll it around like a huge suitcase. Unfortunately, the way the tuning trimmers were located, if you moved the CS-80 the way the manufacturer intended, the vibration was in the same plane as the trimmer adjustment. The CS-80 could be nicely in tune, and then the roadies would come, slam it down on the floor, drop it down the curb, put it on the truck, and bounce it all the way to wherever it was going, and all the trimmers would drop into another position. Changing the trimmers themselves didn't help, because they were so sensitive.

Does it qualify as a vintage synth yet? At a decade old, I think so. Yamaha's DX7 introduced FM synthesis to the market at an affordable price and yanked Yamaha to the head of the industry. Trouble is, it made them over-confident. For a while, they believed they could duplicate the DX7's success at any time.

What the . . .?! Not a Yamaha product, the DX-Programmer was an analog-style programming interface from German music manufacturer Jellinghaus. It appeared early in 1987 at the Frankfurt Musik Messe trade show and was available for a time in Europe, but never made its way across the big pond to the States. Such a shame. It could have made FM programming fun.

The TX7 was Yamaha's module version of the DX7.

Yamaha's DX5 contained the equivalent of two DX7s and a 76-note keyboard.

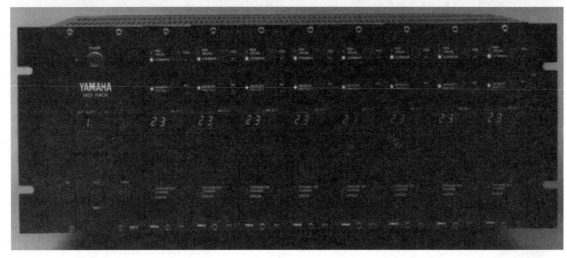

Eight DX7-like TF1 FM synth modules made up the TX816, introduced in 1985 for a mere $4,995.

At their maximum, they required maybe a tenth of a degree turn to vary the tuning over several semitones." For those CS-80s to be transported to gigs or from his shop back to the owner, Luebbing insisted on hiring a cartage company that would "do things my way and move the CS-80 in a horizontal position, which helped a good deal."

To combat the tuning problems, technicians tried various strategies, such as applying drops of fingernail polish to hold the trimmers still and installing internal cooling fans for improved air circulation. One of Luebbing's tactics really went beyond

In 1987, Yamaha replaced the DX7 with the DX7IIFD (the FD stood for floppy drive). Whereas the DX7 had a single output, the DX7II had stereo outputs and a cleaner sound.

the ordinary. "It involved the installation of a heat pipe, a fluid-filled copper tube, purchased from Edmund Scientific in New Jersey for about $70. There was less than a quarter-degree temperature change from one end to the other. I soldered a tab from each oscillator chip to the tube, and it would tend to keep them at the same temperature. Garth Hudson [of The Band] was the only CS-80 owner experimentally oriented enough to give it a try. Subject to its limitations, it did what it was supposed to do. Garth toured with that CS-80 up and down the East Coast. Then he brought it back about a year and a half later, and it was still tuned pretty well. Unfortunately, it was stolen when he was in New York, and we never heard from it again."

Luebbing concedes that, in the proper environment, the CS-80's tuning "actually could be made reasonably stable. If I give it a good in-studio tuning, it will be serviceable through a couple of sessions. If it isn't moved around and it's kept powered up and hot in a cool environment, it'll stay pretty well." For that reason, Luebbing now insists on tuning a CS-80 in its habitat — the studio. In his opinion, road use is out of the question.

Other Mods. Besides his tuning-stabilizing modification, Luebbing often performed a different kind of surgery on the CS-80: routing the synth's audio signals around the potentially noisy built-in tremolo/chorus effect. "If somebody wanted those effects, we'd use an outboard device."

Gary Leuenberger wasn't satisfied with the CS-80's factory presets. "They were thin and not in the taste of American musicians. I had a book of my patches that I'd show the customers when they got their CS-80. I'd say, 'Go through and take the time to set up all these little buttons and see which patches

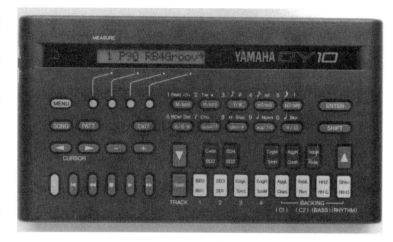

you like. Then we'll modify the presets for you.' My technician would rewire the board with the proper resistors and capacitors to replace the factory presets. I didn't charge for this modification.

"Our mod also added four-voice, two-voice, and unison modes, as well as eight supplementary LFOs per channel, so that we could modulate each oscillator at a different speed."

Conclusions. Luebbing sums the CS-80 up quite nicely: "It was sort of like a 1951 Packard: Just beautiful. You want to see it at a car show, but you aren't going to take it on the freeway back and forth between home and work to make a living. It came from a wonderful era, but now it's over with.

"From a technician's point of view, it was the biggest pain in the ass that any manufacturer ever made. From the technician's revenue point of view, it was the biggest gold mine that was ever made. From the musician's point of view, it was one of the most rewarding synthesizers ever made, even to this day. But, it could also be the most expensive habit, other than cocaine, that you'd ever get involved in."

You won't find a smaller, self-contained multitrack synthesizer/MIDI sequencer combo than Yamaha's QY10, introduced in 1991 for an economical $399. Take along half a dozen AA batteries and Walkman-style headphones for unbeatable portability.

Yamaha's current flagship synth, the SY99, combines FM and sample-playback technology. Even though it looks like such a big honker — thanks in part to its 76-note keyboard — the SY99 is a lot easier to transport than the old CS-80.

CHROMA

The Synth That
Survived ARP's Fall

BY MARK VAIL

When the seas came crashing down on ARP Instruments in 1981, plans for a two-year-old programmable, polyphonic synthesizer design were seemingly squandered. The team that had several times tried to surf through internal company resistance to actually produce the instrument were scattered by the waves.

Philip Dodds was left at the helm of a nearly submerged ARP. While bailing out the lifeboat . . . er, cleaning up the financial and loose-end disorder that remained, he managed to sell the Chroma design to CBS — and get himself hired as the director of its production.

The Chroma represents what could be thought of as the second generation of analog/digital hybrid synthesizer instruments. It came along at the peak of the Sequential Prophet-5's popularity, offering then-radical functions like multitimbral operation, voice layering, and keyboard splitting, not to mention velocity response — common synth features that we take for granted now. Voice structuring wasn't limited to the typical Minimoog con-

figuration (two oscillators, a filter, two ADSRs, and a VCA); the Chroma's internal computer could route signals through two low-pass filters, in parallel or series, or position the VCA before or after the filters. Its original keyboard was a wooden weighted-action design (by Dodds) manufactured by Kimball.

In addition, there was a computer interface that allowed Chroma performances to be digitally recorded and played back, and voicing software was even developed for the Apple II and IBM-PC. Digital sequencing and editor/librarian programs are commonplace today, but the Chroma came out at least a year before MIDI was accepted as a de facto protocol.

The Chroma also helped usher in a concept that annoyed some synthesizer programmers: menu-driven voice programming with a single data slider and multiple dual-function membrane switches (undeniable influences on Yamaha in their design of the DX7). Previously, single-function knobs and sliders (one control per parameter) abounded, and single-line LCD displays were foreign and unfriendly to affirmed knob-twisters.

Philip Dodds is proud of the Chroma, as you'll see from the interview that follows. These days, he deals with a multimedia PC trade association made up of big guns like IBM, Apple, Kodak, and DEC. "I'm the head of the trade association that is setting standards for multimedia in all desktop, workstation, and network computers," he says. Our sympathies! What this man needs is an extended programming session with an ARP 2600 or Chroma — or even the ARP 2500 that he played to the aliens from outer space in *Close Encounters of the Third Kind.* Sad to say, though, Philip Dodds regretfully doesn't have access to any of them.

* * * *

How did the Chroma's development come about?

Conceptually, the Chroma began in the fall of '79. It started into serious development in the latter part of '79 and 1980. We were ready to bring it out in '81 when everything at ARP came uncorked. When ARP went into receivership, among the first things I had to do was shut down R&D, which of course was extremely difficult and painful because I was the VP of engineering. Everything froze. People went off and tried to get other jobs, and many did. We lost a full six to eight months from the development cycle, because there was a lot of lost momentum internally while the company folded itself up and I was off trying to figure out how to get it back up and going. But at the time, I felt we had a sufficient lead and that we could still pull revenue out of the hat. I was proved to be correct. We went through a full

three restarts in the design until we got it right, which normally doesn't occur in business.

Do you mean development was stopped once with ARP and twice afterward?

Actually, it stopped twice with ARP and once restarting again after CBS bought the rights to manufacture the Chroma. With ARP, I stopped the design a couple of times because it was heading down the wrong paths and because there were new developments and new technologies available that could put us significantly forward. Plus it just wasn't ready for prime time, and having suffered through releasing products that weren't ready for prime time, I wasn't about to allow that to happen again.

Did you get any resistance?

Oh, man, I got a lot of resistance internally.

From ARP president David Friend?

Principally, but then also from David Spencer — who's often not heard of, but was chief operating officer right after David left, became president briefly, and was the chief financial officer for a period. He was a very good guy, but really had no idea about the technology. He tended to back my decisions, lacking any other sort of direction. Good guy, but not a music industry veteran. He was sort of left holding the bag. David Friend left the company a substantial number of months before the company actually filed Chapter 11, and David Spencer took over in his absence. David Spencer was sort of this quiet person that nobody knows anything about, but he ended up holding the bag. He was one of the first to go upon the filing, and then I ended up taking over from there.

Like a phoenix, the Chroma rose from ARP's ashes in 1981 and lived a tumultuous, if fairly successful, life during its five years of development and production.

So you had to clean up ARP after the fact. When did you finally get back to working on the Chroma?

Through the summer of '81, I negotiated the sale of the Chroma to CBS and in the fall we pulled the R&D team back together by hook and by crook. We opened up the CBS R&D labs in Woburn, Massachusetts, with 21 people kicking it off. We had a pilot production area where we finished the design of the Chroma. We built the first 50 Chromas right there in Woburn ourselves, because basically CBS was clueless about how to build electronic instruments. They built the Rhodes electric piano, but building instruments with tines that vibrate is a little bit different from making instruments that were built on an Intel 80186 computer chip. Worlds apart! CBS was going through a lot of turmoil as well. So I threw up my hands and said, "We're building the first run of Chromas here until we get it right." We hand-built those things ourselves, the development team did. It was great. The first instruments were among the best. There's a lot of tricky technology there.

The keyboards were built by Kimball, then later by Pratt-Read before they went under. They had a wood-ply base. There was a nine-layer birch-ply bed with a full wooden keyboard action, which I designed. Actually, there were a lot of people who loved the feel of the keyboard. We also used solid cherry end blocks. I was trying to go for as much real, genuine wood as possible for feel and flavor.

How many notes did the keyboard have?

Sixty-four [*E* to *G*]. We wanted to do an 88-key version, but just never got to it. It felt very good and was balanced just right. I went through incredible efforts to get a key-contact set designed so that it didn't impede the feel. It used a leaf switch with Paladium contacts; these were cross-point contacts that were used for telephone switch banks, custom made for the keyboard.

I remember when we first unveiled it and went through the first demonstration at NAMM in Atlanta in 1982. We had a separate room as was often the case. Of course, I was beside myself because my heart and soul were in this beast. That was me there, really. Every ounce of my being — and the team's — was in that instrument. Bob Moog came up, sat down, and played it. We were still ostensible competitors, although I say "ostensible" because the respect was entirely mutual and unbelievably strong. Bob sat down, played it for a few

VITAL STATISTICS

Description: Sixteen-channel programmable polyphonic synthesizer with built-in computer interface, 64-note velocity-sensitive wooden weighted-action keyboard (*E* to *G*), 75 front-panel membrane switches, data slider, two programmable spring-loaded performance levers, three-band graphic EQ, volume, and tuning sliders. Destinations for velocity control were pitch, filter cutoff, the rate of the LFO, the waveshape, amplitude, and attack time. The computer interface allowed pre-MIDI sequencing and voice editing functions via Apple IIe and IBM-PC computers. A tape interface allowed program storage on any ordinary cassette tape machine. (Typically, the cheaper the deck the better; successful cassette storage for a Chroma was just as iffy as any tape-based data storage system. These "conveniences" were incorporated on a slew of machines by a host of manufacturers, on instruments like the Ensoniq ESQ-1 synthesizer/sequencer, Roland TR-505 drum machine, Alesis MMT-8 MIDI sequencer, and Casio PT-30 portable keyboard. Granted, cassette storage is better than no storage at all, but depending on tape for consistent, reliable restoration of patch and sequence memory in a performance situation was like riding bareback in the Kentucky Derby.)

Manufacturer: Original designs completed at ARP. CBS bought the Chroma design, assigned it to their Rhodes division, and hired Philip Dodds and the former ARP engineering team to produce the synthesizer.

Production Dates: 1982 to late '83. Development began in the fall of 1979.

Approximate Number Made: 3,000 including Chroma Expanders.

minutes, and then he just broke out in this grin. He walked over to me and said, "You did it. That is the best-feeling keyboard I have ever felt. You guys have done it. You got the right velocity sensitivity. This is wonderful." A lot of people were critical, saying, "Velocity response is not a big feature, this isn't something people want." But Bob Moog's comment proved to be prophetic. He knew that this was the direction keyboards had to go, and of course now velocity response is a staple.

The Chroma was the *first* keyboard with velocity-sensing keys that also sent it out via an interface. It was the first commercial synthesizer with a keyboard interface with software that ran on an external personal computer, the first one being the Apple II, followed by the IBM-PC. Tony Williams programmed the sequencing software for both computer platforms. When we first shipped the Chroma, the PC hadn't been shipped yet. We had to wait for that. But when the PC first came out, we brought out software for it as well. We actually developed sequencing software — this was before MIDI existed. We actually developed the first computer desktop software for sequencing, as far as I know, anywhere. It had an external port that was fully documented and available to anyone.

There were 256 different velocity levels. We were the ones on Dave Smith's original committee that said that MIDI had to have velocity. Dave Smith said it was too complex and we couldn't do it. We dug our heels in and said it had to have velocity response. And he said, "Well, that's just because you're trying to favor the Chroma." "No," I told him, "One day keyboards will respond to velocity. Trust me on this."

Was it multitimbral?

The Chroma had 16 discrete synthesizer channels, complete analog synthesizers. There were two VCOs, a cool multimode VCF, a VCA, and software-created envelope generators. There were 64 sample-and-holds that controlled all of those channels, and they were real-time updated and driven directly off the central computer.

And the VCOs were under computer control?

Yeah. Not only were they under computer control, but we had implemented a frequency sampler, a zero-crossing detector, that permitted the computer to measure the wave lengths of all of the VCOs and the VCF, so it could figure out what

Original Retail Price: $5,295.

Current Street Value: $300 to $500. ($350 for a Chroma Expander.)

Current Dealer Price: $450 to $800. ($500 for a Chroma Expander.)

Insider Information: CBS picked up the Chroma and ARP electronic piano designs for a mere $350,000. . . . Philip Dodds reports that the best Chromas are serial numbers zero through 50, because they were hand-built by the development team in Woburn, Massachusetts. . . . Philip Dodds appears in *Close Encounters of the Third Kind* (1977, '80) as ARP musician Jean Claude. How was the experience? "Oh, it was fun," he says. "It was a lot of fun. I really enjoyed that. That whole sequence, believe it or not, took nine weeks. [ARP president] David Friend threatened to fire me if I didn't get back in time. He later said, 'Oh, I was just kidding. I was just trying to get them to hurry up and get you back to work.' I didn't think it was amusing at the time. I had been granted a leave of absence to deal with it, but they thought it would only take three or four weeks, and then it stretched to nine."

Genealogy: Philip Dodds went from vice president of engineering at ARP to the Chroma development team for CBS, then to Kurzweil, where he "helped birth the Kurzweil 250, dealt with Ray Kurzweil's personal form of reality distortion, and then said, 'This is crazy. I want to go do something else.' So I went off and started my own company. We did interactive video systems." . . . Does Dodds miss the music industry? "Oh, terribly. But Al Pearlman said it best: 'We all love the music business, but over time it was shown to be unrequited love.' And Al was right."

frequencies they were at. That was for auto tuning. When the Chroma first woke up, it would go to sleep for a minute while it read the frequency of each VCO and then created an internal software table that said, "Okay, let me adjust you to the correct frequency." It could actually read frequencies of each of the oscillators in real time, and it could automatically put the filters in resonant mode and read those frequencies as well. So all the tuning was computer-controlled automatically in the background.

The heart of the Chroma was an Intel 80186. We were a beta site for Intel. We helped Intel debug the 186, which preceded the now-famous 286. We were ahead of the PC, which had an 8086. But within every Chroma, if you flip up the front panel, on the right side you will see an 80186, a stack of RAM, and various other silicon glue: it's a CPU card. Take that card out, put in a SCSI controller and a hard disk drive, and you've got a desktop PC. It was a full-fledged programmable computer in a very proper sense. There was a data bus that fed from the CPU throughout the rest of the instrument to the rest of the circuits, the sample-and-holds, the control panel, and — in real time — it read the keyboard. It scanned the keyboard and did the velocity calculations and all the rest.

Paul DeRocco, the chief hardware architect, designed this system and wrote all the Chroma's assembly code. Paul selected the 186 because it had a very good I/O [input/output] structure that allowed a lot of simultaneous data to come in on a lot of data lines. The 80186 was designed as a peripheral controller, whereas the 80286, 386, 486, and so on are really designed more for desktop PC usage. But it's the same family and same instruction set.

Was it a new experience for you to incorporate a microprocessor in a synthesizer?

Not really. The predecessor product, the Quadra, was fakey but was among our first microprocessor-based instruments. It used the 8048, which was a single-chip microprocessor that scanned all the keys, scanned all the front-panel controls, and set up all the patches. The Quadra was basically an old ARP Omni with a two-note synthesizer layered up on top of it.

So the Quadra was a string synthesizer that used divide-down circuitry?

Yes, married with two VCOs, a VCF, and a VCA on a lead line, and the ability to do a split bass. It was a "quick and dirty," and it was a David Friend concept, whereas the Chroma was designed from the ground up.

Going back further in ARP's history, ARP was in the lead. It was *the* largest synthesizer company for years. But they kept looking for shortcuts. And the Quadra is an example. They also really got taken down a black hole because of a guitar synthesizer called the Avatar. Meanwhile, [Sequential Circuits'] Dave Smith came out of left field with this thing called the Prophet, which was really a multi-channel polyphonic synthesizer — the really first polyphonic synthesizer. But within the higher level at ARP, they all pooh-poohed that, saying, "Oh, we can't be bothered by some guy coming out of left field like that." Well, he ate our lunch. So when my team sat down and we conceived the Chroma, we said, "Look, we've got to get back to knitting, doing what we do best, and really up the ante." That's really what the Chroma was all about.

Do you still have a Chroma?

I don't have a Chroma. That's something that I really, really want. And a 2600. The reason I don't have either is that back in those days, I did that for a living, and when I went home I didn't want to see the instruments. Now, I regret not keeping one of each.

How many Chromas were made?

My guess is about 3,000. We built the first 50 in Massachusetts. We set up a production line in the Gulbransen organ factory, which was also a CBS company at the time, and had just all kinds of quality control problems. Working with CBS wasn't easy. We then moved the manufacturing for a time to Fullerton, California, in the Fender Rhodes plant. That was a trial.

As I said, we built a pilot run of 50 until we could prove that everything was in good shape. Then we moved. CBS in their infinite wisdom said, "Oh, no. You can't manufacture, you aren't a manufacturing plant, you don't know anything about this, send it to our plant in Deerfield." I think it

was Deerfield. Well, it was their Gulbransen plant, which is in the middle of nowhere, in the middle of a cornfield. "They know all about building stuff." "Okay," I said to myself. "I'm not sure how I feel about this, but they're the new bosses." So I went with my team out there and we tried to train these people to build synthesizers. Now these were people who had built home organs for 15 or 20 years, and that's all they knew.

The Chroma was a 16-channel instrument. It had eight dual-channel voice cards that plugged into a motherboard for easy servicing. The first thing the Gulbransen people did as a cost-cutting measure was to start processing the channel cards in a new way. They had just started using this water-soluble flux in their production line. The boards were soldered and put through a water-soluble solution. The process saved a lot of money and it was better than doing the old method of flux removal — a manufacturing process for removing the flux from circuit boards. But the process was still experimental at the time.

Anyway, they ran about 300 or 400 channel boards through this process, and we immediately started hearing about problems in the field from customers — often major-name customers — where their instrument would simply never stay in tune, even with all the computerized adjustments.

It took us the longest while to figure out what was going on, and we finally figured out that it had to be the flux-removal process. But the manager of the plant told me, "No, it can't be. You don't know anything about manufacturing, you're just a nerdy engineer. We know about this stuff, you don't."

Finally Robert Hartford, who did all the detective work, took the boards up to a testing lab in New Hampshire and proved that each of the circuit boards had been contaminated through this process such that whenever the humidity rose, the oscillators would go sour. CBS ended up eating probably about $40,000 to $50,000 worth of channel cards, because there was no way to salvage them. They had to ditch the entire production line and move the whole thing to California, where they built tube amps and Fender Rhodes pianos.

Wasn't there a slave unit for the Chroma as well?

Yes, the Chroma Expander, which provided another 16 voice channels. We basically chopped off the keyboard and connected it to the Chroma through the ports on the back to go from 16 to 32 channels.

Herbie Hancock was one of the first of many early Chroma buyers. I ran into him a year ago and he said he still has his Chroma. I remember the first time he came up to the keyboard at a NAMM show in Anaheim. He laid down some riffs that

Descendant of the Chroma was the Chroma Polaris, which cost $1,495 and sported MIDI, a built-in sequencer, and interfaces for Apple IIe computer and the Chroma. The Polaris was designed and executed after Dodds' departure from CBS, "although its seeds were sown right before I left," he explains. "The Polaris was a spin-off from the Chroma, conceived on the drawing board as a cut-down, slimmed, low-cost version." Street value of the Polaris runs from $200 to $400.

were classically Hancock. Of course, I'd captured what he played using the computer. Then I started changing the voice as it played back, and you should have seen his eyes pop. This was before MIDI. I sped it up, slowed it down, reallocated the voices. This is all stuff that's perfectly routine now.

Was the computer just for sequencing?

Well, it had a precursor to the MIDI interface. It was very similar in ways. You could send out multi-channel information, velocity data, and time-stamp information. In fact, it was on the basis of what came out of the Chroma that we got into arguments with Dave Smith on what MIDI should look like.

As a parenthetical story to that, I was on the first MIDI committee, but CBS came down and said, "Uh oh, we don't like the way in which they're forming this committee." They were worried about anti-trust. As a result of that, they forbade me as a CBS employee from participating, and I was blocked from attending all but the first three MIDI meetings. After that, I wasn't allowed to go. But our velocity stuff got in there, and our opto-isolator [the circuits in a MIDI jack] concepts got in there and were picked up by the Japanese.

There was something about the Chroma that caused the R&D people who were involved with it to say, "This is something really worthwhile to do. This is something that the world needs." There's something magical about the Chroma that really bonded people, making them say, "Let's, at all costs [and sometimes those costs were high, personally], make the best instrument we possibly can." We didn't make the best possible instrument in the world, but the devotion to trying was sincere and that's what kept that team together. That's what kept it moving and, even when ARP died, the Chroma lived on. It transcended a corporation's death and kept that team together, and was the sole reason everything moved forward from there.

DIGITAL SYNTHS & SAMPLERS

SECTION 4

P P G   W A V E

Vintage German Digital

BY MARK VAIL

We depend mostly on digital sound generators for synthesis these days. With affordable digital recording technology apparently just around the corner, let's take a look back at a digital synthesis pioneer who put numerous digital synths in the hands of artists like Tangerine Dream and Thomas Dolby when analog was all anybody knew anything about.

The pioneer was a German engineer named Wolfgang Palm, and the company he founded was called PPG. Palm's line of PPG Wave instruments are without a doubt the most familiar synthesizers to emerge from Germany, known for their piercing digital sound, which brazenly included clock and aliasing noise in higher registers — musical grunge that gave the PPG that special sonic squawk. Perhaps the most popular PPG Wave sound was created by its ability to sweep through digital wavetables using envelope generators.

The span of Palm-developed electronic music products ranges from 1975 to today. Although PPG is no longer in business, Palm's latest develop-ments can be found in the synthesis circuits of the Waldorf MicroWave synth module (1990) and the full-blown Waldorf Wave synth (1993) — '90s-vintage PPG Wave instruments.

As with most of the relative handful of synth pioneers, Palm's quest began small, and slowly snowballed. "In the early '70s, I was playing organ in a small band in Hamburg," Palm recalls. "It started when I first heard Emerson, Lake & Palmer's 'Lucky Man' on the radio. I listened to the portamento sounds, the glide effect, and I thought, 'How do they do that?' Nobody in Germany had a synthesizer at that time. So I built my own VCOs and connected them to my organ keyboard. I made some crazy things, including simple sequencers. After some time, I became known to somebody who owned a Minimoog and wanted it to work with my sequencer. In the process of connecting the sequencer to his Minimoog, I became more familiar with the idea of voltage control of oscillators, filters, and amplifiers. Gradually, I made my own modular system. Then I built some special keyboards for the guy who handled Moog's distribution in Germany. He had customers who wanted

A complete PPG Wave system, ca. 1982. On top at the left is the Expansion Voice Unit, resting on top of the Waveterm (original version). To the right are the PRK Processor keyboard and the Wave 2.3.

duo- and quadraphonic keyboards. That led to my association with the members of Tangerine Dream, particularly Chris Franke and Edgar Froese. They had a great interest in new instruments and getting their Moog and ARP synths modified. So they invested a lot of money and time and ideas, and helped me start my business — building analog synthesizers."

VITAL STATISTICS

Description: The first widely available digital wavetable synthesizer, with analog filters, sequencing, and user sampling option.

Produced: Wave 2.2, 1982–84; Wave 2.3, 1984–87; Waveterm, 1982–87.

Approximate Numbers Made: Wave 2.2, 300; Wave 2.3, 700; Waveterm, 300.

Manufacturer: PPG (Palm Products Germany), Hamburg, Germany (out of business). PPG designer Wolfgang Palm now works for Waldorf, a division of TSI GmbH, in Waldorf, Germany.

Original Retail Prices: PPG Wave 2.2, $8,800; PPG Wave 2.3, $9,000 to $10,000 (later discounted to about $6,500); Waveterm A, $10,650; Waveterm B, $11,995.

Current Street Prices: Wave 2.2, $300 to $750. Wave 2.3, $500 to $800. Waveterm A, $1,000. Waveterm B, $500 to $1,500.

Current Dealer Prices: Wave 2.2, $500 to $1,000. Wave 2.3, $700 to $1,000. Wave 2.3 with MIDI, $1,000 to $2,000. Waveterm A, $1,000 to $1,500. Waveterm B, $750 to $1,800.

Service & Support: Airborne Music Electronics, 751 Onarga Ave., Los Angeles, CA 90042. (213) 257-1761. EPR Electronics, 505 California Ave., Middletown, NY 10940. (914) 343-1237.

Insider Information: *Keyboard* editor Dominic Milano wrote the manual for the Wave 2.3. . . . Thomas Dolby has been using PPG synths for years. In *Keyboard's* Aug. '83 Dolby cover story, he claims his PPG is ". . . actually a prototype that predated the 2.2 by several years. It was originally designed to run light shows for Tangerine Dream." According to PPG designer/developer Wolfgang Palm, Dolby was using the PPG 340 Wave Computer and 380 Event Generator. "The 340/380 was not a compact synthesizer," Palm reveals. "You could call it a digital modular system. It included three 19" rack units, a keyboard, and a computer terminal."

Palm had studied electronic engineering, and welcomed the opportunity to make money from his synth-design hobby. Within a few years, he designed what he calls "the first programmable synthesizer," the PPG 1003. "That already had digital oscillators that you could tune by steps. It was a very strange instrument, with no knobs on the front panel, only increment and decrement buttons. All my customers were very afraid of it, because they didn't know how to handle it. I think we sold only six pieces of that machine."

But it was a start. His next goal — around 1977, when Oberheim's monster, two-case Eight Voice was the rage — was to produce a cheap polyphonic synthesizer that made new sounds. Palm's idea was to replace the VCOs, VCFs, and VCAs with digital oscillators for harmonic control and tuning stability. He hoped that wavetable synthesis, in which waveforms are generated by a computer reading a set of numbers stored in memory, would suffice without the need of analog filtering. During his groundbreaking research — Palm's instruments were the first digital wavetable synths — he found that the sound of simple waveforms produced digitally at 8-bit resolution wasn't as aesthetically appetizing as the fat mass of sound generated by the analog machines from his American competitors. At that time (1980/81), Palm was obliged to settle on 8-bit sound because of cost factors. "RAM and 12-bit converters were very expensive," Palm recalls.

Palm knew he had to develop complex wavetables to improve the sound quality of his synths. But even with more complex waveforms, Palm eventually realized that 8-bit digital sound was too brittle. "I found that wavetable switching wasn't smooth enough," he says, "So I returned to analog and connected a VCF and VCA to the digital oscillator. That was the Wave 2."

By 1982, Palm had advanced to the next generation, the Wave 2.2. Its configuration sounds remarkably similar to some late-'80s synth/sequencer combos: eight-voice polyphony with two digital oscillators per voice, 24dB-per-octave analog filtering, a pressure-sensitive keyboard, 200 patches, an eight-track digital sequencer, a ten-function arpeggiator, numerous split and layered

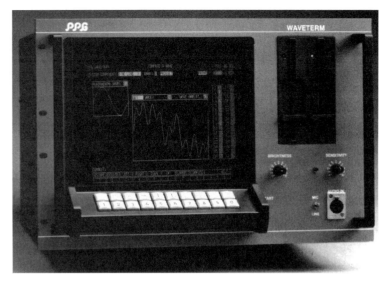

Closeup taken in 1985 of the PPG Waveterm B, easily distinguished from the original Waveterm by the size of its disk drives. Among other major improvements, the Waveterm B used 5¼" disks instead of the 8" monsters that its predecessor relied upon.

keyboard modes, and an event generator that you used to control the sequencer. The 2.2's oscillators could generate almost 2,000 different single-cycle waveforms (some created from samples of acoustic instruments like sax and piano), a huge increase over anything else that was available at the time. The 2.2 was introduced one year prior to MIDI, which resulted in significant problems for Palm, as we shall see.

Besides introducing the Wave 2.2 at the '82 Frankfurt Musik Messe (Music Fair trade show), Palm also unveiled a new machine for generating wavetables, the Waveterm. Thanks to this mutant computer terminal cleverly disguised as an industrial-grade, rack-mount video game, you could create new waveshapes by specifying points on a graph or by sampling acoustic sounds. You could display the resulting waveform on the Waveterm's CRT screen in order to perform a Fourier analysis. Still, the Waveterm was limited. "It was only 8-bit and had quite limited memory," Palm offers. The microprocessor chip used in the original Waveterm (which later became known as the "Waveterm A") was a 6809.

Meanwhile, Palm continued to develop his instrument's sample-playback capabilities. "In the Wave 2.2," he explains, "you could only play very small periods that consisted of 128 samples. The next step was the 2.3, in which the hardware was changed, and there were two modes. One was the digital oscillator mode, and the other was a sampler mode where you could play through the entire memory in a linear fashion, like on a sampler. Of course, you could transfer waveforms from one mode to the other, which was very interesting. You could sample something and then take out periods, make Fourier analyses, and put that back into a wavetable."

In 1983, PPG announced the Expansion Voice Unit (EVU) and the PRK Processor keyboard. The EVU provided 16 additional voices for the Wave 2.2. Since MIDI was still being formalized at that time, the EVU and Wave 2.2 were interfaced via PPG's 12-pin parallel communication bus. The PRK sported a 72-note (*F* to *E*) velocity-sensitive, weighted-action keyboard. In addition, the PRK could be loaded with up to eight PPG voice cards, each with four wavetables.

The Wave 2.3 was introduced at the 1984 Frankfurt Music Fair. Not only did it allow linear playback of samples in memory, but the resolution of those samples was increased to 12-bit, which greatly improved the Wave's sound quality. The 2.3 was also multitimbral, sounding up to eight different wavetables at once. And it had MIDI, the implementation of which is somewhat of a sore subject as far as Wolfgang Palm is concerned. "PPG had an 8-bit parallel bus system before MIDI came out," he says, "because we had to transfer samples from the Waveterm to the Wave — a very thick amount of data. Our bus was much quicker, so we didn't like MIDI very much. It was okay for some things. The problem was, MIDI was the second in-

terface that we had to use and support. It took much more effort to redesign our existing machines than it would have been to implement all the MIDI capabilities from the beginning."

During the next year, Palm continued development on the Waveterm and PRK, resulting in the introduction of the Waveterm B and PRK FD at Frankfurt in 1985. "The Waveterm B had more memory than the Waveterm A," Palm notes, "as well as 16-bit resolution and a better A/D converter. We also upgraded the Waveterm B with a 68000 processor, so it was quite powerful for that time. The Wave 2.3 was still only 12-bit, which was okay because each voice has 12 bits and if you play 16 oscillators together, you get quite good resolution, because it's been added together. The idea was that you sample at 16-bit, and then you can get the best out of that for 12 bits. So we developed some mathematical tools to convert samples from 16-bit to 12-bit."

The PRK FD also sported a 68000 CPU, as well as a 5¼" floppy drive, so that wavetables and samples from Waveterm B disks could be loaded and played. In addition, the PRK FD was outfitted with some impressive MIDI master controller capabilities, including a 99-track sequencer and four independently addressable MIDI outs. Unlike the PRK before it, the PRK FD had pitch-bend and mod wheels. Still, the PRK FD suffered from the same fault that the original PRK had: Both were limited to a simple two-digit LED display — hardly tolerable for keeping a handle on all the unit's functions.

As the synth industry exploded in the mid-'80s, Palm started seeing more of his customers opting for American and Japanese instruments. To maintain his business, he decided to produce some different products. "When the Waveterm had outlived its relevance, and with samplers like the E-mu Emulator II and Sequential Prophet-2000 getting very strong on the market, we tried to get into another market area. The logical step from the sampler was a digital disk recording system. So we developed the HDU (Hard Disk Unit), a 16-bit digital recording system with Winchester hard disks. At the 1986 Frankfurt Music Fair, we presented the whole PPG system — including the Waveterm, Wave 2.3, and PRK FD — along with the HDU. We had prepared a

Although it never made production, the PPG Realizer (1986) could be considered the first virtual instrument. The Realizer was designed to be capable of digitally replicating numerous synthesis methods, but its development ended — along with PPG as a manufacturer — in 1987, before Wolfgang Palm could perfect its operation. Here the Realizer, which was slated to cost $65,000, mimics the Minimoog.

song with 16 sequenced synth voices and the HDU playing some vocal tracks together in sync with the sequencer. It was quite surprising for some people. It was quite a big step for the MIDI world. But the problem with the HDU was that we didn't know exactly how to plant it in the market. The first idea was to promote it as a MIDI-controllable machine for the typical musician. But it was too expensive for the normal musician. Then we decided to get more into the studio and professional recording area. These people wanted to use the HDU in a different way than a musician would use it. There are so many applications — including film synchronization and video — and every application has different requirements. That was a big problem."

The HDU's standard 85Mb storage capacity could sample six minutes' worth of stereo material at a 44.1kHz sampling rate with 16-bit resolution. It allowed you to alter the playback speed without altering pitch — an impressive achievement that apparently resulted in some distortion of the sound quality.

At the same time, Palm was developing a multi-purpose, all-digital music machine. It was called the Realizer, and it combined digital sound production, processing, recording, sequencing, and mixing in one system. "That was a big step into the future," Palm admits. "With the Realizer, you sampled something in and it remained in the digital domain inside the machine, so you never lose any quality."

Although PPG didn't stay in business long

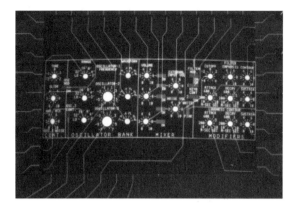

Close-up of the Realizer-image Minimoog, complete with front-panel knobs and sliders dedicated to duplicating those on the Mini.

enough to get the Realizer into production, Palm did get it to perform some pretty interesting tricks. "The Realizer had all four basic kinds of sound generation: an analog model, an FM model, wavetable synthesis, and a sampler. But it was never finished, because it was too big a project. We didn't have the manpower."

Like many American synth manufacturers, PPG went down even though it had such a good reputation among synthesists. Wolfgang Palm summarizes the difficulties: "The PPG keyboards didn't sell so well anymore, because everybody came out with a sampler. The HDU didn't sell well because it wasn't in the right marketplace. And we didn't have the manpower and finances to finish the Realizer. The truth is, I was never a real businessman; I'm just a developer. In the end, running the PPG business was a lot of hassle and stress; it was not the thing I really wanted. It was the thing that had to be done because, of course, you must earn money and you must sell machines."

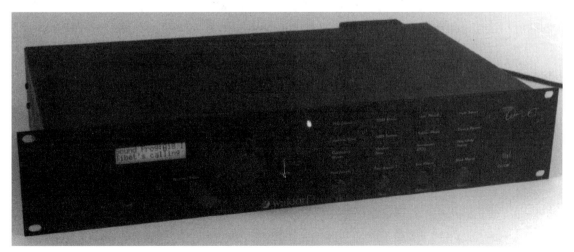

The currently produced Waldorf Microwave bears PPG designer Wolfgang Palm's synthesis ideas in a rack-mount MIDI module.

DIGITAL KEYBOARDS SYNERGY & CRUMAR GDS

Additive Synthesis Epitomized

BY MARK VAIL

Some people latch onto an instrument and stick with it for years, squeezing all the music out of it that they can. Case in point, Wendy Carlos and the Synergy. Nobody has focused as much attention on this additive-synthesis machine as Carlos.

Wendy, who brought the Moog synthesizer more fame than ever before in 1968 with *Switched-On Bach*, scored the Disney computer-world flick *Tron* in 1982 using the Synergy's predecessor, the GDS. Subsequently, she used a pair of Synergys to create two stunning synthesizer albums, *Digital Moonscapes* (1984) and her alternate-tuning tour-de-force *Beauty in the Beast* (1986). In 1988, she teamed up with musical satirist "Weird Al" Yankovic to do an updated version of Prokofiev's *Peter and the Wolf*. The GDS and Synergys were back once more, with the addition of the GDS/Synergy progeny, three Mulogix Slave 32s.

To this day, Wendy Carlos depends on these instruments — along with more contemporary synths like the Yamaha SY77 and Kurzweil K2000 — in composing and producing her music. "I still

count on them for a great many sounds," she tells us, "because nothing has yet come along to equal them in certain respects. The Synergy was very powerful, and probably *the* most sophisticated synthesizer, in some respects, that's ever been built." An instrument that can command that kind of praise and the attention of such a renowned artist must be very special.

Clinical Beginnings. In the late '70s, digital synthesis was a concept that most people had only heard or read about. But at Bell Labs, experiments and developments were well under way that would eventually lead to the GDS, or General Development System. "The GDS came out of some early research at Bell Laboratories in the early '70s," explains Mercer "Stoney" Stockell, who himself shared in developing the GDS and Synergy. "Hal Alles, a researcher there, designed the high-speed additive engine that was put into the GDS and later systems. He was a very bright man. The work originally came out of some stuff he was supposed to be doing for echo-cancellation on telephone lines.

"This was before the divestiture of the Bell system," Stockell adds, "and Bell Labs at that time was a non-profit organization. There was a lot of research, and numerous things were invented there that benefited mankind — things like the transistor. If they had been a profit organization and they'd had a patent on that right now, they would not be in the telephone business at all. They did the Telstar satellites and various other things. It was a very, very interesting place.

"After Hal developed this oscillator, people from both the music industry and other research areas decided that they wanted to do some neat things with it. One interested party was Music Technology, a division of the Italian company Crumar and my employer. They realized that the technology had a ten-year leap on other musical products of the time, things like the Prophet-5. So they wanted to get this technology out of Bell Labs.

"Now, Bell Labs had no experience at all in selling anything. They didn't know how to do that. When we approached them to buy the oscillator technology, they said it would take their legal staff a couple of years to research how to sell it to us. So the suggestion was made to Hal that he publish the thing and make it public domain, then we could use it, which was approved by the Laboratory, because they did that all the time. Procedurally, *that* was okay, but you couldn't throw money at them, because they didn't know how to do that. They had no built-in procedures for accepting money. Probably for a non-profit organization, that's par excellence."

After enlisting Hal Alles as an advisor, MTI hired a development staff comprising Stockell, Kevin Doren, Wing Moi, and Jerry Kaplan. "All of us really had different types of expertise," says Stockell, "but we weren't very well organized. We were located in the back of this warehouse. Ernie Briefel and his son Dennis, who now has a company called Music Industries, were very supportive of the project, probably to a fault, which is why Music Technologies is not here any more . . . or a contributing factor anyway. They put a lot of time, effort, and money into this project and we built this thing called the GDS.

"The GDS was something that we'd really built for our own internal use. It included an Industrial Microsystems Z-80 CPU with dual 8" floppy drives

(256k bytes per floppy!) and a computer terminal, and a keyboard controller with a very arbitrary control panel: 32 sliders, 12 rotary pots, 16 pushbutton switches with lights in them, and LEDs attached to everything, but that was it. The reason that it was so arbitrary was that we had no idea where we were going with this stuff, but we needed a box of some kind to control it. Any of the earlier digital machines that were worked on in labs were pretty much the same way: racks of sliders, knobs, and joysticks — anything we could find — hooked up to PDP-11s [computers] and all other kinds of hardware. We didn't really want to build them to sell them. The commercial aspect was what Music Technologies wanted to do."

Thirty-two sliders and 12 knobs? Performing synthesists might drool at the thought of having front-panel access to so many controls, but they weren't intended for real-time interaction as much

The General Development System, manufactured under the Crumar name, descended from the work of Hal Alles at Bell Laboratories. Costing $27,500, the GDS comprised a CPU with two built-in 8" floppy drives, computer terminal, and the keyboard controller unit, which had lots of generalized sliders, knobs, and buttons because, in the beginning, the designers weren't sure what it was supposed to do.

as for programming sounds. That's why Wendy Carlos still creates all her Synergy timbres on the GDS, which was a necessity at first until a computer interface and software were developed to allow programming on the Synergy itself.

"The GDS did its job," Stockell reflects. "We built up voice libraries, we had people using them and playing with them, and they were a good development platform for us to be able to migrate this technology into an extremely cheaper box at about $5,000 or $6,000."

The Next Generation. With their development system up and running, the Music Technologies team — er, now Digital Keyboards — focused on the less expensive system. "Next we came out with this instrument called the Synergy," Stockell re-

veals. "The Synergy was a push-button machine and it didn't offer any programming like the GDS, but it had some interesting aspects to it. One is that it had a sequencer. It was the first keyboard that had a sequencer anything like this. The sequencer allowed you to overdub and play on top of the sequence. It was real easy to use.

"Another thing was, the Synergy provided the ability to be able to control multiple sounds [up to four] simultaneously from the keyboard — also a first. You could do that with some analog synths, but you couldn't before actually figure out which finger on which key was going to play what sound, and have absolute control over that kind of thing. It could track your hands up and down the keyboard. You could get six floating split

VITAL STATISTICS

Description: Digital additive synthesis machines: Crumar General Development System, Digital Keyboards Synergy, and Mulogix Slave 32. The oscillator system used by all three was based on an article entitled "An Inexpensive Digital Sound Synthesizer" by Bell Labs' Dr. Hal Alles in the *Computer Music Journal*, vol. 3, no. 3, published in Sept. '79.

Production Dates: GDS, 1979. Synergy, 1982 to 1985. Mulogix Slave 32, 1986 to 1989.

Common Features: 32 programmable digital oscillators with patching network. Each oscillator limited to a 32kHz sampling rate for a 0–14.5kHz frequency range and a 12-bit amplitude range for a dynamic range of 72dB per oscillator — the output was 16-bit with a 92dB dynamic range.

GDS Features: 61-note velocity-sensitive keyboard (*C* to *C*). 32 sliders, 12 rotary knobs, 16 push buttons, joystick, spring-loaded rotary pitch-bend knob, and expression-pedal input. Z-80 microcomputer-based general-purpose computer system with 64k of RAM, two double-density 8" floppy drives, and computer terminal.

Synergy Features: 74-note velocity-sensitive keyboard (*E* to *F*). 24 on-board factory presets (about 200 bytes each), four of which are playable simultaneously in various assignment modes: Unison (all voices sound together for each key), rotating (each note triggers the next voice in sequence, round-robin style), first-available, fixed-split, and floating-split. Four user program slots for storing combinations. Velocity cross-switching. Built-in four-track polyphonic digital sequencer with 1,860-event capacity, no editing, no external sync, individual track looping. Cartridge port for loading 24 alternate presets. Stereo outputs. In his Oct. '82 review of the Synergy in *Keyboard,* Dominic Milano said the original presets "range from bowed violins complete with bow scratch to fuzz-guitar-like sounds that get ballsier the faster you press the keys. There are also some sound-effects presets that range from thunder to 'digital synthesizer' sounds. The bowed-string sounds, which sound like a *single* violin or cello, not a string section, are especially nice." Non-MIDI serial interface implemented in 1983 for program and sequence storage using a microcomputer (Kaypro).

Synergy II+ Features: Addition of MIDI, 24 user-voice RAM, RS-232 computer port, and Synergy voicing software (Synergy Host Control System, or SYNHCS) for a Kaypro 2 or 4 portable computer. (Remember CP/M? It was an operating system used by Kaypros and a number of other microcomputers in the early to mid '80s. For further details, see *Vintage Computers.* [Just kidding.])

The third-generation Synergy II+ interfaced with a Kaypro computer so that users could edit and enter their own sounds. Previously, alternate sounds could only be entered via cartridges. To create your own Synergy sounds, you needed a GDS and a ROM burner for the cartridges. (See the cartridge resting to the right of the Kaypro keyboard.)

zones, and there were all kinds of different modes for assigning sounds to keys. The whole idea of the machine knowing things like which hand was playing what sound was very experimental. We thought it was wonderful. We would design this extensive piece of software to do this one thing, and there was really only one neat tune that you could make with it."

Slave 32 Features: Two-space rack-mount MIDI module version of the Synergy II+ with additional waveforms.

Manufacturer: A New York City–based division of Italian manufacturer Crumar. Then Music Technology, Inc., located in New Hyde Park on Long Island. Next, Digital Keyboards, a wholly owned independent subsidiary of Music Technologies. Digital Keyboards, or DK, was in Garden City Park, NY. Finally, Mulogix of Halesite, NY. (All out of business.)

Approximate Numbers Made: GDS, five or six. Synergy, 700 to 800. Slave 32s, 25 to 30.

Original Retail Prices: GDS, $27,500. Synergy, $5,295. Synergy II+, $5,995. Slave 32, $1,500 to $1,800. Synergy voice cartridges, $199 each ($400 for custom cartridges).

Current Street Prices: Synergy, $500 to $800. Synergy II+, $600 to $1,000.

Current Dealer Prices: Synergy, $800 to $1,200. Synergy II+, $1,000 to $1,200.

Current Support: Stoney Stockell, Korg USA, 89 Frost St., Westbury, NY 11590. "I managed to preserve all of the source code, files, and libraries," he says. "I've packed it all onto four or five 3.5" IBM-compatible high-density floppy disks. I'd be glad to copy it for Synergy II+ and Slave 32 owners."

Insider Information: Since 1975, Larry Fast has recorded solo synthesizer albums under the project name Synergy. From '76 to '81, he contributed to and used several developmental synthesis projects at Bell Labs, including the Alles synthesis engine. Fast's work on that instrument appears on *Games* (1979). Although he saw a prototype version of the then-unnamed "Small GDS" in early '80, Fast never gave DK permission to use the Synergy name and had to take legal action to protect his U.S. trademark. "To this day," he declares, "I still get questions about what happened to 'my' synthesizer company." . . . Wendy Carlos wasn't the only famous film-scoring GDS owner. Tangerine Dream's Christopher Franke became the first composer to use the GDS in a movie soundtrack. The flick was called *Thief*. . . . Other noted Synergy artists: Billy Cobham (*Glass Menagerie*), Hall & Oates (*H2O*), and Donald Fagen (*The Nightfly*). . . . What's a Synergy really worth today? "To somebody who doesn't know what it is, probably nothing," Stockell reports. "To people who have them and don't want to part with them, I don't know. I would call it one of those wonderful experiments. It's a museum piece. Without knowing what you're doing with the thing and having ways to be able to manipulate the hardware that's inside that box, by itself, face value, it's probably worthless. I would call it a research piece."

Wendy Carlos describes some of the Synergy's controls and capabilities: "On the far left of the Synergy's front panel, there's a joystick that goes left-to-right for pitch-bend and up-and-down for modulations. I prefer the two Minimoog-style rotary wheels for pitch-bend and modulation, but the Synergy had none of those. It also had some rotary knobs for globally controlling timbre, volume sensitivity, vibrato rate, amplitude, and its random rate — aperiodicity is the term they use. Threshold settings allowed keyboard velocity to dynamically control volume or timbre changes and, depending on how the voice was built, could in effect act to change the brightness or inharmonicity in the sound, or some other quality that a live [acoustic] instrument would have if it were played more forcefully. I generally tend to leave those settings in a place where the velocity of the keystrokes would do that job for me, but I could always change the interrelations on how volume and timbre would be affected by velocity by touching those four knobs.

"The keyboard had no aftertouch, and even though release velocity was implemented in the voices, a hardware tie-in was never made. Release velocity would have been nice, but I pushed for getting the microtonality tables, because I thought that was more important at the moment, and I guess I still do.

"There were 24 internal patches that you could toggle rather quickly. The Synergy was among the first synthesizers to have a memory cartridge slot. You could get a device that would let you burn your own ROM chips and you could save your own cartridges of voices. I even built DK a library of voices that they later sold when the machine was in its latter stage of being commercially available."

To avoid any confusion, Synergy cartridges stored patch data, not waveforms. Although a number of current synthesizers from manufacturers like Roland, Yamaha, and Peavey can read sampled waveform data from cards and disks, cartridges and cards for synthesizers in those days could only store patch data. In addition, the GDS was still required at this point to program Synergy timbres, which then could be "burned" into cartridges.

Wendy continues: "There was a convenient mini-sequencer in the Synergy that I used in *Beauty in the Beast* — the most mature Synergy project that I have done, because of the microtonal tables. I haven't needed to use the built-in sequencer since then, because a current computer-based MIDI sequencer is much more flexible and powerful. It will also remember what you've done, whereas the Synergy sequencer had volatile memory that forgot everything when you turned the machine off.

"The Synergy's oscillator table was 12-bit. Its frequency tables were specified to be 16-bit, and then they were interpolated to 20-bit, which is how they're able to be used on the microtonality tables. So they're really a good bit better — and I don't mean the pun — than the spec might look. And if you're putting together big additive voices, 12-bit isn't a big limitation, because you'd have to crank down the level of 16-bit oscillators so that the total didn't exceed 16 total [at the output DAC] in the end anyway.

"I would love to see somebody devise a new version of the Synergy, but the main thing that has

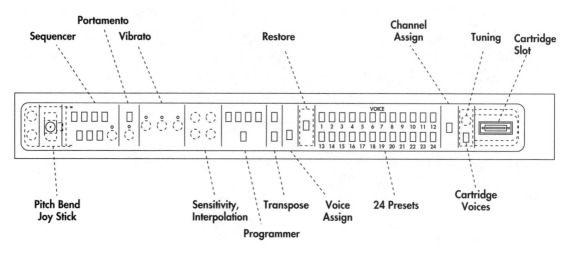

Illustration of the Synergy's front-panel controls.

Sequencer
Portamento
Vibrato
Restore
Channel Assign
Tuning
Cartridge Slot

Pitch Bend Joy Stick
Sensitivity, Interpolation
Transpose
Voice Assign
24 Presets
Cartridge Voices

Programmer

never been duplicated on anything else is that Synergy voices were defined two-dimensionally. First, the voice is defined over the pitch domain so that the timbre actually changed as you went up and down the keyboard. You could voice the instrument for the low region and high region separately, and then run an interpolation from low to high. The timbre would actually change as you went from the bottom note to the top note. If you've ever heard my record *Digital Moonscapes*, there are a few places on one of the movements where the instrument, as it's playing up and down the keyboard, turns from one sound to another, such as from a cello into a trumpet, then into a clarinet, that kind of trick. And that's done because the Synergy lets you interpolate between timbres. That's one dimension.

"The second dimension is that it interpolates for loudness, which means that the loud-attack notes are a different patch than the soft-attack notes. Once again, that's a great way to work compared to any of the other machines I know of. It would be like having a two-dimensional sample of any live instrument. Assume that you wanted to sample something like a marimba. You want it to play on this lowest note, on a middle note, on a high note, and then two places in between each of those, and you wanted to do each of those at pianissimo, at piano, at forte, and fortissimo. And you wanted to run these all over. Well, my god, you're going to have to multisample the thing 30 or 40 times. That's the sort of model in the Synergy, and I know of no instrument now that lets you have that kind of model, which is so much like live instruments, and so unlike the way the rest of the synthesizers are done. It's one of the reasons I'm really unwilling to let go of the instruments now. I would be giving up an awfully rich resource by turning to any of the other alternatives out there.

"These are ideas that could be used and developed by other manufacturers. But obviously, with a recession on, nobody's likely to do much of anything right now."

Carlos has a great deal of respect for Hal Alles and Stoney Stockell. "Hal was the originator of the silicon engine, the hardware, that made the Synergy oscillators. He tried to come up with a varia-

tion on his other five generations of digital synthesizers that he had built at Bell Labs. He did this as a mature stage, trying to find a commercial instrument that would be available to the public at a modest cost, because up until that time, the only way you could build additive voices and complex AM and FM voices was at a great cost, something over $25,000. If they could get involved with some other team to develop a synthesizer, Hal and Stoney would still be among the best people to develop a new synthesizer."

About Additive Synthesis. Traditionally, additive synthesis comprised gobs of sine waves (which produce the fundamental frequency only and have no overtones) sounding at various harmonic frequencies, combined together to generate a complex timbre. "The Synergy oscillators actually knew of two waveforms," Stoney Stockell reveals, "sine and a modified triangle wave. Modified meaning that it was sort of triangle for the first three or four harmonics, and then sine wave thereafter. It sort of petered out. The reason for that was that there were no such things as digital filters in the Synergy. We had one, sort of, in there, but if you had real triangle waves or square waves that went on out to the nth harmonic, there would be no way to control the sidebands.

"For every partial generator on the Synergy, you had ways of modifying the frequency and the amplitude. Each one had a multi-part envelope generator, which could be looped and synchronized with other envelope generators. This means that you could use the envelope generators to draw a low-frequency waveform — piecewise — up to about 1,000 points a second, and synchronize or not synchronize it with other waveforms that are running to drive either frequency or amplitude changes.

"The other thing that was interesting, and the way that the Synergy controlled amplitude without a multiplier, was by doing two lookups on a waveform, one at a delta phase from another waveform lookup — in other words, the first lookup would be the full-amplitude sample and another lookup on the wavetable was done at some delta phase point from that, and the result was summed, which allowed control of the amplitude using phase cancelation. This meant that as the amplitude went up and down, the phase of the output signal for that partial rotated 90 degrees. Now that might sound like a stupid thing to do, but actually you'll realize that it was a very smart thing to do if you've ever tried to play around with a DX7 or any of the other early digital machines. The reason was that you could hit these phase-locking points in the keyboard where partials on other FM synths would be canceled out. Since the Synergy had the amplitudes and phase moving around, you just didn't have that happen, and it gave it a lot of texture and various other weird things happening that made it very rich, considering you only had 32 oscillators to work with.

"Additive synthesis as a theoretical way to make sounds is probably a wonderful thing. But I don't think the technology is here yet to effectively use it. It requires an inordinate amount of computation, because for every single harmonic you have to independently control its amplitude, phase, and frequency to make it work. That's what this early machine did, but it only did it for 32 partials. That really didn't do much as far as additive went."

Even though the GDS and Synergys were additive synthesis machines, they did have filter systems. "The GDS's filter system, which was partially used in the Synergy, was pretty wild," says Stockell. "Imagine a rack of 128-band graphic equalizers. With the joystick, you could pull a band out of the middle and move it. The result would sound like the movement of a crude formant. Between discrete equalizer bands there were interpolations, so it had a completely smooth flow to it. The motion of this joystick phenomenon would be played back on every key when you played it, independently, which gave it a tremendous capability to have these filtering functions run around. For it to do this, we had a poor little Z-80 computer trying to compute what was going on with the envelope generators and the current slopes and ramp generators. The ramp generators were actually implemented with some reasonable hardware, not a poor computer trying to do this. But it was actually trying to manipulate all the partials that way using these lookup tables. A very smart idea, but just not enough computing power. Nowadays, that stuff would be easy."

Pull up the Synergy's lid like a car hood and what do you see? Not as many circuits as the cavernous lid would suggest. "You might say, 'Oh, geez, it only has two circuit boards in there,'" Stockell says. "But most people didn't build their own computers out of 200 small integrated circuits running at 30MHz, when the parts were only guaranteed to run up to 25MHz. I mean, this was a little bit of black magic."

Favorite Marketing Tricks. "Tom Piggott was the musical advisor on the Synergy," Stockell recalls. "We had a problem with Tom: He was a pretty good player — there was no question about his playing ability — and he was a good thinker on this sort of stuff. He was very imaginative about the sound he could make. The problem was he was also a *salesman*. He could take any defect in the machine and turn it into a positive thing by writing some kind of musical line around it. Then it got to be such an interesting thing that he'd forget to tell the developers about these problems. So we were always behind the eight ball."

Shootout at the Digital Corral. The Synergy wasn't the only early digital machine to vie for market share. Yamaha, whose most interesting synthesizer to date had been the polyphonic CS-80, dipped its toe into the pool at about the same time that the Synergy came along. "The other digital keyboards came from Yamaha. They had two, the GS-1 and GS-2, at the same trade show in Chicago that we introduced the Synergy [1982]. The Synergy was about half the price of the GS-2, and it could make more than one sound at once, which was a unique idea."

The Synergy team may have won that round, but at the next NAMM show Yamaha turned the tables. "After being put away at one trade show," Stockell remembers, "Yamaha came back and definitely did a job on almost everybody with the DX7, which absolutely killed the Synergy."

When MTI shut down the DK division in the first quarter of 1985, Stockell teamed with Jim Wright and Jerry Ptascynski (pronounced *Zan' ski*) to form Mulogix. Their lone product was the Slave 32, which was basically a Synergy squeezed into a two-space rack-mount module with an improved MIDI implementation. The Slave 32 could play sounds off Synergy cartridges, so Wendy Carlos added three of them to her GDS/Synergy collection. (Additive synthesists need more oscillators than anyone else.) She reports that the Slave 32s work much like newer multitimbral MIDI synths, but they don't always play Synergy sounds correctly. "The Synergy software had to be rewritten for the Slave 32, and there are some funny things that they do that aren't quite the way the Synergy worked. In some ways, they have some small, unresolved bugs that sometimes cause ramp times to come on too soon or have a slight double hiccup when the sound is released, stuff like that. You have to work around those problems."

Twenty-five to 30 Slave 32s were produced before Mulogix stopped doing business in 1989 or '90. For the past four years, Stoney Stockell has worked for Korg USA in New York. He's a reliable source of Synergy software support. "There are people who end up with a Synergy who find me here and I still send them stuff when they can't find it, if I can find it."

Yamaha's FM Patent. Whereas MTI was freely able to develop the digital oscillator designs patented by Hal Alles, Yamaha licensed the exclusive use of FM, the patent for which was held by John Chowning. Yamaha, whose license expires in 1995, actively pursued and prosecuted any music manufacturer whose instrument could perform frequency modulation. If they didn't abandon the technique altogether, some manufacturers avoided trouble by calling their synthesis method another name; others didn't speak of the capability at all.

Wendy Carlos voices a complaint shared by many in the music instrument industry: "The GDS included FM long before Yamaha ever incorporated it. In fact, FM is a process that I used on my earlier *Switched-On Bach* records. I thought that for one manufacturer to have a patent on FM seemed rather surprising. But these things do happen. But Yamaha got the patent rights from John Chowning, so DK never quite made a big deal of their FM. They called it phase-modulation, which it also was, but they had really the first of that kind of modulation, and in some ways it's still far more sophisticated than anything Yamaha developed, until the SY77."

Obsolescence & Designer's Responsibilities. If

the GDS hadn't shown up on the groundbreaking albums and in the movies that it did, it might have appeared in Ted Greenwald's "It Came from the Music Industry" retrospective. As stated in the Crumar General Development System brochure printed by DK, "Because the functional capabilities of the GDS are under software control, the unit will never become obsolete. As new digital synthesis concepts and software packages are developed, they will be available to all GDS users, ensuring that the unit will remain current. . . . A GDS purchase, therefore, is as much an investment in digital sound synthesis as it is the acquisition of a fine musical instrument."

Chuckle as we might at those bold promises, Stoney Stockell deserves credit for his dedication to the Synergy. "When you spend a lot of effort to build anything, I don't think there's any such thing as being able to walk away from it. Anything you put years' worth of work into, you're sort of married to, whether you like it or not. I think anybody who is a builder of products that people buy should have that kind of an attitude. You have to support the things that you've built. There's a certain amount of trust that people put in you when they bought this stuff. Maybe it's up to the company, but I think it's the designer myself. I take it more personally than that."

Although he still answers GDS, Synergy, and Slave 32 owners in distress, Stoney doesn't share Wendy's devotion to these instruments. "I have a working GDS in my basement if you want one, but you'll have to pay for shipping."

A Mulogix Slave 32 mounted in a rack above the only rack-mount Synergy ever produced, property of San Francisco Bay Area keyboardist Barry Gould. Gould somehow managed to convince Stoney Stockell to make a rack-mount Synergy, a job that wasn't too much fun. "There's only one of those, and Barry has it. Why did we build it? We built it because we happened to like Barry, all right? That was the only reason."

FAIRLIGHT CMI

Trailblazing Megabuck Sampler

BY MARK VAIL

ts name brings to mind a list of major people in the music industry — Peter Gabriel, Stevie Wonder, Jan Hammer, Thomas Dolby — who made it a centerpiece in their studios. By today's 16-bit standards, the 8-bit sample resolution of the original Fairlight Computer Musical Instrument, or CMI, doesn't sound impressive. But it was good enough for them.

Its name is also synonymous with a price tag that would financially bury most musicians. To them, the Fairlight CMI was a mystical computer music system, as magical and inaccessible as the machinery hidden behind the Wizard of Oz's curtains.

Where did this groundbreaking instrument come from? Look south, to the Land Down Under. Specifically, Sydney, Australia. That's where Kim Ryrie and Peter Vogel licensed the dual-processor computer designed by engineer Tony Furse, then developed it into a device that allowed you to digitally record any acoustic sound, store it on disk, tweak its harmonic content using a light-pen on a video monitor, and play it and seven other independent sounds back from an 88-note keyboard.

Fairlight's co-founder Kim Ryrie fills us in on the CMI's history: "My experience in the synthesizer field started in about 1971, when we published the details for a build-it-yourself analog synthesizer in *Electronics Today Magazine*. A lot of its electronic design was done by Barry Wilkinson. It was basically a four-oscillator system, but we used a logarithmic voltage-control system instead of one-volt-per-octave, because even though the one-volt-per-octave environment was very flexible, it was hard to make oscillators that were pitch-stable at that time. I was told there had been a couple thousand of those things built by readers over the years. My frustration set in because of the inability to produce more natural sounds.

"Once we finished that project, I tried to think of ways of improving it. That's when I contacted Peter Vogel, who was an old school friend and a good electronics designer. I said, 'How 'bout we start a company and work on a synthesizer that's based on a microprocessor?' In those days, that meant the Motorola 6800, an 8-bit processor. The original idea was to use digital control of analog oscillators, a little like the Prophet-5. The Prophet-

The Fairlight Computer Musical Instrument, c. 1980. Its early development can be traced back to 1971 and '72. Eight-voice multitimbral/polyphonic, the CMI could store 1Mb of sample data per double-sided, double-density 8" floppy disk — the equivalent of about 40 wavesamples.

5, of course, didn't exist then, but that was sort of the idea we had in mind."

Ryrie and Vogel founded Fairlight in the last half of 1975. Around that time, they discovered Tony Furse, who had been working for several years for the Canberra School of Music on a digital

VITAL STATISTICS

Description: The first keyboard-based digital sampler, with software sequencing and additive synthesis capabilities.

Produced: CMI, 1980 to 82; Series II, 1982 to 83; Series IIx, 1983 to 84.

Approximate Numbers Made: CMI and Series II/IIx, about 300.

Manufacturer: Fairlight Instruments. Current contacts: Fairlight ESP Pty. Limited, 30 Bay Street, Broadway, Sydney, NSW, Australia 2007. 011-61-2 212-6111, fax 011-61-2 281-5503. U.S. support: The Digital Support Group, 626 N. Beachwood Dr., Los Angeles, CA 90004. (213) 460-4884, fax (213) 460-6120.

Original Retail Prices: Original CMI, $25,000 to $36,000; Series IIx, $32,000.

Current Street Prices: CMI, $1,000 to $1,500. Series II, $2,000 to $3,000.

Current Dealer Prices: CMI, $1,500 to $2,000. Series II, $3,500 to $5,500.

Upgrades & Repair: Series II to IIx upgrade, $2,000; IIx to IIx with SMPTE/MIDI, $3,000. (Series I to II upgrade no longer available.) Complete card-swap for Series I, $150 per card (13 to 16 cards total). Labor, $80/hr.

Insider Information: Each 8-bit wavesample in the original CMI was 20K in size: 16K plus 4K for control parameters. . . . According to Kim Ryrie, the first digitally sampled sound was of a barking dog, recorded in late 1977. "The dog belonged to one of our programmers. You could tell him to speak, and he would bark. The sample was stored in 16K of RAM on the first channel card, a giant, hand-wired circuit board."

Fairlight co-founders Kim Ryrie (L) and Peter Vogel seated in front of a Fairlight Series III, probably in 1986.

size single-cycle waveforms into a wavetable. Beyond that 4K of memory, there was about 64K of processor RAM.

"Tony had a fully hand-wired prototype, enclosed in a black anodized box with wood veneer ends. The box measured about 4' wide by 1½' high and deep. There were 20 8" x 8" circuit boards in it, each one full of TTL logic. The whole thing consumed about 2 kilowatts of power, and the RAM ran so hot that it had its own fan to cool it down. That machine was called the Qasar M8, which stood for multimode eight. It took about two hours to boot the machine, because it was booted from paper tape on a Model 33 teletype. Tony had even begun work on a light-pen interface to a graphics card.

"We arranged for a license agreement with Tony whereby we just took over the whole machine to continue development. The thing is, the Qasar was never intended for sampling — a word that hadn't yet been used to mean digital recording. With only 4K of memory, putting natural waveforms into it just wasn't viable."

The Original CMI's Long & Winding Evolution. Over the next couple of years, Ryrie and Vogel worked on their digital instrument. "We designed a graphics display with which you could

synthesizer based on a dual-6800 system. The 6800s operated out-of-phase with one another, accessing data in a common allocation of RAM.

The Qasar. Unlike the hybrid synthesizer Ryrie and Vogel had envisioned, Furse's instrument was totally digital. "For us, this was quite a revelation. At that time, Tony's machine didn't do much; there was still a lot of work to do. It had a common pool of 4K of RAM and there were eight channels that spoke to that RAM. The processors would synthe-

Predecessor to the Fairlight CMI, the Qasar, shown here in action sometime in the late '70s. (photo by Peter Vogel)

draw amplitude profiles for each of these harmonics across the screen. There were 32 vertical lines, each representing one waveform cycle. As you drew envelopes across the screen, it represented the level of each of up to 64 harmonics for each cycle. A channel would play one of these cycles for as long as you told it to, and then it would move on to the next one. It effectively animated a series of static waveforms as it played. The problem was that although it sounded interesting, it was extremely hard to make rich, meaningful sounds that way.

"Since we already had orders for the machine, we went ahead and designed all the circuit boards. The original 20 boards were all hand-wired, and that took about a year. All of the functions of each sound channel were divided across about 12 of those 20 cards. There were things like address generators, pitch generators, and so on. Each board would have one function and would do it eight times for the eight channels, which was good for

the research phase of the product, but not for the production phase, because it meant that you had all these different boards to make.

"Just as we got to that point, I thought, 'This is ridiculous.' Every one of the boards was different, which meant that if we sent one overseas, a spare-parts kit would virtually have to contain another machine. We weren't too clued up on how to run an efficient business in those days. So I said to Peter, 'Can you think of a way to get one channel onto one card? Then we could have eight cards. And forget about this common-memory idea, just put in a lot of memory.' By this time, DRAMs were coming out, and although there were 4K DRAMs, we decided to go with these new 16K DRAMs, eight on each card. At the time, this was an enormous amount of memory, and it was very expensive. Peter designed the new system over a span of about a month, and we had the prototype.

"What we realized was that by having 16K of RAM there, it was possible to actually sample a

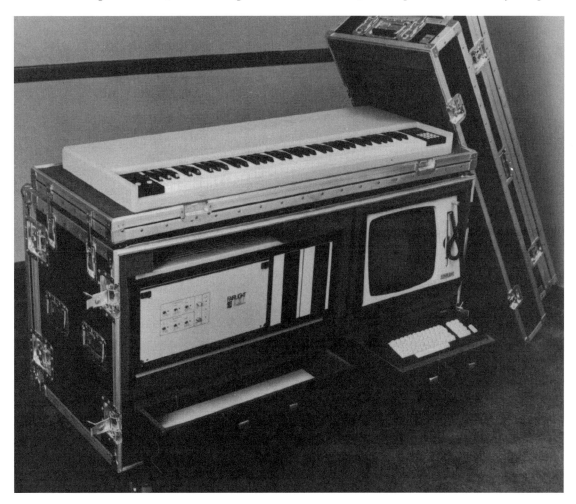

A CMI nearly ready for shipment.

real sound into memory. So Peter designed an 8-bit A-to-D converter, and lo and behold, this solved our sound quality problem.

"Then we decided to completely redesign the product to change its orientation. We kept the original dual-processor architecture that Tony had developed, and we added whatever requirements we needed for it to be a musical instrument. It all started to take shape during '78 and '79, and we brought the first CMI out in 1979."

To reach potential clients, Ryrie stressed the difference between the CMI and existing synthesizers. One way was to box its components in predominantly white cabinetry. "That was a conscious decision," Ryrie reveals. "Most synthesizers at the time were black or dark and we wanted to be different, because we didn't feel that we were selling a synthesizer."

Digital synthesis was a new and rare deal at the time, and obviously very expensive. Early CMI systems started at $25,000. At eight notes of polyphony, the cost per note was considerable — mainly because it took one whole circuit board to play each note. "The original CMI could only produce eight monophonic voices. If you wanted to play eight notes of the same sound, you had to load the same sound into each channel card."

Series II & IIx. Ryrie and Vogel continued to improve on the design of the CMI's channel cards. An increase in the sampling rate resulted in an improved high-frequency response and, in '82, the Series II's introduction. Where the Series I's frequency response suffered from a low top end of 10kHz, the Series II went up to 16kHz. Then in '84, Fairlight released the Series IIx, in which the 6800 processors were replaced by 6809s and MIDI functions were implemented.

Series III. By 1985, Ryrie and Vogel had ditched their earlier designs in favor of a new architecture. "We went back to a common pool of memory," Ryrie recalls, "changed from 8-bit to 16-bit sample resolution, and increased polyphony from eight to 16 channels. We also converted to 16- and 32-bit processors. There were now two 68000 processors — one for master control and waveform generation, the other for SMPTE and MIDI functions —

Since the necessary peripherals weren't available, Fairlight had to manufacture their own music and QWERTY keyboards, and video monitor. Programmers used the light pen to draw sound waveforms and amplitude envelopes for each harmonic.

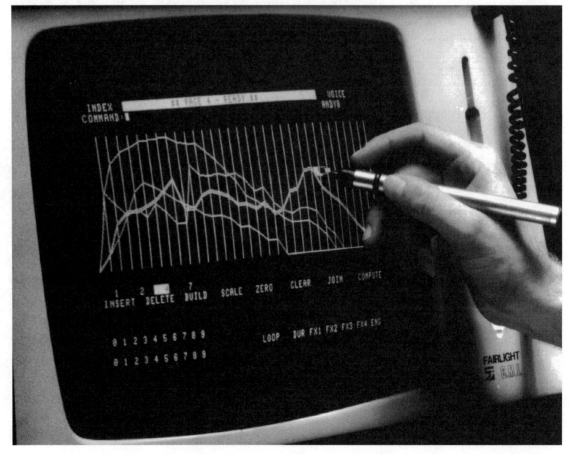

along with a 6809 for each sound channel and two 6809s for sequencing and graphics."

Page R. As the Fairlight design team refined the CMI's sampling and playback functions, they started development of a sequencer program for the instrument. Initially, Page 9 (as it was first known) could only record notes and their velocities. Overdubbing was possible, but editing was pretty awful. Inspired by the pattern programming features of Roger Linn's LM-1 Drum Computer, Ryrie and Vogel assigned programmer Michael Carlos to create Page R, an interactive sequencing environment that evolved throughout the CMI's lifetime, and had a great deal to do with the instrument's popularity.

"Outside" Developments. Like any startup company, Fairlight was financially strapped during the CMI's early development. Luckily, since their machine was based on a computer, Fairlight was exposed to some opportunities that most musical instrument manufacturers wouldn't have been. "It just so happened that Remington Office Machines were looking for a business computer. They had a software team and they heard that we'd developed this dual-processor computer that ran BASIC and C. So they asked, 'Can we write application programs and sell your system as an office product?' Obviously, we said yes, because we had no other income, apart from a few video products. I think about 120 Remington business computers were sold. Then cheaper business computers started appearing, and that market faded away."

Global Distribution, Downfall, & Recovery. Where did the Fairlight sell best? "Our biggest market was Europe — specifically the U.K. and Germany. Japan was next. We had a lot of trouble in the U.S. In fact, the U.S. has always been Fairlight's biggest trouble, which led largely to the downfall of the original company at the end of '88. Our U.S. subsidiary had lost almost $2 million in the previous two years, and the main company wasn't able to cover that during that post-crash period. We had three offices in the U.S., and the overheads there were extremely high. We've always found the U.S. a very expensive place to sell into and support, because it's so physically large. It's very expensive to get out to all the population centers compared to, say, Europe.

"Another problem was that Fairlight Instruments was, for the most part, a one-product company, with a lot of people to support and a lot of trade shows to attend. If we had been able to sell through a normal retail or pro audio chain, those expenses could have been covered by a lot of different products. But that was always one of the biggest problems, finding a dealer who was right for the product."

Fairlight still exists, albeit in an altered format — without Peter Vogel. After helping to establish Fairlight ESP in 1989, Vogel set up his own consulting business in the mountains west of Sydney. It's still possible to buy a CMI Series III from Fairlight; they're up to rev 10 now. $70,000 will get you a serious machine. Start saving those dimes and quarters.

E-MU EMULATOR

First Affordable Digital Sampler

BY MARK VAIL

How would you like to play a turkey? That's what a 1981 ad in *Keyboard* suggested. Dogs, violins, voices, drums, and sound effects were also mentioned. The ad introduced a new instrument by a then-little-known synth manufacturer in a Pacific coast surfer-and-boardwalk town in Northern California. The town was Santa Cruz, the company E-mu, and the new instrument the original Emulator — the first digital sampler that didn't cost as much as a Jaguar. (Two Honda Civics maybe, but not a Jaguar.)

One of the main influences on E-mu in the creation of the Emulator was the Fairlight CMI. E-mu had another prime motivating factor, as well — financial. The company had plans for a completely different instrument (with an oddity of a name, as you'll see), but instead shifted gears to develop their groundbreaking sampler — a move that may have saved them from extinction as a business.

Royalties, Royalties, Who Paid the Royalties? E-mu's co-founder and master engineer Dave Rossum outlines what happened prior to the Emulator's introduction: "E-mu unofficially started back in 1970 and became an official business in '72.

E-mu Systems' first sampler, the Emulator, daddy of the II, grand-daddy of the Three. According to Dave Rossum, the production Emulator's metal case was built like a Sherman tank. He knows of at least one Emulator that survived a fire.

From then until 1980, our primary business in terms of products was a modular analog-based electronic music synthesizer, similar in concept to the old Moog modular systems. In 1973, we developed and patented a digitally scanned polyphonic keyboard that we licensed for use in Oberheim Electronics Four and Eight Voice synthesizers in 1975.

"We also consulted with Dave Smith in the design of the Sequential Circuits Prophet-5 in 1977. Sequential was a starving little company back then, so we helped Dave out in a number of ways — licensing him our polyphonic keyboard patent, letting him use our development system for creating his microprocessor code, and designing the analog circuits, because Dave wasn't as familiar with analog circuitry. We arranged to get a royalty on each Prophet-5 that was sold, because Dave had no money up front and that's the way things were done back then. Of course, as with any business, when you start making products, you always discover all the things you have to spend money on that you didn't expect. So Dave Smith and [Sequential's] Barb Fairhurst came to us and said, 'We'd rather not pay you any royalties right away because we don't think we'll be able to make you as much money. Why don't you let it ride for a little while

and we'll start paying you later?' It seemed like a good idea to us, because it was certainly in our interest for them to be as successful as possible.

"By 1979, Sequential caught up financially and started writing us royalty checks. The Prophet-5 took off like we'd all hoped it would, and those royalty checks got pretty substantial. So we decided, 'With this nice income stream, we can take the time to develop some very large, professional systems that will take a long time to sell.' That's when we designed the Audity — a very sophisticated computer-controlled analog synthesizer that we expected would cost $50,000. We showed it at the AES [Audio Engineering Society] convention in May of 1980. Our plans were to start our marketing efforts well in advance, because we knew it was going to take a year or two before we could sell anything that expensive. But with the royalties coming from Sequential, it seemed like a reasonable thing to do; we could keep our doors open and continue development on the Audity to make it a top-notch system."

While showing the Audity at that 1980 AES show, Rossum and his E-mu compatriots spotted a few novel musical products on display. "The Fairlight CMI had just come out," Rossum explains, "and that was the first time we had a

A close-up look at an Emulator retrofitted with JLCooper's Emulator Generator Modulator (called simply the Genmod), which added ADSR envelope generators and voltage-controlled filters for the Emulator's upper and lower voice banks. The equivalent of Cooper's mod was incorporated into the sound engine of E-mu's second keyboard sampler. "To a certain extent," Dave Rossum offers, "Jim Cooper was the father of the Emulator II."

chance to see one of those. Everybody was pretty excited about the Fairlight; it was the first real digital synthesizer. I guess the Synclavier was out at the same time, but the original Synclaviers were not really that exciting.

"Another product was from a French company called Publison, who had a digital delay line with a voltage-controlled clock rate. You could take an audio sample — capture a sound in memory — and trigger it monophonically from a keyboard. A gate from the keyboard would turn the voice on and play once through the sample.

"Also of note at that AES show was the LM-1, Roger Linn's drum machine. We knew that all of these products were fairly hot and within an area of interest to many musicians, and — being the sort of people who didn't mind borrowing other people's ideas — we said, 'It sounds like this digital sampling idea is ripe. Someone should come in and do it right.'"

Rossum and his co-founding partner, Scott Wedge, actually considered handing the idea over to Sequential. "We thought that maybe this was too big an idea for us," Wedge recalls, "because E-mu was a very small company at the time, and that maybe we should talk with Dave Smith over at Sequential Circuits about it, because it might be a little more appropriate for his company at that point. We realized this could be a really significant product. But the day we got back to the office from AES, we found a letter in the mail from Dave saying that he had decided to stop paying royalties on the Prophet-5 design. Of course, what ensued was a lawsuit and a whole epic unto itself. But it became clear at that point that we were going to have to do this one ourselves. We couldn't sell this idea, at least not to Sequential."

VITAL STATISTICS

Description & Overview: The first affordable digital keyboard sampler. Four- and eight-voice versions were available, as was a two-voice model that was quickly discontinued due to lack of consumer interest. The Emulator's four-octave keyboard was always split into two halves between *B* and Middle *C*. To play the same sample across the entire keyboard, you had to load it into both the upper and lower banks. An optional program, the User's Multisample, allowed the keyboard to be split at every tritone, providing eight possible split points rather than two. Newly sampled sounds were assigned to the lower keyboard range; a swap function switched the upper and lower sounds. Whereas today's sampling machines are stuffed with megabytes of memory, the first Emulator E-mu Model 6000 had only 128K bytes of sample RAM, which was a huge amount of memory for the time. Every sample was a fixed two seconds in length. Editing functions were limited to adjustable playback start point and truncation of sample length. The original Emulator was also limited to 8-bit words. Since digital signal processing (DSP) was hideously expensive at the time, the Emulator transposed samples across the keyboard by changing the playback rate. Samples were stored on 5¼" floppy disks, and one keyboard bank could be loaded while the other was played. Speaking of loaded, thanks to its cold-rolled-steel cabinet, the Emulator weighed in at around 80 pounds.

Produced: January 1981 to spring 1984.

The Emulator II appeared in 1984 at around $8,500 for one with two 5¼" floppy drives. Now they range in value from $500 to $1,000, and up to $1,600 if it has a built-in hard disk.

"The consequence," Rossum adds, "was that E-mu went from having a positive cash flow to having a fairly substantial negative cash flow to pay the lawyers to get Sequential to pay us the money that we thought they owed us."

Although Sequential and E-mu later amicably resolved their differences out of court, the financial reality of the situation prodded E-mu's founders into reevaluating their focus. Rossum quickly realized he could design an instrument that offered one of the Fairlight's most useful attributes, digital sampling. "The trick with the Fairlight," he explains, "was that there was a completely different memory subsystem for each sound it played. Memory was a large basis for the high cost of instruments like the Fairlight. I realized that the Z-80 microcomputers we could buy were fast enough to handle note-on events and functions such as that — as proved by the Prophet-5 — and that if we could get our instrument to play many notes out of one memory, we could tremendously reduce the cost of the system and make it affordable. That was the birth of the Emulator concept, back in May of 1980.

"I immediately started experimenting and found that one of the DMA (Direct Memory Access) chips that was available from the microcomputer people had the basic facilities we needed. If you threw five of them together, you could make a memory subsystem that would be able to play

Approximate Number Made: 500.

Manufacturer: E-mu Systems, 1600 Green Hills Rd., Scotts Valley, CA 95067-0015. (408) 438-1921, fax (408) 438-8612.

Original Retail Price: Eight-voice with 17 seconds sampling time, $9,995. Lowered to $7,995 in early '82.

Current Street Price: $200 to $500.

Current Dealer Price: $250 to $800.

Insider Information: Dave Rossum tells how E-mu's engineers first tested the Emulator's sample loop function: "There was a bathroom right next to the lab, so we sampled the sound of somebody peeing in the toilet. Then we could play that sound for two or three minutes. That was our Big Bladder Simulator." Rossum on early instrument sampling: "Ken Provost, who is an industrial designer/mechanical engineer now, worked for E-mu as a purchasing agent, and he played the violin. He was the source of our first violin sample, before we knew that it really took a professional musician to make a good sample." . . . Scott Wedge admits to name-dropping: "When we shipped serial number 001, I drove it over the hill from Santa Cruz to the airport in San Jose late one night. There was this guy working at the American Airlines airfreight counter, taking his time. It's late and he doesn't really care. To get his attention, I said, 'Hey, do you know who Stevland Morris is?' He said, 'Yeah, that's Stevie Wonder.' I said, 'Check who this is going to: It says, "Ship to Stevland Morris" right there on the box.' This guy says, 'No shit! Wow. I'm gonna get this out on the next flight.' He pushed some buttons once he saw who it was for."

eight notes at once, and would be reasonably economical. Looking back, I wish to heck I'd patented that, because nobody had done it before, and that's the fundamental basis of all samplers these days, memory sharing."

Dawn of the Sampler. By November '80, Rossum had the basics of the instrument mounted on plywood, with circuits held down with screws and nails. When the system finally worked, the E-mu team realized they were riding the leading edge of a new revolution in music. But as with the creation of any new technology, there were bugs to work out. "At that point," Rossum recalls, "there was an ADC [analog-to-digital converter] problem that resulted in a lot of noise in samples. All it was was quantization noise. Even with that problem, we realized there was a light at the end of the tunnel."

Rossum raced to get a working Emulator prototype ready for the upcoming NAMM (National Association of Music Merchants) convention. At that point, however, the instrument had a different name. "Whenever we do a project," Wedge explains, "we have an in-house name for it. Then, as we get it closer to the time that it goes to market, we go through a formal process of actually naming the product. The in-house product name for the Emulator I was the 'Sampler.' For us, that was kind of a pun between Nyquist's sampling theorem — which

is an obscure piece of mathematics that underlies the whole genre — and the Whitman Sampler, a box with a whole bunch of different flavors of chocolates in it, because this was an instrument that could have a whole bunch of different sounds."

Still, the E-mu gang wasn't set on the name. "Scott came in one day," Rossum recalls, "and said, 'We've been assuming we're going to call this thing the Sampler, but we really ought to consider what other names there are. So everybody go home, sleep on the thing, come back tomorrow, and we'll decide what we're going to call it.' Ed Rudnick came in the next day with a big grin on his face and said, 'I've found the name.' He announced that it was the 'Emulator.' It was so obvious. He'd found it by going through the thesaurus. Considering the match with the company name, it was just amazing."

"For a while," Wedge adds, "a lot of people thought the name of our company was 'Emulator' and that we got the name E-mu from that, but it isn't true. It was just a wonderful coincidence and a perfect name, really, for the technology that we were using."

NAMM, Stevie Wonder, & Reindeer Hoofs. Almost nine months after the aforementioned AES show, E-mu brought a plastic-cased Emulator prototype to the February '81 NAMM convention in

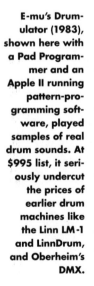

E-mu's Drumulator (1983), shown here with a Pad Programmer and an Apple II running pattern-programming software, played samples of real drum sounds. At $995 list, it seriously undercut the prices of earlier drum machines like the Linn LM-1 and LinnDrum, and Oberheim's DMX.

When it was introduced in 1989, the E-mu Proteus/1 greatly improved the status of sample-playback multitimbral synthesizers and spawned a line that includes the Proteus/2 and /3 and Procussion drum module.

Anaheim, California. "We had a tiny little booth," Rossum recalls. "Nobody had ever heard of E-mu at NAMM. It made our day when Stevie Wonder came up with his entourage. He walked up to the instrument, sort of hugged it to get the feel of it, and then started playing it. Across the way was one of the more established companies. They told us, 'What you just got was better publicity than you could ever buy for any amount of money.'"

"Stevie sampled his voice into the Emulator and played it back on the keyboard," Wedge continues. "That drove us all crazy because we knew that voice didn't work very well on it. Voices ended up sounding funny. 'Munchkinized' was what we called it. We thought there were much more interesting things to sample. To top it off, when Stevie sang into the microphone for the sample, it really overloaded the inputs and distorted the signal. It was a bad sample and a bad example, but when he played it, I guess it was just enough of a mind-blower to turn him on to it."

Wonder was so impressed with the Emulator that he ordered and received serial number 001. "Actually," Wedge confesses, "we had promised number 001 to Daryl Dragon of the Captain & Tennille. I'm not sure if Daryl ever really understood why he didn't get number 001. We were tempted to make two — one for Stevie Wonder and one for Daryl Dragon — because Daryl had been a loyal E-mu modular system owner for a long time before that. On the other hand, Stevie at the time had a slightly larger name-recognition value, so I guess it got a little political. Apologies to Daryl on that one."

Apparently Dragon wasn't too upset, because he used the Emulator — quite ingeniously — in a Christmas concert with the Glendale Symphony

Orchestra at the Dorothy Chandler Pavilion in Los Angeles. "Daryl's dad, Carmen Dragon, was the conductor of the Glendale Symphony Orchestra, so it was a family deal," says Wedge. "Daryl used the Emulator to play sounds that were not present in the orchestra, such as a little pump organ, sleigh bells, and reindeer hoofs. It turns out that the source of the sound of the reindeer hoofs was Daryl thumping the inside of the Emulator's disk pocket."

Slow Sales & Second NAMM. In spite of Stevie Wonder's unsolicited publicity appearance, Emulator sales were slow in the beginning. "We sold about 20 of our first units, but sales just hit the wall at the end of '81," Rossum explains. "Part of the reason for that was a problem with the way we originally designed the Emulator: When you played a key, the sound would play out of sample memory, but it continued to play even after you'd released the key. Short sounds worked okay, because they would loop as long as you held the key and decay when you let go. But for many sounds, it was very annoying because even if you let up during the attack stage of a sound, it would continue to attack and then start to decay. We hadn't designed the instrument with any kind of VCA (voltage-controlled amplifier) in it to handle that problem. Scott Wedge kept after me until I came up with a 50-wire kludge that we could retrofit every unit with. It was fortunate that we had left a couple of open spaces on the edge of the circuit board so we could add this ugly kludge."

After Rossum's worldwide tour to retrofit Emulators in the field with both the "ugly kludge" and the just-completed sequencer, E-mu brought the revised Emulator to the January '82 NAMM in Chicago. Besides offering the instrument at a re-

VINTAGE KEYS
CLASSIC ANALOG KEYBOARDS

C16 Vol127 Pan=P
254 SUPERMOOG 3

Newest in the Proteus-fathered line of sample-playback synthesizers, E-mu's Vintage Keys (January '93) offers samples of keyboards like the Hammond B-3, Wurlitzer electric piano, and Mellotron, along with analog synths like the Minimoog and Prophet-5.

duced price (just under $8,000), E-mu began promoting its sample library of 25 or 30 disks. These strategies paid off. "In hindsight," Rossum admits, "pushing the sound library more than anything else — except possibly for getting notes to shut up when you released the keyboard — made the Emulator successful. The original people we sold to were visionary musicians, people who knew what they would do with the instrument as soon as they heard its description. But now we had enough samples that you could play a couple dozen different instruments, so people with less imagination, who really needed to hear it before they could comprehend what this thing was going to do for them, could relate to the instrument. I think we came back from that trade show with orders for immediate delivery of 25 units, and production stayed around that level per month from then until the end of the life of the instrument in the spring of 1984."

What a Difference . . . Unlike many manufacturers of vintage-class electronic music gear, E-mu

has survived and prospers today. Consider what might have transpired if it hadn't been for a letter and the decisions that resulted. Scott Wedge puts it in perspective: "The Emulator offered us a much more powerful synthesis approach, a much more powerful sound generator, and it answered some business questions. In 1980, we built a $40,000 modular system for the University of Texas. At that time, it was clear that growing a company on that kind of business was really going to be tough and that there was a tremendous demand for a more affordable method of synthesis. So we were looking for an opportunity to expand our distribution into music stores by finding a standard product that we could produce. The Emulator represented E-mu's first standard music-store product, so it was a major turning point in the company's development."

"What actually made E-mu wasn't the Emulator," Rossum adds. "It was the Drumulator. But the Emulator made the Drumulator, and the Drumulator then made the Emulator II, which really was our first truly successful instrument."

MISCELLANEOUS

SECTION 5

MELLOTRON

Pillar of a Musical Genre

BY MARK VAIL

Recording tape has been put to many extraordinary uses. Few compare with the way Britain's Leslie Bradley and his brothers Frank and Norman rigged the renowned Mellotron Model 400.

Beneath each of its 35 keys is a 6' long, ⅜" wide strip of magnetic tape. When you play a key, a rotating spindle inside the Mellotron catches the front end of the appropriate tape, pulling it over its dedicated playback head for up to approximately eight seconds before coming to the tape's end. Bradley's spring-based system quickly pulls it back in preparation for the next note (see the figure on page 207).

During that eight seconds, you would hear one of the sweetest flutes, string sections, or boys' choirs that you might — in those pre-sampling days — have imagined. Instead of bland electronic representations, the Mellotron played analog recordings of acoustic instruments.

What did it sound like? Listen to the Beatles' "Strawberry Fields Forever" — the Mellotron's first hit single. Paul McCartney played the flute intro-

duction and the brass sounds at the end. John Paul Jones played Mellotron strings in Led Zeppelin's "The Rain Song" on *Houses of the Holy*. Long-term fans of the Moody Blues, King Crimson, and Yes know exactly what the Mellotron sounded like.

In addition, there were other sonic possibilities at your fingertips with the Mellotron, sounds like brass, tenor sax, and Hammond organ. If you've got a working Mellotron today, you have access to marimba, glockenspiel, and timpani roll tapes. Or maybe you would prefer canned laughter, cuckoo clocks, frogs and toads, ship hooters, or a thunder-

The most popular Mellotron is the Model 400. Or is this a Novatron? No matter, they're essentially the same instrument.

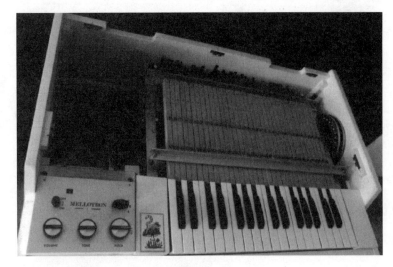

storm. Such sonic demonstrations are familiar today. In essence, the Mellotron was an analog sample-playback keyboard.

With Aftertouch. According to some players, the volume of each note that you play on a properly adjusted Mellotron depends, to a limited extent, on how hard you push its key down. Although Leslie Bradley tells us that the Mellotron wasn't intentionally designed this way, the harder you push down, the harder the tape's pressure pad pushes the tape against its playback head. Since each key has its own tape and playback head, you have some control over the volume of each individual note in a chord. Thus, even though pressure only affects volume and nothing else (such as vibrato), the Mellotron collects the First Keyboard with Polyphonic Aftertouch award.

Genealogy. Why weren't the tapes looped to play continuously? So that notes had attack transients, instead of playing steady tones like an electronic organ. Plus, each note has an independent attack. As a matter of fact, the Mellotron's predecessor, the Chamberlin Rhythmate — designed and built by Californian Harry Chamberlin — had continuous tapes. Later Chamberlin machines

used the retracting tape mechanism that subsequently appeared in all Mellotrons. The Bradley brothers refined Chamberlin's design in developing the Mellotron.

"In about 1960, Chamberlin was producing something like one instrument every three to six months," Leslie Bradley tells us. "A gentleman by the name of Bill Fransen got together with Chamberlin with the object of increasing the production rate. Fransen brought a couple of Chamberlins over to England in the early part of 1962, in search of someone to finance and produce it. At the time, our company was called Bradmatic Ltd. [based in Birmingham, England]. We manufactured semi-professional tape recorders and magnetic heads. Fransen approached us with a bid for 70 matched reproduce heads. As we got to know him better, he said, 'What else can you do? You'd better come down to London to see me.' We assisted in negotiations to get the thing under way. Finally, in late '62, Fransen got financing, we found a factory, and eventually we produced our first machine, the Mark I — a fair copy of Chamberlin's unit."

Second in Line. The Mark II appeared in early '64. Like the Mark I, it featured two side-by-side, 35-note (*G* to *F*) keyboards — thus, the 70 playback heads. Where the right-hand keyboard was typically loaded with lead or melody sounds, the left was split in two, with rhythm and accompaniment tracks in the lower half, recorded to play in the key of the note that you play, and fill patterns in the upper half. The Moodies' Mike Pinder had lead tapes loaded into both of his Mark II manuals.

Unlike those in the Model 400, Mark II tapes — still ⅜" wide — were 42' long. Six "banks" of sounds were strung out along the tape, with sections of silence between them. Six selector buttons for each keyboard provided access to the different banks. Changing banks generated an audible

whirring sound from within the Mark II. (The Model 300 was similar in offering six banks of sounds, but it used ¼" two-track tapes.) With its plethora of 1,260 sounds (70 keys x 3 tracks x 6 banks), the Mark II intrigued the British Broadcasting Corporation so much that, in 1967, the BBC commissioned Bradmatic to load one with special effects tapes for television Foley work. The BBC was so pleased that they purchased three additional units. All of the sound effects on the *Dr. Who* series were performed with these Mark IIs, one of which went up for sale in early '93.

During these evolutionary years, Bradmatic Ltd. became Bradmatic Productions and, later, Streetly Electronics. Mellotronics, a related company that handled financing and tape production, was based in London.

Further Offspring. "From the Mark II, we went to the Model 300," Bradley recollects, "which was a rather different arrangement. It used ¼" tape, with only two tracks." The 300 also featured a 52-note, *A* to *C* keyboard and an optional headphone output.

Then came the Model 400. Streetly apparently prospered through the mid-'70s, but London-based Mellotronics — rather than the Bradleys — were handling sales and promotion.

Analog? Tape? Surely you remember magnetic tape, that long, brown strip of thin plastic. It can be fragile stuff. One tape can cause trouble enough. Imagine 35 or 70 strips of it inside a cabinet with a keyboard. "If you don't use the right tape, it will stretch," David Kean of Mellotron Archives explains. "You can't use coarse-backed tape, because it won't fall back into the storage box properly. If its width isn't right on the money, you'll also have problems with it running through the tape guides. There's no such thing as pre-made ⅜" tape. You have to start with ½" tape and cut it to ⅜". I contacted Maxell about special-cutting UD-50 tape to my specifications, but they wanted a $15,000 order. I wasn't ready to spring 15 grand for a tape order at that point."

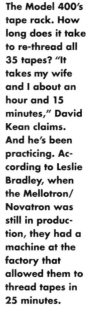

The Model 400's tape rack. How long does it take to re-thread all 35 tapes? "It takes my wife and I about an hour and 15 minutes," David Kean claims. And he's been practicing. According to Leslie Bradley, when the Mellotron/Novatron was still in production, they had a machine at the factory that allowed them to thread tapes in 25 minutes.

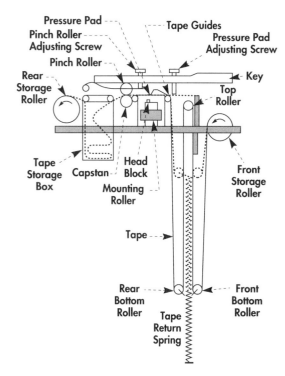

An illustration of the Mellotron system, the one used on the Mark II. The design was considerably simplified for the Model 400. (illustration by Yecta Sadat)

Every ⅜" Mellotron tape has three tracks, each containing an instrument sound. Since multitrack tape heads were prohibitively expensive at the time, the Bradleys incorporated a single-track head in the Mellotron. (From '80 to '83, American-based Mellotron USA Ltd. attempted to manufacture a Mellotron that could play up to four tracks at a time; only four 4Tracks were produced.) A front-panel rotary switch shifts the tape-head positions, allowing you to select one of the three tracks.

Eight-track and ⅜" master tapes were used to record ⅜" Mellotron tapes — continuous tape that was wound on a reel before getting cut into individual strips of tape for each Mellotron note. As long as the desired source sounds reside on the same master tape, the ⅜" tapes can be recorded in one pass, recording all three tracks simultaneously. Otherwise, it can take two or three passes. Of course, it's imperative that the attack of every note on each track begin at the same instant as corresponding notes on the other two tracks. "I designed and built two recording machines,"

VITAL STATISTICS

Description: Magnetic tape playback instrument, based on instruments by American Harry Chamberlin, designed and built by three British brothers, Leslie, Frank, and Norman Bradley.

Produced: Mark I (prototype), 1963–1964; Mark II, 1964–1967; Model 300, 1968–1970; Mellotron/Novatron Model 400, 1970–1980; Novatron Mark V, 1976–1981; Mellotron USA Ltd. 4Track, 1980–1983; Novatron Model T.550 (flight-case version of Novatron Model 400), 1976–1978.

Approximate Numbers Made: Mark I, ten; Mark II, about 650; Model 300, about 160; Model 400/Novatron, about 1,850; Mark V, nine; 4Track, four; Model T.550, about seven.

Manufacturer: Aldridge Electronics, Bradmatic Productions, Mellotronics Manufacturing, Streetly Electronics, Mellotronics, and Mellotron USA, Ltd. (All out of business.)

Original Retail Prices: Mark I, £1,000 ($1,500 to $2,000). Mark II, £1,000 ($1,500 to $2,000). Model 300, £1,150 (about $2,500). Mellotron Model 400, £625 (about $4,000). Mark V, £1,650 (about $9,000). 4Track, $4,000. Novatron Model 400, about £850 (about $4,000). Model T.550, £1,150 (about $4,500). (U.S. prices weren't direct conversions of British pounds; dealer markups varied.)

Current Street Prices: Model 300, $600 to $750. Mellotron/Novatron Model 400, $800 to $1,000.

Current Dealer Prices: Mark II, $3,500 to $5,000. Model 300, $3,500 to $5,000. Mellotron/Novatron Model 400, $1,400 to $2,000. Mark V, $4,000 to $5,000. 4Track, $1,500 to $2,500. Model T.550, $3,000 to $5,000. (See Tronnie Alert! above.)

Tapes: Mellotron tapes are available from Mellotron Archives (see Sales, Servicing, & Support, below) for $250 per reel. Empty tape rack, $250. Loaded rack, $500. $25 tape-racking fee.

Sales, Servicing, & Support: David Kean, Mellotron Archives, 721 Michael, Moses Lake, WA 98837. (509) 765-6451, fax (509) 766-9977.

Insider Information: Mike Pinder, the Moody Blues' original keyboardist, worked at Streetly for 18 months before joining the Moodies in '64. . . . You'll find a picture of the Mellotron Mark II on the back of their *In Search of the Lost Chord* album jacket. . . . Frank Bradley died of a heart attack on Nov. 29, 1979. . . . David Kean owns one of Rick Wakeman's Birotrons. The Birotron was another tape-playback keyboard that used eight-track cartridges, like those squashed by cassette tapes in the '70s. It appears in one of the video tapes now available from Mellotron Archives.

Bradley tells us. "One is on display in the British Science Museum in London. We had to get the note starts in the right position and then transfer them to ⅜" tapes. On the Mark II, with all its rhythms, it was one helluva job to keep all the rhythms in step and in time. It put a few gray hairs on my head, and removed a few too."

Tronnie Alert! For information and support, David Kean is a man of utmost importance to current and future Mellotron owners. Perhaps the ultimate Mellotron fanatic, he has secured the remaining stock of Mellotron parts, master tapes, and tape-making machines. Kean transported all these goodies to his home in the state of Washington. "The only thing I didn't get is the tape-cutting machine, which caught fire in Florida. It was just an old Ampex or GE tape machine with the head block ripped off and a cutting jig installed." He tried to manufacture a new tape-cutting machine, but the attempt failed. Not to worry, though, because Mellotron creator Leslie Bradley has access to the original cutter in England, and is cutting Mellotron and Chamberlin tapes for Kean. As David Kean promised in early '91, he's made the Mark II library available for the Model 400. "That's a pretty big deal," he explains, "because Mellotron recordings from a long time ago — Beatles, Stones, Genesis, etc. — were done with the Mark II, not the Model 400. The Mark II tape library was different than the Model 400 library."

Somehow Kean also finds the time to head a Mellotron user's group, for which he publishes an aperiodic, informative, and slightly out-of-left-field newsletter. Quoting a portion of his October 31, 1992, edition provides some indication of just how exuberant this man is: "We have concocted what I believe to be the world's only MIDI Mellotron. Actually, it's a Chamberlin. This all started when I bought a Chamberlin M-1 remote unit. This thing has solenoid operated 'keys' that were just *begging* to be MIDIfied. I used a Sunn MIDI lighting controller to fire the solenoids and it works great. I just know they're going to come to the house in the little white truck for me now. This could be done to a Mellotron or regular Chamberlin M-1, but it is a *major* pain to install and would be one more thing to maintain in your machine.

However, I'd be happy to give you the details on how to do it."

Mellotron owners should be flogged and tortured if they don't contact David Kean at Mellotron Archives to register for the user's group — he'll want to know what Tron or Chamberlin you own and serial numbers — and to get current pricing information on tape racks and tapes. He can also sell you a refurbished Tron, or help you find one for sale.

Kean-refurbished Mellotrons cost considerably more than what you might be able to find one for on the used market. "Before we sell a refurbished Mellotron," Kean explains, "we strip and clean all the aluminum parts, install new felt strips around the capstan, replace worn or damaged pinch rollers and pressure pads, install a new SMS 4mr motor control board, repair and refinish the cabinet, replace stretched springs and PVC separators in the tape frame, install the customer's choice of new tapes, and replace any broken or damaged parts with new ones. These are typical repairs that I've performed on every Mellotron I've had here (over 30), and virtually every used Mellotron will need these renovations. A $600 Tron you buy at the Joe Blow's Down Home Studio sale will get expensive in a hurry."

According to Kean, shipping costs are steep, too. You can expect an average of $300 in air freight charges to ship a Model 400 between major U.S. cities, and $700 to and from Europe.

Fixes or Repairs Daily? Leslie Bradley points out the Mark II's weakness: "Tapes would last a couple of years. The only trouble we saw was when the Mellotron got shoved into a truck and left overnight after a gig in a very hot room. This could result in condensation that would cause the tape to stick to the capstan and wind up. The Mark II was more susceptible to that than the Model 400. The Mark II would also get out of adjustment because they were often tossed off the back of trucks. Some Mark IIs used to come in looking like a blacksmith had shaped horseshoes on the top." It couldn't have had anything to do with the Mark II weighing somewhere between 300 and 400 pounds, could it?

Words of advice to would-be buyers from today's Mellotron champion, David Kean: "The first thing that people who buy an old Mellotron need to do is remove the keyboard and make sure there's an aluminum plate installed across the top of the tape storage box. If it isn't there, the tape won't properly feed into the tape storage box; it will spill out into the guts of the machine, get balled up, etc. You'll need to get one fabricated, something a metal workshop could do, as long as it's made of a non-magnetic metal.

"Try to get one with a CMC 4 or SMS-2, -3, or -4 motor control unit. If you get a Mellotron with a CMC 10 motor control, you *will* be replacing it.

"Check the capstan for excessive wear. I can't replace this one for you.

"Make sure to demagnetize the heads of any machine that you aren't sure about, because the tape heads get magnetized fairly easily and they will immediately erase valuable Mellotron tapes.

RIME OF THE ANCIENT SAMPLER: THE MELLOTRON RETURNS

1986 saw the demise of Streetly Electronics, the British company that made the Mellotron. It seemed like the end of an era. But thanks to a few diehard purists and an intriguing new album, even sampling enthusiasts may have to admit that there's still plenty of punch in those old tape-playback machines.

Martin Smith, a restorer who recently brought Robert Fripp's Mark II and Model 400 Mellotrons up to speed, was the driving force behind *Rime of the Ancient Sampler*, a compilation homage to the grand old instrument, which is available on the Voiceprint label [Box 32827, Kansas City, MO 64111. (816) 561-0723]. The music reflects the wide stylistic range of the participants: On "Owner's Guide," Patrick Moraz features

his sound effect tapes on a Model 400; listen and spot the licks from his solo albums as well as his Moody Blues cuts. His predecessor with the Moodies, Mike Pinder, on "Waters Beneath the Bridge," proves that his techniques on Mellotron remain unique. David Cross, who played violin and keys with King Crimson in 1972–74, revisits his old turf in "Not So," a demented violin solo over a doomy background. Matt Clifford, whose recent credits include tour gigs with the Rolling Stones, kicks off "Then and Now" with genuine vinyl crackles to underscore his comparisons of sounds from the '60s to those of the present. Nick Magnus, a prominent player on Steve Hackett's solo albums, takes a wide-screen approach on "Night of the Condor," with textures from Mellotrons and synths woven smoothly together. And British session player Chris Taylor juxtaposes original Mellotron string sections, guitar, mandolins,

vibes, and organ sounds against a modern MIDI setup on "Bradmatix." ("Bradmatic" was the original name of the Bradley brothers' company that produced the Mellotron.)

On my track, "The Mighty Mellotron," I wanted to pay tribute to the sounds, styles, and riffs from the transitional period of rock. So it was quote time: "Strawberry Fields Forever," "Nights in White Satin," and other songs provided the jumping-off point for a performance built on chord changes aplenty.

The album finishes with part of the original vinyl disc produced in the '60s to demo the instrument. At that time, the possibilities suggested by the Mellotron foreshadowed a time of unbounded creativity for studio and gigging musicians. So what is its role today? Is the Mellotron dead? If it's just sleeping, who will awaken it? Use your ears and decide.

— David Etheridge

You have to demagnetize each head separately. (Be sure to remove the tapes before you do!)

"Don't judge the machine's sound based on the condition of its tapes. Most of the old machines out there have old tapes in them and are apt to sound that way.

"Lots of times, the pinch rollers get stuck because they're corroded on their axles. I've got tons of good ones available. Also, the pressure pads need to be properly adjusted so that the tape sits squarely on the head.

"One of the main problems with 60 to 70% of the Mellotrons out there is they use the CMC 10 motor control card. That one component gave Mellotron a bad name, because it causes tape wobble, takes a long time to warm up, and never works well. If your machine has the CMC 10, you should by all means get it replaced. We have a replacement card that costs $250.

"New motors are available, so don't worry too much about a cheap machine with a damaged one. They cost about $175, depending on the current dollar-to-British-pound conversion rate.

"I can provide a list of Mellotron maintenance procedures, and we now offer a homemade maintenance video. Most of the stuff can be done by anybody who has any kind of mechanical know-

Novatron T.550 in a rack case.

how. That was one of the reasons for the Mellotron's longevity: You didn't have to send it to London to get it fixed."

You can order two newly released video tapes from Mellotron Archives, one that demonstrates all the Mellotron-related machines and sounds that are available on tape, the other identifying all

The Mellotron Mark II intrigued the British Broadcasting Corporation so much that, in 1967, the BBC commissioned Streetly to load one with special effects tapes for television Foley work. The BBC was so pleased that they purchased three additional units. All of the sound effects on the Dr. Who TV series were performed with these Mark IIs, one of which went up for sale in 1993. (photo by David Kean)

the Mellotron parts and showing how to make adjustments/repairs and generally maintain the machine. Each tape goes for $39.95 for VHS ($49.95 each for PAL tapes), and no respected Tron owner or wanna-be should be caught dead without both.

Degeneration & Rebirth. From '76 on, business got rough for the Bradleys. Attempts at worldwide distribution failed, Mellotronics in London wasn't able to meet loan obligations, and all the London-based assets — including the Mellotron name — were sold to an unknown party from Connecticut. Although very few Mellotrons were manufactured in this country, the name, tapes, parts, and tape-making equipment were passed from one company to another before finally ending up with David Kean in December '90.

Back in Birmingham, the Bradleys continued to produce the Model 400, as well as a version built inside a flight case, the Model T.550. However, they had to fabricate a new name for the instrument and settled on "Novatron."

Following a number of recessions in England, the Bradleys' valiant efforts to stay in business finally failed in '86. "We had to put the company into liquidation," Leslie Bradley says. "We were left more or less penniless."

"The thing that really rings my bells," Kean says, "is that Leslie and his brothers are finally getting some credit for this thing. You know, if it hadn't been for that instrument, we wouldn't have heard those bands."

PAIA ELECTRONICS

Synthesizer Kits

BY MARK VAIL

The smell is unforgettable: hot, smoking solder melting onto a circuit board. In the '60s and '70s, numerous companies in the U.S. sold electronic kits for consumer construction, and several magazines frequently published schematics and details for building electronic projects from scratch. For those who constructed magazine-published projects or put together electronic kits, it was a hobby as rewarding as quilt making, afghan knitting, and — later on — personal computer programming.

As far as musicians were concerned, one of the most popular kit companies was Paia. While there were lots of other kit manufacturers around, Paia was the most familiar one. The kits were way affordable and easy to assemble, even though many were delivered a few parts short of complete. (A quick phone call assured that all the missing parts would arrive within a few days.) Image-conscious performers may have scoffed at Paia's reputation, but truth is, a lot of people put the kits together, benefiting from the pride of assembling a bunch of parts into a functional electronic instrument.

Although their product line has shrunk considerably from its heyday in the '70s and early '80s, Paia still offers musical kits — including one that's especially pertinent to owners of old analog synth gear: the MV-8 MIDI and control voltage processor. In Paia's tradition of offering inexpensive gear, the MV-8 comes in kit form for a mere $299, or $399 assembled (but then you wouldn't get to smell melting solder).

One man has stood behind the majority of Paia's products and has maintained the company through the years: John Simonton. I rang him up to discuss the history of his company.

* * * *

What led you to the electronic music industry?

Oh, I had an avocational interest. I played in a garage band when I was a kid. I started writing articles for magazines — *Popular Electronics* back in those days, and *Radio Electronics.*

What year did you make your first product?

Right around 1970. As a matter of fact, the very first product that Paia put out was a burglar alarm, a self-contained intrusion alarm. The first audio product showed up pretty quick after that. There were things like wah-wah pedals and a Leslie speaker simulator. At first, we called the latter the Leslie Effect Simulator. But CBS, who owned the Leslie name at the time, had their attorneys ("Flim" and "Flam," if I remember correctly) notify us that in their opinion there was no such thing as a "Leslie Effect" and that we were infringing on their trademarks. So we changed the product's name to the Synthespin.

Where did the Paia name come from?

There is a little town on the island of Maui called Paia. The naming dates back to that. My mom was raised in Hawaii, and I was born in Hawaii, for that matter, in a little place called Ewa on the island of Oahu.

So the correct pronunciation is pie-ee´-yah?

Yes, it is if you're in Hawaii. If you're here in Oklahoma, it's "pie-ya."

What is your background in electronics?

I have a bachelor's degree in electrical engineering, but like a lot of people who have that, the interest goes back a lot further, back as far as I can remember — light bulbs, wires, and stuff like that.

What was the first keyboard instrument that you manufactured?

The first keyboard instrument didn't have a keyboard at all. It was a modular voltage-controlled synthesizer that we did for *Radio Electronics* back in about '72. I say it didn't have a keyboard because it didn't; it had a bunch of switches that were homemade and, believe it or not, shirt buttons as the things that you pressed on to activate the keys. But it got such good response that within about six months we were offering one with a regular keyboard. It was a big unknown at the time; we didn't know if anybody even wanted anything like that.

We have always been a small company and can't afford major investments, and getting set up to manufacture keyboard instruments required a major investment for us at that time. So we put it out there, there was some response, and because there was a response, we went ahead and made arrangements to bring in keyboards, retrofitted the first synthesizer with a real keyboard, tweaked it up, and changed some things.

In the '70s, Moogs were selling for maybe $5,000 to $10,000. Our original modular synth sold for $139. When we put a keyboard on it, it cost

VITAL STATISTICS

Manufacturer: Paia Electronics, 3200 Teakwood Ln., Edmond, OK 73013. (405) 340-6300, fax (405) 340-6378.

Products: Dozens of kits, some available assembled: 2700 and 4700 series modular synths, 8700 computer/controller, Gnome micro-synthesizer, Oz mini-organ, Programmable Drum Set, Stringz 'n' Thingz, Organtua combo organ, Proteus 1 programmable monophonic synth, and many more.

Production Dates: Gnome, 1974–82. Programmable Drum Set, 1975–83. 8700 computer/controller, 1976–83. Drum, 1976–83. Proteus 1, 1978–83.

Approximate Numbers Made: Gnome, 3,000. Programmable Drum Set, 1,500 to 2,000. 8700-based modular systems, 250 to 300. Stringz 'n' Thingz, 500 to 1,000. Proteus 1, 70 to 80. Paia estimates it has had 30,000 to 40,000 customers.

Original Retail Prices (kits only): 2720/A, $230. 4700/S, $499. 8700, $149.95 (optional cassette interface, $22.50). Gnome, $59.95. Oz, $89.95. Programmable Drum Set, $84.95. Stringz 'n' Thingz, $295. Organtua, $299.95. Proteus 1, $399.

Current Street Prices (estimated): Modular system with keyboard, $100 to $400. Gnome, $50 to $100.

Insider Information: In 1989, E-mu introduced the Proteus/1, which is still in production. A decade earlier, Paia made a Proteus 1 synthesizer. How does Paia's John Simonton feel about E-mu "borrowing" the name? "We have a great relationship with E-mu. If anything, we were flattered when they picked up the Proteus name.". . . Composer/synthesist Larry Fast introduced Peter Gabriel to the programmable drum set in the late '70s, and Gabriel subsequently used the box on "Biko" and "Games Without Frontiers," among other songs of that era.

about $200. Our modular system consisted of a single oscillator, a single filter, a couple of transient generators, a VCA, and that was about it.

Was the second system modular?

The next system would have been the one that had the real AGO keyboard, and the one after that would have been kind of an updated version of that, with a little more precision, a little quieter, and so on — as it was obvious that there was a demand for that sort of thing.

I have a Paia catalog from 1978. The modular system of the time was called the 4700.

The original one was the 2700, and that 4700 that you see there was the successor to the original one.

Who helped you develop these?

As a matter of fact, I did those pretty much single-handedly. As a result of those products, Paia went through a spurt of growth. And it was during that spurt of growth that a lot of people that were associated with Paia for some time came aboard, people like Marvin Jones. It was also about that time that we started working with Craig Anderton.

As far as the modules were concerned, did you study what other manufacturers were doing?

Sure. There really was only one then, and that was Bob Moog and his Moog equipment. To the extent that I was able to lay my hands on information on Moog synthesizers, I studied it. When I set out to develop what's going to be a new product for us, in a lot of cases I avoid studying what people have done in the past — until I have an idea of how we're going to approach it. Once I have an idea of how we're going to approach it, then I'll go

back and take a look at how other people have done it, and if some of our ideas were better, then great, we use those. If some of their ideas were better and can be adapted to what we're doing, then we'll do that.

I was familiar with the company Heathkit when I was growing up. I feel like Heathkit and Paia are probably responsible for a lot of people knowing more about electronics than they would have if they hadn't bought a kit from one of those companies.

I think that's true. A number of other companies were around at that time. Southwest Technical Products out in San Antonio did a lot of that kind of work, Heathkit, and also Knight Kits. In that time frame — late '60s, let's say — Heathkit was very active.

What about other kit companies in the music industry? Weren't Aries synthesizers available in kits?

Aries, yeah. I hadn't thought about them for a while. Yeah, Aries was around in that same time frame. My recollection is that all of these people came after we'd done some of that, but it could easily be that I just wasn't aware of them. Even Moog sold some kits for a while.

Things from Aries and Moog were much more expensive than Paia products.

A lot more expensive.

How were you able to keep the costs down?

It's the result of a lot of different things. It's the result of trying to have high commonality between parts. That is, carry as small an inventory of different things as possible; use the same part again and again. When you do that, you're able to buy that component in larger quantities and get the price down.

Another thing that we always did that I don't believe other kit manufacturers did was that we've always had our own sheet metal shop. For a long time we did our own circuit boards. These days we don't because it's gotten to be such an environmental mess that it's just better to have someone who's prepared to deal with that side of it do it. We don't make our own circuit boards any more, but certainly in the early days those were the three key things: we were very vertical, we made our own circuit boards and sheet metal, and we maintained that philosophy of high commonality of parts.

The thing that a lot of experienced designers know that hobbyists probably don't is that there are very, very few magic values. That is, there are very few places in electronic design where only one value will do. In most cases, you have the option of juggling different values to get the same effect, even though you're not really using the same value. For us, a good bit of time always went into seeing how we could take parts that we already had — one standard op amp, for example, instead of having five or six different op amps, a couple of different standard values of potentiometers and

controls, that kind of thing. We tried to keep the number of different parts low so that we could get the purchasing power up on parts that we did need. But it largely is a result of so much of it being done in-house.

When you go out for sheet metal, a lot of times you'll find people that are accustomed to doing sheet metal for the space industry, for example, or for the government or for the metal industry. The tolerances there are just so much tighter than what we need for the kinds of things we do that if you have to pay their overhead to have a shop that meets all of those federal requirements and so on, it gets real expensive. We know what we need and we have the equipment that we need to make the products that we use, so it's just a lot less expensive to do it here.

Is the 4700 system still in production?

No, it hasn't been for some time.

Do you still offer any of the modules?

As a matter of fact, we still make some modules that use Curtis chips. Curtis chips were used in the Prophet-5 and a lot of stuff from Sequential Circuits. Doug Curtis was an acquaintance of sorts and very, very talented. His chips — oscillators, filters, transient generators, and so on — were just extraordinary. We still have a quantity of those, and

While it started out as purely an electronic instrument to make wind sounds, the Gnome turned into one of the smallest, most portable analog synthesizers ever manufactured.

we still manufacture some modules that use those chips. They're quiet, they're precise, they do what you want them to do.

For us, it's gotten very difficult to get keyboards. The Japanese and other importers have done such a marvelous job of bringing very high-tech instruments to the public at a very low cost. In particular, during the mid-'80s, it's no exaggeration to say that I could go to our local discount store and buy a complete instrument for less than Paia was able to buy just a keyboard action. So when the situation got like that, at that point it didn't make much sense to go on with it.

Fortunately for us and a number of other companies, MIDI came along. One of the things that MIDI does for companies like us is it relieves us of the responsibility of having to provide a keyboard at all. Silicon electronics are cheap; iron, steel, plastic, and things like that are expensive. So anything that you can do with silicon is going to be a lot less expensive than something that you have to do with iron, steel, and plastic. Essentially, that's what MIDI does, it takes the steel, iron, and plastic of the keyboard and puts it over in one instrument while we get to deal with the silicon end of things. We don't have to worry about the mechanical action of the keyboard and so on. It's just all electronic, all information processing. Having MIDI come along really opened doors, not only for performing artists but for manufacturers also.

I'm looking at the Gnome, your tiny battery-powered synthesizer.

Oh, yeah. That came out in 1974. The Gnome started out as an instrument that wasn't going to do anything more than make the sound of wind — not like a flute, but real wind. *Sssssshhhhew.* That kind of wind, which could be played with a little vinyl controller strip that was part of it. The Gnome was one of those things that just grew. After the instrument that did the wind sound was done, it became pretty apparent that you could stick other components in there and essentially come up with a small synthesizer, a thing that captured the central ideas of voltage-controlled synthesis at that time — oscillators, filters, transient generators, and so on — but stripped down to the essentials or the core. It was an attempt to get rid

Paia's Oz turned out to be a big hit. Its controls were minimal, but with its touch-sensitive plate and small size, its reputation grew as a polyphonic keyboard source whose sounds could be modified, enhanced, and mixed via other modular synthesizer gear.

of that keyboard that was always by far the single most expensive part of anything we made, by an order of magnitude or more.

The Gnome attracted a lot of people who were interested in synthesis. When people stopped using voltage-controlled synthesizers, I feel that they began to fall out of touch with what sound was in the first place. Those were great days when you had laboratory-quality equipment, very precise, that you could use to build sounds. You could start off with an oscillator that had the waveforms you wanted, you could subtract formant frequencies with filters and move those filters with transient generators, and control dynamics with voltage-controlled amplifiers and transient generators. There's just no substitute for that in terms of figuring out what the central characteristics of sounds are. A person who has spent some time with a synthesizer like that frequently gets to where they can program sounds in their head; they can hear a sound and have a pretty good handle on what it's going to take to make that sound. I think that that's largely missing when you get into samplers and sample-playback synths. There's nothing wrong with samplers; samplers are great. And there still are people, of course, who are messing around with analog synthesizers largely for that reason, because you've got such a good handle on why a sound sounds that way.

Did the Oz mini combo organ come after the Gnome?

Yeah.

I see the Oz keyboard only had a range of an octave and a fourth — from C to F. Was an 18-note keyboard the smallest you could find?

No, as a matter of fact we could have gotten a smaller keyboard than that. It just seemed like a convenient number. At about that time, Marvin Jones was working with me on a good many things, and that was his contribution. Marvin is probably the one who said, "No, John, it really needs to be at least an octave and a half." If I had been left to my own devices, it most likely would have been a smaller keyboard.

The problem that was being addressed there was the monotonic nature of synthesizers at that time. There really weren't any built-in microprocessors to control multiple signal-generating chains, so every synthesizer was monotonic. And when you found synthesizer work that was polyphonic, it was done with multitracking. So one of the purposes of the Oz was to give a polytonic front end, something that could do chords that then would be processed by the rest of the synthesizer chain — filters and so on. One of the tricks on Oz was that it had a little pad that you could push to bend the note, or bend the whole chord for that matter. That was an added gimmick.

The Oz also had the ability to trigger the Gnome, didn't it?

Yeah. It had a gate signal out or a trigger signal out, a signal that says, "Okay, a key's down now, go ahead and do what you're going to do."

Could you refresh my memory about exponential and linear response?

The Paia things were linear, and I had always thought that we were really out in left field on that. But it wasn't really until these days that I realized there were a number of other products that also were linear. Old analog Korgs, for example. The reason that I know it now is that we're offering a product, the MV-8, that retrofits MIDI to voltage-controlled synthesizers. It's set up for equipment with exponential response, unlike our original linear-response stuff. It surprises me how many people can't use it, because they have other devices — old Korgs and other things — that are linear.

Here's why the problem arises: Perception of pitch is based on octaves, which are an exponential function. The frequency doubles with each octave, and that's an exponential curve. VCOs, or voltage-controlled oscillators, by their nature, are linear, so that in order to double the frequency you have to double the voltage. There are a couple of technical problems with that: Resolution gets very small down on the low end of the scale, and up at the high end it tends to stretch.

The better approach without a doubt is to have things that respond on the basis of one volt per octave. Adding one volt produces an octave shift in the output. The reason that's good is that it allows you to simply sum in a voltage if you want to offset an oscillator. If you want to offset it by a third or a fifth, for example, crank in the appropriate control voltage just as a summation, and then everything will track properly from there on. With linear stuff, you can't do that. You can't have two oscillators and sum a voltage into one of them, because they won't track any more. On the other hand, in those days exponential was really where the money was. It wouldn't be true these days, but back then getting that exponential response was invariably done with a semiconductor junction, which is very temperature-sensitive. So you had to temperature-compensate with resistors that had an opposite temperature coefficient. It got real cumbersome and clumsy.

A current Paia product, the MV-8 MIDI and control voltage processor provides CV outputs for up to eight synths and performs CV-to-MIDI conversions. Kit, $299; assembled, $399.

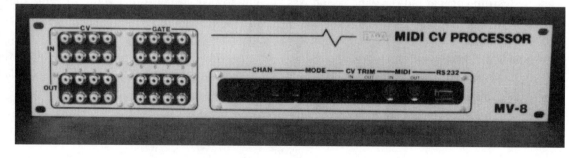

You were one of the first companies to incorporate a computer inside your synthesizer. When did you develop the 8700 computer/controller?

That was around '76 and '77.

What was the computer processor you used?

The 6502. In those days, there really weren't very many to choose from. You either had a 6502 or you had an 8080 or Z-80. Just because we had experience with 6500- and 6502-based stuff, that's why it wound up with a 6502 in it. That subsequently was the same processor that Apple used in the Apple II, so it gained some popularity. These days, it's considered an antique.

In the catalog, it says 6503.

The 6503 is a 6502 in a smaller case.

The 8700 only had a two-digit readout. Was everything in hexadecimal?

Everything was in hex.

Standard RAM in the 8700 was only 512 bytes. It's hard not to say "kilobytes." And the catalog says it was expandable to 1k.

Isn't that nice? It's enough to make you gasp. A *full* 1k! It's very difficult to do these days, but you really have to put yourself back in that time frame to realize what computers were in those days. The first computers that I had experience with in school were IBM machines that filled, honestly *filled* entire rooms, and had their own air conditioning and of course their own power coming in. A computer then was just an incredibly big deal. And I think it had 4k of memory, which was just *huge* in those days.

I have one of the very early Apple IIs, which is another story. Serial no. 12. It came, as I recall, with 1k of memory, and I just really debated for a long time before I expanded that to 4k. I thought, "What will I ever do with 4k of memory?" It had a disk drive that would hold something like 160k bytes. I said, "What would you do with that? My god, that's all the information that there is in the whole world!" Now I've got eight megabytes sitting here and a total of about 200 meg of hard disk. And at every step, I've felt the same thing: "My god, what am I going to do with all that memory?"

What kind of things did the 8700 computer/controller allow the modular system to do?

First of all, it made it polyphonic. It made it so

that key activity — pushing down a key on the keyboard — could be assigned by the computer to one of the signal chains. The signal chains were essentially traditional analog synth voices: a couple of oscillators, a filter, a voltage-controlled amplifier, a couple of transient generators to run the filter and the amplifier, that kind of thing. The computer's big job was to keep straight what key was assigned to what signal chain. When a key was released from a chord, that signal chain would become "available." Once available, it could be reassigned as another key went down. The 8700 software provided several different algorithms for doing that, such as rotational and high-note priority. There were a limited number of resources in terms of what sound-processing modules were available, and it was the computer's job to assign those resources as they were needed for activity on the keyboard.

We also had some compositional algorithms that would generate tunes on the 8700. There were a number of other tricks. It was neat stuff, and a lot of fun to work on. I think a lot of people learned something about programming, too. We hear from a good many people — like you said earlier — who are now engineers (some of them out-of-work engineers, unfortunately) saying, "If it hadn't been for you guys, I never would have gotten into engineering." We always apologized. We'd say we didn't know what we were doing.

There are a good many people who also had their first experience with programming on that kind of product. That was another reason for using a 6500 as a processor, as a matter of fact. For beginners, it's a little bit easier to get a handle on how that processor works, a little more straightforward than the 8080s and the Z-80s, which were also available then.

When did the computer-based modular system go out of production?

Early '80s, '82 or '83, probably.

You manufactured a couple of innovative drum machines.

I've always loved drums.

I'm looking at a picture of the Programmable Drum Set. When was that introduced?

That was in 1975. In those days, we numbered

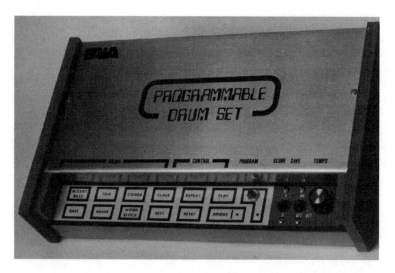

The history books confirm that John Simonton's Paia Programmable Drum Set was the first of its kind.

grammable part is fantastic, but I only use it as a guide track. We'll come back and do real drums on top of it later. We'll use this as a tool to figure out rhythms, but these drum sounds are horrible." The Programmable Drum was an awful lot of work, but it got used on some records.

Did it play the same sounds that were in the Drum?

No, the Drum was essentially a full drum synthesizer. It had an analog synthesizer voice — oscillators, filter, voltage-controlled amplifier, and transient generator — that was optimized to do drum kinds of sounds. Some of the flexibility that you would want to have in a real synthesizer voice really wasn't there in the Drum; it was optimized for percussion kinds of sounds. A percussion sound doesn't have any sustain, so you don't have to worry about the parts of the processing chain that have to do with what happens during the sustain period. That goes away. So the Drum's voice generator got cut back and simplified to do drum kinds of sounds, but it was still essentially a synthesizer.

When was the Drum manufactured?

Must have been around 1976 or '77.

It was the 5700.

That was about when we'd stopped doing the product numbers that way, so the number doesn't have any kind of date in it. But as I recall, it was in that same late-'70s time frame.

Did it go out of production when everything else did?

Yeah. The sensors for the Drum were silicon-encapsulated piezo disks. It got to be difficult to manufacture them, so that's why that one went out of production.

One of the Paia kits that I put together was the Stringz 'n' Thingz, a string machine that had an analog piano voice. That was probably pretty popular, wasn't it?

Stringz 'n' Thingz was amazingly popular. It was designed, for all practical purposes, exclusively by Marvin Jones. Yes, it was very popular and sounded absolutely fantastic. Marvin had such a feel for things. We still get three or maybe even four calls a month these days from people who say, "You know, I had a Stringz 'n' Thingz. That was so great. Do you still sell that?" It's the same deal: It's got a keyboard

products so that they contained some date information. So I can remember the model numbers on those things and remember about when they came about. The Programmable Drum was 3750, which would have made it March of '75 that the work was being done on it.

How long was that in production?

Probably five or six years, and we probably sold 1,500 to a couple thousand of those. That's been credited as being the first programmable drum machine, and it may be. For about a year, it was dominant, because there weren't any other programmable drum sets.

The Programmable Drum did not play digital samples of sounds like other programmable drum machines that followed it. The drum sounds were done using a technique that was popular at that time called ringing oscillators. You have a filter that's very close to oscillating all by itself, and when you hit it with a little pulse to excite it, it rings the way a drum does. It makes drum kinds of sounds.

A real drum has a lot of character. Ringing oscillators tend to be a pure-tone kind of sound, a sine wave that dies out very quickly. Real drums aren't really so much that way; they're like any mechanical instrument. They have resonant properties of their own that tend to accentuate some parts of the spectrum and de-accentuate others. It's a stylized kind of drum. People hear it and say, "Oh, yes, that's supposed to be a drum sound, isn't it?"

We had a number of name people that would use the Programmable Drum and say, "The pro-

The Stringz 'n' Thingz was a popular string synthesizer — really just an organ, but it made great string-like sounds. When I finished assembling mine, two keys wouldn't play the piano sound, but that didn't matter because I never used the piano sound anyway.

on it, so we don't sell them. But yes, that was a fantastic piece of equipment.

We had a good time in those days. We still have a good time, but there were a number of people whom I've been fortunate to work around and with that were just amazingly talented, talented people.

I'm looking at the Proteus 1 in a Paia catalog. That was a programmable monophonic synthesizer. What memories do you have of the Proteus 1?

It's kind of funny. That one took a long time to do. Incredibly long, particularly by today's standards. We use CAD [computer-aided design] a good bit here these days for doing sheet metal and the circuit boards and so on, and most things don't really take more than a couple of weeks to get together. That one took, as I remember, a year or more. By the time the product was there, the market had moved on. I can remember talking to Doug Curtis about that, as a matter of fact, about nine months before it came out, telling him what it was — a preset, monotonic synthesizer. He made some comment about, "Does anybody want that?" I said, "Sure they do, Doug. Of course they do." Well, it turned out he was right. Nobody really did want that, particularly when there were Prophet-5s available. The Proteus 1 was a neat piece of equipment and I'm very proud of it, but it just missed the mark.

When did that come out?

That must have been '78 or '79.

When did it go out of production?

Probably about the same time as the other products. All the keyboard stuff went out of pro-

duction at more or less the same time, which would have been '82 or '83. That started a time of inactivity for Paia. Personal computers were really starting to come on strong, and an awful lot of people who had prior to that point spent time plugging components into circuit boards started playing with computers. A lot of people who had been soldering parts onto circuit boards decided they didn't want to solder any more. So it really went into and stayed in decline for a number of years.

During that time, we did some consulting work and whatever to keep things together. We continued to mail catalogs, but we weren't really active in replacing old products and bringing in new products at that time. It really wasn't until '91 that we started to crank up again and started to get involved with some of the authors that we had worked with in the past, as well as some new authors on doing DIY [do-it-yourself] stuff for some magazines. Along about that time, I started to no-

Not to be confused with E-mu's Proteus/1 multitimbral synth module, the Paia Proteus 1 was a programmable monophonic synth with 16 memory locations. The Proteus 1 kit cost $499 in 1982, later lowered to $399.

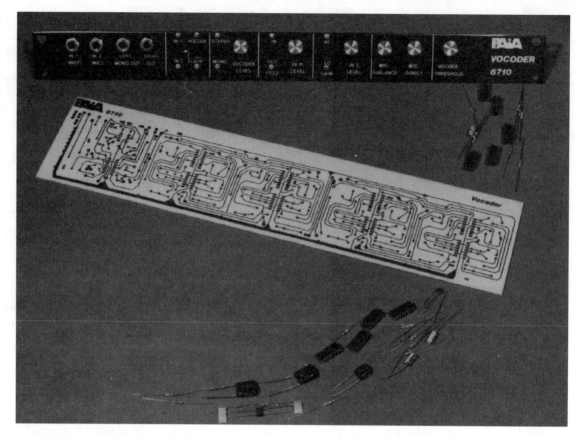

Author/musician Craig Anderton designed Paia's 6710 vocoder, and it's still available for $99.95 (plus $15.95 for single-space 19" rack panel).

tice that we were getting more calls from people who would say things like, "Gosh, remember how neat that stuff used to sound, that old analog stuff, how great that was? Golly, remember how neat it was to plug those circuits in and the smell of rosin, how neat that was?"

So it seemed like maybe there was a little interest starting to develop again. Some of the electronics magazines were interested in doing some music stuff, and some of the music magazines were interesting in doing some do-it-yourself things that they hadn't been doing for a while. So here we are back in it again, and back in it again to the extent that, at this point in time, we're turning out a new product about every three weeks. We're working with Craig Anderton, who's very busy being an author and working with a number of magazines, and not so active in designing things these days. But we keep hitting him over the head, and he certainly does have more good ideas than most people. It's been nice working with Craig again.

We're also working these days with a guy named Jules Ryckebusch, who's in the Navy. He has turned out to be incredibly prolific and has a very

good eye for the kind of things that people need in terms of useful gadgets.

Left to my own devices, I'm kind of a techie, and I tend to do things that are technically very interesting but maybe not as useful. So it's handy to have people like Craig and Jules and others who see the need. I mean, it's a very simple process: They have a need and come up with a product to fit that need. That seems to be working very well these days.

Is there much of anything from the old line that you still carry on today?

A good many things. A good bit of Craig's earlier work, like a parametric equalizer and guitar gadgets. About ten years ago, Craig did a thing called the QuadraFuzz, which was like four fuzz boxes in one box, and each fuzz has its own filter in front of it, so you abstract a frequency spectrum from the signal, fuzz that, and then recombine them. It's a neat gadget because it doesn't get muddy like some fuzz boxes.

Craig also did a vocoder many years ago that we still sell. So there's a good bit of stuff from the past, and I think some fairly interesting things coming up in the future.

VOX CONTINENTAL

Original Doors Combo Organ

BY MARK VAIL

If you're like me, Ray Manzarek's keyboard work on the Doors' "Light My Fire" remains firmly etched in the memory. Instead of using the inexpensive Vox Continental to emulate a Hammond B-3, Manzarek shoved the Vox's brittle, edgy sound right in the listener's face, from opening to closing riffs, with his unforgettable solo in between.

For the Doors' first two albums and part of the third, Manzarek stuck with his Vox Continental, an instrument that many of us 30/40-somethingers have rocked out with at some time or other.

Researching the Vox wasn't easy. Not only has the U.K.-based company passed through four or five owners over the past three decades, but the key people in the Vox organ division are probably jamming with Jim Morrison — among too many others — in Rock and Roll Heaven right now.

I spoke with three different people formerly involved with Vox. Dick Denny worked at Vox for ten years starting in 1957. He designed the Vox AC-30 — one of England's most popular guitar amplifiers — and assisted Vox's organ guru, the late Ken Mc-Donell, in developing the Continental's sound.

"Originally, Ken McDonell was a master cabinet maker," Dick Denny reveals. "He used to design the cabinets and everything. He had a good knowledge of organs and their electronic circuits." Dick's son, Richard, joined the company in '65 and worked there for 12 years. Andy East was a technical manager for Vox from '83 to '88. Each interviewee gives a slightly different historical perspective. Therefore, some of the Vox Continental dates and details are sketchy. I also contacted a few people who either collect or repair Vox organs; these sources provided a few additional tidbits of information.

Vox started making huge electric church organs in the '50s. They also developed a small organ known as the Univox, which was featured in the Animals' "House of the Rising Sun." "The Univox was a tiny, three-octave keyboard that you could fit under a piano," explains Dick Denny. "It had its own amplifier, a load of tabs [sounds], sustain, vibrato, and percussion. It also had repeat [apparently like tremolo], so that you could get a banjo sound and play something like 'Way Down Upon the Swanee River.' It was very popular with pianists, especially in pubs."

A vintage Vox Continental shares the New York skyline with Paul Shaffer of the David Letterman show. Now, where did he leave the genuine Vox volume pedal? (photo by Ebet Roberts, 1983)

Then, in 1960, Vox released the first organ under the Continental moniker. Like later Vox organs, it had a four-octave, 49-note keyboard. Of course, it used analog circuits, and vintage analog synth owners can surely relate to tuning problems. "We called the really old, single-manual Continental the 'milk crate,' because of its tone generator design," Richard Denny recalls. "The tone generator was mounted on a metal frame with two potentiometers on the top so that you could adjust the pitch. In those days, you could hold a lamp over the top of the generator and it would change pitch."

Like the early polyphonic synths from Korg and Yamaha that would appear more than a decade later, the Vox used divide-down circuitry. Inside its cabinet were 12 tone generators, or oscillators, one for each note of the musical scale. In tandem with each generator were three frequency di-

viders, each of which halves the frequency of an incoming signal. The octave that you play in determines which combination of frequency dividers, if any, an oscillator's output is routed through — none in the top octave, one in the second, two in the third, and three in the bottom octave. This procedure actually only covers 48 of the organ's 49 notes. A 13th circuit generated the bottom *C*, and also had a low-frequency oscillator for adding vibrato to the Vox's sound.

Two dual-manual Continentals came later, one a portable with the same orange-and-black Rexine (a waterproof fabric) found on the original, the other like a console with bass pedals and a rotating speaker cabinet. This organ broke down into two parts for semi-portability.

Another portable Vox organ, the Jaguar, sounded nearly identical to the Continental, but it was less expensive because it provided voice switches rather than drawbars. The Jaguar may have been just as popular in the U.S. as the Continental, and it's actually worth more on the U.S. vintage market than the Continental. But it was a Super Continental that found its way onto the bumper of the Voxmobile, a custom car with fake, oversized Vox guitars on either side.

It's clear that Vox organs were manufactured both in England and elsewhere, but there's confusion as to whether "elsewhere" was limited to Italy, or included both Italy and the U.S. According to both Dick and Richard Denny, Continentals were manufactured in both England and Italy, but Jaguars were only produced in Italy. However, Andy East seems to have proof otherwise. "In about '66, Vox struck up an agreement with the Thomas Organ Company in the States so that Thomas could manufacture Vox products in California. I've got photocopies of American service manuals for that period, and part numbers correspond to those in Thomas Organ manuals." Not only that, but American electronic kit manufacturer Heathkit offered the Jaguar as a kit during

What's fast, loud, and red all over? The Voxmobile, of course. The "guitar" fenders were fake, but the Vox Super Continental riding on the back certainly wasn't. Neither were the three Super Beatle amplifiers and the dozen or so speakers. Get your motor runnin'!

the '60s and early '70s.

Can you tell where your Vox was made? "The normal person," says Richard Denny, "will not know whether a Vox is English or Italian." What if we look inside the cabinet? "We used to sign our names in every organ we made," Richard Denny confesses. According to Jason Savall, Vox collector and former keyboardist with New York-based rock group the Fuzz Tones, it's easy to tell where his Voxes came from. "The older of my two Continentals is British. There's a little metal plate on the back of the organ that tells you the wattage and where it was made."

VITAL STATISTICS

Produced: 1960 to around 1972.

Total Number Made: Dick Denny (with Vox from '57 to '67) estimates "thousands."

Manufacturer: Vox, founded in the '40s by Tom Jennings, managed by Birch/Stowlech — Michael Birch and George Stow — from '68 to '75, owned by Dallas Arbiter from '75 to around '80, purchased in '80 by current owner Rose Morris & Co. Ltd., the U.K. distributor for Korg and Ovation; only guitar and keyboard amplifiers are currently produced under the Vox name.

Description: 49-note keyboards (C to C), single- and dual-manual portable organs with drawbars. (A two-piece, dual-manual semi-console Continental with a pedalboard and a rotating-speaker cabinet was also produced.) Several styles of tone generation were used during the Continental's production cycle: germanium transistors, silicon transistors, and finally ICs. The Continental and its less expensive brother, the Jaguar, used frequency-division technology to generate notes in the scale. Visually, the Vox organ's most prominent characteristics were its reversed keyboard colors (black ♮s, white ♯s) and its chrome, Z-shaped stand. 1/4" audio out; secondary bass output on some models. Vox volume pedal, stand, and utility carrying case standard.

Original Retail Price: Just under £100 (about $250).

Current Street Price: $75 to $125.

Current Dealer Price: $200.

Not all Vox organs had keys made of plastic. "I used to have three Continentals," Savall explains, "but I only kept two. They have wood keys. I got rid of the hollow plastic-keyed one." Of course, a Vox with wood keys is worth more than one with plastic keys.

Back in the '60s and '70s, musicians didn't have multiple-tiered A-frame, columnar, and "invisible" keyboard stands the way we do today. One of the Vox organ's outstanding features — visually, anyway — was its chrome, Z-shaped stand. It made the Vox stand out on stage. In fact, a standless Vox isn't worth as much as one with a decently maintained stand.

In the beginning, the Vox Continental was a hot item. According to Dick Denny, "It was light, easy to set up onstage, and had great popularity. It didn't have too many voicings, it only had a few drawbars, but it was a godsend to early pop musicians and bands." Andy East remembers the Vox's significance. "The first Continental, the single-manual, was the one everybody associates with the British beat — the Animals, the Dave Clark Five, that period." In this country, besides Ray Manzarek, we had Doug Ingle of the Iron Butterfly pumping out cheesy organ sounds on the Vox Continental. What else could have given "Inna-Gadda-Da-Vida" that unforgettable touch of class?

But the Vox organ's popularity waned rather quickly in the '60s. Even though some popular British bands used them, East tells us, "Until the new wave craze, the Vox organ was a very unpopular instrument in the U.K. People had written it off as not being a desirable instrument to own. You could pick it up in pawn shops very cheaply, in the region of $60 to $80." They came on strong again in the late '70s, when new wave bands like Blondie and Elvis Costello's Attractions brought them back onstage. The B-52s and Prince continue to use Vox-like sounds. How popular is the Vox in England these days? According to East, it isn't as hot as its old nemesis, the Farfisa organ. "There's a big thing happening in the Manchester area with dance music. The most popular bands are using Farfisas. The resurgence hasn't spread to Voxes yet."

As with any vintage electronic instrument, you have to beware of things that can go wrong with an ancient Vox organ. "Key contacts were the biggest problem," Eric Snowball, an English organ technician, tells us. "Some wires might come off the circuit boards, but the circuits themselves were pretty solid."

COMBO ORGANS OF THE '60S

Turn On • Tune In • Rock Out!
Tweezy • Twerpy • Trendy

BY BARRY CARSON

Time is a funny thing. We spend all our lives plowing ahead into the future . . . and yet, we are irresistibly drawn back into the past. Nostalgia, to human beings, is a pretty big deal. A lot of today's MIDI fanatics are aging baby-boomers who first got turned on to music by the Beatles on *The Ed Sullivan Show*. I would be willing to guess that a fair number of individuals reading this magazine began their musical careers playing a Farfisa or a Vox organ, or one of the multitude of their lesser-known brethren, which — in a veritable rainbow of colors — captivated the first generation of rock keyboard players. There seems to be a growing nostalgia for the musical milieu of the 1960s among those musicians who were there and those who wish they were.

Some keyboard players may scoff, but there is a growing fringe cult among our numbers who are making it their business to exhume and resurrect that most ubiquitous of keyboards from the 1960s era of rock music, the infamous combo organ.

A Brief History

For us, history begins in England in the early 1960s, when the first Vox Continentals were built. Before that time, smaller electric organs with a certain amount of portability had been used in dance bands, but the Vox was made for the stage, not the living room, and its "mod" appearance was perfect for the seminal British rock music scene. Since these were among the first combo organs, that term had yet to be invented. Vox called the Continental a "transistor organ." Lowrey and other early entrants in the field simply referred to their instruments as portable organs. In November of 1964, Tom Jennings, managing director of Jennings Musical Industries — with the weight of such powerhouse Vox acts as the Beatles, the Dave Clark Five, the Animals, the Searchers, and so on behind him — signed a million-dollar contract with the Thomas Organ Co. to distribute Vox instruments and amplifiers in the United States (CBS distributed Vox equipment elsewhere). By the beginning of 1965 the Italian Farfisa Combo

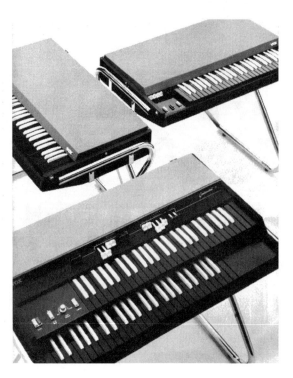

A sight to bring joy to the heart of an aspiring keyboard player during the summer of '67: a family of Vox organs. Note the early Jaguar (upper R), with no black face plate or contour control, and the Continental II, which was to become the Super Continental.

Compact was also available, and it was becoming clear to musicians, instrument dealers and builders, and the vast number of fans — many of whom were themselves becoming musicians — that a new era in keyboard playing had begun.

By 1967 (perhaps the peak year of combo organ production), young keyboard players wishing to rock out in style could choose from at least 30 different combo organs, from the Ace Tone Top 5 and the Domino Combo King to the Magnus 3-D Combo and the Guild Binson (which had its controls on a panel below the keys, not unlike today's Hammond Suzuki XB-2). Combo organs were available in red, green, white, blue, turquoise, orange, gray, and of course basic black. One could spend anywhere from a couple of hundred bucks to over $1,000. If you loved the new teenage music and you had taken a few piano lessons as a kid, you could find the combo organ that was just right for you and become a star overnight. While everybody played the guitar or bass, organ players were almost as much in demand as drummers. (Drummers still had the edge, because a band could get by without an organ, even though they couldn't play "Liar Liar" by the Castaways very well.)

By the 1970s the combo organ began to fall from favor. With the popularity of groups like Yes and ELP, Uriah Heep, and Deep Purple, the organ

sound of choice was now the massive roar of the Hammond through an overdriven Leslie. Voxes were being discarded as Hammond L and M organs were being chopped up and made as portable as possible. Those keyboard players not wishing to lug a Hammond organ around were turning more and more to electric pianos like the Rhodes or RMI (it should be mentioned that all through the '60s, some bands featured the piano sounds of the old Wurlitzers and Hohner Pianets, and, of course, some bands used the Hammond through the '60s). If the New Wave phenomenon of the late '70s was the last gasp of popularity of the combo organ, it was also a foreshadowing of the rising interest in these instruments we see today; call it the pre-nostalgia era, if you will. Even into the '80s, beginner high school groups and budget country bands would occasionally use an old Farfisa if nothing else was available, but now that role is usually taken by an anemic-sounding porta-keyboard. Most combo organs are now either carefully preserved in someone's back closet or dumped in a damp garage or basement.

Organs I Have Known

Vox. The names Vox and Farfisa rest at the pinnacle of the combo organ heap. If any combo organs are truly collectible at this point, they would be Vox organs. The old British Continental with wooden keys and a single hole in the back to which the stand is attached is by far the most desirable. This is the ubiquitous organ of the British Invasion of the mid-'60s. Its orange-and-charcoal-gray finish, gleaming chrome stand, and reversed-color keyboard looked wonderful on those newfangled color television sets, and the Dave Clark Five and the Animals used the Continental sound constantly. The Beatles often had one onstage, and, in the States, the Monkees and Paul Revere and the Raiders (and later the Grateful Dead, Iron Butterfly, and of course the Doors) were among the faithful.

The later Italian Continentals had highly breakable plastic keys and two holes in the back for the stand. Any Vox organ with a stand and a complete set of keys is a bit of a rarity. (Somewhere on this planet there must be a huge pile of scrap metal made up of nothing but old combo organ stands; organs by Vox, Panther, Fender, and others all can be found much more often without the stand than with.)

Perhaps the rarest Continental of all is the legendary American Continental. I have never laid eyes upon one, but Vox organ collector Mike JoDon of Costa Mesa, California, has every reason to believe in their existence; he owns two of them. These instruments were evidently made at the Thomas factory. According to JoDon, they have wooden keys like their English brothers, and the orange-and-gray Rexine fabric has a different texture than that found on Italian Continentals.

JoDon estimates his American Voxes are from the early '70s, near the end of the Continental production run. He notes that the wooden keys offer much better action than the plastic keys, and that the insides of the American Vox do not fold up for servicing as do the insides of the Italian organs.

The dual-manual version of the Continental was out by 1967. Again, a few versions of this instrument were built, but as far as I can make out, most, if not all, double-keyboard portable Continentals were made in Italy. (It should, by the way, be no surprise that so many of the combo organs of this period originated in Italy; that country has a tradition of being home to master musical in-

ORGAN TABS

Although combo organs were seen (by some of us at least) as hip new innovations in the world of music, they drew heavily from hundreds of years of organ-building tradition. What may be most confusing to a reader not familiar with organ terminology are the names given to the various voices available. There are two main components in an organ voice: the tone color, or timbre, and the range or pitch at which the note will play.

In this day of 16-bit samplers and complex digital synthesizers, when we play a flute sound, we expect exactly that — the sound of a flute. Back in the pipe organ days, ranks of differently shaped pipes would create different timbres or tone colors; these sounds were named after the orchestral instruments that they vaguely resembled. This was done simply as a convenient memory aid. In no way did anyone ever expect a string voice to sound like a violin section; that wouldn't happen

until the Mellotron showed up. The softest sounds would be called flute voices; horns, reeds, and brass all were brighter, and the brightest sounds would be called string voices. This practice was continued by the builders of church and home electric organs. (Often the black preset keys on a Hammond B or C organ will be labeled with the names of orchestral instruments.) Later, the designers of combo organs used the same technique when naming their voices. No one ever expected the trumpet voice on a Farfisa organ to sound like anything other than a Farfisa organ, brighter than the flute voice, less bright than the string voice.

Even more confusing may be the little numbers that show up on organ voice tabs or drawbars. Again, this practice harks back to the days of the pipe organ. The 8' marking refers to an organ pipe eight feet long, the length at which a C note would play at unison pitch. A 4' pipe would produce a pitch one octave higher, and a 16'

pipe would produce a pitch one octave lower. By playing 16', 8', and 4' voices at the same time, the organist produces three pitches for each key depressed, creating a very full sound. 5 1/3' and 2 2/3' voices play pitches a fifth higher than 8' and 4'. 2' and 1' voices play the highest octaves, and so on. One key depressed on the upper manual of a Vox Super Continental would actually sound 8 pitches at once, helping to create that cutting, bright sound.

Almost all combo organs had 16', 8', and 4' voices, which were enough to create good, full sounds. Some organs, as we have seen, played quite a few more pitches for each key depressed. A few of the less expensive models only had two pitches available, and the cheapest organs only had 8' voices, which created a very thin sound. It should be noted that a good combo organ with only a few voices could sound much better than a cheaply designed one with dozens of voices.   — Barry Carson

strument builders dating back hundreds of years.) According to the faceplates on the organs, some are called the Continental II and some (which appear to be the later models) are called the Super Continental. It is the dual-manual portable that rode to glory on the back of the Voxmobile, the custom hot-rod with built-in Super Beatle amplifiers. The Voxmobile was created by George Barris, who also designed the Batmobile and the Munsters' car of 1960s TV fame. The double-keyboard Continental console organ is more rare; I've yet to find anyone who has ever seen one, and it may well have been made in England.

The famous Vox Jaguar, the lowest priced and best selling Vox organ, was a true native of Italy. While the outside looked much like a Continental, the electronics inside bear little resemblance to the circuits inside the other Vox organs. As a matter of fact, the oscillators and some other parts in the Jaguar appear to be identical to those in another Italian import, the Howard combo organ, which was sold by Baldwin. The Jaguar was the same shape and size as the Continental; it had, however, a set of voice switches instead of the six drawbars of the Continental, and the bottom octave of keys was reversed in color (remember, white naturals with black flats and sharps was reversed-color for a Vox organ) to denote a manual bass section. The earliest Jaguar had a top just like the Continental's, all orange with a small gold Vox emblem on the far right front; the later Jaguar had a black faceplate like the Super Continentals with the words "Vox Jaguar" written in a silvery white. The later Jaguars also had a tone control called "contour" located next to the bass volume knob. I've heard rumors of a Jaguar model on which the treble keys are white with black flats and sharps, just like a regular keyboard, and the bass section reversed, but I've never seen any evidence to back this up. One group of Jaguars was built, or at least assembled, in places other than Italy; for a short time the American company Heathkit offered a Vox Jaguar kit, along with its guitar amp kits and stereo receiver kits, for do-it-yourself electricians. These organs can be identified by a metal Heathkit label attached to the black Vox faceplate.

The strangest Vox organ ever made would have to be the V305, otherwise known as the Continental Baroque. This instrument was truly the issue of the Vox/Thomas union. The V305 looks like a Super Continental with two five-octave manuals. The bottom manual is a reversed-color Continental keyboard complete with the Vox drawbars; the top manual plays Thomas Organ special effects sounds like banjo, harpsichord, and celeste. There are at least two versions of the Baroque, one with a normal-colored top keyboard and one with the traditional Vox reversed-color keyboard; a white bass section also covers the bottom octave-and-a-half of the lower manual on some models. Built into the instrument, which has four straight chrome legs instead of the famous Vox stand, is an amplifier and speaker system. Some Baroque models also offered a knee controller along the lines of that offered on the Farfisa.

The legacy of the Vox combo organ is its sound. The thin, reedy sound of a Continental with all the drawbars out is the signature timbre of an era. If we could pick only one combo organ to survive and represent the keyboard sound of the 1960s for some distant, future generation, the Vox Continental might be the best choice. "Incense and Peppermints" played on a Hammond B-3 wouldn't have been the same song. While this stereotypical sound is wonderful, it should be remembered that the Continentals had a fairly flexible voicing architecture for the time. The Continental had four drawbars controlling pitches of 16', 8', 4', 2⅔', 2', 1⅗', and 1'. (A single drawbar controlled the level of the top four pitches collectively.) The Super Continental adds a fifth drawbar and the 5⅓' pitch. These are all the pitches but one (1⅓') that are found in the Hammond B-3 drawbar system! Not to say that a Continental sounds anything like a B-3, but given these five eight-position drawbars along with two others (one of which controls a flute-like sound, while the other controls a bright reed sound), you have a very flexible system. The Super Continental also adds a bass voice an octave lower than that offered by almost any other combo organ for real pedal-like sounds. This bass voice is layered on top of whatever drawbar voice is selected for the lower keyboard in the bottom octave.

The Jaguar has a less complex sound. When the voice tabs and tone control are used, sounds from soft flutes to bright strings can be played, but any voice will always play a combination of 16', 8', and 4' pitches with no user control in the top three octaves. The bottom octave will only play 8' (which can be turned off) with the bass volume controlling an amazingly punchy 16' bass sound. (I'll bet this sound blew up more than a few 12" speakers during the '60s.) The Jaguar bass sound is interesting because it is monophonic with low-note priority and it can also double the regular organ voices; this means a chord can be played in the bottom octave and the bottom note of this chord will play the bass voice.

As with all combo organs, vibrato was an important effect on the Vox organs. Unlike most of the other instruments that offered vibrato speed and depth control, the Vox organs only offered a simple on/off switch. Luckily for a generation of keyboard rockers, the Vox engineers hit the nail on the head; the Vox vibrato is wonderful.

Even apart from its sound, the Vox combo organ was an icon of the '60s. Visually, the sleek profile of the Vox is highly evocative of the nostalgia that now surrounds that era. During the late '60s, the Vox Continental was even immortalized as a plastic scale model kit (just like the Spitfire and PT-109), an honor given to very few electronic keyboard instruments.

Farfisa. For some reason the Farfisa never got the glory that the Vox organ received. While the famous groups would be playing Continentals on the TV, the punks down the street would be setting up a Farfisa in somebody's basement. Farfisa combo organs were made in Italy and distributed by the Chicago Musical Instrument Co., which owned Gibson. Confusing the issue a bit is the fact that the first Farfisa organs to show up in the States in late 1964 were called CMI organs. These first organs were what was to become known as the Farfisa Combo Compact. While it didn't share the sleek lines of the Continental, the Combo Compact was ruggedly built into a sturdy box. Good news for collectors is the fact that the legs of a Farfisa were actually built into the organ and can't be misplaced. The bottom of the organ would

Whatever sound this guy is hearing, it must be pretty psychedelic: All of the Farfisa Combo Compact's voice tabs are turned off. Note that this Combo Compact has the octave of gray keys and the plastic music stand (but is missing the 2 2/3' voice) of the later Deluxe.

open to reveal the legs, which could be folded out; the bottom panel of the organ could then be fastened to the legs to form a sturdy support. The fact that this distinctive trait was built into other CMI portable organs like the Lowrey and later Kalamazoo and Gibsons has led to some confusion over the years about who actually played which organ. (The popular misconception that Ray Manzarek of the Doors replaced his Vox with a Farfisa can be traced to the physical resemblance of the Farfisa to the Gibson he actually played.) As sturdy as this kind of stand was, it lacked the graceful good looks of the curving, chrome Vox stand. The early Farfisa's sound was also more solid and workmanlike; only the 16', 8', and 4' sounds were produced, but there was a powerful keyboard bass sound, and the infamous knee-level tone booster (a gimmick borrowed from pump organ days when the player's feet would be busy pumping, so knee levers would be used to increase the volume, add ranks of reeds, etc.) could blast the sound from the classic Farfisa flute voice up through the higher reaches of seriously brilliant sounds.

The early Combo Compacts had a light gray plastic top. The lower part of the organ was made of wood covered with darker gray fabric, and the bottom was black. The voice tabs were white, the tone booster tabs — which selected the voices to be controlled by the knee level tone booster — were light green, vibrato switches were light blue, and reverb tabs were pale yellow. The Combo Compact series were among the very few combo organs that had built-in spring reverb units. This organ had a five-octave keyboard, the bottom octave of which was reversed in color and played the bass voice. After the initial success of the Combo Compact, the Mini Compact and Duo Compact were introduced. The original Mini Compact had a four-octave manual with no bass notes; the Duo had two 49-key manuals.

By late 1966 — the peak of the Farfisa's fame — four Farfisa models were available. At the bottom of the line was the Mini Deluxe Compact, an upgraded Mini Compact that now had a bass octave of gray keys with white flats and sharps (the gray coloring indicated that the keys could be switched between the bass sound and the selected treble voices). At about $500, the Mini was priced to compete with the Vox Jaguar and other "beginner" combo organs. The venerable Combo Compact, now a bright red color (to keep up with the competition's growing arsenals of gaudily hued instruments), was still holding its own. It now had an added tab to switch the tone booster section to full; this allowed players who wanted a really bright sound to play without having their knees permanently jammed up into the organ. The new Combo Deluxe Compact had all the features of the Combo Compact plus an added octave of gray keys (allowing the 12 bass notes to be extended to 24), a percussion effect, and a couple of 2⅔' voices. At around $800, this organ was in the price range of the Vox Continental and some other serious single-manual organs. At the top of the line still was the Duo Compact, with all the features of the Deluxe Compact in a two-keyboard package that included a separate preamp with a spring reverb that worked much better than those built inside the other Farfisa models.

As with the Vox organs, there are some differences between Farfisa organs that may not be readily apparent, and some rarer models that showed up between '64 and '66. There are, for example, Combo Compact models that share traits of both the Compact and Deluxe. Some Combo Compact models have the octave of gray keys that can be switched from bass to treble; they also have a rotary volume knob instead of the three volume switches of the original Compact for the bass sound (the Deluxe actually has both the knob and the switches), bass percussion, and a bright bass voice. These organs, however, are missing the 2⅔' voice of the true Deluxe, and the coloring is the same as the Compact models — that is, light gray, dark gray, and black on the earlier models or bright red with a black stripe around the middle on the newer models. The color scheme of the Deluxe is a uniform gray with a black stripe around the middle. The early Deluxe models retain the name in the gold print of the original compact; the later Deluxe models feature black print. Some Farfisa organs have a tube preamp and some use transistors; the tube Farfisas can be readily identified because they need to "warm up" before they can be played when turned on. One of the most striking visual aspects of the Combo Compact/Deluxe series was the music rack that was built onto the organ. It was an ornate plastic affair that could be folded flat for transport but was not readily removable. Most rock musicians got these things off one way or another and discarded them. The most valuable Combo Compact/Deluxe organs today will have an intact music stand. It should be noted, however, that some Combo Compact models (including the very early ones) did not have this music rack; these organs can be identified by the lack of holes in the sloping front where the rack was attached. The Mini and Duo did not have this ornate music stand. The Mini had a simple wire stand, and the Duo a transparent plastic one.

By the 1968 NAMM show, Farfisa was showing a whole new line of combo organs. Called the FAST series, these instruments boasted to be Farfisa All-Silicon Transistorized organs (it should be noted that Farfisa still offered the Combo line and did so through the end of the '60s). Visually, these organs were quite striking. Obviously wanting to get away from the somewhat dull appearance of their earlier organs, Farfisa came up with an entirely new look. Made of metal and covered with a white material, the FAST organs had gray keys with white flats and sharps, violet, orange, dark blue, and bright yellow tabs, colorful plastic end pieces, and graceful, chrome folding legs. Collectors should note that, in general, the FAST organs haven't aged well; the milky white finish was easily stained and marred and the plastic end pieces easily broken. Coming at a time when the Hammond sound was becoming more popular with rock groups, some FAST models came with 5⅓' and 2⅔' voices and a kind of harmonic percussion. The top-of-the-line Professional had a pseudo-drawbar system that covered eight of the nine Hammond drawbar pitches. The Farfisa ads at the time stressed that these organs didn't sound like combo organs and could emulate the B-3 sound that was so popular in soul and rhythm-and-blues music.

Bob Sauter from Canton, New York, rebuilds and collects organs, and has a special fondness for Farfisas. "It was 1967," he remembers. "I was in a rock band and making payments on an awful-sounding Esty console organ. The guys at the music store let me transfer what I had paid to a new Farfisa Compact Deluxe." He has had that Compact Deluxe (which he describes as a big box with a little handle) ever since. "There were two great ways to end a tune with a Farfisa," he recalls. "One was to grab the spring reverb box (which was located in the underside of the organ) and shake it around to get a great explosion effect; the other was to hold some notes and turn the organ off." This latter effect creates some utterly bizarre sounds as all the notes scramble up to the higher levels of the stratosphere.

Sauter has a few tips for collectors. The first is to keep an old combo organ dry. "Most of the problems you see are mechanical," he offers. "Switch contacts will corrode and things like that, and that happens when they get damp. Most of the electronic parts are easy to replace, and Farfisa organs are easy to repair if you don't mind that everything is jammed in such a small space and that all the wires are the same color." Sauter cautions that the mechanical parts are almost impossible to find and that the best source of parts is another Farfisa.

He recalls being presented with an old Combo Compact that had been stored in an attic for years and had become a home for a family of mice. He (along with this author) spent a malodorous afternoon greedily stripping the organ of usable parts and cleaning the mouse droppings from those parts. The Farfisa company is now owned by Bontempi, and a call to their U.S. distributor reveals that the supplies of parts for Farfisa models over 20 years old are indeed depleted.

Tuning a Farfisa can also be a problem. Most Farfisas are tuned directly at the oscillator boards, although a few have a small panel inside the front of the organ with tuning knobs. A non-metallic flat screwdriver must be used (as with any organ like this, approaching the tuning control with a metal tool will throw the note out of tune before you even touch the thing). Extreme care must be taken trying to move these screws after 25 years of sitting; I've seen the insides of more than one Farfisa coil reduced to dust by over-eager organ tuners.

The debate still rages (in some quarters at least) over which organ had the better sound, the Vox or the Farfisa. While the Continental excelled at thin, reedy sounds, the original Farfisa line was best at a deeper, more flute-like sound. With the tone booster tabs on and at their most mellow, you get a wonderful sound that evokes a garage full of teenagers with long hair on a sultry summer day in 1966. Add a little vibrato and punch the knee level tone booster a few times with the beat and you could be in combo organ heaven. The sound of the FAST organs suffers by comparison. Since they came out at a time when the combo organ's popularity was waning, their sound never really had a chance to become part of our collective experience. Of course, nostalgia is a very personal phenomenon, and a person who spent many hours playing a FAST 4 in 1968 may find the sound of that instrument extremely powerful and evocative.

Seth Allen, from Albuquerque, New Mexico, considers himself a "hardcore" collector of Vox, Farfisa, and other combo organs. He has a definite opinion on this topic: "The Farfisa is a better organ. It is sturdier, and has a better action. It didn't look as good as the Vox, but it had a better sound." Allen admits the best organ for rock music is the

Hammond (which he also collects), but he says that for Tex-Mex as well as vintage music, the sound of a combo organ is perfect. Since he feels that moving and amplifying a combo organ can be more trouble than it's worth, he will often use a Yamaha SY77 to recreate combo organ sounds when playing jobs, but his real love is for the combo organs themselves. "These things were out of reach when I was a kid; it was like unrequited love. Now almost nobody wants them."

Collector Warren Dasho, however, casts his vote for the Vox. "Not only did the Continental look better, it sounded better," he says. "The Vox drawbars gave you better control and a better sound."

The Organ Giants Jump In

Baldwin. By the mid-1960s, it was clear to just about everyone in the music business that strange and wonderful things were happening. Stores that once catered to moms and dads looking at pianos for junior and sis, students looking for clarinets, and the occasional pro looking for a new accordion found themselves overrun with teenagers desperate to spend as much money as they possibly could on anything that looked like the instruments the groups on TV or at the local high school played. Baldwin had been selling pianos and organs for years, and they knew a good thing when they saw it. By late 1965, Baldwin had come out with a couple of guitar amps of its own and bought the English guitar company Burns (legendary English lead guitarist Hank Marvin played a Burns — but wait, this is the wrong publication). They also came out with a couple of combo organs (not to mention a solidbody electric combo harpsichord).

The Baldwin combo organ, at close to 100 pounds and $900, was large, heavy, and expensive for a single-keyboard organ. Made at the Baldwin factory in Arkansas, of several layers of wood and protective metal trim, these things were built to last. Finished in bright blue and black, the combo organ matched the Baldwin amplifier line. Although they are fairly rare, a number of Baldwins have made it to the 1990s relatively intact because of their tank-like construction and because of the fact that, unlike for most combo organs, some spare parts are available.

The Howard combo organ came out in 1966, and was about half the price of its big brother Baldwin. This, as I mentioned before, was an Italian import with a blue and black finish to match the rest of the Baldwin line. Making an educated guess, I would say this organ came from the same Italian company that made the Vox organs of the same era, since a fair number of the parts seem to be interchangeable. Another combo organ called the Doric looks enough like the Howard to make me think that it may also share a common parentage with the Jaguar. (Having never had the opportunity to look inside one of the things, I can't prove or disprove my hunch.)

The fact that parts for the Howard are still available may be a godsend to desperate Vox owners. The oscillator boards look identical to those in the Jaguar (although I have never tried switching them), and I have replaced Italian Continental keys with Howard keys. The bottom two octaves of the Howard are reversed to denote a bass section. While the Continental and Howard keys aren't identical, they're essentially interchangeable and the difference is scarcely noticeable.

The sound of the Baldwin combo organ is good, if uninspired. Set up rather like a Farfisa, the voice tabs are to the right; flute, reed, and string voices are available at 16', 8', 4' and 2⅔' pitches. In the center, where the tone booster voices are on the Farfisa, are four preset flute voices. To the left are vibrato and bass controls. This organ is unlike most in that the entire two-octave bass section can be switched to respond to the treble voices. While the flute voices are very nice, I can see where the sound of this organ would have been too much like

The Baldwin combo organ (right) was heavy, sturdy, and ruggedly built. Its Italian cousin, the Howard (L), was smaller, lighter, cheaper, and can claim kinship with contemporary Italian Vox organs.

that of a "real" organ for the Baldwin to have become really popular in rock bands in the '60s.

The sound of the Howard is something else altogether. Raucous and raspy, the Howard creates the trashy garage-band sound perfectly. If it uses the same oscillators as the Jaguar, it certainly uses different filters, because the Jaguar at its raunchiest can't come close to this thing. A knob on the front panel is pulled out to physically couple 16', 8', and 4' pitches to create a sound that is not only cheesy but cheesy and big to boot.

According to Bill Stevens, an organ technician who worked for Baldwin during the 1960s, these combo organs were built primarily to appease Baldwin exclusive dealers who carried only Baldwin instruments and were eager to serve the growing number of customers who wanted to buy combo equipment. Stevens, who now owns Stevens Custom Organs [330 North West Ave., Fayetteville, AR 72701], still has a few parts for these old organs in stock, but he is sentimental neither about the Baldwin combo organs nor about any of the other combo organs. "They did not use innovative organ technology," he muses, "and they did not make good organ sounds." He feels they were only designed to be loud. Stevens also warns that parts for combo organs in general will be extremely hard to find because these instruments were thought at the time to be only a fad with little lasting power. He estimates that Baldwin only made their combo organs from about 1966 to 1968, selling just a few hundred a year. Stevens affirms that the Italian company that built the Howard organ also built combo organs sold by a number of other companies, and that many of the parts are interchangeable.

Wurlitzer. While the Wurlitzer company may be best known for its huge theater organs, and rock and jazz keyboard players will fondly recall the long line of Wurlitzer electric pianos, Wurlitzer also made a combo organ. The complete antithesis of the Baldwin, the Wurlitzer, which used integrated circuits, was one of the smallest and lightest combo organs. Besides its small size, its most striking visual feature was its stand: a single pedestal that attached to the middle of the underside of the organ. These features give the Wurlitzer

The smallest of the mighty Wurlitzers, this combo organ was remarkably compact and light. Note the single-pedestal stand. Surprisingly, the unit was very stable.

an uncanny, contemporary look, not unlike a Roland S-10 or the original Yamaha DX7 sitting on one of those Ultimate Support Apex column stands. Like a modern synth, this organ fit completely inside a separate carrying case.

If the Baldwin fit into the Farfisa mold, the Wurlitzer shared many traits with the Continental. Both had four-octave keyboards with no manual bass, both could play pitches of 16', 8', 4', 2⅔', 2', 1⅗', and 1' controlled by four drawbars. (Again, the level of the top four pitches was set with one drawbar.) The Wurlitzer drawbars looked more like slide switches than real drawbars and were called VIP Tone Levers (Variable Intensity and Pitch, not to be confused with the later Farfisa VIP, Very Important Portable organs of the 1970s). A fifth Tone Lever acted as sort of a combination of the fifth and sixth drawbars on the Continental: all the way in gave a flute voice, all the way out a very bright string sound. This organ also featured a set of 8' voice switches that selected string, reed, and brass voices that could be played alone or along with the drawbar voices.

While the sound of the Continental is thin and reedy, the sound of the Wurlitzer is strong, with lots of foundation. During the late '60s this organ had the reputation of not really sounding like a combo organ (which could have been considered good or bad depending on your taste at the time), and it remains one of the few combo organs that actually sounds much better played through a Leslie than through a guitar amp.

Morelock Organ Parts & Service [Rt. 1, Box 6, Rienzi, MS 38865. (601) 462-7611] still has a fairly large supply of parts for the Wurlitzer combo organ (whose official model number is 7300). Unfortunately, the unique pedestal stand is no longer available.

The Guitar Giants Jump In

Gibson. As legend has it, Ray Manzarek was looking for an organ to replace his Italian Vox, which had highly breakable plastic keys. Of the instruments that interested him, only one had a top flat enough to accommodate his Fender/Rhodes piano bass. Thus, one of the most photographed organ players of the late '60s brought the Gibson combo organ a degree of fame it never would have achieved had its top been rounded. The single-manual Gibson began life in the spring of 1967 as the Kalamazoo K101. By that summer it had been

The Gibson G101. Note the metal Gibson plate in front, which has replaced the script Kalamazoo logo, and the flat top, which is perfect for supporting a Fender/Rhodes piano bass.

renamed the Gibson G101. The Kalamazoo (which must be mighty rare) looked just like a Gibson with a pale green and gray finish, except in the front of the organ. Right under the keyboard, a metal script Kalamazoo logo is attached. This is replaced by a flat, rectangular metal plate with Gibson etched on it in the later models. All is not as cut and dried as it appears: My Gibson has the rectangular plate in front but is still labeled as a model K101 inside. Occasionally, photos of Manzarek show him playing Gibsons that are different colors (tan or completely black, for example); whether these were custom paint jobs or whether the instruments were actually offered in these colors, I can't say.

More rare is the dual-manual Gibson Stage Organ, which is similar to the 101 but finished in black and orange fabric. It came with its own orange-and-black amplifier — which attached to the organ by a special cord — and a matching fold-up organ bench. This amplifier is very similar to the Sabre Reverb I that shows up in the Farfisa catalogs of the time. The double-keyboard Gibson organ itself looks quite similar to the Lowrey portable organ, but since I've never had the chance to poke around inside a Lowrey, I can't really begin to discuss the relationship between these two organs other than to note that both were part of the CMI family.

The sound of the Gibson was immortalized on the later Doors records, especially *Absolutely Live*. One thing that makes this album interesting to keyboard players is the fact that Manzarek is shown on the cover and in the other photographs playing a Vox Continental. The organ played on most, if not all, of the record, however, is the Gibson. Although the Gibson has a very nice straight combo organ sound and can sound like a Vox or Farfisa to some extent, it also has a rough, percussive sound with a bit of sustain (all the flute voices on, mixture and bright on, and staccato off) that can't be imitated by any Continental. The Gibson, which at $995 was one of the most expensive single-manual combo organs, was also loaded with special effects like percussion, repeat, sustain, fuzz bass, and pedal-controlled trumpet "wow-wow" — what it was called in Gibson's ads, but an effect more commonly known as wah-wah.

Fender. If Vox, with their organs, guitars, amps, and drums, represented the British rock music scene, the Fender company was the icon for the American scene. Less well known than the Precision Bass and Stratocaster guitar, the Twin Reverb and Bandmaster amplifiers, and the Fender/Rhodes electric piano is the Fender Contempo combo organ. According to Steve Woodyard, who worked at Fender during the 1960s, Leo Fender had always

A Fender Contempo organ (R) shares the beach with a Fender Rhodes electronic piano, piano bass, and the exquisitely rare celeste in this 1968 Fender catalog photograph.

been interested in building keyboard instruments; of course the most famous result of this interest was Fender's partnership with Harold Rhodes and the popular Fender/Rhodes electric piano and piano bass. The Contempo combo organ joins the Fender/Rhodes celeste (a treble version of the piano bass) in semi-obscurity today. Woodyard remembers that Fender wanted to become a complete musical supplier during the mid-'60s, and a combo organ was a logical addition to the line. Built at the Fender factory in Fullerton, California, the bright-red-and-black Contempo featured a keyboard by the Pratt-Read Company (who also built the keyboard for the Fender/Rhodes instruments) and a chrome stand that allowed the organ to be tilted at an angle. The Contempo used an interesting voicing structure. Each voice had three volume-boost tabs which, used in a number of combinations, gave each voice eight possible volume levels, the same number of levels as available from the Hammond drawbars. The Contempo was also one of the few combo organs that offered a separate 5⅓' voice, making it possible to play the popular 16', 8', 5⅓' Hammond combination. Again, this is not to say that the Fender sounded like a Hammond. The Contempo had a five-octave manual with a 17-note, reversed-color bass section; as on the Baldwin, the bass section could be turned off, allowing the player to play the treble voices from the whole keyboard. Tremolo was

available as well as the standard vibrato, and a pedal that controlled tone as well as volume was included. Harold Rhodes, inventor of the Fender/Rhodes pianos, says that the Contempo organ would be very rare; he only recalls them being shown at one or two shows in the late '60s. "At this time," he recalls, "combo organs were on the wane and electric pianos were taking over." Another Fender combo organ, the Starmaker, apparently never made it into production, although the Vibratone, a small Leslie speaker designed to match the Fender amplifier line, was popular for a couple of years.

For those who hated plugging their organ into their amp, their amp into their speakers, and their pedal into their organ, Kustom had the perfect answer: The Kustom combo organ, which could also serve as an extra sofa in a pinch.

who let the 'cat'
out of the bag?

Who started the rumor that the PANTHER Portable Combo Organ was the one to hear and buy? How does the word get around so fast? All we know is that we're shipping PANTHERS as fast as we can—and that they're selling as fast as you can show them. Now a national advertising program, "celebrity" group tie-ins and dealer promotion aids are building up demand even faster! It's that hot, winning combination of sound styling, portability, engineering and special features that catches fire!

For information, call or write.

MERSON / UNICORD

33 Frost Street, Westbury, N. Y. 11590
(516) 333-9100
A subsidiary of
Gulf & Western Industries, Inc.

Catalog available on request.

The Panther was one of a number of look-alike Italian combo organs that proved to be very popular. It was distributed by the company that eventually became Korg.

Woodyard [10461 Lexington, Stanton, CA 90680. (714) 821-7859], who still has a small supply of Contempo components, says that most of the electronic parts are pretty standard and can be easily replaced. Tuning the Contempo can be a bit of a mystery. "You have to dig the wax plug out of the coil," he says. "That gives you access to a small hex nut that can be adjusted with a non-metallic tool."

Although the Contempo was rarely used by any famous bands, it did show up in numerous "Fendermen" combos that prided themselves on their exclusive use of Fender equipment (usually along with Rogers drums).

Others. There are so many other wonderful combo organs out there waiting to be explored; this article could go on forever: the wonderful Kustom Kombo organ — keyboard, amp, speakers, police-siren treble-driver horns, all in one

handy, padded package on wheels (I often wondered if the thing would roll away from you as you played it); the famous Italian Panther organs (which came in a choice of colors — white with black, red with black, or black with red) and their identical cousins, the Capri and Lo Duca; the mysterious Doric with its possible ties to the Vox Jaguar; the Rheem, the Excelsior, the Nomad; and so on.

Where to Find the Darn Things

You never really know where you'll stumble across a real combo organ treasure. Music stores will sometimes have a storeroom or basement full of what some people would consider junk. Although the chances of finding a '50 Fender Broadcaster guitar in there are pretty slim, you may well come across some keyboard treasures. When you go to a music store, ask around and keep asking: Oftentimes the existence of such a room isn't even known to all the salespeople. I've come across lots of pretty good organs hidden away in music stores. Of course, when you find them you may be faced with one of two scenarios: The English Continental you just found is considered a piece of junk by the store, so they will sell it for $50; but, since they consider it junk, it has been treated like junk for the last twenty years and it may well be junk by now. On the other hand, if the store considers it to be a valuable antique, it will have been taken much better care of, but it may be quite expensive.

Going to garage sales can be tedious, but I've heard of people finding great stuff at them. As a rule I would say that an old organ that has been sitting in a person's home for 30 years will have aged better than one sitting in a store. Often store organs will have lived a violent second or third life as a rental instrument before being deposited in the damp cellar.

Check the want ads. Run want ads of your own, and don't just run them in music magazines. I would guess that a lot of combo organ players of 25 years ago aren't even involved with music anymore, but they may still have some wonderful instruments they would be happy to be rid of.

Before you buy anything, check it out completely. Play every key with every voice to see what's missing, check the inside for corrosion and rust, look for signs of obvious abuse, see what kind of accessories are still with the organ. A missing foot pedal on some organs will mean the volume will be permanently all the way down. A missing stand will affect the visual impact of the organ and may lower its value to collectors. I'm not saying you shouldn't buy an organ if something doesn't work on it, but you should know what's wrong with it before you buy it. Often a pair of less desirable instruments will complement each other well. A Farfisa that looks beautiful but is electronically dead would be a great purchase for a collector who has a similar model that plays perfectly but is a physical wreck; a new combo organ could be resurrected that would be worth more than the sum of its parts. The prices of combo organs vary widely; while I've seen collectors selling Farfisas and Continentals for five or six hundred dollars, I've found the same models for as low as $40 at music stores and garage sales. It's probably worth looking around to find the combo organ of your dreams.

Coda

A friend of mine collects automobiles. He mentioned that some older collectors have put vast amounts of time and money into renovating cars from the '20s and '30s only to have people begin to lose interest in them. It turns out that the younger collectors are mainly interested in cars from the '50s and '60s. As my friend puts it, "We're nostalgic about the things that were important to us when we were younger." Many keyboard players who came of age with the DX7 and Mirage may well have no interest in these ancient instruments, and those '60s musicians who never liked combo organs in the first place probably have even less use for them now. But for those of us who grew up under the powerful spell of the combo organ, the magic is still there.

Combo organ collector Seth Allen has a Mini Compact setup that he doesn't play; he has it displayed with photographs of the '60s. "Yeah, it's like a shrine," he says. "We're musicians; we can't forget our roots."

SEQUENCER HISTORY IN A NUTSHELL

Mechanical, Analog, Digital

BY JIM AIKIN

Ever since the invention of clockwork, people have been fascinated by the idea of machines playing music. In the 18th century, classical composers were commissioned to compose for the ornate music boxes of the day. Sticking metal pins into a rotating drum wasn't a real user-friendly process, however.

The player piano, with its paper rolls and pneumatic action, was a big step forward. In a 1925 in-

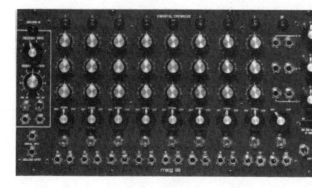

Moog's 960 sequencer module generated a single voltage-control output with up to 24 steps, or three eight-step outputs.

terview, Igor Stravinsky expressed his enthusiasm: "There is a new polyphonic truth in the player piano. There are new possibilities. . . . It has a future,

yes. Men will write for it." During the same period, concerto performances for player piano and live orchestra attracted great attention. And at least one artist, Conlon Nancarrow, found an original musical voice in the player piano. Still, the mechanical limitations were daunting, and the player piano never made any inroads among composers.

The first step into electronic sequencing was a short one: In 1955, the RCA Synthesizer, with its banks of vacuum tubes, played whatever notes had been punched into a roll of paper tape. Holes in the tape tripped electro-mechanical relays, and the relays controlled a number of aspects of the sound, including pitch, envelope, and portamento.

In the early '60s, electronic music experimenters were still assembling melodies by the primitive method of recording oscillator tones on tape at various fixed pitches, and then chopping the tape apart and splicing the pieces back together in whatever order might be musically necessary. In the course of building his first electronic music system for the San Francisco Tape Center in

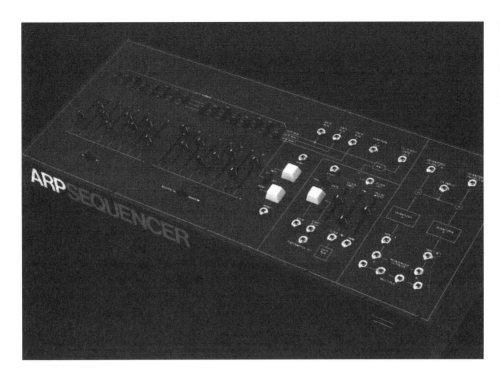

Introduced in 1979, the ARP Sequencer could output a single 16-note line or two eight-note sequences.

1963, Don Buchla came up with an automated system that eliminated this type of tape splicing. His invention came to be known as the analog sequencer.

Ten years later, analog sequencers had become a standard feature on modular synthesizers, which were the most advanced electronic music devices available at the time. Moog, Buchla, ARP, Polyfusion, E-mu, and several other companies made them. A typical analog sequencer put out control voltages that changed the pitch of the oscillators, and gate signals that opened up the envelope generators — a pre-digital, pre-MIDI form of standardized interfacing.

The memory of an analog sequencer consisted of a row or rows of hardware potentiometers. The

The AS-1 analog sequencer from Polyfusion provided up to 16 steps.

Roland's MC-4 Micro Composer was a hybrid sequencer, using digital techniques and control-voltage technology. Its production followed that of the MC-8.

What may look like a vintage analog sequencer is actually a MIDI device that is currently in production. In ways, the German-made Doepfer MAQ 16/3 resembles the old Moog 960 sequencer module. Members of Kraftwerk helped design the MAQ.

advanced the sequence to a new vertical column of pots, and the output voltages changed to whatever values those pots were set to.

By using a control voltage to change the speed of the clock, irregular or syncopated rhythms could be created. But the analog sequencer quickly developed a reputation for sounding dull and mechanical because, compounding its other limitations, most people simply let the clock run without controlling its speed, producing incessantly repeated patterns of eighth-notes.

pitch of a note in the sequence was changed by turning the pot corresponding to that note. That's right, one note per pot. Anybody who ever worked with an analog sequencer will remember how much fun it was to separately tune each and every note in a sequence, only to find when you finished that the oscillators themselves had drifted, forcing you to tune everything again.

The smallest analog sequencers had only eight pots, while the largest had three or four rows with 16 pots each, and so could play three- or four-note chords. The sequence was "played" by a low-frequency clock oscillator. Each tick of the clock

The first digital sequencers were built in the early-'70s by David Cockerell and Peter Zinovieff of EMS, followed by Dave Rossum and Scott Wedge at E-mu, Tom Oberheim, and Ralph Dyck (whose design was the inspiration for the Roland MC-8). Like their immediate predecessors, these devices had CV/gate outputs. They had more memory capacity, however (between 250 and 1,000 notes), and the output could easily be calibrated in $1/12$-volt steps, so the tuning problems were far less severe.

The E-mu 4060, which appeared in 1976, was a

microprocessor-equipped polyphonic keyboard controller with a built-in sequencer. The sequencer had real-time input, data storage to audio tape, and ten "bins" in which separate sequences could be recorded. No editing was possible however, and of course the keyboard was not velocity-sensitive.

Today's universally used system of auto-correcting rhythms was developed by Roger Linn in 1978 for his first drum machine, the LM-1. The LM-1 also introduced the idea of building complete song arrangements by chaining together short segments. Many of today's musicians got their first dose of digital sequencing by programming patterns in one of the host of drum boxes that followed the LM-1's lead.

The high point of pre-MIDI sequencer evolution was unquestionably the visual score editor built into the Buchla 400. Designed mainly to play the 400's own internal voices, the score editor was a six-voice system with individual note editing, block move, delete, loop, and copy functions, patch change commands, and other goodies. A CRT that plugged directly into the instrument provided a real-time scrolling display of the sequence in bar-graph notation.

Better known to rock musicians was the Oberheim DSX, which interfaced with the OB-8 and DMX drum machine to form the Oberheim System. The DSX spoke the same digital language as the OB-8, but also had eight CV and gate outputs. It stored ten polyphonic sequences of ten tracks each, and could record patch changes and tempo changes, but had no individual note editing.

Several other digital sequencers were floating around in the early '80s, including popular models from Roland. They were all hardware-based units, however. Prior to MIDI, only two systems based on personal computers gained any wide acceptance: The alphaSyntauri and the Passport Soundchaser. Both of these instruments were based around the Apple II computer, and could generate sounds only by using plug-in oscillator cards, which didn't sound very good. Because they were already working in this area, Passport was able to offer the first-ever MIDI sequencer, MIDI/4, early in 1984.

The arrival of a universal specification for note data has caused an explosion in sequencing far beyond anything that most of us could have imagined a decade ago. It's beginning to look as if Stravinsky's prediction may have been right after all.

ROLAND MC-8 MICROCOMPOSER

Digital/Analog Hybrid Sequencer

BY MARK VAIL

Long before MIDI, there was voltage control, and digital sequencers were rarer than homemade costumes at a Hollywood Halloween party. Typical analog sequencers of the day — knob-laden boxes — generated control voltages for determining oscillator frequency and gate signals that opened envelope generators. The majority were limited to sequences from eight to 16 steps in length, which of course could be looped for continuous playback. Better analog sequencers could simultaneously output two to four different voltages for chords.

Then, in the early '70s, electronics dabblers started playing with discrete TTL logic circuits (transistor-transistor logic, or just plain digital for the rest of us) — the forerunner of the microprocessor chip. Since these digital sequencers still had to drive analog synths, they output control voltages.

The first of these that we're aware of was the EMS Synthi 100 from England. Designed by David Cockerell and Peter Zinovieff, and released in 1971, the monstrous Synthi 100 measured something like eight or ten feet long (according to Cock-

erell, "You had to take walls down to get it into studios") and featured a three-track digital sequencer. EMS delivered two Synthi 100s in '71: one to Belgrade Radio in Yugoslavia, the other to the BBC Radiophonic Workshop in London. Then came the Oberheim DS-2, which Tom Oberheim introduced sometime in 1972. It was a monophonic device that came prepared to interface with either Moog or ARP synths. You entered notes — up to 72 of them — from the synth keyboard, and the DS-2 could spit them back, hogging the single voice of the synth it was driving.

Meanwhile, up in Vancouver, BC, Ralph Dyck wanted something other than a keyboard to trigger his homebrew synthesizer — designed in '70 or '71 and based on the specs used in ARP synthesizers. So, in 1972, he built a prototype sequencer that was, like the DS-2, based on TTL circuits. But unlike the Oberheim, notes and related data were entered using a 10-key calculator keyboard. "I could enter values for pitch, step time, and gate time for controlling the envelope generators, oscillators, filters, and voltage-controlled amps," Dyck explains. "I had my own synthesizer studio, Little Mountain

Sound, and I was using the sequencer regularly, working on jingles, records, and film."

Enthused by his success, Dyck built a second prototype. "It was much better," he recalls. "It had a massive amount of memory — enough for 1,024 notes."

As with other digital sequencers of that time, Dyck's was limited to playing monophonic lines. "Since I could only play one voice at a time, I worked out a synchronization system using FSK (frequency shift keying), which is used a lot now. I know I used it as early as 1973. I should have done something about patenting it."

Dyck figured other musicians could benefit from his sequencer, so he went in search of an interested manufacturer. "I tried to present the idea to ARP, but they had no use for it. I couldn't get anybody in North America interested. Then a friend of mine, who was the Roland distributor in Canada, put me in touch with Ikutaro Kakehashi, the president of Roland.

"In January or February of '76, Kakehashi came over to have a look at my prototype and decided to manufacture a sequencer based on my ideas. After a few days of negotiation, we came to an agreement. They didn't exactly use my circuitry. They hired a wizard computer guy — I believe from Toshiba — named Tamada. He incorporated the

8080A microprocessor to implement the same method of encoding the pitch, time, and phrasing information, except that he was able to make it output eight channels of control voltages, unlike my very simple one-channel prototype. Tamada improved the design a great deal. Roland was able to produce a better version of my sequencer, because they had infinitely better technical resources than I did."

The results were introduced to the electronic music world as the MC-8 MicroComposer. It retained the step-entry and ten-key pad features found in Dyck's prototype sequencers. Although the MC-8 wasn't the first polyphonic digital sequencer, it was one of the most popular and visi-

If you think your MIDI sequencer is hard to deal with, consider the Roland MC-8 MicroComposer. Notes and other events in an MC-8 sequencer had to be entered one-at-a-time on the ten-key pad in the middle of the MC-8's control panel.

VITAL STATISTICS

Produced: 1977 to 1982.

Total Number Made: About 300.

Manufacturer: Roland Corporation.

Description: One of the first commercially available polyphonic digital sequencers.

Features: Step-time programming only; data entry using 10-key pad. 16k of RAM memory, enough for over 5,300 notes. Note editing by measure and step numbers. Measure copying. Eight control-voltage outputs, eight gate outputs, six multiplex outputs. External CV and gate inputs. Tape sync (FSK) and data storage connectors. Remote start/stop input.

Insider Information: Design inspired by prototype sequencer developed by Ralph Dyck in Vancouver, BC. ARP Instruments had first shot at buying Dyck's ideas, but ignored the opportunity.

Original Retail Price: $4,795.

Current Street Value: $200.

Current Dealer Price: $250 to $600.

ble. Second after the aforementioned EMS Synthi 100 was the E-mu 4060 polyphonic keyboard, which included a souped-up version of Oberheim's DS-2. The 4060 was designed by Dave Rossum for E-mu's modular synth systems. It was first shipped in December '74.

As we said, the MC-8 was more popular than these other systems. While Rossum estimates that E-mu shipped at least 20 or 30 and maybe as many as 70 or 80 polyphonic keyboards with the digital sequencer, Kakehashi tells us there were 300 MC-8s manufactured. (Only a very limited number of the behemoth $25,000 Synthi 100s were produced.)

Three hundred? A pretty meager figure compared to the 7,000-plus Prophet-5s or 10,000-plus Minimoogs that were produced respectively by Sequential Circuits and Moog Music. Can Roland have made a profit on the MC-8? "When we were developing the MC-8," Kakehashi admits, "I underestimated the production costs. Even though it wasn't a success financially as a product, I believe that it was very successful, because it was the first such product in the world."

Ralph Dyck concurs: "It cost them, I'm sure, more than they made. But I think it gave Roland an excuse to get into the microprocessor. It was good for them to do that."

Even though there was a limited number of MC-8s, the sequencer made its mark. Composer/synthesist Isao Tomita was the first MC-8 user in Japan. Toto's Steve Porcaro had — or still has — three of them, according to Dyck, who worked with Porcaro for almost ten years, during which he extensively modified Porcaro's MC-8s to interface with Toto's huge Polyfusion synth system to "do a whole bunch of things the MC-8 wasn't really designed to do. I got into the MC-8 and expanded the I/O so that we could trigger a lot more things on the synthesizer in a digital fashion, basically to afford ourselves more control over the Polyfusion."

Suzanne Ciani was another diehard MC-8 fan. "I did my whole first album, *Digital Waves*, using the MC-8," she tells us. "I had it hooked into my Prophet-5. The MC-8 came with program sheets for you to write down every note and then convert them to numbers. I have scores from that period where, above every single note, there's a number for the MC-8."

Ciani has worked with a formidable number of sequencing systems in the years since she finished

Digital Waves, but she fondly remembers her experiences with the MC-8. Number one in the we'll-laugh-at-this-later category took place during the two-year, weekend-only production cycle for the album. "Before one of the Saturday recording sessions, I had my assistant enter the note numbers for the piece I was recording that day. I was paying dearly for the studio time and trying to be calm. Unfortunately, my assistant had entered all the wrong note numbers, so everything was completely useless. I thought, 'What an incredible task to have to enter all the right notes during the recording session!' But it had to be done. So we very calmly, *very*, *very* calmly started the six-hour process of getting that stuff in, and then the whole session went great.

"It was a wonderful machine. You could do velocity and, if you were really good, you could do crescendos. Unless you used the MC-8, you don't appreciate how easy everything is now."

Like to know one MC-8 characteristic that makes today's sequencers look so easy? "There wasn't any SMPTE back then," Ciani recalls. "In order to drive the MC-8, I would put a series of clicks on four separate tracks of the 16-track deck. I'd put the quarter-note click on one track, an eighth-note click on the second, a 16th-note click on the third, and a 32nd-note click on the fourth. If I wanted a 16th-note passage, I had to drive the sequencer with the 16th-note click track. Then I would do a bar count on another track with my voice. I had to use up five tracks just for control information."

Thank your lucky stars that floppy and hard disks are so prevalent these days. You could store MC-8 sequences, but only on cassette tape. "There wasn't any other media available at that time," Kakehashi explains. "Disk drives were very, very expensive. There weren't any popular computers that had a disk drive."

Your turn, Suzanne: "It was very tricky. You'd have to set a level for the data tape, and there was no way to calibrate the MC-8's input. You had to do crazy things to find a consistently successful routine. When we found one, we'd use it religiously. We'd use the exact same cassette recorder every time, with the EQ set the same. It was very iffy."

See how MIDI has spoiled us? Thank goodness nobody then knew how easy things would get. In fact, people were downright grateful for the tools they had.

Dyck was appreciative too. "It never would have come to anything if Roland hadn't been interested. I'm eternally grateful to them for pursuing something that was fairly esoteric for the time. I give them an enormous amount of credit for doing that."

FAMOUS ROLAND SYNTHS

Since we're cutting Roland short without decent coverage of a single vintage synthesizer from their extensive and historic line, we present here a pictorial look at some of those instruments.

The monophonic Roland SH-5 came to market in early '76. Not many of us noticed here in the States. We were too busy concentrating on the Minimoog and ARP Odyssey.

Roland's SH-7 came out in 1978 at a price of $1,795.

If you can find one, a Roland Paraphonic 505 might go for less than $100.

Roland deserves credit for a history of offering vocoders in one form or another. In the VP-330 Vocoder Plus, they combined a vocoder with an ensemble-style keyboard (strings and choir). Today it's worth $250 to $400 on the street, and up to $600 from a dealer or store.

Four-voice polyphony, programmability, and an arpeggiator were some of the features of the Roland Jupiter-4 Compuphonic synth, released in 1978 with a suggested retail of $2,795.

Even though the Roland Saturn 09 looks like a monophonic synth, it's actually an organ. It showed up in 1980 for an asking price of $795.

Roland's Jupiter-8 had eight voices, 16 oscillators, both high- and lowpass filters with selectable 12dB- or 24dB-per-octave attenuation slopes, and 64 patch memories. And an arpeggiator. Not many synths these days have arpeggiators, which is a shame. Asking price when the Jupiter-8 was new in 1980 was $5,295. Today it will only set you back $400 to $800 on the street, or $650 to $1,200 from a dealer or store.

The Juno-6 six-voice polyphonic synth appeared in 1982. Our market expert tells us it's worth a measly $125 today.

Strap-on convenience, courtesy of Roland's SH-101 synth (introduced in 1983). (photo by Jon Sievert)

When Roland's Juno-106 was introduced in 1984, it packed one of the most potent MIDI implementations of any synth to that point.

Practically qualifying for vintage status, Roland's D-50 linear synthesizer (1987) appeared during the Yamaha DX7's declining years and carried the most-popular-synth title until Korg introduced the M1 in '88.

For a number of years, Roland offered optional slider-laden programmers for their synths. The 56-slider PG-1000 made programming the D-50 easier than dealing with multiple parameter screens and a single slider.

In 1991, Roland thrilled all those synthesists in search of knobs and sliders with the introduction of the JD-800. While others have been patiently waiting for machines like the Oberheim OB-MX and Waldorf Wave to finally make it to market, we've been happily tweaking away at the JD-800's 59 sliders. We call *that* "retro."

LINN LM-1 DRUM COMPUTER

Going Beyond the Beat Box

BY MARK VAIL

n this day of 16-bit arrogance, mention the word "great" in reference to an 8-bit device and you're bound to raise a few cynical eyebrows. But if it weren't for an 8-bit marvel known as the Linn LM-1 — with which Roger Linn introduced a number of drum machine features taken for granted today — it might have taken us a lot longer to reach this enlightened age of the digital drum machine.

Before the LM-1, 99% of all drum machines were essentially organ add-ons that exclusively featured preset rhythm patterns. The final 1% comprised John Simonton's programmable drum machine (distributed by Paia), the Roland CR-78 programmable drum box, and a 6' x 2' beast that Bob Moog built in the late '60s but never put into production. Not only that, but they all made sounds using analog synthesis, just like the Prophet-5, ARP Quadra, and Oberheim OB-X — popular polyphonic synths of the day (c. 1980). If you haven't tried it, fabricating realistic drum sounds with analog circuits is about as satisfying as eating roast beef with a teaspoon. Roger Linn changed all that by introducing his LM-1.

"I was a starving musician," Roger remembers. "I had a little four-track recorder and some music gear in one room of my house where I was making demos. Of course, the hardest thing to record is drums in your home studio. I remember looking at drum machines, but they were too expensive. They cost something like $500."

Furthermore, as Roger said back in early '88, "I wanted a drum machine that did more than play preset samba patterns and didn't sound like crickets."

So what did he do? He went out and made his own drum machine, one with a price tag of $5,000. But it wasn't that simple or quick, and many a notable musician didn't sneeze at the price because, unlike those $500 drum machines, the LM-1 played samples of real drums — a radical departure for that time.

But how did Roger jump from being a "starving musician" to the manufacturer of a digital drum machine? "I had an interest in computers, and a little S-100 buss system. I had taken a couple of classes on how to write computer programs in BASIC and assembly code, and I had fooled

The earliest LM-1s, assembled in Roger Linn's house, lacked the quantize and swing-time controls on the front panel. Also note the engraved buttons. The level sliders on all LM-1s were accompanied by triple-throw switches for assigning each drum sound hard left, center, or hard right.

around with hardware a little bit. I sent away to Roland for a voice generator from one of their existing analog-synthesis drum machines, hooked it up to my computer, and wrote a program that displayed a grid on the computer screen showing time versus drum events. You'd plug little stars into positions on the grid, hit the space bar, and it would play the pattern. It eventually evolved to include chaining of patterns into a song. A lot of the ideas that I came up with at that time — like quantizing or shuffle play — were really acci-

dents of programming that eventually turned into LM-1 features."

Sampling was a little-known term back then. Besides developing his own drum-machine programming ideas, Linn had to pave his own way into the sampling world. "I tried different methods of sampling," he explains. "I basically knew it had to be 8-bit, and a ComDAC (companding digital-to-analog converter) could provide more dynamic range than 8-bit linear. That was a suggestion from some engineer at the time, so I tried it out and it

VITAL STATISTICS

Produced: 1980 to 1983. Development started in 1978.

Total Number Made: 525.

Manufacturer: Linn Electronics, Hollywood and, later, Tarzana, CA. (Out of business since early 1986.)

Description: First programmable drum machine to feature sampled sounds.

Features: Twelve 8-bit samples (kick, snare, hi-hat, cabasa, tambourine, 2 toms, 2 congas, cowbell, clave, and handclap). All sounds tunable. Built-in 13-channel stereo mixer. 100 patterns. Pattern chaining. Real-time programming. Variable swing-time and quantization programming functions. Two main pairs of outputs (right and left, hi- and low-level) and 12 individual outputs. Tape sync and data storage connectors. Clock output with variable pulse frequency; external clock input. Footswitch input.

Insider Information: First 35 assembled in Roger Linn's home. Then Bob Easton of 360 Systems took over LM-1 manufacturing. Earliest LM-1s featured engraved buttons, but lacked front-panel controls for swing-time and quantization functions and weren't up to the quality standards set by those manufactured by 360 Systems.

Original Retail Price: $4,995. Later bumped to $5,495, returned to $4,995, and finally lowered to $3,995 before production ended.

Current Street Value: $150 to $500.

Current Dealer Price: $200 to $700.

worked. I believe that I was the first one to use them, and they became sort of the standard for 8-bit sound enhancement. A ComDAC is just a single-chip part, originally created for use in the telephone industry to create a wider dynamic range out of eight bits.

"I believe the LM-1s sounded better because I didn't incorporate strict textbook digital sampling theory. By the book, I should have filtered out any playback frequencies above the Nyquist frequency, which is a little less than one-half of the sampling frequency. I used a sampling rate of around 27kHz. However, filtering on playback would have made some of the drums sound pretty dull. Instead, I let some of the frequencies above that point get through, because the results — which can get distorted — sounded like the sizzle of drums anyway. Thanks to that decision, the LM-1 sounded better than some machines with the same sampling rate, because it had the highs. In a sense, I'm thankful that I wasn't very good at the engineering."

So why did Roger opt for sampled sounds? "Originally, I was planning on using analog sounds. But [Toto keyboardist] Steve Porcaro may have been the first one who suggested sampling to me. Steve's always been a real creative thinker; he's given a lot of great ideas to a lot of manufacturers."

While sampling caused one set of problems, devising the LM-1's operating system wasn't much fun either. "My original development system was an old Radio Shack TRS-80 Model 1, which was absolutely hideous to use. The disk storage space was tiny and the disk access speed was so slow that I had to severely limit the comments in my code — a very dangerous thing to do in itself — because it would have taken too long to save it. Saving a file often took two minutes. Plus, the power supply was so unreliable that, during a long save, I might lose something along the way."

Linn's shuffle feature was unique in the drum machine world, and it's found on every device he's manufactured — including the currently produced Akai MPC-60 II. On the front panel of all but the earliest LM-1s is a column of six red LEDs, labeled from 50% to 70% in increments of 4%. Linn explains: "In order to create a sixteenth-note swing or shuffle feel, you unevenly split the timing of an eighth-note, thereby delaying every second sixteenth-note by some time factor. The LM-1 percentages signify the interval between the first and second sixteenth-note and between the third and fourth sixteenth-note, and so on. If you want both notes to play perfectly even — no shuffle — you would select 50%, which means 50/50. If you make it one clock later, it would be 54/46, or 54%. Delaying it two clocks makes it 58/42, or 58% for the first half and 42% for the second half."

These percentages are somewhat approximate, because the LM-1's clock resolution was 48 ppq. (The minimum acceptable resolution on today's MIDI sequencer is 96 ppq.) Still, there's something about that LM-1 feel that other drum machines haven't quite matched. "Nobody really programs their swing algorithms quite right. Roland's R-5 and R-8 have swing, but you only have one gradation between triplets and straight sixteenths, which isn't practical. Other drum machines that I've heard have really accurate timing. But the LM-1's rhythmic success might have been due to something haphazard, like maybe I didn't clip the front end of the snare sample properly, so the resulting delay would make it sound a little more laid back."

Linn realized early on that musicians could get more out of his sampled drum sounds if they were tunable, and if each sound had a separate output, so that they could be routed to different effects processors. Another feature found only on his drum machines is a knob for varying the hi-hat's decay. It was on the LM-1's back panel — not very accessible. On later machines — the LinnDrum and Akai MPC-60 — he put it on the front panel, right there with the volume and tempo knobs.

Compare the two LM-1s shown in this chapter and you'll notice some variations in their front panels. There were two separate LM-1 production cycles. "When I first started making the LM-1, I was doing them out of one room in my house," Linn recalls. "I hired assemblers to come in and do the work. The trouble was, I didn't know that much about manufacturing costs or purchasing, but I wanted the thing to be slick. I figured each button should have a name on it. I think it cost me $1.87 per button to have them engraved. It was ridiculous, especially since there were more than 40 buttons on the front panel. Eventually, I went to a non-engraved button and silk-screened the functions on the front panel above the buttons."

Buttons weren't the only problem. You can't tell from our photos, but the LM-1 is deep — over 22". But it's a lot lighter than you might imagine. "When I was designing it, I was doing it all at the same time. I remember I had to get the design in for the metal chassis, and I didn't know how big it needed to be, because I didn't know how big the circuit boards were going to be. So I guessed, and made it as big as I thought it could possibly need to be. If you look inside the thing, there's a lot of wasted space. I also used a power supply that had far more power than was ever needed, because I didn't know how much circuitry would need to be in there. It was just a comedy of errors. But by going with a lot of overkill, even though it was more expensive, at least it worked well."

In other words, the things were built like tanks — for the most part. "In the early ones, there were some software bugs. I think we removed most of the bugs by the time we made about the 75th LM-1. Then we replaced all the ROMs in the earlier units. The very early ones — before Bob Easton's 360 Systems started manufacturing them for me — weren't manufactured to such high standards. When Bob started assembling the units for me, the quality really improved. I don't remember exactly when Bob took over production, but it was very early, probably after about 35 units.

"I suppose the most common problems in the earlier units were due to my not knowing enough about the manufacturing process. For example, all the ICs were socketed on the very earliest LM-1s, which is a mistake because any connector has a chance of getting corroded. Bob recommended that I stop using sockets, which reduced the cost and made the LM-1 much more reliable."

Even before the LM-1 went into production, Linn was able to drum up (pun intended) buyers. They must have wondered what they were in for, though. "I had a prototype that wasn't actually producible, basically a cardboard box with a bunch of wire-wrap boards mounted inside. But it worked. I would show it to people who had come over to my house, and they would give me 50% deposits on the finished product. On occasion, I would take this cardboard box down to somebody's session and show it to them. It was pretty hilarious.

"Later, when I had a *real* prototype, I'd keep it in my car. At one party, I showed it to some members of Fleetwood Mac, and I generated some sales from that."

Linn attracted quite a few musicians of note. We've heard that Prince swore by his LM-1 and refused to get rid of it. Anybody else we know, Roger? "I used to play with Leon Russell, so he bought one. Stevie Wonder bought one of the first ones. Boz Scaggs bought one. So did Daryl Dragon (the Captain) and Peter Gabriel. There were other people, but it's been so long ago."

There was at least one request for a specialized LM-1. "There are a couple of unique LM-1s out there. David Rubinson, who was Herbie Hancock's producer at the time, asked me to make one with a built-in auxiliary mono mixer. Just above the individual outs on the back, there was a row of level pots, with a single output jack for routing signals to outboard effects. I think Rubinson and Herbie had the only two with that feature."

If you check our list of LM-1 sounds, you may note that there weren't any cymbals. Bob Easton, whose 360 Systems took over manufacturing of the LM-1, filled the gap. "Bob manufactured two cards that he would install into LM-1s to provide cymbal sounds; one card was a crash and the other a ride. Each card had about 32K of memory."

Before the LM-1 ceased production, Linn designed a new drum machine — the LinnDrum — which had many of the LM-1's features but at a significantly lower price: $2,995. (The LinnDrum price dropped to $2,495 about halfway through its production "in response to competition from Oberheim and others.") Many preferred the original. "We were horribly afraid that, when we brought out the LinnDrum, nobody would buy the LM-1. So we tried to keep it secret. The funny thing about it is there were a lot of guys who wanted the LM-1. I always thought, 'God, who would want the older technology when the new one's cheaper and better?' But a lot of people liked certain things about the LM-1, like the individual voice tunability."

In 1984, Linn introduced the forward-looking but ill-fated Linn 9000 sequencer/drum machine. Since Linn Electronics closed its doors in early '86, he has consulted for Akai and helped design products such as the MPC60 sampling and sequencing drum system and the ASQ10 sequencer.

THE PATCHBAY

SECTION 6

IN SEARCH OF...
VINTAGE
SYNTHESIZERS

BY MARK VAIL

Psst. Hey, kid! Wanna buy an old synthesizer?

The following lists represent the fruits of four years of research for the Vintage Synths columns in *Keyboard*. We're sure the list will grow as we hear from people, so we might as well try to coordinate the collection of information. If you find a helpful vintage synth dealer, store, repair person, or whatever — or you've bought or are selling a vintage instrument — and you'd like to share this information with us, please write the essentials down and send them to Vintage Synths/*Keyboard*, c/o Miller Freeman Inc., 411 Borel Avenue, San Mateo, California 94402. We're also accessible via E-mail on the PAN network (as *Keyboard*), MCI (ditto), and CompuServe (ID #70007,1121). We'll do our best to keep a database of vintage sales, rentals, and support contacts — and maybe even the What They're Worth list — updated and available via mail, fax, or on-line.

WHAT THEY'RE WORTH

Street Values & Dealer Prices for Vintage Synthesizers & Other Toys

To determine the values of a good sampling of vintage synthesizers, keyboards, and other gear, we contacted eight dealers across the U.S., provided a long laundry list of instruments, and asked for their estimates. The list eventually ballooned to include practically double the number of instruments we started with.

We've tried not to sway the prices to the favor of either buyers or sellers. The values given by all eight experts were considered in arriving at the figures presented below. Some experts quoted street value, others gave dealer prices (the equivalent of retail, or what you would pay when you buy from the dealer). If no price is listed for a specific instrument under one column or the other, that simply means none of our experts provided such a value or price, not that the instrument isn't available either on the street or from a dealer or store. You'll pay more for an instrument from a dealer or store because you should be getting a product in better condition (or at least checked out to make sure it works) than if you bought it from another individual, plus you should get some kind of limited warranty on the product.

In any case, the street values and dealer prices are merely educated guesses. Your experience may vary. Beyond the condition of the merchandise, the value of a specific item might depend on the seller's desire to sell and the buyer's need to buy. Or a road case might be included, which is a major enhancement because it will mean that (1) the instrument will be shipped/delivered to you in the case, (2) you will have a case in which to transport the instrument, and (3) the instrument is likely to be in better shape than one that has been knocked around.

Vintage synth prices may also vary from one location or one dealer to another — although we didn't find a noticeable difference in prices quoted by experts from separate sections of the country. One expert offered that, in his experience, vintage instruments tend to be cheaper in New York, Boston, and Los Angeles than in other areas.

Who are the experts? Alphabetically: Larry Caruso of Caruso Music, New London, Connecticut; Sean Denton of the Starving Musician, Santa Clara, California; independent dealer Dave Gould of Seattle, Washington; David Kean of Mellotron Archives, Moses Lake, Washington; independent dealer Mark Levreault of Derry, New Hampshire; Louis Newman, Media Sonics/Discrete Audio, Broken Arrow, Oklahoma; Wes Taggart of Analogics, Geneva, Ohio; and Chris Youdell of Analogue Systems, Los Angeles, California. Thanks loads for your input, guys.

WHAT THEY'RE WORTH

Manufacturer & Instrument	Estimated Street Value	Estimated Dealer Price
Akai AX60	$200	$300
Akai AX73	$250	$350
Akai AX80	$250 to $300	$400
Akai MPC60	$1,200	$1,800
Akai VX600	$200	$350
Akai VX90	$150 to $300	$400
Aries modular	$300 to $800	$800 to $2,500
ARP Avatar	$100 to $200	$300 to $500
ARP Axxe	$50 to $150	$75 to $300
ARP Odyssey[1]	$100 to $300	$200 to $450
ARP Omni	$25 to $125	$100 to $300
ARP Pro-Soloist	$50	$100 to $450
ARP Quadra[2]	$150 to $400	$500 to $650
ARP Sequencer[3]	$75 to $300	$250 to $500
ARP Solina IV	$100	$200
ARP Solus	—	$350
ARP 2500 modular[4]	$500 to $8,000	$5,000 to $10,000
ARP 2600[5]	$300 to $1,000	$700 to $1,500
Buchla (any model)	$2,000 to $6,000	$3,000 to $6,000
Buchla 100 modular	$1,000	$1,800
Buchla 400	$1,500	$2,000

Manufacturer & Instrument	Estimated Street Value	Estimated Dealer Price
Buchla Touché	$800	$1,800
Casio CZ-101	$75	$100 to $400
Casio VZ-1	$350	$500
Casio VZ-10M	$200	$300
Chamberlin	$1,300 to $1,500	$2,500 to $5,000
Chroma	$300 to $500	$450 to $800
Chroma Expander	$300 to $500	$400 to $800
Chroma Polaris	$200	$400
Crumar Bit One	$100 to $200	$200 to $300
Crumar DS-II	$100	$200
Crumar Orchestrator w/ pedals	$125	$350 to $400
Crumar Performer	$100 to $200	$150 to $500
Crumar Spirit[6]	$100	$200
Crumar Stratus	$50 to $80	$100 to $150
Crumar Trilogy	$50 to $100	$150
Delta Research Lab modular	$400	$800
Digital Keyboards Synergy	$500 to $800	$800 to $1,200
Digital Keyboards Synergy II+	$600 to $1,000	$1,000 to $1,200
E-mu Drumulator	$50	$100
E-mu Emulator	$200 to $500	$250 to $800
E-mu Emulator II	$500	$800
E-mu Emulator II+ HD	$800 to $1,200	$1,000 to $1,600
E-mu modular system[7]	$1,000 to $5,000	$2,000 to $8,000
Electro-Harmonix Mini-Synthesizer	$75	$150
Electro-Harmonix Vocoder	$200	$300
Electronic Dream Plant Caterpillar	—	$150
Electronic Dream Plant Spider	—	$200
Electronic Dream Plant Wasp	$100	$200 to $350
Elka Rhapsody 490	$100	—
EML 400 sequencer	$100 to $350	$400 to $600
EML ElectroComp 101	$300 to $600	$800
EML ElectroComp 200	$200 to $500	$400 to $600
EML ElectroComp 300	$200	$300
EML ElectroComp 500	$100 to $200	$350 to $400
EML Model 1500 SynKey	$250	$350
EML Model 2001 SynKey	$300	$500
EML Poly-Box	$75 to $500	$150 to $800
EMS Synthi A	$300 to $1,000	$800 to $1,500
EMS Synthi AKS	$400 to $800	$1,000 to $1,500
EMS VCS3 (the "Putney")	$500 to $800	$1,000 to $1,500
Ensoniq ESQ-1	$300	$500
Ensoniq Mirage	$200 to $350	—
Ensoniq Mirage rack-mount	$150 to $250	—
Ensoniq SQ-80	$200	$400
Evolution EVS-1	$300	—

Manufacturer & Instrument	Estimated Street Value	Estimated Dealer Price
Fairlight CMI	$1,000 to $1,500	$1,500 to $2,000
Fairlight Series II	$2,000 to $3,000	$3,500 to $5,500
Farfisa Duo Compact	$700	—
Farfisa VIP 345	$150	—
Freeman String Symphonizer	$50 to $100	$100
Gleeman Pentaphonic	—	$395
Gleeman Pentaphonic Clear	—	$500
Hohner D6 Clavinet	$150	—
Kawai K3	$200	$300
Kawai K5	$300	$550
Kawai SX-210	$100	$300
Korg BX-3	$1,000	—
Korg CX-3	$700	—
Korg DS-8	$350	$500
Korg DW-6000	$100 to $200	$250
Korg DW-8000	$200 to $300	$450 to $500
Korg EX-800	$80	—
Korg EX-8000	$250 to $300	$350
Korg KPR-77 drum machine	$50	—
Korg Micro-Preset	$80	—
Korg Mono/Poly	$70 to $150	$200 to $300
Korg MS-10 patchable	$50 to $300	$125 to $400
Korg MS-16	$50	—
Korg MS-20 patchable	$100 to $400	$200 to $500
Korg MS-50 patchable	$100 to $200	$300 to $450
Korg Poly-61	$100 to $125	$200
Korg Poly-61 w/MIDI	$150 to $175	—
Korg Poly-800/EX-800	$100	$200
Korg Polysix	$100 to $250	$250 to $800
Korg PS 3100 modular	$300 to $1,000	$750 to $2,000
Korg PS 3200 modular	$400 to $1,500	$1,000 to $2,500
Korg PS 3300 modular	$500 to $3,000	$2,000 to $5,000
Korg SQ-1D	—	$195
Korg Trident	$250 to $400	—
Korg VS-10 patchable	$150	$250
Korg X-911 analog guitar synth	$80	—
Kurzweil K250	$1,000	$1,500
Linn 9000	$500	$800
Linn LM-1	$150 to $500	$200 to $700
LinnDrum	$200 to $300	$200 to $500
Mellotron Mark II	—	$3,500 to $5,000
Mellotron Model 300	$600 to $750	$3,500 to $5,000
Mellotron Model 400	$800 to $1,000	$1,400 to $2,000
Moog Liberation	$150 to $350	$500
Moog Memorymoog	$200 to $700	$800

Manufacturer & Instrument	Estimated Street Value	Estimated Dealer Price
Moog Memorymoog Plus w/MIDI[8]	$500 to $900	$1,100 to $1,500
Moog MG-1	$50	$150
Moog Micromoog	$50 to $100	$100 to $150
Moog Minimoog	$300 to $700	$500 to $750
Moog Minitmoog	$75 to $100	$400 to $1,500
Moog modular system	$500 to $5,000	$2,000 to $12,500
Moog Multimoog	$100 to $250	$175 to $400
Moog Opus 3	$150 to $200	—
Moog Polymoog	$150 to $350	$600 to $750
Moog Polymoog Keyboard	$150 to $200	$450 to $750
Moog Prodigy	$50	$150
Moog Rogue	$50	$75
Moog Satellite	$50	$100
Moog Series 15 modular	$1,000	$1,500
Moog Series 35 modular	$2,500	$4,000
Moog Series 55 modular	$3,500	$5,500
Moog Sonic Six	$125 to $250	$250 to $450
Moog Source	$150 to $250	$300
Moog Taurus II pedals	$200	—
Moog Taurus pedals	$300	$600
Moog Vocoder	$500	$800
New England Digital Synclavier II	$2,000	$3,000
Novatron Model 400	—	$1,800 to $2,000
Oberheim DMX drum machine	$50 to $80	$100 to $150
Oberheim DMX w/MIDI	$250 to $300	$300 to $450
Oberheim DSX sequencer	$0 to $100	$100 to $250
Oberheim DX	$50	—
Oberheim Eight Voice	$600 to $2,000	$900 to $2,750
Oberheim Four Voice	$400 to $1,500	$600 to $1,700
Oberheim Matrix-1000	$300	$350
Oberheim Matrix-12	$2,000	$3,000 to $3,250
Oberheim Matrix-6	$400	—
Oberheim Matrix-6R	$200	$350
Oberheim OB-1	$100 to $350	$250 to $400
Oberheim OB-8	$350 to $650	$600 to $750
Oberheim OB-8 w/MIDI	$500 to $1,000	$1,000 to $1,200
Oberheim OB-X Eight Voice	$300 to $500	$500 to $700
Oberheim OB-X Four Voice	$100 to $400	$450 to $600
Oberheim OB-Xa	$150 to $500	$700 to $1,050
Oberheim SEM	$50 to $350	$150 to $450
Oberheim Two Voice	$250 to $1,000	$400 to $1,000
Oberheim Xpander	$800 to $900	$1,000 to $1,500
Octave Electronics Cat	$50 to $125	$100 to $250
Octave Electronics Kitten	$100	$150
Octave-Plateau Voyetra Eight	$1,000	$1,500

Manufacturer & Instrument	Estimated Street Value	Estimated Dealer Price
OSCar	$400 to $700	$700 to $1,000
Paia Gnome	$50 to $100	—
Paia modular w/kbd. controller[9]	$0 to $250	$100 to $400
PPG PRK	$500	—
PPG Wave 2.2	$300 to $750	$500 to $1,000
PPG Wave 2.3 w/MIDI	$500 to $800	$700 to $2,000
PPG Waveterm A	$1,000	$1,000 to $1,500
PPG Waveterm B	$500 to $1,500	$750 to $1,800
Roland Alpha Juno-1	$200	$400
Roland Alpha Juno-2	$250 to $300	$500
Roland Axis	$350	$500
Roland CR-78 Beat Box	$50	$350
Roland CR-8000 Beat Box	$50	$200
Roland D-50	$500	$800
Roland GR-300	$200	$300
Roland GR-500	$200	$300
Roland GR-700	$350	$500
Roland JSQ-60	$50	—
Roland Juno-6	$100 to $125	$300
Roland Juno-60	$100 to $125	$300
Roland Juno-106	$150 to $300	$300 to $550
Roland Jupiter-4	$125 to $250	$350 to $400
Roland Jupiter-6	$300 to $450	$500 to $700
Roland Jupiter-8	$400 to $800	$650 to $1,200
Roland JX-10	$500 to $600	$800 to $1,000
Roland JX-3P	$200 to $250	$350
Roland JX-8P	$225 to $300	$500 to $550
Roland MC-202	$50	—
Roland MC-4	—	$250
Roland MC-8	$200	$250 to $600
Roland MKB-200	$150	$250
Roland MKS-7	$150 to $200	$300
Roland MKS-10 Planet P	$50	$100
Roland MKS-20	$100	$250
Roland MKS-30 Planet S	$100	$250
Roland MKS-50	$200	$300
Roland MKS-60	$350	$450
Roland MKS-70	$500 to $600	$800
Roland MKS-80	$700 to $800	$1,200
Roland MKS-100	$350	$500
Roland MPG-80	$300	$500
Roland Paraphonic 505	$100	—
Roland PG-800	$150	$300
Roland RS-09	$100	—
Roland SH-2	—	$250

Manufacturer & Instrument	Estimated Street Value	Estimated Dealer Price
Roland SH-5	—	$250
Roland SH-09	$50 to $100	$250 to $350
Roland SH-101	$50 to $150	$125 to $350
Roland SH-2000	$50	—
Roland Studio System-100M	$750	$1,000
Roland SVC-350 Vocoder rack	$300 to $500	$500 to $750
Roland System-100 modular system	$300 to $1,200	$500 to $1,500
Roland System-700 modular system	$2,500 to $5,000	$5,000 to $7,500
Roland System-700 modules	$800 to $1,500 each	—
Roland TB-303 Bassline	$50 to $300	$200 to $700
Roland TR-606 Drumatix	$50 to $200	$125 to $300
Roland TR-808	$350 to $500	$600 to $750
Roland TR-909	$250 to $400	$450 to $700
Roland VK-1 organ	$200	$350
Roland VP-220	$250	$400
Roland VP-330 Vocoder Plus	$200 to $500	$400 to $750
RSF Kobol	$300 to $500	$800 to $1,200
Sequential 400 Drumtraks	$50 to $100	$125
Sequential Fugue	$125	—
Sequential Max	$75 to $100	$200
Sequential Model 610 Six-Trak	$100	$200
Sequential Multi-Trak	$150	—
Sequential Prelude	$100	—
Sequential Pro-One[10]	$50 to $150	$150 to $500
Sequential Prophet-5 rev 1 or 2	$400 to $500	$500 to $1,000
Sequential Prophet-5 rev 3 w/MIDI	$400 to $800	$750 to $2,000
Sequential Prophet-10 w/MIDI	$500 to $1,200	$1,000 to $2,500
Sequential Prophet-600	$200 to $300	$450 to $600
Sequential Prophet-2000	$400 to $700	$800
Sequential Prophet-2002	$500	$800
Sequential Prophet-3000	$1,000	$1,500
Sequential Prophet-T8	$700 to $1,400	$1,300 to $3,500
Sequential Prophet-VS	$700 to $1,200	$1,500 to $2,000
Sequential Prophet-VS Rack	$1,500	$2,500
Sequential Split-8	$150	—
Sequential Studio-440	$800	$1,500
Sequential Tom 420	$100 to $150	$250
Serge Modular system	$1,000 to $2,000	$3,000 to $6,000
Serge series 79 modules	$350 per panel	$750 per panel
Siel DK 600	$200	$300
Simmons SDS-5	$350	$500
Simmons SDS-8	$50	$125
SMS Voice 400	$500 to $2,000	$2,000 to $3,000
SMS Voice 400	$500 to $2,000	$2,000 to $3,000
Steiner-Parker Synthacon	$300	$500

Manufacturer & Instrument	Estimated Street Value	Estimated Dealer Price
Synton modular system	$300 to $1,500	$800 to $3,000
360 Systems MIDI Bass	$50	$100
Vako Orchestron	$150	$300
Vox Continental	$75 to $125	$200
Vox Jaguar	$100 to $200	$225
Wurlitzer stage piano	$150	—
Yamaha CE-20	$100	$200
Yamaha CP-20	$200	—
Yamaha CP-30	$250	—
Yamaha CS-01	$50	$100
Yamaha CS-5	$50	$100
Yamaha CS 15	$100	$175 to $200
Yamaha CS 20M	$150	$200 to $250
Yamaha CS 40M	$175 to $200	$250 to $300
Yamaha CS-60	$150 to $600	$300 to $800
Yamaha CS 70M	$200 to $350	$300 to $400
Yamaha CS-80	$300 to $1,000	$500 to $1,500
Yamaha DX1	$650	$1,000
Yamaha DX5	$200 to $350	$700 to $800
Yamaha DX7	$350 to $500	$700
Yamaha DX7II	$400 to $600	$700 to $800
Yamaha DX9	$100	$200
Yamaha DX11	$100	$200
Yamaha DX21	$100	$200
Yamaha DX27	$100	$200
Yamaha DX100	$50	$150
Yamaha GS 2	$350	$500
Yamaha SK-15	$70	—
Yamaha SK-20	$99	—
Yamaha SK-50	$125	—
Yamaha TF1 FM module	$50	$100
Yamaha TX7	$200	$300 to $500
Yamaha TX802	$350	$600
Yamaha TX816	$500	$1,000

(1) There were three versions of the ARP Odyssey: the first had no CV/gate interface, number two had the CV/gate interface but no PPC (proportional pitch control), the third had both. Louis Newman says dealer price for a white-faced Odyssey is $450, $295 for a black-and-orange-faced Odyssey.

(2) According to Wes Taggart, the Quadra's mylar membrane front panel is no longer available, making the synth a risky purchase.

(3) The ARP Sequencer is a most desired analog sequencer, Wes Taggart says, because of its quantized outputs and random sequencing capabilities.

(4) The 2500 is prone to cross-talk problems in its matrix patching system.

(5) Two keyboard versions of the ARP 2600 were available, one monophonic, the other duophonic.

(6) Bob Moog helped design the Spirit for Crumar.

(7) *Keyboard* columnist Dave Stewart recently found an E-mu modular system for sale in a London music store. We can't believe he wasn't ready to hand over £6,000 for it.

(8) The Memorymoog is a hot ticket on the vintage synth market. Wes Taggart warns that it needs the autotune update, which is an expensive upgrade.

(9) Paia synths were built from kits, many times successfully but often improperly, which leads some dealers to recommend against buying them.

(10) Wes Taggart claims the Sequential Pro-One is one of the best values in a mono synth.

BUYING A VINTAGE SYNTH

What the Experts Say

There are a number of considerations in becoming a vintage synth enthusiast, such as where to look for them, how to get your money's worth, and how to test an unknown instrument. It's also important to consider what benefits you should expect in buying a refurbished synth from a store or dealer as opposed to getting one cheaper from the current owner or in a pawnshop. In addition, as in the antique auto business, there are synthesizers that suffer from inadequate manufacturing and/or design problems and perhaps had best be avoided by the average collector.

We turned to experienced dealers and brokers to get answers to these questions and for some general buying tips for vintage synth shoppers. In alphabetical order, we spoke to: Sean Denton, who's in charge of keyboard sales for the Starving Musician in Santa Clara, California; independent synthesizer dealer Mark Levreault of Derry, New Hampshire; Louis Newman, owner of Media Sonics/Discrete Audio in Broken Arrow, Oklahoma; synth dealer Wes Taggart of Analogics in Geneva, Ohio; David Wilson, founder of the New England Synthesizer Museum in Nashua, New Hampshire; and independent synth dealer Chris Youdell of Analogue Systems, Los Angeles, California. Each interviewee made important contributions to our knowledge base, for which we're extremely grateful.

* * * *

Where's the best place to find old synthesizers?

Newman: If you want to get one that's completely restored and has a warranty, the best place to get one is from me or another dealer. You may want to buy them from people you know. If you're in a city like Los Angeles or New York, there's probably going to be more available from musicians. In California, you have classified ads in the *Recycler*. In New York, you have the *Village Voice*. Both of those are good sources. The Midwest has *Bargain Posts*, a used trade magazine. People may have better luck in a music store than in a pawnshop.

Pawnshops typically go by the blue-book, and they don't always update the book yearly, so something like a Moog Satellite or some less desirable piece of gear may still show a $400 or $500 blue-book value.

Wilson: Some pawnshops undervalue the equipment and some of them overvalue the equipment. In the ones that overvalue the equipment, it's hard to get it through their heads that it's just not worth quite that much. Prices have been driven up recently and that has made it harder to get older analog synthesizers. I guess it's just the demand. It's the hoopla. It's like you're not cool unless you own an ARP 2600. Talk to salesmen in all your local music stores. Go also to pawnshops. I've had both good and bad experiences scrounging stuff at pawnshops. In addition, there are a lot of places that advertise in the back of *Keyboard*.

Levreault: I make old synths come to me by advertising in a rag here in New Hampshire called the *Want Ads*, which is very similar to California's *Recycler*. I put wanted ads into those sorts of magazines. I usually make them humorous, like, "Unearth those old dinosaurs in your basement and call me to turn them into cash." So oftentimes people will dig out stuff that's either not working or in a state of disrepair, or just that they haven't used. They'll give me a call and I'll give them cash for it.

Taggart: Here in Ohio we have a newspaper called the *Trading Times*. They sell used items like cars, boats, keyboards, and so on, and you can find a lot of stuff there. You can try local music stores. You'd be surprised what some of these people still have brand new that they don't know what it is, especially mom-and-pop type of stores. The farther out in the boondocks you go, the better chances you'll have of finding something really unique. Or you can go to dealers like me who specialize in vintage synthesizers. If you buy an instrument from a reputable vintage synth dealer, then you have recourse in the sense of a warranty. The dealer will sell you something he guarantees is going to work. It's the same thing as buying something from your music dealer. You go to a dealer like that because you are more or less guaranteed that you are going to have support after the sale, although not all of them do that any more. If you buy something from someone like me, you get the manual, you get the cords, if it came with a cartridge you get that also. Going to an individual is like buying something mail-order. You're assuming that you don't need support, that you know what you're doing. That's why you're getting the bargain. If you don't know what you're doing, you really want the support, and you want to call somebody who is familiar with the stuff and can help you out, my suggestion is to buy it from a dealer. When you're looking to buy an instrument that's 20 years old, support is fairly important because it isn't something that you can go up to the corner, walk into a store, and ask somebody. There are relatively few people out there who really know the inner workings. When someone sells you something, they should be obliged to provide support. That's not always the case. That's how I feel. I'm obliged to my customer because I'm not interested in one sale, I'm interested in multiple sales. I want them to keep coming back to me because they're happy with what I do.

Youdell: In the Los Angeles area, pawnshops are no longer a source of reasonably priced keyboards. They're really quite expensive. I'm not saying that's true throughout the country. I've got a network of people across the country who hear about things. A lot of it is word of mouth. People just call up. If someone is looking for a specific item, I'll hunt it down. I know about quite a few vintage instruments that are just sitting there ready for someone to actually want them. Then I get back to the broker and put the two people in contact with each other. For instance, there's a very large Buchla 200, which obviously is very rare, sitting about and the owner wants to get rid of it at some point soon. Realistically there aren't that many people who are going to pay $12,000 for a Buchla 200. And it's not really worth it for me because it's so expensive to buy, to keep hold of it for the next 18 months. Rather, if someone calls up for one, I'll happily put the two people in contact and they can sort it out. Generally, however, I pick things up, take them for restoration, and then put them on sale.

Can you suggest some buying tips for vintage synth shoppers?

Youdell: People should be aware that they are buying something that is old and has inherent in-

stability, which actually is part of the beauty of those machines. But they do cost money to fix. It's like having a great old car. You can buy things that get you from A to B quicker and with less trouble, but they probably don't have the aesthetic beauty that the older machines have. It's similar with synths. You have to pay to get the things repaired. Having said that, if the oscillators are reasonably stable when someone buys one, there probably aren't really going to be that many problems with it. I also suggest you specify that anything sent to you be shipped properly. I once bought a 2600 that I was told was in absolutely great shape. But the seller just stuck a label on it and sent it without any packaging. That certainly did ruin the instrument.

Newman: It really is a "buyer beware" market. Some people will take advantage of you and some people will treat you fairly. You really need to go into it with some education. It's important, if the seller knows the instrument, that you have them take you through it step by step and show you what it's doing and what it isn't doing. You should also not be afraid to ask them what kind of problems it has. If you're the seller, always be very exact in how you describe the condition of any equipment that you're selling. Take photos, not only for potential buyers but for your own records and protection should there be damages in shipping. Always use heavy-duty boxes and over-pack. Cushion the instrument with bubble wrap instead of packing peanuts; if your box gets a hole punched in it during shipment, the peanuts could leak out and leave the contents with no protection. Insure the instrument for the full value of your transaction. When shipping internationally, use air freight, not ground; although ground is considerably less expensive, remember that ground shipping means by boat, and electronic equipment does not like sea air because of its salt content. When in doubt, call someone with more experience; we don't charge for answering questions regarding prices, repairs, shipment, or anything regarding synthesizers.

Denton: Make sure you get everything: power cord, manuals, patch cords, footswitches and pedals, stand, whatever. If it has a problem, take into consideration how much you're going to have to pay to have it repaired to bring it back up to stat so it's working correctly. You don't want to get a synth for $500 that needs $1,000 worth of work. Always check out gear before you buy it. Try to get a warranty. The vintage keyboard market is still pretty young. I think we need a couple more years to educate people and let them know what the market values really are for old synths. Until that time, you're going to see what I consider inflated prices for certain great-sounding machines.

Wilson: Try to get as many oscillators and as much versatility as you can. A machine like the Moog Prodigy doesn't let you do quite as much as perhaps a Multimoog. If you can, get an ARP Odyssey instead of an Axxe, but a 2600 is better than an Odyssey.

Levreault: Just get out there and grab them, but be prepared to open them up. All the old pots and circuits are usually dirty, and so are keyboards, especially the key contacts and things like that. Get some Cramolin, a toothbrush, some Q-tips, and a good cleaner and start cleaning things. Radio Shack's TV tuner cleaner and lubricant is a good buy. They sell those cans for $3.69 or something. That's what I use to clean pots and things like that. The tuner cleaner and lubricant is the better stuff because it has a lubricant built in which will save the parts for a much longer period than just a cleaner, which tends to dry them out. With a few simple tools and some time and care, you can take an old synthesizer that's literally been sitting around for years and breathe life into it just by cleaning the thing up. And if you're handy at all with a soldering iron, sometimes you can do some simple wiring repairs and things like that. But certainly, people shouldn't be afraid of older keyboards, because in most cases they've just been abandoned only because they've been superseded by something that somebody thought was a better instrument.

Taggart: You should approach it the same way you would if you were buying a used car. If you can, get the person you're buying it from to take it to a shop for a checkup. But that's scary because a lot of the people who were repairing stuff in the '70s aren't doing it in the '90s. They've got good jobs now. The musical instrument repair industry is one of the worst-paid technical industries there is. Someone with electrical engineering experience can be making $30,000 to $70,000. In the repair field, go out and get a job with the kind of experience you need to test this stuff and you'll make maybe $9 or $10 an hour. In some communities, like L.A. and New York, you'll make more, but compared to the cost of living in those areas, it's still pretty low on the scale. So the people who really know how to work on this older stuff are few and far between. Stay away from the mom-and-pop music stores for service, because generally they're either farming their service work out or they're fixing the bells on trombones. They're more into wind instruments and servicing the school system than they are into providing qualified electronic repairs. Those are good places to find old synths for sure, but not such a good place to hope to find technical expertise on this kind of stuff. You should ask the person you're buying from whether the battery has been changed. Ask to see some service documentation, if it exists. A lot of people don't save that kind of stuff; musicians are not really known for their bookkeeping. But if you can find someone in your area that knows this type of instrument — and there are some people still around — then probably the best thing to do is get it checked. You can expect to pay $25 or more to have them check it out.

How do you test an old synthesizer?

Newman: Check out every knob and slider. If the person showing it knows more about it than you, make him or her take you through it. You can learn a lot that way. If it's something that you have any questions about, take it to a repair person first and have them check out the power supply to make sure that it's not putting out too much voltage. Resistors can go bad and the power supply can be putting out three or four times as much voltage as it needs to be. If it is and you turn it on, you may toast a lot of the modules that are in line. I think it's really worth someone's while to have a good service person check it out. It's probably going to cost about $50, but it may be the best money they ever spent.

Taggart: A lot of people don't realize that it's probably just as bad for an instrument to sit around as it is to be running all the time. Electronics go bad, capacitors get leaky, contacts can get corroded, tons of things can happen.

Levreault: See what functions work or don't work. A lot of these instruments have been sitting in basements and really just need a thorough cleaning before anything gets done with them. Usually, that's all they require.

Taggart: If it has one, hit the auto-tune button to see if the instrument comes up tuned. With a Memorymoog, if it runs the tuning operation and all the oscillators sound in tune, that's a good indication that the instrument is working. I always move all the pots to see if they make changes and hit all the switches. If the instrument has LED-type switches like in the Prophet-5, each pushbutton's LED should come on and go off every time you hit the button. You should see parameter changes when you do things. Go through the presets to see if things sound normal.

Denton: I'll burn it in for a while. Minimoogs especially. When you first turn them on, they always sound funky. Let it run for ten or 20 minutes and then play it. Go through all the sliders, knobs, and pots to make sure that everything is happy. Make sure that you're not getting double triggers and that it tunes properly. Most important is to make sure that the synth is as stock as possible. If it's been modded, make sure that it's as close to original condition as possible. Try to find out as much information as you can about the mod, such as whether it was done at the factory or who did the mod, so that if you have to work on it, you know what has been done to it in the past. In the '70s, modification was a big thing. Everybody customized their own gear, like putting Oberheim pitch-benders on a Prophet-5 because they liked the spring action. If it's a stupid, silly mod and it destroys the machine, the machine is not going to be worth much. Try to find synths that are as close to stock as possible.

Newman: Modifications are typically bad, although the person that does them at the time probably thinks that they're very important. But often they wind up being problems unless they were done by someone that really knew what they were doing. Most modifications are probably go-

ing to drive down the value of an instrument, certainly to a collector. They want a synth to be in its original state.

Levreault: I don't have a MIDI retrofit on my Minimoog because I prefer the character of the Mini by itself and playing it live. Using the mod and pitch-bend wheels and knobs is part of the character of the Minimoog. Yeah, it's a nice concept to be able to have the sound of a Minimoog run by a sequencer, but I think you lose something when you get away from playing the instrument live. Old synthesizers were designed to be interacted with by adjusting the knobs while you played it. Watch some old footage of Rick Wakeman and see what he does with a Minimoog. A Minimoog is all about user interface and user control, and it becomes a whole lot less human when you retrofit it with MIDI or modify it in some way. Certainly if you're going to modify and improve some instabilities in an instrument and it gives you more pleasure to play it, I don't have any problem with people doing that for their own use. But when you change the character of the instrument, I think there's a point beyond which you've gone too far.

Are there any synthesizers you recommend people avoid?

Youdell: Not really, because I think everything can be fixed. Probably one of the worst was the Memorymoog. I think virtually every one they ever made had to get fixed at some point or other. But right now, the Memorymoog is one of the most fashionable polyphonics to buy. It's funny how things change around so much in a few months. No doubt by the time this is published, it will have changed again. But certainly right now, the Memorymoog is way ahead of the Jupiter-8 or Prophet-5 as the most sought-after polyphonic internationally, particularly in Europe. Before that, the most popular vintage synth was probably the Prophet-5. I guess a lot of people have gotten one of those, they've used it on records, and now they want a slightly different sound. So they went to the next popular vintage synth, which happens to be the Memorymoog. Similarly, the ARP 2600 was really commanding a very high price in Europe about three years ago, and now they're probably down to a quarter of the price that they were then, due to the supply-and-demand factor.

Denton: Service-wise, the Memorymoog was just awful. It's a great-sounding machine, but if you take it on the road, everybody knows they crash. If it's left in the studio and taken care of, then it should be fine.

Newman: I don't think people should avoid any old synth, really. All of them can be restored. It depends on what your tastes in sound are. Some people don't like ARPs, some people don't like Moogs. But people who like them can do anything they want with them. There are so many synthesizers, and they all have different sounds. They're all worthwhile. Rhodes Chromas are very difficult to work on. Oberheims are wonderful-sounding but they tend to take a banging, and so do the Prophets when you start shipping them around. They look heavy-duty and they certainly weigh enough, but for some reason when we ship them we almost always have to have them tuned up. In fact, typically when we sell someone a Prophet-5 or an Oberheim, we'll make arrangements with a repairman in the area to spend about an hour tuning it up and recalibrating it prior to the new owner taking possession of it. We have technicians lined up worldwide, and it's helpful for us because we offer a 60-day warranty. Without that, customers would have to ship their instruments back here in case of a problem. Shipping is not only costly, it's also extra wear and tear on the instrument. That's one thing to avoid with a lot of these old synths. If you're going to do a gig, buy E-mu's new Vintage Keys. But if you're going to do studio work, buy the actual unit and have a good repairman that you can trust to look after it for you. It's kind of like a car. You really should have them calibrated about every six months to a year, have the power supply checked out to make sure it's putting out the correct voltage, and make sure all the groundings are correctly connected inside.

Wilson: I would recommend staying away from anything with custom chips in it, like some of the later Sequential Circuits instruments. Not that they're bad or anything, but where do you get those chips? Wine Country Productions will sell them to you for a while, but when they run out,

who's going to sell them to you? On the other hand, just about anything that was able to sell at all has to be some kind of viable instrument. If you love the sound, for God's sake go for it.

Levreault: My philosophy is that you can learn something from every one of them. Granted, there may be some synthesizers that I wouldn't own because they require too much care. For instance, a lot of the ARP equipment was very poorly made. The quality of the connectors used was not good. Oftentimes you get a lot of problems in those with oxidation on connectors. And beware if they use sockets. Sockets are always a major headache because they will oxidize and you'll get problems that appear to be intermittent, which oftentimes can be tracked down to bad mechanical connections. But again, there isn't a lot that I would tell people to avoid, because my interest in it is more educational. I'm always interested in the philosophy behind why a company would have designed a synthesizer with certain types of features and how they implemented those features.

Taggart: It can be quite costly if you buy a regular Memorymoog and you want it MIDIed. You're liable to find out it hasn't had the auto-tune kit and a whole bunch of other updates that that instrument needed. I've had customers who bought them for $200 or $300 and thought they got a great deal, wanted to get it MIDIed, and ended up paying $1,200 to $1,300 for updates, MIDI, and everything else. They could have bought one for $1,200 to $1,300 from someone like me. It ended up costing them more money. I hate to say it, but a lot of these things have had bad service records. Memorymoogs had horrifying service records until you had all the updates done, and then they were relatively reliable. The same thing with Oberheims. For a Prophet-5, I would suggest you buy a rev 3. Stay away from rev 1s and 2s because they're going to be horrifyingly costly to repair, if you can find someone to repair one. Stay away from the Italian stuff like Crumar and Siel. I don't support them, and I don't know where you would go. Japanese manufacturers typically have had relatively good records. Earlier stuff from Roland was really well made, like the Jupiter-6, the Jupiter-8, the MKS-80, the MKS-70, and the JX-10. That generation was very well made. Even to this day, I think when the Japanese — Yamaha and Roland especially — put out a product, it generally works from the get-go. I only have one bad thing to say about Ensoniq: It seems to me they put stuff out a little too early. That's been the problem with a lot of the American synth manufacturers. Of course, in the past that was because the Americans were on the cutting edge of technology, especially with the real early stuff by Moog and ARP. They were using ICs when ICs were only two or three years old. American manufacturers were always right on the cutting edge of technology, and I think that's what ended up creating problems for them, because engineering changes had to be made in the field. They were so close to the edge that they were finding ways to fix things that they thought would work a certain way. Of course musicians had a lot to do with it, because musicians never used equipment the way the designers intended.

How much should someone expect to pay to get their vintage synth restored?

Newman: Something like a Minimoog wouldn't be very expensive to fix. But there's a big difference in the way that the modules and submodules are put together on Moogs and ARPs. ARP 2600s in some instances have submodules epoxied inside of the main modules. So if you have one component that's defective in the 2600, it can be very expensive. Sometimes you can't even have it repaired; you have to replace the whole module, and they're very hard to get. Back when these things were made, manufacturers were always afraid someone was going to copy their design, so they would epoxy in these submodules so that you couldn't get at them and copy them. That was great for them at that time, but when you start having a problem with something now, you're stuck.

Taggart: Electronically speaking, for most instruments I would say it's probably not horrifyingly expensive, unless there are multiple problems. If you want to get into the woodworking and cosmetic stuff, that's a lot more expensive. To use an ARP 2600 as an example, if all the sliders and controls are there, everything generally works, and you just want it tuned up, you're looking at maybe $50 to $75. Say one of the epoxied modules is bad

(which is fairly common) or you want the cabinet re-Tolexed — you're better off buying one in better condition. If you need a filter module, you're looking at $300 plus installation. If you want the outside re-Tolexed and some other things adjusted, you're up to the price that I would sell one for. So in some instances, reconditioning can be more expensive than buying something that's refurbished already. On the Minimoog I would say generally, even if you have a problem like a bad oscillator, you're probably looking at anywhere from $50 to say $200, provided it hasn't been struck by lightning. That's real generic. If you want wood refinished or something like an Oberheim Four Voice re-Tolexed, it can get real expensive, because you're paying for labor and expensive materials. Tolex itself is like $20 a yard. A 2600 uses 2½ yards. A Four Voice has four yards, so you're looking at $100 just in materials — and this is my expense. Then there are all the corners and other parts. Now you're talking about $200 my cost, customer cost $300 to $400, and labor probably anywhere from four to eight hours. I charge $50 an hour. So you can really get up there money-wise. What's nice about those instruments is that you can restore them to a like-original condition. On the other hand, all-metal units like a Prophet-VS or a Jupiter-8 that have been damaged are going to be virtually impossible to fix. I had a customer who bought an Oberheim Matrix-12 at a real good buy. He wanted a new front panel, but there are none. He asked me, "Do you have another Matrix-12 that isn't working?" He wondered whether I'd sell him the front panel. My answer was, "No, because if I had a Matrix-12 I'd get it working and sell it for $3,000. Why would I want to take all the parts off and then sell you the front panel?" Occasionally you can find a Prophet-5 front panel or things like that from something that's been gutted. You might be able to find something that is in a little better condition than what you might have purchased. That's a good way to restore something, if you can find parts. But for a lot of the stuff, you can't. Here's an example of the mentality that I run into here in America (in Europe, it's different): A guy calls and says, "I just got a Pro-One for $25. I don't want to spend $250 to MIDI it. I want to spend $50."

Denton: It depends on what's wrong with it. Sometimes you can get away with a repair that's going to cost you $10. Sometimes it's going to cost you $400 or $500. But finding parts is a big thing. You don't see the parts around as much as you used to, and everybody who has parts basically stockpiles them and they charge you what they want, because you can't find them anywhere else.

Wilson: If you want expert restoration done on a vintage synth that you've found, the New England Synthesizer Museum is fully qualified. For the Minimoog, I've charged anywhere from $25 for something small to $150 for major repairs and recalibration. The Minimoog doesn't have a lot of parts, and there are no custom parts. So anything in there that's blown, you can practically buy at Radio Shack. ARPs are a little better in some ways, but a little worse in others. If one of those sealed modules goes bad, you have to cut it open with a hacksaw. That's a bear. But the purpose of my museum is for composers to have access to the sounds of analog synthesizers. A lot of times the people who have these older machines don't have lots of bucks. If I charged $300 or $400 for repairs, I could make lots of money, but that's not the reason why I'm doing this.

Levreault: I don't know that I've ever spent more than $100 on getting an old synth working, but that's because I have the skills to fix them. I have fixed instruments for others in the past, but I don't now because most people want to get something fixed quickly so that they can use it. The time pressures of that are usually too much for me. I would rather have an instrument that I can set aside and when I get a chance to sit down and putter, then I'll work on it. Often, I'll sit down one weekend a month and repair a lot of things in a burst. But if somebody needs something turned around in two days, I'm usually not in a hurry to take on that kind of task.

Youdell: With big modular systems, you know automatically that quite a lot of restoration work has to be done, and the labor is quite expensive. Generally speaking, if things look as though they're in fairly good condition physically, then it's pretty true to say that they will be in reasonably good condition inside. But every modular system has to have all the pots and jacks gone through, just because the course of time takes its effect on them. There are some people I know who have everything fully reconditioned and upgraded as much as possible, and obviously that costs a lot of money. I'd estimate that the restoration of something like a Moog Series 55 would cost at least $750 to go through and clean everything, provided there aren't too many things wrong with it. Obviously that is very much dependent on how much is actually wrong with the machine and which parts need changing. For one Moog system, we have to get new 921 oscillators, and we're paying about $600 apiece. It's really quite expensive. So I would estimate that the proper restoration of a modular system would cost probably $4,000.

How are people using these old synths?

Taggart: Most of the people that buy 2600s now aren't using them as synthesizers, they're using them as processors for their drum machines, for instance. Trent Reznor of Nine Inch Nails runs his drum sounds through the pre-amp and other modules to modulate or filter them. Even though these guys use samplers so much, they have a real aversion to people copying their sounds or figuring out what they're doing. So when you run sounds through a 2600, to tell you the truth, you can't even duplicate the effects the next time, because there's no way that you're going to get the sliders back where they were. So this is a quick and really effective way to get sounds that no one else is going to be able to copy unless they just directly sample. That's what a lot of these people are using, especially the modular type of stuff like a 2600 or the EML 101.

A couple of years ago, Keyboard *printed a list of what vintage synthesizers were worth in Japan. At that time, something like a Prophet-5 could bring $5,000. A friend of mine in Japan says that that market has really dried up.*

Youdell: It has. I think to an extent the prices were slightly exaggerated as well. A lot of the big Japanese music stores are asking very high prices for analog keyboards in their advertisements, but in reality they aren't really selling them at those prices. So people get the false impression that actually they're worth that amount of money. Actually, the Japanese market is pretty well saturated because they have so many people out in America buying keyboards at American prices. That also probably brings down prices in the second-hand market, because there is a glut now of Memorymoogs, Prophet-5s, Oberheims, and whatever else. That probably undercuts the big stores when they're dealing those machines. Certainly Japanese prices are higher than American prices, but then there are customs regulations and the air fare to send the thing, and the transferring of the money. So it isn't the gold mine that people think it is.

VINTAGE SYNTH SUPPORT, SERVICE, & SALES

The following people are good to turn to for vintage synth help. If no one listed below can help you, chances are someone you talk with will know who can. If you set out in search of something exotic, be prepared to run into obstacles. It may take persistence and determination to find an obscure tidbit of information or that intriguing vintage synth that you've read about.

You don't have to rely solely on the dealers and stores listed below for old gear. *Lots* of music stores deal to some extent in used equipment, which will include some vintage pieces. Ask the salespeople to show you the old stuff, which might be hidden away in a basement, attic, or auxiliary storeroom.

Want ads and garage sales may turn up worthwhile items as well. When you're traveling, check out neighborhood pawnshops — especially those in a large city — for the odd vintage treasure. The vendor may not know what they're selling you, and there's no law that says you have to divulge what you know either. "I found a Moog Sonic Six for $50 in a pawnshop in San Diego," synthesizer technician Timothy Smith recalls. "It was working perfectly. The guy said, 'I don't even know what it is. Is it some kind of organ or what?' I said, 'Oh, I don't know. I'll give you fifty bucks.' I played dumb. Sometimes that's a rational strategy, not to let them know what it is they've got."

Before buying a keyboard, try everything out. Play each key individually, and try all the inputs, outputs, and patch cords. Hook up footpedals, switches, and other supplementary hardware to see if they work, too. (Make sure you get everything the seller has that goes with your purchase, including manuals and documentation.)

Rental companies often rent vintage instruments — no guarantee as to their condition — at reasonable costs. This can give you the opportunity to play with a specific instrument for a sufficient length of time to judge whether pursuing one that's in better shape is worth the effort.

To borrow from the *Keyboard* Classifieds guidelines for mail-order transactions, before buying get: (1) a written description of the instrument, which should include the serial number, (2) front and back photos of the instrument, and (3) a written purchase agreement with a 24-hour approval clause that allows you to return the instrument for a full refund if it doesn't meet your expectations.

If you ship an instrument to a repair shop, speak with someone on the phone before shipping anything so that they will be expecting your parcel. Record the instrument's serial number and the condition it was in when it left your possession, and take photos if possible so that you have a visual record of its pre-shipped condition. Carefully pack the unit (optionally wrapped in plastic) in a suitable box with sufficient packing material, seal the box with good strapping tape for shipment, and insure the article for its legitimate value. Make sure to enclose specific details on the exact procedures you want done by the technician. Request an estimate and make sure they get your authorization before they start whacking away at your prized possession. One technician reports his service rates are $50 an hour, he charges a $25 estimate fee, and he offers a 30-day limited warranty on instruments, updates that he installs, and labor. Specify a date by which you need the item back; you may not get it as soon as you'd like, but it's worth a try to get expeditious service. And make sure there's some kind of warranty in case everything wasn't properly repaired. You should be allowed a reasonable amount of time to establish whether the instrument has indeed been fixed to your satisfaction.

Advanced Electronic Services
2303 Brookpark Rd.
Cleveland, OH 44134
(216) 741-2211

Repair of digital keyboards, amps, speakers, mixers, processors, and recorders. Authorized warranty service for all manufacturers but E-mu.

Airborne Music Electronics
Bill Cawthorne
751 Onarga Ave.
Los Angeles, CA 90042
(213) 257-1761

Services PPG Wave and Dynacord instruments; formerly with Europa Music.

Analogics
Wes Taggart
5261 Maple Ave. East
Geneva, OH 44041
(216) 466-6911

Analog synthesizer support. Buy, sell, trade, and service. Epoxy-encapsulated ARP 2600 modules available. Synth rentals, including Mellotron 400, Korg BX-3 with MIDI, ARP 2600 with MIDI, Roland Jupiter-8 with MIDI, Oberheim Matrix-12, Oberheim Eight Voice, Aries modular, Serge Modular, Buchla 200, Sequential Prophet-5 remote keyboard, and MIDI-to-CV converters.

Analogue Systems
Chris Youdell
(213) 850-5216
Fax (213) 850-1059

Keyboard broker. Buys, sells, and services analog keyboards and modular systems.

The Audio Clinic/Weyer-Smith Labs
Timothy Smith
3461 Canyon Dr.
Billings, MT 59102
(406) 652-1564

Service and support for EML, Moog, ARP, and practically everything else. "I'm willing to supply any schematics that I have for ARP, Moog, EML, Sequential Circuits, Roland, and other vintage synthesizers," says Timothy Smith. "I have manuals for the Minimoog, Moog Sonic Six, Maestro sound processors, Electro-Harmonix, and many more."

CAE (Custom Audio Electronics)
Peter Miller
285 N. Amphlette
San Mateo, CA 94401
(415) 348-2737
Fax (415) 348-2034

Vintage synth, Hammond organ, and amplifier servicing. Vintage synth retrofits. Consulting.

Caruso Music
Larry or Richard Caruso
20 Bank St.
New London, CT 06320
(203) 442-9600
Fax (203) 442-0463

Vintage synth sales, trades, and service. Worldwide delivery.

Daddy's Junky Music
Box 1018
Salem, NH 03079
(603) 894-6492
Fax (603) 893-3517

Used musical equipment dealer.

The Digital Support Group
626 N. Beachwood Dr.
Los Angeles, CA 90004
(213) 460-4884
Fax (213) 460-6120

U.S. support, servicing, and upgrades for Fairlight CMI systems.

Tom Dunn
12651 Briarglen Loop, Unit M
Stanton, CA 90680

Oberheim parts, schematics, and documentation.

EJE Research
20 French Rd.
Buffalo, NY 14227
(716) 668-6600

Modular and later Moog servicing, documentation, and information.

EMS (Electronic Music Studios)
Trendeal Vean Barn
Ladock, Truro
Cornwall TR2 4NW
England
011-44-726-883-265

Service, support, and custom orders for VCS3, Synthi A, Vocoder 2000, and Sound Beam.

EMS (Electronic Music Studios)
Don Hassler
2409 Hewatt Rd.
Snellville, GA 30278
(404) 972-9176

U.S. contact for EMS products.

EMSA (Electronic Music Studios, America)
Everett Hafner
11 North Main St./P.O. Box 767
Williamsburg, MA 01096
(413) 268-3588

Service and support for EMS products.

EPR Electronics
Jeff Carano, Richard Bruyn
505 California Ave.
Middletown, NY 10940
(914) 343-1237

Synth servicing and modification. PPG service and support. MIDI consultation.

Goldman's Gear Exchange
Dick Bauerle
1620 Niagara Falls Blvd.
Tonawanda, NY 14150
(716) 833-6111
Fax (716) 832-6009

Analog synth broker. Owners submit list of gear and Goldman's finds buyers. Mailing list of about 25,000 people. Periodically publish catalog with classified want ads.

Goff Professional
74 Edward St.
Newington, CT 06111
(203) 667-2358

Hammond and Leslie repair, restoration, modifications, and sales.

David Gould
3710 26th Place West, Ste. B4
Seattle, WA 98199
(206) 285-0262
Fax (206) 285-2944

Vintage synth collector/dealer. U.S. Waldorf sales representative.

Interval Music Systems
Scott Morgan
12335 Santa Monica Blvd. #244
Los Angeles, CA 90025
(310) 478-3956
Fax (310) 478-5791
   VS WaveWrangler editor/
librarian, wave converter, and
resynthesis software for
Sequential Prophet-VS and
Macintosh.

Doug Jackson Electronics
1906 Fremont St.
East Troy, WI 53120
(414) 642-9732 or (414) 642-7348
   Buys, sells, and modifies
tube-type Hammonds and
Leslies.

Kelsey-Pape Engineering
John Pape
274 N. Goodman St.
Rochester, NY 14607
(716) 271-1990
   Repair of keyboards, P.A.
systems, amplifiers. Authorized
service for Korg and Yamaha
keyboards. MXR schematics
and documentation.

**Keyboard Exchange
International**
8651 Portside Ct.
Orlando, FL 32817
(407) 671-0730
   Buys and sells Hammonds
and Leslies.

The Keyboard Network
11231 Otsego St.
North Hollywood, CA 91601
(818) 761-2532
   New and analog synth sales.
Finds analog synths for people.

Keyboard Products
10950 Tuxford St., #24
Sun Valley, CA 91352
(818) 504-9931
   Hammond and Leslie modifications and restoration.

Keyboard Rebuilders
Liddell Newsham
3454 Morning Glory Ave.
Baton Rouge, LA 70808
   Refurbishes, rebuilds, and
modifies Hammonds and
Leslies.

Keyboard Specialties
Paul Homb
775 50th Ave. North
St. Petersburg, FL 33703
(813) 521-1118
   Hammond and Leslie servicing, modifications, and
restoration.

Mark Levreault
3 Ledgewood Dr.
Derry, NH 03038
(603) 432-3085
Fax (603) 432-3086
   Vintage synth
collector/dealer. Servicing
available.

Kevin Lightner
(818) 985-2548
   Analog synth rebuilder.
Constructed film composer
Hans Zimmer's Roland 100 and
Polyfusion modular systems.
Specializes in ARP 2500, Moog
modulars, EMS synths, but
works on anything old and
analog.

Magic Parts
Tom McNeil
1537 Fourth St., Suite 198
San Rafael, CA 94901
(800) 451-1922
Fax (415) 453-1111
   Oberheim owner's and service manuals. Distributor of
general electronics parts for
the music industry.

Mellotron Archives
David Kean
721 Michael
Moses Lake, WA 98837
(509) 765-6451
Fax (509) 766-9977
   Service and support for all
Mellotrons and Chamberlins.
Videotapes demonstrating all
available Mellotron sounds
and internal workings. Periodic
newsletter includes list of Mellotron and Chamberlin owners.

**The Museum of
Hammond Organs**
John C. Drotos
Box 44
Peninsula, OH 44264
(216) 225-7937
   An association of Hammond
musical instrument, tone cabinet, accessory, literature, clock,
and memorabilia for collectors
and enthusiasts.

Musician's Service Center
(MSC)
998 S. 2nd St.
San Jose, CA 95112
(408) 297-7532
Fax (408) 286-4861
   Former service technician
at Sequential Circuits.
Factory-authorized repair for
most electronic instruments.

MusicTek Services
12041 Burbank Blvd.
North Hollywood, CA 91607
(818) 506-4055
Fax (818) 506-2963
   Synth repair and modifications. Rhodes Chroma and
Fender Polaris parts and
service.

**New England
Synthesizer Museum**
David Wilson
6 Vernon St.
Nashua, NH 03060-2672
(603) 881-8587
   14,000 sq. ft. display area
with nearly 100 keyboard
synths, synth modules, and sequencers.

Louis Newman
Media Sonics/Discrete Audio
2416 S. Chestnut Ave.
Broken Arrow, OK 74012
(918) 451-0680
Fax (918) 451-0671
   Collector and distributor of
Moog and other analog modular synths. Synthesizer sales
and rentals. Recently
purchased remaining Poly-
fusion inventory. International
shipping. "We will buy your
used synthesizer and studio
equipment. We buy, sell, and
trade pre-owned, demo, and
dealer closeout musical equipment. Our service personnel
are authorized to service Moog,
ARP, Oberheim, Sequential,
Roland, and E-mu synthesizers.
We are analog experts."

Old Colony Sound Lab

P.O. Box 243/305 Union St.

Peterborough, NH 03458-0243

(603) 924-6371

Fax (603) 924-9467

Electronics supplier of tubes, op amps, test CDs, and power supply kits. A subsidiary of Audio Amateur Publications.

Prototypes, Inc.

Bill Leaf, Tom Lepson

10449 Metropolitan Ave.

Kensington, MD 20895

(301) 942-1731

Fax (301) 933-2867

Synthesizer service, repair, and modification.

Resurrection Electronics

Bob "O" Overton

3504 King St.

Austin, TX 78705

(512) 451-5900

Replacement circuit board for SM304 key processor chips for Korg CX-3 and BX-3 organs. Purchases, refurbishes, and resells CX-3s and BX-3s.

Harold Rhodes

5067 Topanga Canyon Blvd.

Woodland Hills, CA 91364

(818) 340-8483

Founder and developer of Rhodes electric pianos and Rhodes Piano Bass; parts available.

Rockfleet Music Service, Inc.

Mary Lock, John Hannon

664B Main St.

Reading, MA 01867

(617) 942-1192

Fax (617) 942-0318

Servicing, parts, and modifications for vintage synths.

Rogue Music

251 W. 30th St.

New York, NY 10001

(212) 629-3708

Fax (212) 947-0027

Dealer of used musical and recording gear. Synth servicing and modifications. Authorized service center for Roland, Yamaha, and others.

Charles M. Solak Companies

AACCSS Distributing and Marketing

133 Myrtle Ave.

Johnson City, NY 13790-1507

(607) 770-9542

Vintage keyboard and strap-on MIDI controller dealer.

Sound Deals, Inc.

Jerry Schilleci

230 Old Towne Rd.

Birmingham, AL 35216

(800) 822-6434

Fax (205) 979-1811

New, used, and vintage gear traded and repaired.

Sound Transform Systems

Rex Probe

1615 Broadway, Ste. #712

Oakland, CA 94612

(510) 465-6896

Fax (510) 465-4656

New manufacturer of and support for Serge Modular Music Systems.

SST

Ed Winquest

13601 Ventura Blvd.

Sherman Oaks, CA 91423

(818) 907-7780

Fax (818) 752-0142

Rental of new and vintage synths and computers. Sales of vintage synths.

The Starving Musician

Sean Denton

3427 El Camino

Santa Clara, CA 95051

(408) 554-9041

Fax (408) 554-9598

Vintage synth sales and service.

Stoney Stockell

c/o Korg USA

89 Frost St.

Westbury, NY 11590

Documentation and support for the Crumar General Development System, Digital Keyboards Synergy, and Mulogix Slave 32.

Gene Stopp

(818) 701-1618

Collector/restorer/enthusiast of early '70s dinosaurs.

Studio Electronics

Greg St. Regis

18034 Ventura Blvd., Suite 169

Encino, CA 91316

(818) 776-8104

Fax (818) 776-1733

Rack-mounted and MIDIfied Minimoog (Midimini), Oberheim OB-8 (Obie-Eight), Oberheim SEMs (Obie SEM Rack), Prophet-5 (P-Five), and Roland TR-808. Newly manufactured rack-mount Minimoog type MIDI synth (SE-1).

Studio Instrument Rentals

(SIR)

1235 Howard St.

San Francisco, CA 94103

(415) 863-8200

Rental of new and vintage keyboards, instruments, audio gear, lights, and concert equipment.

Studio Instrument Rentals

(SIR)

Fred Rose

7950 Sunset Blvd.

West Hollywood, CA 90068

(213) 466-3417

Fax (213) 650-6866

Rental of new and vintage keyboards, instruments, audio gear, lights, and concert equipment.

Synthlocator

David Thomson

12292 Hilltop Dr.

Fredericktown, OH 43019

Vintage synth broker. Manuals and documentation for old synths. Send SASE for information.

Syntronics

John Koumoutseas

466 Commonwealth Ave.

Boston, MA 02215

(617) 266-5039

Fax (617) 266-5076

Servicing for vintage synthesizers, computers, tape decks, effects, and amplifiers. Music software sales.

Patrick Warren

c/o Addis-Wechsler and Assoc.

955 S. Carrillo Dr., 3rd Floor

Los Angeles, CA 90048

(213) 954-9000

Chamberlin tapes.

Wine Country Productions

David Sesnak

1572 Park Crest Ct. #505

San Jose, CA 95118

(408) 265-2008

Fax (408) 266-6591

Service and support for all Sequential Circuits gear.

MIDI-TO-CV CONVERTERS, MIDI MODS & RETROFITS

Analogics
Wes Taggart
5261 Maple Ave. East
Geneva, OH 44041
(216) 466-6911

MIDI retrofits for ARP Odyssey, Axxe, Solus, and 2600, Korg Mono/ Poly, Poly-6, Trident, CX-3, and BX-3, Linn LM-1 and LinnDrum, Minimoog, Micromoog, Multimoog, Moog Prodigy, and Source, Oberheim OB-8, OB-X, and OB-Xa, Roland SH-101, VP-330, Jupiter-8, Juno-6 and -60, TR-808, and CR-78, Sequential Prophet-5, -10, and Pro-One, and Simmons SDS-5. Standalone MIDI-to-CV converters available.

Big Briar, Inc.
Bob Moog
Rt. 3, Box 115A1
Leicester, NC 28748
(704) 683-9085

Memorymoog upgrade. New Theremins, with or without MIDI.

Clarity
Greg Kramer
Nelson Lane
Garrison, NY 10524
(914) 424-4071
Fax (914) 424-3467

The Retro MIDI-to-CV converter.

Doepfer Musikelektronik
Lochhamer Str. 63
D-8032 Gräfelfing
Munich, Germany
011-49-89-85-5578

MIDI-to-CV converter.

Encore Electronics
Tony Karavidas
30 Glenhill Court
Danville, CA 94526
(510) 820-7551

MIDI retrofits for Moog Source, Roland Jupiter-8, Oberheim OB-8, OB-X, OB-Xa, and OB-SX. MIDI-to-CV converter.

Gulbransen
2102 Hancock St.
San Diego, CA 92110
(619) 296-5760
(800) 677-7374
Fax (619) 296-7157

MIDI retrofits for pianos and Rhodes.

Kenton Electronics
John Price
Rear of 137-165 Hook Rd.
Surbiton, Surrey KT6 5AR
England
011-44-81-974-2475
Fax 011-44-81-974-2485

MIDI retrofits for numerous mono and poly synths and some drum machines. MIDI-to-CV converter.

Keyboard Specialties
Paul Homb
775 50th Ave. North
St. Petersburg, FL 33703
(813) 521-1118

Velocity-sensitive MIDI retrofit for Hammond B-3 (transmission only).

Miditec
453 Darwin Crescent
Thunder Bay, Ontario
Canada P7B 5W5
(807) 345-6434

MIDI retrofits for Roland Juno-60, Jupiter-8, Korg Polysix, Poly-61, CX-3, BX-3, EPS-1, and SP-80s, and Viscount VK-1. General-purpose MIDI mods for accordions, pipe organs, and pedal boards.

Paia Electronics
John Simonton
3200 Teakwood Ln.
Edmond, OK 73013
(405) 340-6300

MV-8 will perform MIDI-to-CV or CV-to-MIDI conversions. Comes in kit form or assembled.

Pianodisc
2444 Marconi Ave.
Sacramento, CA 95821
(916) 973-8710
Fax (916) 973-8784

MIDI and reproducing retrofits for pianos.

Wine Country Productions
David Sesnak
1572 Park Crest Ct. #505
San Jose, CA 95118
(408) 265-2008
Fax (408) 266-6591

MIDI retrofits for over 35 synth models from Sequential, ARP, Moog, Korg, Roland, and Yamaha. MIDI-to-CV converter.

EUROPEAN CONTACTS

Cedos Corp.
Bachstr. 40
6334 Assiar Werdorf
Germany
011-49-6443-3438
Fax 011-49-6443-1611

Cedos Corporation
426 E. North St., #209
Waukesha, WI 53188
USA
(608) 277-8305
Fax (608) 277-8307

Cheetah International Ltd.
(see Soundscape Digital Technology, Ltd.)

Comus USA, Inc. (U.S. distributor for Furstein)
107B Corporate Blvd.
S. Plainfield, NJ 07080
(908) 668-1404
Fax (908) 668-1103

ddrum
25 Lindeman Dr.
Trumbull, CT 06611
(800) 882-0098
(203) 374-0020
Fax (203) 374-1093

Digital I/O (U.S. distributor for Plasmic & D2D)
2554 Lincoln Blvd., #122
Marina Del Rey, CA 90291
(213) 398-3993
Fax (213) 822-1360

Digigram
Parc Technologique
de Pré Milliet
38330 Montbonnot France
011-33-76-52-4747
Fax 011-33-76-52-1844

Doepfer Musikelektronik
Lochhamer Str. 63
D-8032 Gräfelfing
Munich, Germany
011-49-89-85-5578

Dynacord
200 Sea Ln.
Farmingdale, NY 11735
(516) 249-3660
Fax (516) 420-1863

D2D Systems
(see also Digital I/O)
St. John's Innovation Centre
Cowley Road
Cambridge
England

EMS (Electronic Music
Studios)
Trendeal Vean Barn
Ladock, Truro
Cornwall TR2 4NW
United Kingdom
011-44-726-883-265

FCN/Simmons International
756 Lakefield Rd., Unit C
Westlake Village, CA 91361
(800) 832-3786
(805) 374-7788
Fax (805) 374-7786

Furstein/Comus SpA
viale Don Bosco 35
62018 Potenza Picena (MC)
Italy

Generalmusic (GEM, Elka,
LEM, Schulze/Pollmann, Bach-
mann)
47048 S. Giovanni
Marignano (FO) Italy
Via delle Rosa, 12
011-39-541-957336
Fax 011-39-541-957404

Generalmusic
1164 Tower Ln.
Bensenville, IL 60106
USA
(708) 766-8230

Intersound & Soft
Constantin Coreth
Loretostraße 47/49
I-39040 Salurn (BZ) Italy
0039-471-884646

Mellotron Archives
David Kean
721 Michael
Moses Lake, WA 98837
(509) 765-6451
Fax (509) 766-9977

Music Industries Corp.
99 Tulip Ave.
Floral Park, NY 11001
USA
(516) 352-4110
(800) 431-6699
Fax (516) 352-0754

Musitronics
TSI-GmbH
Neustraße 12
W-5481 Waldorf
Germany
011-49-26-36-7001
Fax 011-49-26-36-7935

Musitronics (U.S. dist.)
Valhala
Box 20157
Ferndale, MI 48220
USA
(313) 548-9360
Fax (313) 547-5949

**Novation Electronic Music
Systems, Ltd.**
Sovereign House
4-6 Station Rd.
Marlow
Buckinghamshire SL7 1NB
England
44 (0) 628-481992
Fax 44 (0) 628-481835

Plasmic (see Digital I/O)

Quasimidi Products
Elsenbahnstr. 13
D-3575 Kirchhain 1
Germany
011-49-64-22-6712
Fax 011-49-6422-1735

**Soundscape Digital
Technology, Ltd.**
U.S. distribution
Steve Nelson
Nelson & Associates
Box 21211
El Sobrante, CA 94820
(510) 235-4413

Steinberg
TSI-GmbH
Neustraße 12
W-5481 Waldorf
Germany
011-49-26-36-7001
Fax 011-49-26-36-7935

Steinberg/Jones
17700 Raymer St., Suite 1001
Northridge, CA 91325
USA
(818) 993-4091
Fax (818) 701-7452

Überschall
Dieckbornstrs.
3000 Hannover 91
Germany
0511-455410
Fax 0511-447444

Valhala Music, Inc.
Steve Stribling (vintage)
Box 20157
Ferndale, MI 48220
USA
(313) 548-9360
Fax (313) 547-5949

Waldorf Electronics
TSI-GmbH
Neustraße 12
W-5481 Waldorf
Germany
011-49-26-36-7001
Fax 011-49-26-36-7935

Wersi GmbH
Industriegebiet
W-5401 Halsenbach
Germany
011-49-6747-123-0
Fax 011-49-6747-123-193

Wersi Keyboard Systems
c/o Jim Rosenberg
Gibson Musical Instruments
1818 Elm Hill Pike
Nashville, TN 37210
(615) 871-4500
Fax (615) 889-3216

Zadok
P.O. Box 1192
2260 BD
Leidschendam
The Netherlands
31-70-3200-209
Fax 31-70-3200-345

GLOSSARY

AC coupling: A method of transferring signals from one circuit to another in which the AC (alternating current) portion of the signal is passed while the DC (direct current) portion is suppressed.

ADC: See analog-to-digital converter.

A/D converter: See analog-to-digital converter.

additive synthesis: The technique of creating complex tones (for example, a fundamental with a specified series of harmonics) by combining simpler tones. Traditionally these tones were sine waves, but in more recent instruments entire sampled waveforms are used additively.

AD: Attack/decay, one of the simplest types of envelope generator. An AD generator produces a rising voltage followed by a falling voltage, but unlike an AR generator, has no sustain segment. Thus the output of an AD generator typically lasts for a fixed amount of time, regardless of whether or not the key that triggered it is still being held down.

ADR: Attack/decay/release, a type of envelope in which the decay segment falls to the sustain level and the release segment thereupon begins immediately. The sustain portion of the envelope thus has a zero duration. ADR envelopes are useful for creating percussive timbres.

ADSR: Attack/decay/sustain/release, the four segments of a common type of envelope. The controls for these four parameters determine the duration (or, in the case of sustain, the height) of the segments of the envelope. See envelope, envelope generator.

aftertouch: A type of control data generated by pressing down on one or more keys after they have reached and are resting on the keybed. See channel pressure, poly pressure.

algorithm: A set of procedures designed to accomplish something. In the case of

computer software, the procedures may appear to the user as a configuration of software components, for example an arrangement of operators in a Yamaha DX-series synthesizer, or as an element (such as a reverb algorithm) that performs specific operations on the signal.

aliasing: Undesired frequencies that are produced when harmonic components within the audio signal being sampled by a digital recording device or generated within a digital sound source lie above the Nyquist frequency. Aliasing differs from some other types of noise in that its pitch changes radically when the pitch of the intended sound changes. See Nyquist frequency.

AM: See amplitude modulation.

amplitude: The amount of a signal. Amplitude is measured by determining the amount of fluctuation in air pressure (of a sound), voltage (of an electrical signal), or numerical data (in a digital application). When the signal is in the audio range, amplitude is perceived as loudness.

amplitude modulation (AM): A change, usually periodic, in the amplitude of a signal. When the modulating signal is in the audio range, AM produces additional partials somewhat like those produced by FM. When the modulating signal is below the audio frequency range, AM is called tremolo. See tremolo.

analog: Capable of exhibiting continuous fluctuations. In an analog audio system, fluctuations in voltage correspond in a one-to-one fashion with (that is, are analogous to) the fluctuations in air pressure at the audio input or output. In an analog synthesizer, such parameters as oscillator pitch and LFO speed are typically controlled by analog control voltages rather than by digital data, and the audio signal is also an analog voltage. Compare with digital.

analog/digital hybrid: A synthesizer or sampler that makes use of both analog

and digital technology, for example digital oscillators with analog lowpass filters, or (in the case of some older instruments) analog synthesis hardware with digital memory and control hardware.

analog sequencer: A sequencer in which the control voltages to be played back are stored mechanically using a bank of knobs.

analog-to-digital (A/D) converter (ADC): A device that changes the continuous fluctuations in voltage from an analog device (such as a microphone) into digital information that can be stored or processed in a sampler, digital signal processor, or digital recording device.

AR: Attack/release, the two parameters controlled by the simplest type of envelope generator, one in which the sustain level is automatically set at 100%.

arpeggiator: A device that automatically steps one note at a time through a group of notes, usually notes specified by keys that are held down (or latched). The notes may be stepped through in ascending or descending order, or in some other manner. Unlike a sequencer, an arpeggiator cannot usually play irregular rhythms or chords; it is primarily a performance aid.

assignment priority: The scheme used by a synthesizer for assigning voice channels to the keys that are being pressed. See keyboard logic, high-note, low-note, and last-note priority; also dynamic voice allocation.

attack: The first part of the sound of a note. In an envelope, the attack segment is the segment during which the envelope rises from its initial value (usually zero) to the attack level (often the maximum level for the envelope) at a rate determined by the attack time parameter.

attenuator: A potentiometer (pot) that is used to adjust the amplitude of the signal passing through it. The amplitude can usually be set to any value between full (no attenuation) and zero (full attenuation). Pots can be either rotary or linear (sliders), and can be either hardware or "virtual sliders" on a computer screen.

audio input: An input to a signal modifier that accepts the signal the modifier is intended to act on.

auto-correct: See quantization.

auto-bend: A function that causes the beginning of each note to start at a pitch above or below the intended pitch, after which the note moves smoothly to the intended pitch, usually at a programmable rate.

auto-glide: A type of glide (portamento) in which there is a pitch slide between notes only when the new key is depressed while the previous key is still being held down. Playing with a staccato touch produces discrete pitches with no glide.

auto-tune: A function, often triggered by a button or switch, which causes an instrument to automatically tune (and perhaps calibrate the scaling of) its oscillators and sometimes filters.

azure noise: Random fluctuations in sound, weighted so that there is greater energy in the upper part of the frequency spectrum. Compare with pink noise and white noise.

balanced modulator: A device that differs in circuit design from, but has the same audio effect as, a ring modulator. See ring modulator.

bandpass filter: A filter that allows only the frequencies within a specified range to pass through, attenuating all frequencies above and below that range.

band-reject filter: A filter that eliminates the frequencies within a specified range and allows all other frequencies to pass through. Also called a notch filter.

bandwidth: The available opening through which information can pass. In audio, the bandwidth of a device is the portion of the frequency spectrum that it can handle without significant degradation. In digital communications, the bandwidth is the amount of data that can be transmitted in a given period of time.

bank: (1) A set of patches. (2) Any related set of items, e.g. a filter bank (a set of filters that work together to process a single signal).

baud rate: The number of bits of computer information transmitted per second. MIDI transmissions have a baud rate of 31,250 (31.25 kilobaud), while modems typically have a much lower rate of 300, 1,200, or 2,400 baud.

bend: To change pitch in a continuous sliding manner, usually using a pitch-bend wheel or lever. See pitch-bend.

bit: The smallest possible unit of digital information, numerically either a 1 or a 0. Digital audio is encoded in words that are usually eight, 12, or 16 bits long. Each added bit represents a theoretical improvement of about 6dB in the signal-to-noise ratio.

block diagram: A schematic representation of a synthesizer patch, shown as abstract voltage routings, that can be applied to any synthesizer with the proper routing facilities.

bpm: Beats per minute. The usual measurement of tempo.

break point: (1) The third setting in Korg's six-stage envelope generator. The break point is a level setting that occurs between the attack level setting and the sustain level setting. (2) In Yamaha's DX synthesizers and Roland's D-50, the break point is a point of reference on the keyboard above or below which amplitude scaling takes place.

brick-wall filter: A lowpass filter at the input of an analog-to-digital converter, used to prevent frequencies above the Nyquist limit from being encoded by the converter. See Nyquist frequency, aliasing.

buffer: An area of memory, used for recording or editing data before it is stored in a more permanent form.

bug: A defect in software that causes a piece of digital equipment to behave in an unintended or anomalous manner.

byte: A group of eight bits. See MIDI byte.

capacitance sensing: An unusual type of touch sensitivity in which the amount of key surface covered by a fingertip is sensed and a corresponding output voltage generated.

card: A plug-in memory device. RAM cards, which require an internal battery, can be used for storing user data, while ROM cards, which have no battery, can only be used for reading the data recorded on them by the manufacturer.

carrier: A signal that is being modulated by some other signal, as in FM synthesis.

cartridge: A plug-in memory device, functionally identical to the card except that it's thicker.

cassette storage: Data about memory contents stored on cassette tape in the form of an audio signal.

cent: The smallest conventional unit of pitch deviation. 100 cents equal one half-step.

center detent: A notch at the center of throw of a controller (especially a pitch-bend wheel or pan pot) that allows the user to return the controller precisely and reliably to the position at which the controller has no effect on the signal, or, in the case of the pan pot, the position at which the two outputs receive equal amounts of signal.

chain: An ordered series. For example, a program chain is a set of patches that the user can step through in order with a footswitch or button-press. A song chain is a series of sequences or patterns in a sequencer or drum machine.

channel: An electrical signal path. In analog audio (such as a mixer), each channel consists of separate wired components. In the digital domain, channels may share wiring, and are kept separate through logical operations. MIDI provides definitions for 16 channels, which transmit not audio signals but digital control signals for triggering synthesizers and other devices.

channel pressure: A type of MIDI control message that is applied equally to all of the notes on a given channel; the opposite of poly pressure, in which each MIDI note has its own pressure value. Also called aftertouch, channel pressure is generated on keyboard instruments by pressing down on a key or keys while holding them. See aftertouch, poly pressure.

chorusing: A type of signal processing. In chorusing, a time-delayed or detuned copy of a signal is mixed with the original signal. The mixing process changes the relative strengths and phase relationships of the overtones to create a fatter, more animated sound. The simplest way to achieve chorusing is to detune one oscillator from another to produce a slow beating between them.

clamping: The limitation of a voltage (or some other value, such as MIDI velocity) to a specified level. Oscillator clamping is a type of sync in which, when it receives a command pulse, the slave oscillator resets not to the beginning of its cycle (as in normal sync) but to whatever point in its cycle corresponds to the clamping level.

clangorous: Containing partials that are not part of the natural harmonic series. Clangorous tones are often more or less bell-like.

clavier: A keyboard.

click track: The simplest type of timing reference signal that can be recorded on tape. A click track contains a single click for each beat.

clock: (1) Adjustable source of a regular low-frequency pulse; often used as an automatic trigger for sample-and-hold, analog sequencer, etc. (2) One of two types of timing control devices. A low-frequency pulse clock normally puts out one gate and/or trigger signal for each event to be initiated, and may be used as an adjustable-speed automatic trigger for a sample-and-hold, analog sequencer, envelope generator, etc. An audio-rate sync clock puts out a pulse with which various digitally controlled devices can be synced to one another, or to a tape track containing the sync clock signal. Typical clock rates are 24, 48, and 96 pulses per quarter note. MIDI clock signals, sent at 24 per quarter-note, are one type of MIDI data type. (3) Any of several types of timing control devices, or the periodic signals that they generate. A sequencer's internal clock is always set to some number of pulses per quarter-note (ppq), and this setting is one of the main factors that de-

termine how precisely the sequencer can record time-dependent information. The actual clock speed is usually determined by the beats-per-minute setting. See ppq, bpm, MIDI clock.

clock resolution: The precision (measured in ppq) with which a sequencer can encode time-based information.

coarse tune: A control used for making large changes (usually by half-steps) in the pitch of an oscillator.

companding: A type of signal processing in which the signal is compressed on input and expanded back to its original form on output. Digital companding allows a device to achieve a greater apparent dynamic range with fewer bits per word.

compression: The process of reducing the amplitude range of an audio signal by reducing the peaks and bringing up the low levels.

contour amount: A control parameter that regulates the amount of envelope applied to the destination (usually a filter or VCA). Note that the sustain control is a level control *within* the envelope generator which sets the sustain level relative to the peak found at the end of the attack portion of the envelope, while the contour amount control increases or reduces the entire envelope, including the peak, proportionately.

contour generator: See envelope generator.

control input: An input to a signal source or modifier that accepts the signal telling the module what to do.

controller: Any device (for example, a keyboard, wind synth controller, or pitch-bend lever) or analog synth module (envelope generator) capable of producing a change in some aspect of a sound by altering the action of some other device.

control voltage: An electrical signal, typically found on an older analog or modular synthesizer, that tells a voltage-controlled device or module (such as a VCO or VCF) what levels to go to or changes to make in the settings of its parameters. A control voltage is an analog signal, but many digital synthesizers are designed to operate,

from the user's standpoint, as if their control signals were voltages. See analog.

crash: The failure of a piece of digital equipment, resulting from a disastrous bug. See bug.

cross-modulation: A term used by some manufacturers to refer to a type of modulation in which one of the audio oscillators is being modulated by another, or by an envelope generator.

cross-switching: A velocity threshold effect in which one sound is triggered at low velocities and another at high velocities, with an abrupt transition between the two. If the transition is smooth rather than abrupt, the effect is called cross-fading rather than cross-switching. Cross-switching can also be initiated from a footswitch, LFO, or some other controller.

cutoff frequency: The point in the frequency spectrum beyond which a filter attenuates the audio signal being sent through it. On most older analog synthesizers, the cutoff frequency is both manually adjustable and voltage-controllable.

cutoff slope: See rolloff slope.

CV: control voltage.

DAC: See digital-to-analog converter.

dB: See decibel.

DC coupling: A method of transferring signals from one circuit to another that preserves frequencies down to 0Hz (DC voltage offsets).

DCO: (1) Digitally controlled oscillator; that is, digital signals are used to set the pitch and waveform. (2) A term used principally on Korg and Roland synthesizers, whose oscillators can be directly controlled digitally because they are digital oscillators. The analog oscillators on analog/digital hybrid instruments are ultimately controlled digitally as well, but the control signals are often sent through a DAC and converted to analog voltages before arriving at the oscillators' control inputs.

dead band: An area at the center of travel of a controller such as a pitch-bend wheel. Within this area, physical movement by the controller generates no output data. A dead band is usually provided to allow a pitch controller to be returned reliably to its center pitch. Unlike a center detent, a dead band has no notch to impede the physical travel of the controller.

decay: The second of the four segments of a typical ADSR envelope. The decay control determines the amount of time it takes for the envelope to fall from the peak reached at the end of the attack segment to the sustain level.

decibel: A unit of measurement used to indicate audio power level. Technically, a decibel is a logarithmic ratio of two numbers, which means that there is no such thing as a dB measurement of a single signal. In order to measure a signal in dB, you need to know what level it is referenced to. Commonly used reference levels are indicated by such symbols as dBm, dBV, and dBu.

delay: (1) The first stage of a five-stage DADSR envelope, which delays the beginning of the envelope's attack segment. (2) A control function that allows one of the elements in a layered sound to start later than another element. (3) A signal processor or digital delay line (DDL), used for flanging, doubling, and echo, that holds its input for some period of time before passing it to the output, or the algorithm within a signal processor that creates delay.

detune: A control that allows one oscillator to sound a slightly different pitch than another.

digital: (1) Quantized into discrete steps; the opposite of analog. Digital equipment uses microprocessors to store and retrieve information about sound in the form of numbers. (2) Using computer-type binary arithmetic operations. Digital music equipment uses microprocessors to store, retrieve, and manipulate information about sound in the form of numbers, and typically divides potentially continuous fluctuations in value (such as amplitude or pitch) into discrete quantized steps. Compare with analog.

digital/analog hybrid: See analog/digital hybrid.

digital oscillator: An oscillator (a source of a periodically repeating waveform) in

which the specific waveshape to be generated exists in the form of a series of numbers (the wavetable) that describe the height of the waveshape at various points in time. See oscillator.

digital-to-analog converter (DAC): A device that changes the sample words put out by a digital audio device into analog fluctuations in voltage that can be sent to a mixer or amplifier. All digital synthesizers, samplers, and effects devices have DACs at their output to create audio signals.

digital sequencer: A sequencer in which the notes and controller gestures to be played back are stored in the form of numbers in computer memory. See analog sequencer, sequencer.

distortion: An alteration in an audio signal. Distortion can be intentional (when produced by an effects device, for example) or unintentional (caused by overloading a circuit or otherwise inputting a signal that the circuit is not capable of handling properly).

dithering: A way to avoid the problems with low-level signals in a digital system. The transition between zero and the lowest bit is made to occur in a statistically random manner, so that low-level signals vanish into noise as on analog equipment.

double mode: A type of keyboard logic in which two different timbres (or programs) sound simultaneously from each key; usually found on instruments with a split keyboard function.

dry: Consisting entirely of the original, unprocessed sound. The output of an effects device is "100% dry" when only the input signal is being heard, with none of the effect(s) created by the processor itself. Compare with wet.

DSP: Digital signal processing. Broadly speaking, all changes in sound that are produced within a digital audio device, other than changes caused by simple cutting and pasting of sections of a waveform, are created through DSP. A digital reverb is a typical DSP device.

duophonic: Possessing two voices, one sounding the highest note depressed on

the keyboard and the other the lowest. A duophonic synthesizer is a simplified polyphonic synthesizer in which the two voices generally share a single VCF and VCA.

duty cycle: The percentage of the time of a complete cycle of a pulse wave which it spends in the up portion of its cycle. In the case of audio-rate pulse waves, there is no functional difference between two waves that have duty cycles of 50% + X and 50% – X, as their harmonic spectra will be identical. Also called pulse width.

dynamic voice allocation: A system found on many multitimbral synthesizers and samplers that allows voices to be reassigned automatically to play different patches whenever required by the musical input from the keyboard or MIDI.

echo: A discrete repetition of a sound, as opposed to reverberation, which is a continuous wash of closely spaced non-discrete echoing sound. See delay (3), reverb.

edit buffer: An area of memory used for making changes in the current patch. Usually the contents of the edit buffer will be lost when the instrument is switched off; a write operation is required to move the data to a more permanent area of memory for long-term storage.

edit mode: A mode of operation in which front-panel controls or computer editing software can be used to make changes in the values in the device's memory. (Usually, the changes are made in the portion of memory called the edit buffer. See edit buffer.)

editor/librarian: A piece of computer software that allows the user to load and store patches and banks of patches (the librarian) and edit patch parameters (the editor).

effects: Any form of audio signal processing — reverb, delay, chorusing, etc.

EG: Envelope generator. See envelope, envelope generator.

emphasis: See resonance.

enharmonic: Alternate with respect to harmonic function. Enharmonic equivalents are notes that are spelled differently (such as A♭ and G♯) but sound the same. Compare with inharmonic.

envelope: (1) A shape that changes aperiodically as a function of time. The envelope shape is controlled by a set of rate (or time) and level parameters. The envelope is a control signal that can be applied to various aspects of a sound, such as pitch, filter cutoff frequency, and overall amplitude. (2) The envelope shape is often in the form of a control voltage that can be applied to a VCA to control amplitude, to a filter to control timbre, or to any other voltage-controlled parameter of the sound, to give shape to a note.

envelope follower: (1) An AC-to-DC converter coupled with a lag processor to produce a DC envelope proportional to the amplitude of the AC input. (2) A module that "listens" to an audio input and creates a control voltage envelope proportional to the amplitude of the input signal.

envelope generator: A device that generates an envelope. Also known as a contour generator or transient generator, because the envelope is a contour (shape) that is used to create some of the transient (changing) characteristics of the sound. See ADSR, AR, AD, envelope.

envelope tracking: A function (also called keyboard tracking, key follow, and keyboard rate scaling) that changes the length of one or more envelope segments depending on which key on the keyboard is being played. Envelope tracking is most often used to give the higher notes shorter envelopes and the lower notes longer envelopes, mimicking the response characteristics of percussion-activated acoustic instruments such as the piano.

event editing: An operation in a sequencer in which one musical event at a time is altered.

exponential: A relationship between two quantities such that as one quantity increases, the amount of change in the other increases as the absolute value of the first increases. An exponential response curve is concave; that is, a small change in input at a low input level will have little effect on the output, while the same amount of change at a high input level will cause a much larger change in

the output. For practical purposes, an exponential curve is the opposite of a logarithmic curve. See logarithmic, linear.

fc: Center frequency or cutoff frequency. In a resonant filter, the fc is the center frequency of the resonant peak. See cutoff frequency.

feedback: A circular signal path in which the output of a device is fed back into its own input. Multiple echoes are produced in a digital delay using an internal feedback process.

FFT: Fast Fourier transform. A quick method of performing a Fourier analysis on a sound. See Fourier analysis.

filter: A device for eliminating selected frequencies from the sound spectrum of a signal and perhaps (in the case of a resonant filter) increasing the level of other frequencies. In addition, synthesizer filters are generally capable of emphasizing certain frequencies just inside the cutoff frequency, creating a resonant peak. See resonance, lowpass filter, highpass filter, bandpass filter, band-reject filter.

filter scaling: See keyboard scaling.

fine-tune: A control used for making small, precise changes in pitch.

floating split: A type of keyboard logic in which the instrument attempts to follow the player's performance in order to determine which notes should be transmitted on which MIDI channel, or should play which internal timbre.

floppy disk: A removable, portable disk on which computer data is encoded in magnetic form. Called "floppy" in reference to the malleable circular sheet of plastic coated with magnetic material and enclosed in the disk's protective envelope. When first applied to early computer-based music systems, 8" was the most common size of floppy disk. Later, 5.25" and 3.5" became prevalent. Some Japanese products (Akai's MD280 mini-disk drive for the S612 sampler and Roland's MT-100 MIDI sequencer/synth module, to mention two) used 2.8" micro-floppies ("quick disks"). These weren't as common, were more vulnerable to damage (there was an open slit that leaves the disk surface unprotected), provided less storage

space, and cost more than 3.5" disks — the current norm.

FM synthesis: A technique in which frequency modulation (FM) is used to create complex audio waveforms/tone colors. See frequency modulation.

footage: A way of designating what octave an oscillator will sound in. Borrowed from pipe organ terminology, footage settings range from 2' (high pitch) through 4', 8', and 16' to 32' (low pitch). Each increase by a power of 2 shifts the pitch downward by one octave.

formant: A resonant peak in a frequency spectrum. For example, the variable formants produced by the human vocal tract are what give vowels their characteristic sound.

Fourier analysis: A technique, usually performed using a DSP algorithm, that allows complex, dynamically changing audio waveforms to be described mathematically as sums of sine waves at various frequencies and amplitudes. See DSP.

four-pole: See rolloff slope.

frequency modulation (FM): A change in the fre-quency (pitch) of a signal. At low modulation rates, FM is perceived as vibrato or some type of trill, depending on the shape of the modulating waveform. When the modulating wave is in the audio range (above 20Hz or so), FM is perceived as a change in tone color coupled with an overall change in pitch.

FSK: Frequency shift keying. A type of synchronization signal that consists of a rapid periodic alteration between two pitched audio tones, usually an octave or more apart. FSK is more reliable than an LFO clock when recording a sync tone on tape. An ordinary FSK sync tone contains information about tempo but not absolute time location. See smart FSK.

gain: The amount of boost or attenuation of a signal.

gate: A control signal put out by a keyboard that tells the envelope generators that a key is now depressed, or an equivalent signal put out by a sequencer or some other module. A gate signal is put out continuously until the key is lifted, or until a moment when no key is depressed. Compare with trigger.

gigabyte: One billion (for British readers, one thousand million) bytes.

glide: A function, also called portamento, in which the pitch slides smoothly from one note to the next instead of jumping over the intervening pitches.

global: Pertaining to or governing all of the operations of an instrument.

graphic editing: A method of editing parameter values using graphic representations (for example, of envelope shapes) displayed on a computer screen or LCD.

hard disk: A magnetic storage medium for computer data, typically built into its own housing or into the console of an instrument. A hard disk can store much more data than a floppy disk and access it much more quickly.

hard sync: The standard type of oscillator sync. See oscillator sync.

hard-wired: (1) An electrical connection that is built into the instrument's circuitry; the opposite of patchable. Some hard-wired connections can be overridden by patching or using defeat switches, while others are a permanent part of the instrument's operation. (2) Connected electrically in a manner that cannot be altered by the user. Also called "normalled."

harmonic: See overtone.

headroom: The amount of additional signal above the nominal input level that can be sent into a module before clipping distortion occurs.

hexadecimal: A numbering system that uses base 16. Hexadecimal digits include the numerals 0 through 9 followed by the letters A through F. Bytes are often represented by two-digit hexadecimal numbers, in which case a dollar sign or letter 'H' is used to indicate that the number is in hex rather than decimal (base 10).

high-note priority: A type of keyboard logic in which a voice channel will always be made available to allow the highest key played to sound. High-note and low-note priority are most often found on mono-

phonic synthesizers, and on polyphonics when they are in unison mode. Compare with low-note priority, last-note priority.

highpass filter: A filter that attenuates the frequencies below its cutoff frequency.

hold: See latching.

Hz: Abbreviation for Hertz, the unit measurement of frequency. One Hz equals one cycle per second. The frequency range of human hearing is considered to be from 20Hz to 20kHz (20,000Hz).

inharmonic: Containing frequencies that are not whole-number multiples of the fundamental. Compare with enharmonic.

input: A signal entering a module, or the point at which it enters.

interface: (1) The place where two things come together. The synthesizer's front panel is the interface between the musician and the instrument. Two instruments are said to be interfaced when their operations are linked electronically — for example, when the guts of one can be played from the keyboard of the other. (2) A linkage between two things. A user interface is the system of controls with which the user controls a device. Two devices are said to be interfaced when their operations are linked electronically. An interface box is often required to convert signals from one form to another.

interpolate: To insert estimated values of a function between two known values.

inverter: A device that changes positive voltages or positive-going signals into negative voltages or negative-going signals and vice versa, thus reversing the phase on periodic signals, causing an envelope to descend instead of rising, and so on.

joystick: A controller like a small, freely moving gearshift lever, which puts out two independent control signals simultaneously, one determined by its left-right position (the X axis) and the other by its toward-away position (the Y axis). Three-dimensional joy- sticks are occasionally found; they put out a third control voltage determined by their in-out position perpendicular to the panel in which they are set.

keyboard: A controller consisting of a number of levers or touch-plates mounted horizontally in a row. It's typically based on the design of traditional piano and organ performance input devices, and used primarily for playing traditional melodic and harmonic patterns. On an analog synthesizer, the keyboard sends a control voltage to the oscillators, and gate and trigger signals to the envelope generators.

keyboard amount: See keyboard tracking.

keyboard level scaling: See keyboard scaling.

keyboard logic: The system that determines what types of electronic signals are sent out from the keyboard, and where they are routed. For more on keyboard logic, see assignment, top-note, low-note, and last-note priority; also single trigger, multiple trigger, and dynamic voice allocation.

keyboard rate scaling: See envelope tracking.

keyboard scaling: (1) The calibration of an oscillator so that moving from any key to an adjacent key produces a pitch change of an equal-tempered half-step. (2) The smooth variation in the amplitude of a sound, or some component of a sound, over the range of the keyboard. (3) A function with which the sound can be altered smoothly across the keyboard by using key number as a modulation source. Level scaling changes the loudness of the sound, while filter scaling changes its brightness.

keyboard tracking: Controlling some element of the sound, usually the cutoff frequency of the filter, with a voltage or equivalent pitch information from the keyboard. On some synthesizers, the keyboard tracking amount is continuously variable, while on others it can be controlled only by a two-position (on/off) or three-position (on/half/off) switch. See envelope tracking.

key follow: See envelope tracking.

kHz: KiloHertz (thousands of Hertz). See Hz.

kilobyte: Linguistically speaking, a thousand bytes. In practice, a kilobyte generally contains 1,024 bytes.

lag processor: A module in a modular analog synthesizer that smooths out sudden changes in voltage. The glide (portamento) control on most analog synthesizers is actually a type of lag processor acting on the control voltage output of the keyboard.

last-note priority: A type of keyboard logic in which each new key as it is depressed activates a voice, taking over if necessary a voice that had previously been sounding another note. Compare with high-note priority, low-note priority.

latching: A simple form of memory in which a synthesizer continues to operate according to whatever latchable pattern (for example, the interval between two oscillators, a repeating sequence of notes, or a set of keys sounding a chord or arpeggio) was in effect at the moment when the latching command was received. The operation continues until the latching controller (such as a footswitch) is released or a release-latching command is received. A sustain pedal does a simple form of latching.

layering: Sounding two or more voices, each of which typically has its own timbre, from each key depression. Layering can be accomplished within a single synthesizer, or by linking two synths together via MIDI and assigning both to the same MIDI channel.

LCD: Liquid crystal display — the type of display screen used on most electronic music devices.

LED: Light-emitting diode.

LFO: Low-frequency oscillator. An oscillator especially devoted to sub-audio applications, and used as a control source for modulating the sound to create vibrato, tremolo, trills, and so on.

librarian: See editor/librarian.

limiting: Compression in which the compression ratio is 20:1 or greater, effectively preventing the output amplitude from exceeding the threshold value. See compression.

linear: A relationship between two quantities such that a change in the amount of one causes an equivalent change in the amount of the other. A linear pot produces the same amount of change in sound per amount of physical motion throughout its operating range. Compare with exponential, logarithmic.

linear FM: A type of frequency modulation in which the center frequency of the carrier oscillator is not altered by a change in the amount of modulation; it remains constant.

logarithmic: A relationship between two quantities such that a change in one corresponds to a change in the log of the other. For practical purposes, a logarithmic response curve is convex; that is, it produces the greatest change in output at low input levels. Compare with exponential, linear.

loop: A piece of material that plays over and over. In a sequencer, a loop repeats a musical phrase. In a sampler, loops are used to allow samples of finite length to be sustained indefinitely.

low-note priority: A type of keyboard logic in which a voice channel will always be made available to allow the lowest key played to sound. Compare with high-note priority, last-note priority.

lowpass filter: A filter that attenuates the frequencies above its cutoff frequency.

map: A table in which input values are assigned to outputs arbitrarily by the user on an item-by-item basis.

master: Any device that controls the operation of another device. For example, a master clock is a timing reference signal that controls the playback rate of devices that are synced to it.

matrix modulation: A method of connecting modulation sources to destinations in such a way that any source can be sent to any combination of destinations.

matrix panel: A patching system found on a few modular synthesizers, including the ARP 2500 and EMS VCS3, in which inputs and outputs for all modules are brought to a central grid and connected to one another using switches or pins at the junc-

tions in the grid. (Wes Taggart of Analogics warns that the ARP 2500 is susceptible to audible crosstalk problems thanks to its matrix-patching arrangement.)

matrix switching: A type of signal routing in which signals can be routed from any input to any output.

Mb: Megabyte (a million bytes).

megabyte: Linguistically speaking, a million bytes. In practice, a megabyte often contains 1,024 kilobytes.

memory: A system or device for storing information — in the case of musical devices, information about patches, sequences, waveforms, and so on. Synthesizer memories are generally digital, although there are rare diversions like the EML SynKey, which had a punched-card reader for programming sounds.

MG: Modulation generator. A term used by Korg to refer to the LFO section on their instruments.

MIDI: Musical Instrument Digital Interface. (1) A specification for the protocols by which digital (performance) information — notes, how hard they're played, how hard you push them down while sustaining them, what you do with the pitch-bend or mod wheel or volume pedal, that kind of thing — is transmitted from one synthesizer to another, or between synthesizers, sequencers, drum machines, and computers. (2) MIDI is a specification for the types of control signals that can be sent from one electronic music device to another.

MIDI byte: A group of ten bits. Each MIDI byte includes a start bit and a stop bit, with eight bits in the middle to convey information.

MIDI clock: A timing reference signal sent over a MIDI cable at the rate of 24 clock pulses per quarter-note.

MIDI filter: A device that eliminates selected messages from the MIDI data stream.

MIDI mapper: A device that translates MIDI data from one form to another in real time.

MIDI merger: A MIDI accessory that allows two incoming MIDI signals to be combined into one MIDI output.

MIDI mode: Any of the ways of responding to incoming MIDI data. While four modes — omni off/poly, omni on/poly, omni off/mono, and omni on/mono — are defined by the MIDI specification, omni on/mono is never used, and at least two other useful modes have been developed — multi mode for multitimbral instruments and multi-mono for guitar synthesizers.

MIDI out/thru: A MIDI output port that can be configured either to transmit MIDI messages generated within the unit (out) or to retransmit messages received at the MIDI in (thru).

MIDI patch map: A map with which any incoming MIDI program change message can be assigned to call up any of an instrument's patches.

MIDI retrofit: A modification for specific pre-MIDI synthesizers and drum machines that makes them MIDI-compatible — capable of responding to note data and, in most cases, velocity, continuous controllers, and program changes.

MIDI-to-CV converter: An interface with a MIDI in connector and multiple control-voltage (CV) and gate/trigger outputs for triggering pre-MIDI analog synthesizers and modules from a MIDI source such as a keyboard, sequencer, or alternate controller.

millisecond: One one-thousandth (0.001) of a second.

mixer: A device that adds two or more audio signals together.

mod: (1) Modulation. (2) Modification.

mode: The manner in which a device is currently operating.

modifier: A device (such as a VCF or VCA) that acts on an audio signal to change it in some way.

modular: A type of system design in which the various sound sources, modifiers, and controllers are separate or semi-independent pieces of hardware

that must be hooked together with patch cords or some other patching system in order to produce a sound.

modulation: (1) The process of introducing a control voltage to a sound source or modifier so as to change the character of the audio signal. (2) The process of sending a control signal to a sound source so as to change the character of the sound.

module: (1) A hardware device, generally keyboardless and bigger than an accessory. A module can be either physically separate or integrated into a modular synthesizer, and is designed to make some particular contribution to the process of generating electronic sound. (2) A synthesizer without a keyboard, to be controlled via control voltages, triggers, and gates (analog synth) or MIDI (in the case of a MIDI-compatible device).

mono mode: One of the basic reception modes of MIDI devices. In mono mode, an instrument responds monophonically to all notes arriving over a specific MIDI channel. See multi mode, omni mode, and poly mode.

monophonic: (1) Capable of producing only one note at a time. (2) Capable of producing only one independently moving pitch line at a time. On a classic monophonic analog synthesizer, only one key on the keyboard will have an effect at any given time. (3) Doesn't play chords when you play several keys at once. (Multiple oscillators can be tuned to play intervals, but their harmonic relationship will remain constant as the oscillators track single keys played on the keyboard.)

mother: Roland uses the term "mother keyboard" instead of "master keyboard." See master.

mouse: A hand-held control input device consisting of a tabletop roller and one or more buttons.

ms: See millisecond.

multi mode: A MIDI reception mode in which a multitimbral module responds to MIDI input on two or more channels and maintains musical independence between the channels, typically playing a different patch on each channel. See mono mode, omni mode, and poly mode.

multimode filter: A filter that can operate in lowpass, highpass, bandpass, or (less often) band-reject mode. See filter.

multiple: A small, electrically passive splitting and mixing module found on some modular synthesizers.

multiple trigger: A type of keyboard logic, found in most polyphonic synthesizers, in which each key depression causes a new trigger signal to be sent to the tone-generating circuitry. Compare with single trigger.

multisample: The distribution of several related samples at different pitches across the keyboard.

multitimbral: Capable of playing two or more discrete timbres simultaneously.

musique concrète: An historically significant type of electronic music produced by manual tape splicing and electronic processing of acoustic sounds (sounds not produced by conventional instruments) and electronically produced sounds.

NAMM: National Association of Music Merchants (5140 Avenida Encinas, Carlsbad, CA 92008), whose mission is "to unify and strengthen the music products industry and increase the number of active music makers" via trade shows, educational activities, and market development.

nibble: Four of the eight bits in a byte.

noise: A random or quasi-random sound made up of many frequencies, perceived by the ear as hiss. See azure noise, pink noise, white noise.

noise generator: A source for random or quasi-random fluctuations in voltage, which are perceived by the ear as hiss. See azure noise, pink noise, white noise.

non-parallel mixing: A type of mixing, also called series mixing, in which the two signals being added together interact to produce sidebands. This differs from ring modulation in that in non-parallel mixing the original signals are still present along with the new frequency components. See parallel mixing.

non-volatile memory: A type of memory whose contents are retained, usually by means of a built-in long-lasting battery, when the power is shut off.

notch filter: See band-reject filter.

Nyquist frequency: The highest frequency that can be accurately reproduced when a signal is digitally encoded at a given sample rate. Theoretically, the Nyquist frequency is one-half of the sampling rate. If a signal being sampled contains frequency components that are above the Nyquist limit, aliasing will be introduced into the digital representation of the signal. See aliasing, brick-wall filter.

omni mode: A MIDI reception mode in which a module responds to incoming MIDI channel messages no matter what their channel. See mono mode, multi mode, and poly mode.

operating system: The set of software instructions that tells a device what to do.

operator: A term used in Yamaha's FM synthesizers to refer to the software equivalent of an oscillator, envelope generator, and envelope-controlled amplifier.

oscillator: An electronic sound source. In an analog synthesizer, oscillators typically produce regularly repeating fluctuations in voltage; that is, they oscillate. In a digital synth, an oscillator more typically plays back a complex waveform by reading the numbers in a wavetable.

oscillator sync: A control connection between two oscillators in which the synced oscillator is forced to begin a new cycle of its waveform each time the master oscillator does so. Since the fundamental frequency of the synced oscillator cannot change, sweeping its pitch control input with a controller such as a mod wheel will result in a timbral change.

overdrive: Intentional distortion of an audio waveform, created by overloading an amplifier or signal processor, or the artificially generated equivalent of such overloading.

overflow mode: A mode of operation in which a MIDI module plays as many notes as it can and then transmits excess notes through its MIDI out or thru so that they can be played by another module. Using overflow mode with two sound

modules allows chords to be played that have more notes than either module could produce by itself.

overtone: A whole-number multiple of the fundamental frequency of a tone. The overtones define the harmonic spectrum of a sound. See sine wave, Fourier analysis, partial.

page: One of a set of control panel configurations. Generally, the pages are distinguished from one another by the contents of the LCD screen; the same set of hardware buttons takes on different functions depending on what page has been called up.

parallel interface: A connection between two pieces of hardware in which several data lines carry information at the same time. Compare with serial interface.

parallel mixing: A type of mixing in which two signals are combined in such a way as not to produce any new frequency components. Compare with non-parallel mixing.

parameter: A user-adjustable quantity that governs some aspect of a device's performance. Normally, the settings for all of the parameters that make up a patch can be changed by the user and stored in memory, but the parameters themselves are defined by the operating system and cannot be altered.

part: A software "slot" in a Roland synthesizer whose parameters determine how the synth will respond to input on a given MIDI channel.

partial: (1) One of the sine-wave components (the fundamental, an overtone, or a tone at some other frequency) of a complex tone. See overtone. (2) A single voice channel in a synth (especially one from Roland) whose patches provide separate parameter definitions for two or more voice channels.

patch: *Verb:* To connect together, as the inputs and outputs of various modules, generally with patch cords. *Noun:* The configuration of hookups and settings that results from the process of patching, and, by extension, the sound that such a configuration creates. Often used to denote a single tone color or the contents of a

memory location that contains parameter settings for such a tone color, even on an instrument that requires no physical patching.

patch cord: An electrical cable used to connect the output of one module to the input of another.

PCM: Pulse code modulation — a standard method of digital sampling.

phase-locking: An extreme form of oscillator sync in which a special circuit measures the difference in frequency between the master and slave oscillators and actually changes the frequency of the slave so that they match.

pink noise: Random fluctuations in sound, weighted in such a way that there is equal energy in every octave of the pitch range. Pink noise sounds lower in pitch than white noise. Compare with azure noise and white noise.

pitch-bend: A shift in a note's pitch, usually smooth, caused by the movement of a pitch-bend wheel or lever; also, the MIDI data used to create such a shift.

pitch-to-MIDI converter: A device that interprets the analog audio waveform coming from an acoustic transducer (usually a microphone or guitar pickup) and generates a MIDI note message whose note number corresponds to the fundamental pitch, as well as other MIDI messages for velocity, volume, and pitch-bend where appropriate.

pitch-to-voltage converter: A device that determines the frequency of an audio waveform (such as that picked up by a microphone or generated by an electric guitar) and creates a control voltage which, when applied to the control input of a properly calibrated oscillator, will cause the oscillator to output its own signal at the same frequency.

pole: A portion of a filter circuit. The more poles a filter has, the more abrupt its cutoff slope will be. Each pole causes a slope of 6dB per octave; typical filter configurations are two-pole (12dB per octave) and four-pole (24dB per octave). See rolloff slope.

poly-mod: Polyphonic modulation. A

term used by some manufacturers to refer to a type of patch in which one audio oscillator is modulated by another, or by an envelope generator. Same as cross-mod.

poly mode: A MIDI reception mode in which a module responds to note messages on only one channel, and plays as many of these notes at a time (polyphonically) as it can. See mono mode, multi mode, and omni mode.

polyphonic: (1) Capable of producing a number of independently moving pitch lines simultaneously. On some polyphonic synthesizers, all the keys can be sounded simultaneously, while on most others only a limited number of voices (four, five, eight, or 16, for example) are available. (2) Capable of producing more than one note at a time. On most electronic organs, all of the notes can be sounded polyphonically at once, but all synthesizers place an upper limit on how many voices of polyphony are available. See voice.

polyphonic sequencer: A digital sequencer capable of storing and playing back several independent musical lines simultaneously. See sequencer, digital sequencer, sequence.

poly pressure: Polyphonic pressure. A type of MIDI channel message in which each key senses and transmits pressure data independently. Compare with channel pressure.

port: *Verb:* (1) To translate one type of computer code into another. (2) To translate a program written for one computer so that it can be run on a different model. *Noun:* An electrical connector of some specialized type, e.g. RS-232 port, MIDI port, SCSI port.

portamento: See glide.

pot: Potentiometer. A device (commonly attached to a knob or slider) used to adjust some aspect of the signal being passed through it, or to send out a control signal corresponding to its position. Some pots are used to adjust the amplitude of a signal; others, such as the pan pot (which adjusts where a signal is sent in the stereo space between two speakers) are also found.

ppq: Pulses per quarter-note; the usual measure of a sequencer's clock resolution. Common pre-MIDI timing clock signals were sent out at a rate of 24, 48, or 96 ppq.

preset: (1) A single button that, when pushed, sets up most or all of an entire patch instantly through the synthesizer's internal hardwiring. (2) A factory-programmed patch that cannot be altered by the user. (3) Any patch. Note: Some manufacturers make distinctions between presets, programs, and/or patches, each of which contains a different set of parameters.

pressure sensitivity: See aftertouch, channel pressure, poly pressure.

priority: See assignment priority.

program: *Verb:* To create a synthesizer patch. *Noun:* A patch. See patch, preset.

program chain: See chain.

program change: A MIDI message that causes a synthesizer or other device to switch to a new program (preset, patch) contained in its memory.

programmable: (1) Containing a memory (usually in chip form, and often associated with a microprocessor) that allows the user to store a number of aspects of a patch and recall them all simultaneously to active status by touching not the patch controls themselves but a button or switch in a separate memory-control section. Individual controls are said to be programmable if their settings can be stored in memory. (2) Equipped with software that enables the user to create new sounds or other assignments by altering parameter settings and storing the new settings in memory. An individual control parameter is said to be programmable if its setting can be stored separately with each individual patch.

pulse wave: A signal put out by an oscillator in which a higher steady-state voltage alternates with a lower steady-state voltage. Audio-rate pulse waves are missing every nth harmonic from their spectra, where the duty cycle is $1/n$. Pulse waves with a 50% duty cycle (square waves) sound rich and hollow, while narrow pulses sound thin and reedy.

pulse width: The percentage of a complete cycle of a pulse wave which it spends in the "up" portion of its cycle. In the case of audio-rate pulse waves, there is no functional difference between two waves which have pulse widths of 50% + X and 50% – X, because their harmonic spectra are identical. Also called duty cycle. See pulse wave, pulse width modulation.

pulse width modulation: A change in the width of a pulse wave's duty cycle. In the case of an audio wave, pulse width modulation has the effect of changing the tone color, and in extreme cases the perceived pitch.

Q: See resonance.

quantization: (1) The process of adjusting a continuous input so as to produce an output in discrete steps. Rhythmic quantization is often called auto-correct. Quantization of an audio signal is called digitization or digital-to-analog conversion. (2) A function found on sequencers and drum machines that causes notes played at odd times to be "rounded off" to regular rhythmic values.

quantization noise: One of the types of error introduced into an analog audio signal by encoding it in digital form. The digital equivalent of tape hiss, quantization noise is caused by the small differences between the actual amplitudes of the points being sampled and the bit resolution of the analog-to-digital converter.

quantized: Set up to produce an output in discrete steps. A quantized tuning pot is an analog pot whose output has been confined to certain specific levels so as to determine what pitch within the equal-tempered scale an oscillator will have (no microtonal tuning adjustments are possible). In most digital and analog/digital hybrid instruments, all front panel knobs and sliders are quantized.

quantizer: A module that accepts an incoming voltage and matches this as closely as possible at its output while confining the output to one of a series of equally spaced discrete steps. (Note: A quantizer is an analog module found on a few modular synthesizers, and is not to be confused with an analog-to-digital converter.)

RAM: Random access memory. RAM is used for storing user-programmed patch parameter settings in synthesizers and sample waveforms in samplers. A constant source of power (usually a long-lasting battery) is required for RAM to maintain its contents when power is switched off. Compare with ROM.

ramp wave: See sawtooth wave.

rate scaling: See envelope tracking.

rate/level EG: A type of envelope generator in which the envelope shape is defined in terms of pairs of numbers, each pair consisting of a level (amount of envelope) and a rate (speed, time, or slope) parameter that determines how quickly the envelope will reach that level starting from the previous level. Synthesizers that use rate/level envelope generators include the Yamaha DX7 and the Casio CZ-101.

real time: Occuring at the same time as other, usually human, activities. In real-time sequence recording, timing information is encoded along with the note data by analyzing the timing of the input. In real-time editing, changes in parameter settings can be heard immediately, without the need to play a new note or wait for computational processes to be completed.

real-time mode: A situation in which events (such as keystrokes) are entered in computer memory at a speed directly proportional to the speed at which they will be played back. See single-step mode.

reconstruction filter: A lowpass filter on the output of a digital-to-analog converter that smooths the staircase-like changes in voltage produced by the converter in order to eliminated clock noise from the output.

regeneration: See resonance, feedback.

release: (1) The final segment controlled by an envelope generator. The release portion of the envelope begins when the key is lifted. The release control determines how long the envelope voltage takes to fall from the sustain level back to zero. (2) The portion of an envelope that begins after the key is lifted.

release velocity: The speed with which a key is raised after being depressed, and the type of MIDI data used to encode that speed. Release velocity sensing is rare but found on some instruments. It is usually used to control the rate of the release segment(s) of the envelope(s).

remote keyboard: A keyboard that is not built into the same case as the tone generator that it controls, but rather communicates with this circuitry via MIDI or some other data transmission system. A remote keyboard may be either a dedicated keyboard controller module with no internal synthesizer circuitry, or a full-function synthesizer that is being used as a master keyboard for controlling some other instrument.

resolution: (1) The fineness of the divisions into which an analog input is digitized (as in a sampling machine), or into which real-time input is quantized for memory storage (as in a sequencer or drum machine). (2) The fineness of the divisions into which a sensing or encoding system is divided. The higher the resolution, the more accurate the digital representation of the original signal will be.

resonance: A function on a filter in which a narrow band of frequencies (the resonant peak) becomes relatively more prominent. If the resonant peak is high enough, the filter will begin to oscillate, producing an audio output even in the absence of input. Filter resonance is also known as emphasis and Q. It's also referred to in some older instruments as regeneration or feedback, because feedback was used in the circuit to produce a resonant peak.

resynthesis: The process of electronically approximating a sound (especially the sound of an acoustic instrument) by analyzing its frequency and amplitude characteristics and then using this information to control the operation of a synthesizer. Resynthesis differs from sampling in that the complete time-coherent digital representation of the original waveform is no longer present in the synthesizer when the sound is being generated. Instead, this waveform is reconstructed using more abstract forms of control data.

reverb: A type of digital signal processing that produces a continuous wash of echoing sound. Reverberation contains the same frequency components as the sound being processed, but no discrete echoes. See echo, early reflections, DSP.

ribbon: A controller most often used for pitch-bending. A ribbon has no moving parts; instead, a finger pressed down on it and moved along it creates an electrical contact at some point along a pair of thin, flexible longitudinal strips whose electrical potential varies from one end to the other.

ringing: Filter oscillation. See resonance.

ring modulator: A special type of mixer that accepts two signals as audio inputs and produces their sum and difference tones at its output, but does not pass on the frequencies found in the original signals themselves. The "ring modulator" feature found on today's synthesizers is generally not a true ring modulator, but typically produces the same kind of clangorous tones. See clangorous.

rolloff slope: The acuity of a filter's cutoff frequency. Rolloff is generally measured in dB per octave. A shallow slope, such as 6dB per octave, allows some frequency components beyond the cutoff frequency to be heard, but at a reduced volume. When the rolloff slope is steep (on the order of 24dB per octave), frequency components quite close to the cutoff frequency are reduced in volume so much that they fall below the threshold of audibility. See filter, pole.

ROM: Read-only memory. A type of data storage whose contents cannot be altered by the user. An instrument's operating system and in some cases its waveforms and factory presets are stored in ROM. Compare with RAM.

routing: Sending a signal from one place to another, usually with switches rather than patch cords.

running status: A protocol that condenses the MIDI data stream by allowing one status byte to serve as the identifier for all of the data bytes that follow, until a new status byte is received. See status byte.

sample: A digitally recorded representation of a sound. Also, a single word of the data that makes up such a recording. See word.

sample-and-hold: A circuit on an analog synthesizer that, when triggered (usually by a clock pulse), looks at (samples) the voltage at its input and then passes this voltage on to its output unchanged, regardless of what the input voltage does in the meantime (the hold period), until the next trigger is received. In one familiar application, the input was a noise source and the output was connected to oscillator pitch, which caused the pitch to change in a random staircase pattern. Sample-and-hold devices are usually found in conjunction with an internal clock that tells them to take a sample at regular intervals of time, but on some synthesizers irregularly timed sampling options are available.

sampler: An instrument that records and plays back samples, usually by allowing them to be distributed across a keyboard and played back at various pitches.

sampling: The process of encoding an analog signal in digital form by reading (sampling) its level at precisely spaced intervals of time. See sample, sampling rate.

sampling rate: The number of samples taken per second. When analog audio signals are converted to digital form, the sampling rate must be at least twice the frequency of the highest harmonic in the sound to be sampled (the Nyquist limit) in order to prevent aliasing. Typical sampling rates vary from 15kHz to 48kHz. See sampling, Nyquist frequency.

sawtooth wave: A signal generated by an oscillator in which the voltage rises smoothly from a lower value to a higher value and then falls abruptly back to where it started (a positive-going ramp) or else declines steadily from the higher value to the lower and then jumps back to the higher (negative-going ramp). An audio-rate sawtooth wave contains all of the harmonics in the harmonic series, with successively higher harmonics at successively lower amplitudes. It has a bright, buzzy sound.

scale mode: A control mode that allows the user to alter the pitches of individual keys on the keyboard in relation to one

another, resulting in non-equal temperaments.

scaling curve: A user-defined relationship, generally non-linear, between input and output. See velocity curve.

Schmitt trigger: A device that puts out a pulse whenever the input voltage it is sensing rises above a certain (adjustable) threshold.

scrub: To move backward and forward through an audio waveform under manual control, in order to find a precise point in the wave for editing purposes.

SCSI: Small Computer Systems Interface, a high-speed communications protocol that allows computers, samplers, and hard disks to communicate with one another. Pronounced "scuzzy."

SDS: The MIDI sample dump standard. SDS is used to transfer digital audio samples from one instrument to another over a MIDI cable.

second touch: A type of aftertouch found on some electronic organs, in which bearing down on a key changes the timbre or introduces a second timbre. See aftertouch.

sequence: A set of voltages, keystrokes, or music performance commands (notes and controller data) stored in a sequencer.

sequencer: (1) A device that puts out the same user-determined set of voltages (the sequence) over and over in the same order. Like the sample-and-hold, the sequencer is usually found in conjunction with a clock. (2) A device that records and plays back user-determined sets of music performance commands, usually in the form of MIDI data. See digital sequencer, analog sequencer.

serial interface: An electronic connection between two devices in which digital data is transferred one bit after another, rather than several bits at a time. MIDI is a serial interface. Compare with parallel interface.

series mixing: See non-parallel mixing.

S/H: See sample-and-hold.

sidebands: Frequency components outside the natural harmonic series, generally introduced to the tone by using an audio-range wave for modulation. See clangorous.

sine wave: A signal put out by an oscillator in which the voltage or equivalent rises and falls smoothly and symmetrically, following the trigonometric formula for the sine function. Sub-audio sine waves are used to modulate other waveforms to produce vibrato and tremolo. Audio-range sine waves contain only the fundamental frequency, with no overtones, and thus can form the building blocks for more complex sounds. See additive synthesis.

single-step mode: A method of loading events (such as notes) into memory one event at a time. Also called step mode and step-time. Compare with real time.

single trigger: A type of keyboard logic sometimes found on monophonic synthesizers, and on polyphonic synthesizers when they are operating in unison mode, in which a new trigger signal restarts the envelope generators only after an interval of time, however brief, in which no key was depressed. On a single-trigger keyboard, legato phrases can be played in which the timbre and amplitude of several notes are governed by one continuing envelope. Compare with multiple trigger.

slave: Any device whose operation is linked to and governed by some other device. Compare with master.

slope: (1) See rolloff slope. (2) The fourth segment of Korg's six-stage envelopes. The slope control determines the speed at which the envelope will rise or fall from the break point to the sustain level.

smart FSK: An advanced type of FSK time code in which information about absolute time is encoded and recorded on tape along with (or instead of) information about tempo. Smart FSK allows an external device to sync correctly to tape when the tape is started in the middle of a piece rather than at the beginning. See FSK.

song: A list of patterns or sequences in a sequencer or drum machine, which the device will play back in the desired order in order to create a musical arrangement. Some instruments also allow such information as tempo changes and programmable patch changes to be stored as steps in a song.

song position pointer (SPP): A type of MIDI data that tells a device how many sixteenth-notes have passed since the beginning of a song. An SPP message is generally sent in conjunction with a continue message in order to start playback from the middle of a song.

sostenuto pedal: A pedal found on the grand piano and mimicked on some synthesizers, with which notes are sustained only if they are already being held on the keyboard at the moment when the pedal is pressed. Compare with sustain pedal.

source: The oscillator, noise source, or external input that serves as the point of origin of the audio signal path.

spillover: See overflow mode.

split keyboard: A single keyboard divided electronically to act as if it were two or more separate manuals. The output of each note range is routed into a separate signal path in the instrument's internal sound-producing circuitry, or transmitted over one or more separate MIDI channels.

split point: The point at which a split keyboard is split.

SPP: See song position pointer.

square wave: A pulse wave with a 50% duty cycle. An audio-rate square wave contains only odd-numbered harmonics, and has a hollow sound. A low-frequency square wave modulating the frequency of an oscillator produces a trill.

stage: One of the paired sets of rate and level controls in an envelope generator.

state-variable filter: A filter whose response characteristics can be varied, for example from lowpass to bandpass to highpass, depending on the setting of a panel control or the fluctuations of a control voltage.

step input: See single-step mode.

stripe: To record time code on a tape track.

sub-audio: Frequencies below about 20Hz (the lower threshold of human hearing), which are generally perceived as discrete rhythmic events rather than as a continuous tone.

sub-octave generator: A circuit, also called a sub-octave divider, that puts out a signal whose frequency is half the frequency of the input signal.

subtractive synthesis: The technique of arriving at a desired tone color by filtering waveforms rich in harmonics. Subtractive synthesis is the type generally used on analog synthesizers. Compare with additive synthesis, FM synthesis, sampling.

sustain: The third of the four segments in an ADSR envelope. The sustain portion of the envelope begins when the attack and decay portions have run their course, and continues until the key is released. The sustain control is used to determine the level at which the envelope will remain. While the attack, decay, and release controls are *rate* or *time* controls, the sustain control is a *level* control.

sustain pedal: The electronic equivalent of a piano's damper pedal. In most synthesizers, the sustain pedal latches the envelopes of any currently playing or subsequently played notes at their sustain levels, even if the keys are lifted. On other instruments, the sustain pedal causes the envelope to switch to an alternate release time.

switch trigger: A type of trigger signal that consists of a sudden, brief drop in voltage. See trigger and voltage trigger.

sync: Synchronization. (1) Two devices such as sequencers, drum machines, and arpeggiators are synced when the clock output of one is patched to the external clock input of the other, so that the timing of the notes they play will remain coordinated. Two oscillators are synced when the beginning of each new cycle on the master automatically triggers the beginning of a new cycle on the slave. When the slave oscillator is several octaves higher than the master, it will tend to lock onto one of the harmonics in the harmonic series for which the master is sounding the fundamental. (2) Two devices are said to be in sync when they are locked together with respect to time, so that the events

generated by each of them will always fall into predictable time relationships. See oscillator sync.

sync track: (1) A timing reference signal recorded on tape that consists of a sync tone containing (usually) 24, 48, or 96 pulses per quarter-note. A sync track is intended to be patched directly to devices such as drum machines and sequencers that will accept the appropriate clock input, as distinguished from a click track, which is mainly designed to be listened to by human musicians. (2) A timing reference signal recorded onto tape. See FSK and smart FSK.

synthesizer: A musical instrument that generates sound electronically and is designed according to certain principles developed by Robert Moog and others in the 1960s. A synthesizer is distinguished from an electronic piano or electronic organ by the fact that its sounds can be programmed by the user, and from a sampler by the fact that the sampler allows the user to make digital recordings of external sound sources.

sys-ex: See system-exclusive.

system-common: A type of MIDI data used to control certain aspects of the operation of the entire MIDI system. The currently defined system-common messages are song position pointer, song select, tune request, and end-of-system-exclusive.

system-exclusive: A type of MIDI data that allows messages to be sent over a MIDI cable that will be responded to only by devices of a specific type. Sys-ex data is used most commonly for sending patch parameter data.

system real-time: A type of MIDI data that is used for timing reference. Because of its timing-critical nature, a system real-time byte can be inserted into the middle of any multi-byte MIDI message. System real-time messages include MIDI clock, start, stop, continue, active sensing, and system reset.

THD: Total harmonic distortion. An audio measurement specification, used to determine the accuracy with which a device can reproduce an input signal at its output, that describes the cumulative level of the harmonic overtones (whole-number frequency multiples) that the device being tested adds to an input sine wave. THD+n is a specification that includes both harmonic distortion of the sine wave and nonharmonic noise.

timbre: (1) Tone color. (2) One of the building blocks of a patch in a Roland synthesizer. Pronounced "tam-br."

time code: A type of signal that contains information about location in time. Used for a synchronization reference when synchronizing two or more machines such as sequencers, drum machines, and tape decks.

top-note priority: A type of keyboard logic found on some monophonic synthesizers, in which the highest key depressed is the one that sends out a control voltage to the oscillators.

touch pad: A control input device that senses the presence of a finger — and on some models the position of the finger, the amount of downward pressure, and/or the area covered by the fingertip — without any externally visible moving parts, and puts out a corresponding control voltage. Also called a touch plate.

touch-sensitive: (1) Equipped with a sensing mechanism that responds to variations in velocity or pressure with corresponding variations in a control voltage output that is separate from the main output of the module. (2) Equipped with a sensing mechanism that responds to variations in key velocity or pressure by sending out a corresponding control signal. See velocity, aftertouch.

track: *Verb:* To be controlled by or follow in some   proportional relationship (as when a filter's cutoff frequency tracks the keyboard, moving up or down depending on what note is played). *Noun:* One of a number of independent memory areas in a multi-track sequencer. By analogy with tape tracks, sequencer tracks are normally longitudinal with respect to time and play back in sync with other tracks.

tracking generator: A multi-stage control signal modifier that maps the input signal onto an output in a continuous but usually non-linear manner.

transient: Any of the non-sustaining, non-periodic frequency components of a sound, usually of brief duration and higher amplitude than the sustaining components, and occurring near the onset of the sound (attack transients).

transient generator: See envelope generator.

tremolo: A periodic change in amplitude, usually controlled by an LFO, with a periodicity of less than 20Hz. Compare with vibrato.

triangle wave: A signal put out by an oscillator that rises smoothly and then falls smoothly, but with sharp corners between the positive-going and negative-going halves of the cycle. An audio-rate triangle wave has a muted sound similar to a sine wave, but with a few weak overtones.

trigger: A signal sent out by a keyboard or some other module that initiates the process of generating a note. A trigger is typically of brief, fixed duration, as opposed to a gate, which usually continues until the key is lifted.

TVA: Time-variant amplifier. Roland's term for a VCA or its digital equivalent. See VCA.

TVF: Time-variant filter. Roland's term for a VCF or its digital equivalent. See VCF.

two-pole: See rolloff slope.

unison mode: A type of keyboard logic in which several or all of an instrument's voices are activated by a single key. On some synthesizers, all the voices sounding in unison mode may have the same pitch, while on others, a chord may be latched and then played in unison mode.

variable: Equipped with knobs, sliders, or other controls designed to facilitate the creation of a patch. Generally, the term "variable synthesizer" is used to denote an instrument that is neither equipped with presets nor programmable.

VCA: Voltage-controlled amplifier. A device that responds to a change in voltage at its control input by altering the amount of gain of a signal being passed through it. Also, the digital equivalent of a VCA.

VCF: Voltage-controlled filter. A filter whose cutoff frequency can be changed by altering the amount of voltage being sent to its control input. Also, the digital equivalent of a VCF.

VCO: Voltage-controlled oscillator. An oscillator whose frequency can be changed by altering the amount of voltage being sent to its control input.

vector synthesis: A process in which the amplitudes of two or more oscillators are controlled in complementary fashion from a single two-dimensional envelope, or manually using a joystick.

velocity: A type of MIDI data (range 1 to 127) usually used to indicate how quickly a key was pushed down (attack velocity) or allowed to rise (release velocity). Note: A note-on message with a velocity value of 0 is equivalent to a note-off message.

velocity curve: A map that translates incoming velocity values into other velocities in order to alter the feel or response of a keyboard or tone module.

velocity data: A type of MIDI data, conventionally used to indicate how hard a key was struck.

velocity sensitivity: (1) A type of touch sensitivity in which the keyboard senses how fast the key is descending while it is still in motion. Velocity sensitivity emulates the touch response of the piano, though the velocity information can often be used to control other parameters of the sound than the loudness. (2) A type of touch sensitivity in which the keyboard measures how fast each key is descending. Compare with pressure sensitivity.

vernier: A pot used for fine tuning.

vibrato: A periodic change in frequency, often controlled by an LFO, with a periodicity of less than about 20Hz. Compare with tremolo.

vocoder: A device that continuously analyzes the frequency spectrum of one incoming signal (called the speech signal) and imparts analogous spectral characteristics to another (the carrier signal). The vocoder's output has the pitch of the carrier signal, with some or most of the timbral character and articulation of the speech signal.

voice: (1) The output of a single audio signal path. On a typical one-voice (monophonic) instrument, only one key at a time can be used to sound a note; on a multiple-voice (polyphonic) instrument, as many keys will sound simultaneously as the instrument has voices. The simplest standard voice is made up of a VCO, a VCF, and a VCA, together with the envelope generators that activate the latter two. (2) An element of synthesizer circuitry capable of producing a note. The polyphonic capability of a synthesizer is defined by how many voices it has. See voice channel. (3) In Yamaha synthesizers, a patch.

voice assignment: See assignment priority.

voice channel: A signal path containing (at a minimum) a VCO and VCA or their digital equivalent, and capable of producing a note. On a typical synthesizer, two or more voice channels, each with its own waveform and parameter settings, can be combined to form a single note.

voice stealing: A process in which a synthesizer that is being required to play more notes than it has available voices switches off some currently sounding voices (typically those that have been sounding longest or are at the lowest amplitude) in order to assign them to play new notes.

volatile memory: A type of memory whose contents vanish irretrievably if the instrument is shut off or electrical power is interrupted. Compare with non-volatile memory.

voltage-controlled: Capable of being regulated or altered in some aspect of its operation by a specific type of analog electrical input (the control voltage).

voltage pedal: A foot-operated control voltage source.

voltage trigger: A type of trigger signal that consists of a sudden, brief increase in voltage. See trigger and switch trigger.

waveform: A signal, either sampled or periodic, being generated by an oscillator. Each waveform has its own unique harmonic content. See oscillator.

waveform modulation: The process of changing the harmonic content of a waveform over time using such sources as real-time control, an envelope, or an LFO. Waveform modulation does not normally cause a change in pitch.

wave sequencing: A process in which a single oscillator switches or crossfades from one waveform to another during the course of a single note.

waveshape: See waveform.

wavetable: A set of numbers stored in memory and used to generate a waveform.

wavetable lookup: The process of reading the numbers in a wavetable (not necessarily in linear order from beginning to end) and sending them to a voice channel.

wet: Consisting entirely of processed sound. The output of an effects device is "100% wet" when only the output of the

processor itself is being heard, with none of the dry (unprocessed) signal. Compare with dry.

wheel: A controller, normally mounted at the left end of the keyboard and played with the left hand, that is used for pitch-bending, modulation, or other control such as output volume. The wheel is normally set vertically in a panel with somewhat less than half of its disc protruding in a position accessible to the left hand.

white noise: Random fluctuations in sound, weighted in such a way that there is equal energy per unit bandwidth throughout the frequency spectrum. White noise sounds like hissing. Compare with azure noise and pink noise.

word: The smallest possible unit of digital audio. A word usually consists of eight, 12, or 16 bits. See sample, bit, byte.

workstation: A synthesizer or sampler in which several of the tasks usually associated with electronic music production, such as sequencing, effects processing, rhythm programming, and data storage on disk, can all be performed by components found within a single physical device.

zero crossing: A point at which a digitally encoded waveform crosses the center of its amplitude range. Setting the start and end points of a sample loop at zero crossings is a conventional way of finding smooth-sounding loops.

zone: A contiguous set of keys on the keyboard. Typically, a single sound or MIDI channel is assigned to a given zone.

ABOUT
THE
AUTHORS

Since 1978, **Mark Vail** has performed with numerous bands in the San Francisco Bay Area, including Fourth Lord of Callendar, Palantir, Media Blitz '81, All to Noah Vail, the Instamoids, and his current improvisational crews, Maximum Footprint and Within Shouting Distance of Reality. He holds an MFA in electronic music and the recording media (Mills College, Oakland, California, 1983). Now technical editor, Mark joined the editorial staff at Keyboard magazine in 1988. A classically trained tenor, Mark hasn't yet fused his singing with the bizarre synthesizer music he enjoys playing, so he usually sticks to keyboard.

Jim Aikin is an acclaimed science-fiction author, recording musician, and senior associate editor for Keyboard, where he has spent the past 15 years writing features and articles on synthesizer art, performance, and technology. Jim's new science fiction novel, The Wall at the Edge of the World, is now available at bookstores. His new CD, Light's Broken Speech Revived, is available at your local record store or directly from Linden Music (Box 520, Linden, VA 22642).

Jeff Burger owns Creative Technologies, a multimedia consulting and production firm based in Northern California. He is also a contributing editor to NewMedia magazine. His book The Desktop Multimedia Bible is available from Addison-Wesley.

Barry Carson teaches English Literature, composes electronic music, writes fiction, is finishing his degree in counseling, and has actually owned most of the combo organs described in his article at one time or another. He has written extensively about Ensoniq sampling instruments for the Transoniq Hacker. Although he loves his MIDI studio, he lusts after old combo organs.

Connor Freff Cochran is making yet another career transition. Having been a professional writer, actor, artist, designer, television correspondent, narrator, businessman, musician, composer, songwriter, and clown, he is now attempting to unify the lot by producing feature films. In the background he will write books, paint paintings, record songs, and hike in the desert whenever possible.

David Etheridge's credits include stints as arranger and bassist with Stephane Grappelli, Nigel Kennedy, and a jazz-rock outfit whose members included Brand X's Robin Lumley and Graeme Edge of the Moody Blues.

Former Keyboard staffer **Ted Greenwald** holds a degree in music composition and has worked on the engineering staff at the Power Station recording studio in New York City. His music can be heard on Windham Hill's sampler of electronic music, Soul of the Machine, and the CD Views from a Distance with Scott Hiltzik, as well as in commercials for Bell South, Ban, and the Comedy Central television network. Following five years of freelance writing and composing music, Ted is now with Musician magazine. His fourth book, The Musician's Home Recording Handbook, was published in late '92.

Dominic Milano dropped out of Chicago's Roosevelt University, where he was studying electronic music composition, to join the original Keyboard magazine staff in 1975. An accomplished synthesist and wannabe guitar player, he is currently the editorial director of Keyboard, Guitar Player, Best of Guitar Player, and Bass Player magazines. Also an accomplished painter, Milano chairs the CyberArts International conference on interactive and multimedia technology in the arts.

Bob Moog is an internationally celebrated designer of electronic musical instruments and the founder of Moog Music Inc., manufacturers of early Moog synthesizers. He has written and lectured widely on all phases of the electronic music medium and currently runs Big Briar, Inc.

As a seventh grader in 1974, synthesizer technician **Timothy Smith** was exposed to EML ElectroComp synthesizers in the electronic music lab in junior high school. As a sophomore in high school, he began working part-time for a music store repairing electronic musical instruments. Eventually, Tim became the regional technical representative for the Western area for ARP and Moog. Somewhere in there he picked up a BS in physics. He still works on old and new synths in the Audio Clinic/Weyer-Smith Labs, based in Billings, Montana, and is developing audio upgrades for digital synthesizers.

Craig R. Waters was a senior staff writer for Inc. magazine at the time he wrote "The Rise & Fall of ARP Instruments" in 1982.

Paul Wiffen is a freelance sound developer and synth programmer based in London. His clients have included Paul McCartney, Stevie Wonder, Jean-Michel Jarre, Vangelis, Mark Isham, and Geoff Downes. He has done consulting and design work for numerous European synthesizer manufacturers. His current activities center mainly around hard disk recording, although he also translates technical manuals from German and French manufacturers into English. Paul writes quite often for Sound on Sound magazine in England, and was involved in the launch of Music Technology in the U.S.

INDEX

Also available from Miller Freeman Books

Acoustic Guitars and Other Fretted Instruments: A Photographic History
George Gruhn and Walter Carter
A lavishly illustrated book telling the story of American fretted instruments from the 1830s to the present. The evolution and sibling rivalry is traced, Features hundreds of unique color photographs of acoustic guitars, mandolins, and banjos.
ISBN 0-87930-240-2 $39.95

All Music Guide: The Best CDs, Albums & Tapes
Edited by Michael Erlewine and Scott Bultman
Reviews the best recordings in twenty-six musical categories including classical, rock, gospel, country, rap, and jazz and a total of 23,000 listings. This is the guide for everyone who's walked into a music store and felt overwhelmed by "what to choose?"
ISBN 0-87930-264-X $22.95

The Musician's Guide to Reading & Writing Music
Dave Stewart
For the brand new rocker, the seasoned player, and the pro who could use new problem-solving methods, a clear and practical guide to learning written music notation.
ISBN 0-87930-273-9 $7.95

Bass Heroes:
Styles, Stories & Secrets of 30 Great Bass Players
Edited by Tom Mulhern
Thirty of the world's greatest bass players in rock, jazz, studio/pop, and blues & funk share their musical influences, playing techniques, and opinions. Includes Monk Montgomery, Jack Bruce, James Jamerson, Stanley Clarke, Paul McCartney, and many more. From the pages of *Guitar Player* magazine.
ISBN 0-87930-274-7 $17.95

The Musician's Home Recording Handbook:
Practical Techniques for Recording
Great Music at Home
Ted Greenwald
This book gives the basics for musicians who want to produce high quality home recordings using the equipment at hand. Musicianship, not equipment, is the essential ingredient in a great recording; the author shows how anyone with creativity and a can-do attitude can produce great recordings.
ISBN 0-87930-237-2 $19.95

Secrets from the Masters: 40 Great Guitar Players
Edited by Don Menn
Featuring the most influential guitarists of the past 25 years: Chuck Berry, Joe Satriani, Eddie Van Halen, John Scofield, Pete Townshend and many more. Combines personal biography, career history, and playing techniques. From the pages of *Guitar Player* magazine.
ISBN 0-87930-260-7 $19.95

The Fender Book:
A Complete History of Fender Electric Guitars
Tony Bacon and Paul Day
Tells the complete story of these hugely popular, versatile, and fascinating guitars, from the classic 1950s Telecaster and Stratocaster to current models. Illustrated with unique color photographs of outstanding and unusual Fender models.
ISBN 0-87930-259-3 $19.95

Gruhn's Guide to Vintage Guitars: An Identification Guide for American Fretted Instruments
George Gruhn and Walter Carter
This portable reference for identifying American guitars, mandolins, and basses contains comprehensive dating information and model specifications for nearly 2,000 instruments by all major U.S. manufacturers.
ISBN 0-87930-195-3 $22.95

Guitar Player Repair Guide: How to Set Up, Maintain, and Repair Electrics and Acoustics
Dan Erlewine
Whether you're a player, collector, or repairperson, this hands-on guide provides all the essential information on caring for guitars and electric basses. Includes 264 photos and drawings.
ISBN 0-87930-188-0 $19.95

The Gibson Super 400: Art of the Fine Guitar
Thomas A. Van Hoose
This book traces the evolution of the Gibson 400 including production details and tables, historical anecdotes, step-by-step restoration techniques, and pricing information. Numerous color and black and white photographs make this volume complete.
ISBN 0-87930-230-5 $49.95

The Blues Guitar: The Men Who Made the Music
Edited by Jas Obrecht
"These pieces get straight to the blues through the eyes of the men who lived it."—*Los Angeles Times*. Interviews, articles, discographies, and rare photographs of 25 of history's greatest bluesmen, including Robert Johnson, John Lee Hooker, Albert King, B.B. King, Buddy Guy, Muddy Waters and many more.
ISBN 0-87930-187-2 $19.95

CyberArts: Exploring Art & Technology
Edited by Linda Jacobson
A rich anthology of essays and commentaries from over 50 leading multimedia visionaries on the topics of music, graphics, animation, 3D sound, virtual reality, video and film, toys, and games.
ISBN 0-87930-253-4 $22.95

TO ORDER, or for more information, contact:
Miller Freeman Books, 600 Harrison St., San Francisco, CA 94107
Phone 415 905-2200 • Fax 415 905-2239.